*Mark Jacobs*
*Editor*

# Electronic Resources Librarianship and Management of Digital Information: Emerging Professional Roles

*Electronic Resources Librarianship and Management of Digital Information: Emerging Professional Roles* has been co-published simultaneously as *Collection Management*, Volume 32, Numbers (1/2)(3/4) 2007.

*Pre-publication*
*REVIEWS,*
*COMMENTARIES,*
*EVALUATIONS . . .*

"THE MOST WIDE-RANGING, IN-DEPTH CONSIDERATION OF THIS COMPLEX AND IMPORTANT SUBJECT PUBLISHED TO DATE. . . . A crucial and timely contribution to contemporary library literature."

**Jim Dwyer, MLS**
*University of Washington*
*Bibliographic Services Librarian*
*California State University, Chico*

# Electronic Resources Librarianship and Management of Digital Information: Emerging Professional Roles

*Electronic Resources Librarianship and Management of Digital Information: Emerging Professional Roles* has been co-published simultaneously as *Collection Management*, Volume 32, Numbers (1/2)(3/4) 2007.

# Monographs from *Collection Management*®

For additional information on these and other Haworth Press titles, including descriptions, tables of contents, reviews, and prices, use the QuickSearch catalog at http://www.HaworthPress.com.

1. *The State of Western European Studies: Implication for Collection Development,* edited by Anthony M. Angiletta, Martha L. Brogan, Charles S. Fineman, and Clara M. Lovett (Vol. 6, No. 1/2, 1984). *"An exceptionally well-edited volume . . . lively and engrossing. . . . An informative and thought-provoking overview of the current state of Western European studies and its possible future directions." (Special Libraries Association)*

2. *Collection Management for School Library Media Centers,* edited by Brenda H. White (Vol. 7, No. 3/4, 1986). *"A wealth of information concerning managing a school library media center collection. . . . Readable, interesting, and practical." (The Book Report: The Journal for Junior and Senior High School Librarians)*

3. *Reading and the Art of Librarianship: Selected Essays of John B. Nicholson, Jr.,* edited by Paul Z. DuBois and Dean H. Keller (Vol. 8, No. 3/4, 1986). *"A selection from over 300 completely delightful essays, representing the late author's wide and varied interests. There is much food for thought in these pages, a lively collection that is personal, intimate . . . a passionate look at the world of books." (Academic Library Book Review)*

4. *International Conference on Research Library Cooperation,* The Research Libraries Group, Inc. (Vol. 9, No. 2/3, 1988). *"A useful . . . look at selected cooperative schemes in Britain, Europe and the United States and propose guidelines for the future." (Library Association Record)*

5. *Euro-Librarianship: Shared Resources, Shared Responsibilities,* edited by Assunta Pisani (Vol. 15, No. 1/2/3/4, 1992). *"A rich compendium of information about European studies, especially in relation to librarianship. . . . A worthwhile volume that will be helpful to Western European Studies librarians for many years to come." (Western European Specialists Section Newsletter)*

6. *Access Services in Libraries: New Solutions for Collection Management,* edited by Gregg Sapp (Vol. 17, No. 1/2, 1993). *"Develops a theoretical foundation for the growing phenomenon of access services in public and academic libraries–an approach to the increasingly complex problem of making materials available to patrons." (Reference and Research Book News)*

7. *Practical Issues in Collection Development and Collection Access,* edited by Katina Strauch, Sally W. Somers, Susan Zappen, and Anne Jennings (Vol. 19, No. 3/4, 1995). *With surveys, studies, and first-hand accounts of "how we did it," this book shows how fellow professionals view the evolving world of information selection, maintenance, access, and delivery.*

8. *Electronic Resources: Implications for Collection Management,* edited by Genevieve S. Owens (Vol. 21, No. 1, 1996). *"Discusses the strengths and weaknesses of electronic resources, as well as the implications these resources have on collection management. Also provides guidance on incorporating electronic resources into library collections." (Reference and Research Book News)*

9. *Collection Development: Past and Future,* edited by Maureen Pastine (Vol. 21, No. 2/3, 1996). *"An important navigational tool for steering through the turbulent waters of the evolving collection development environment. I highly recommend it." (Blake Landar, PhD, Philosophy, Classics, and Religion Bibliographer, University of Florida)*

10. *Collection Development: Access in the Virtual Library,* edited by Maureen Pastine (Vol. 22, No. 1/2, 1997). *"Documents unequivocally that collaboration–between library and customer, library and vendor, and among libraries–is essential for success in today's academic library." (Kathryn Hammell Carpenter, MS, University Librarian, Valparaiso University, Indiana)*

11. *Going Digital: Strategies for Access, Preservation, and Conversion of Collections to a Digital Format,* edited by Donald L. DeWitt (Vol. 22, No. 3/4, 1998). *"This excellent book presents a comprehensive study of crucial issues confronting librarians and archivists today. . . . From the first article to the last, it is a compelling read!" (Carol A. Mathius, MLIS, CA, Archivist, Head of Special Collections, Nicholls State University, Thibodaux, Louisiana)*

12. *Government Information Collections in the Networked Environment: New Issues and Models,* edited by Joan F. Cheverie (Vol. 23, No. 3, 1998). *Explores the challenging issues related to effective access to government information.*

13. *Cooperative Collection Development: Significant Trends and Issues,* edited by Donald B. Simpson (Vol. 23, No. 4, 1998). *Shows how the art of cooperation requires librarians' ability to comprehend and support "big picture" goals and the skills to incorporate "common good" objectives into local activities so that there is constructive and affirmative benefit to your own programs and services.*

14. *Creating New Strategies for Cooperative Collection Development,* edited by Milton T. Wolf and Marjorie E. Bloss (Vol. 24, No. (1/2)(3/4), 2000). *Discusses current initiatives in cooperative collection development and points the way to expanding the scope of this activity in the future.*

15. *Electronic Collection Management,* edited by Suzan D. McGinnis (Vol. 25, No. 1/2, 2000). *A practical guide to the art and science of acquiring and organizing electronic resources.*

16. *The New Dynamics and Economics of Cooperative Collection Development,* edited by Edward Shreeves (Vol. 28, No. (1/2)(3), 2003). *Explores state-of-the-art techniques and new possibilities for cooperative collection development.*

17. *Managing the Mystery Collection: From Creation to Consumption,* edited by Judith Overmier and Rhonda Harris Taylor (Vol. 29, No. 3/4, 2004). *A unique collection of essays from mystery authors, readers, critics, scholars, and librarians examining the progression of the mystery story from the author's creation through its inclusion on library shelves on to its consumption by readers.*

18. *Electronic Resources Librarianship and Management of Digital Information: Emerging Professional Roles,* edited by Mark Jacobs (Vol. 32, No. 1/2/3/4, 2007). *A comprehensive examination of the impact of the digital age on the library profession, libraries, and librarians, as well as the needs and expectations of users of digital content.*

Published by
The Haworth Information Press®, 10 Alice Street, Binghamton, NY 13904-1580 USA
The Haworth Information Press® is an imprint of The Haworth Press, 10 Alice Street,
Binghamton, NY 13904-1580 USA.

*Electronic Resources Librarianship and Management of Digital Information: Emerging Professional Roles* has been co-published simultaneously as *Collection Management*, Volume 32, Numbers (1/2)(3/4) 2007.

The development, preparation, and publication of this work has been undertaken with great care. However, the publisher, employees, editors, and agents of The Haworth Press and all imprints of The Haworth Press, including The Haworth Medical Press® and Pharmaceutical Products Press®, are not responsible for any errors contained herein or for consequences that may ensue from use of materials or information contained in this work. With regard to case studies, identities and circumstances of individuals discussed herein have been changed to protect confidentiality. Any resemblance to actual persons, living or dead, is entirely coincidental.

The Haworth Press is committed to the dissemination of ideas and information according to the highest standards of intellectual freedom and the free exchange of ideas. Statements made and opinions expressed in this publication do not necessarily reflect the views of the Publisher, Directors, management, or staff of The Haworth Press, Inc., or an endorsement by them.

**Library of Congress Cataloging-in-Publication Data**

Electronic resources librarianship and management of digital information : emerging professional roles / Mark Jacobs, ed.
     p. cm.
     "Co-published simultaneously as Collection management, volume 32, numbers 1/2, 3/4, 2007."
     Includes bibliographical references and index.
     ISBN-13: 978-0-7890-3217-1 (alk. paper)
     ISBN-13: 978-0-7890-3218-8 (pbk. : alk. paper)
     1. Libraries–Special collections–Electronic information resources. 2. Electronic information resources–Management. 3. Librarians–Effect of technological innovations on. I. Jacobs, Mark, 1956- II. Collection management.

Z692.C65E43 2008
025.17′4–dc22

2007029281

# Electronic Resources Librarianship and Management of Digital Information: Emerging Professional Roles

Mark Jacobs
Editor

*Electronic Resources Librarianship and Management of Digital Information: Emerging Professional Roles* has been co-published simultaneously as *Collection Management*, Volume 32, Numbers (1/2)(3/4) 2007.

The Haworth Information Press®
An Imprint of The Haworth Press

www.HaworthPress.com

# The HAWORTH PRESS
## Abstracting, Indexing & Outward Linking
### PRINT *and* ELECTRONIC BOOKS & JOURNALS

This section provides you with a list of major indexing & abstracting services and other tools for bibliographic access. That is to say, each service began covering this periodical during the year noted in the right column. Most Websites which are listed below have indicated that they will either post, disseminate, compile, archive, cite or alert their own Website users with research-based content from this work. (This list is as current as the copyright date of this publication.)

Abstracting, Website/Indexing Coverage . . . . . . . . Year When Coverage Began

- **(IBR) International Bibliography of Book Reviews on the Humanities and Social Sciences (Thomson)**
  *<http://www.saur.de>* . . . . . . . . . . . . . . . . . . . . . . . . . . . . . . . . 2006

- **(IBZ) International Bibliography of Periodical Literature on the Humanities and Social Sciences (Thomson)**
  *<http://www.saur.de>* . . . . . . . . . . . . . . . . . . . . . . . . . . . . . . . . 1995

- ***\*\*Academic Search Premier (EBSCO)\*\****
  *<http://search.ebscohost.com>* . . . . . . . . . . . . . . . . . . . . . . . . . 2006

- ***\*\*INSPEC (The Institution of Engineering and Technology)\*\****
  *<http://www.iee.org.uk/publish/>* . . . . . . . . . . . . . . . . . . . . . . . 2006

- ***\*\*LISA: Library and Information Science Abstracts (Cambridge Scientific Abstracts)\*\****
  *<http://www.csa.com/factsheets/list-set-c.php>* . . . . . . . . . . . . . 1989

- ***\*\*MasterFILE Premier (EBSCO)\*\****
  *<http://search.ebscohost.com>* . . . . . . . . . . . . . . . . . . . . . . . . . 2006

- ***\*\*Professional Development Collection (EBSCO)\*\****
  *<http://search.ebscohost.com>* . . . . . . . . . . . . . . . . . . . . . . . . . 2006

- **Academic Source Premier (EBSCO)**
  *<http://search.ebscohost.com>* . . . . . . . . . . . . . . . . . . . . . . . . . 2007

- **Advanced Polymers Abstracts (Cambridge Scientific Abstracts)**
  *<http://www.csa.com/factsheets/ema-polymers-set-c.php>* . . . . . 2006

(continued)

(continued)

(continued)

(continued)

# Bibliographic Access

- **Cabells's Directory of Publishing Opportunities in Psychology <http://www.cabells.com>**

- **Magazines for Libraries (Katz)**

- **MediaFinder <http://www.mediafinder.com/>**

- **Ulrich's Periodicals Directory: International Periodicals Information Since 1932 <http://www.Bowkerlink.com>**

*Special Bibliographic Notes related to special journal issues (separates) and indexing/abstracting:*

- indexing/abstracting services in this list will also cover material in any "separate" that is co-published simultaneously with Haworth's special thematic journal issue or DocuSerial. Indexing/abstracting usually covers material at the article/chapter level.
- monographic co-editions are intended for either non-subscribers or libraries which intend to purchase a second copy for their circulating collections.
- monographic co-editions are reported to all jobbers/wholesalers/approval plans. The source journal is listed as the "series" to assist the prevention of duplicate purchasing in the same manner utilized for books-in-series.
- to facilitate user/access services all indexing/abstracting services are encouraged to utilize the co-indexing entry note indicated at the bottom of the first page of each article/chapter/contribution.
- this is intended to assist a library user of any reference tool (whether print, electronic, online, or CD-ROM) to locate the monographic version if the library has purchased this version but not a subscription to the source journal.
- individual articles/chapters in any Haworth publication are also available through the Haworth Document Delivery Service (HDDS).

AS PART OF OUR CONTINUING COMMITMENT TO BETTER SERVE
OUR LIBRARY PATRONS, WE ARE PROUD TO BE WORKING WITH
THE FOLLOWING ELECTRONIC SERVICES:

## AGGREGATOR SERVICES

- EBSCOhost   • Ingenta   • J-Gate   • Minerva
- OCLC FirstSearch   • Oxmill   • SwetsWise

## LINK RESOLVER SERVICES

- 1Cate (Openly Informatics)   • ChemPort (American Chemical Society)
- CrossRef   • Gold Rush (Coalliance)   • LinkOut (PubMed)
- LINKplus (Atypon)   LinkSolver (Ovid)   • LinkSource with A-to-Z (EBSCO)
- Resource Linker (Ulrich's)   • SerialsSolutions (ProQuest)   • SFX (Ex Libris)
- Sirsi Resolver (SirsiDynix)   • Tour (TDnet)   • Vlink (Extensity)
- WebBridge (Innovative Interfaces)

The Haworth Press   Phone: 800-429-6784 • Fax: 800-895-0582 • Web: www.HaworthPress.com

# Electronic Resources Librarianship and Management of Digital Information: Emerging Professional Roles

## CONTENTS

# ABOUT THE EDITOR

**Mark Jacobs** has worked for the University of Illinois at Urbana-Champaign (UIUC), the United States Newspaper Program, Washington State University, and, most recently, as Electronic Resources Librarian at the University of Wyoming.

He holds an MS in Library and Information Science from UIUC and a BA in History from Wichita State University. He has been active in service and professional development with the American Library Association, the Association of College and Research Libraries, and the North American Serials Interest Group.

His professional interests and viewpoints include recognition of the importance of: a holistic, process-orientation to library management; asking the library user; work with the commercial sector and the scholarly community to guarantee fair, affordable, and open access to scholarship.

Mr. Jacobs has published in *Information Technology & Libraries*, *Serials Librarian*, *Cataloging & Classification Quarterly*, and others. He has also published monographs and has made presentations at professional conferences.

# Acknowledgments

The editor wishes to thank:

Wayne Jones, Queen's University, for providing this opportunity; for guidance, support, and encouragement; for editing instructions; and for last-minute editing.

Heather Scott, Kansas City University for Medicine and the Biosciences, for citation verifications.

Charles W. Bailey, University of Houston, for editing instruction.

Mike Nelson, University of Wyoming, for last-minute editing.

Susanne Clement and Rachel Miller, University of Kansas, for coming through on short notice.

Cheryl Goldstein, University of Wyoming, for coming to the rescue.

Cyril Oberlander, University of Virginia, for the candy.

Tawnya K. Plumb, University of Wyoming Law Library, for encouragement and friendship.

And all authors in this monograph for staying the course.

# Foreword

I was very pleased to learn that a collection of articles focused on different facets of the "human element" in electronic resources librarianship was to be published, and even more pleased to get advance access to it in order to provide this foreword. In addition to helping me solidify my understanding of some topics I felt I already knew well, it has provided me with much information that is new, as well as many new ideas and perspectives to consider and go back to–as I feel will be the case for many current and future colleagues working with electronic resources.

And as the book's title indicates, the primary focus of the essays in it is on those colleagues–who I believe will become more and more numerous over the next few years as electronic resources become even more pervasive, powerful, and transformative than they are now. Like many of my colleagues sharing the delights and challenges of these resources and the "interesting times," they typify, I think the more deeply electronic future that libraries and their users will be working in will be a very good thing–though from time to time I feel that we've all been caught up in the "sorcerer's apprentice" segment of *Fantasia!*

One path to dealing with that kind of tableau has been to develop Electronic Resource Management Systems ("ERMS") aimed at gaining some semblance of control over these resources and the dynamic environment in which we find them. And as leader of the Digital Library Federation's Electronic Resources Management Initiative ("ERMI"), I can say that my ERMI teammates and I have taken great satisfaction in seeing that work gain traction, and in libraries implementing local ERMS based on it. But as important and satisfying as that has been, it has also been clear that systems and software can only go so far–and that is where the significance and value of the present volume can be seen.

---

[Haworth co-indexing entry note]: "Foreword." Jewell, Tim. Co-published simultaneously in *Collection Management* (The Haworth Information Press, an imprint of The Haworth Press) Vol. 32, No. 1/2, 2007, pp. xxv-xxvi; and: *Electronic Resources Librarianship and Management of Digital Information: Emerging Professional Roles* (ed: Mark Jacobs) The Haworth Information Press, an imprint of The Haworth Press, 2007, pp. xxi-xxii.

The book is divided into three sections of seven chapters, and each chapter contributes something different and important to the rich and complex picture. The first section, on "The Position" of Electronic Resources Librarian, provides a variety of vantage points from which to view the work involved in dealing with the many facets of electronic resources, the variety of roles that may be taken on by the individual ER librarian or team member, as well as some of the more important qualities and skills required. Some of these roles and supporting technical, interpersonal and political skills may be easy enough for librarians with experience in this area to anticipate, while (such as those related to teaching or the support of users with disabilities) are likely to be less so, but add interesting detail.

The second section, on "The Management" of electronic resources, helps to flesh out the first by adding worthwhile discussions of a variety of topics, including management functions and processes, standards, licensing practices, working with consortia, and usability testing. The final section, on "The Future," enriches the picture still further by providing analyses of the relevance and value of collection policies and plans within the electronic environment, evolving practices related to usage data and preservation, and librarians' responsibilities with respect to helping overcome the "digital divide." The final article in that section (and the book) is an admirably detailed but concise discussion by Charles Bailey of Open Access, what libraries might do to further its cause, and some thoughts about how its success might affect libraries.

The other day a colleague of mine forwarded an article on "change leadership" that began by quoting Mark Twain: "You know, I'm all for progress. It's change I object to." Those of us who deal with electronic resources know that it's our job to maximize the former while trying to minimize the pains and dislocations of the latter, and I am happy for that reason to be able to recommend this worthwhile volume and its focus on the "human element" to practitioners and students alike.

*Tim Jewell*
*University of Washington Libraries*
*Seattle*

# Introduction

In just over ten years, the advent of online information has transformed scholarly communication as well as the library and information science (LIS) profession. In the chapters of this book, the reader will be reminded of many of the signposts and details of that transformation.

But, the changes have only started and some of the authors contained within have, also, pointed to the future and suggested the developments in open access, workflow, license, preservation, collection management, equity, and education that will inform the best practices of librarianship in the coming years.

What is electronic resources (ER) librarianship? For some, it means to be possessed of the title *electronic resources (ER) librarian*, but for many others it means to be responsible for some or many aspects of the processes inherent in the identification, selection, acquisition, organization, description, delivery, and evaluation of online information; referred to, variously, in these pages as e-resources, digital content, e-information, etc.

The number and types of digital information objects, their formats, and the ways in which they are delivered are as remarkable as they are daunting; and their management is a complex business. Just as significant and remarkable are the people who have undertaken the challenges of that management, who hold the positions, and work in the library units that have been responsible for the effort to meet user needs and expectations for the delivery of online information. Some librarians and support staff may be part of a library unit fashioned for this purpose, but in many cases the work is parsed-out across the library with aspects of it to fall to collection management, technical services, systems, access

[Haworth co-indexing entry note]: "Introduction." Jacobs, Mark. Co-published simultaneously in *Collection Management* (The Haworth Information Press, an imprint of The Haworth Press) Vol. 32, No. 1/2, 2007, pp. 1-2; and: *Electronic Resources Librarianship and Management of Digital Information: Emerging Professional Roles* (ed: Mark Jacobs) The Haworth Information Press, an imprint of The Haworth Press, 2007, pp. 1-2. Single or multiple copies of this article are available for a fee from The Haworth Document Delivery Service [1-800-HAWORTH, 9:00 a.m. - 5:00 p.m. (EST). E-mail address: docdelivery@ haworthpress.com].

Available online at http://col.haworthpress.com
doi:10.1300/J105v32n01_01

services, reference, and administrative units. The ER librarian is required, by necessity, to have or to develop skills and knowledge in license negotiations, metadata schema, Web design, database creation/management, and public relations/advocacy and, at the same time must maintain and develop *traditional* skills and knowledge, e.g., bibliographic instruction, subject expertise, reference, budget management, etc. The paradox is that called upon to *manage* a process of workflows that impact every conceivable frame of reference in a library's administration, the work is often performed without benefit of administrative/managerial rank. The recourse for the ER librarian is to finely hone abilities to communicate, coordinate, and bring to consensus.

Who are the professionals who undertake this essential work? Their positions and rank cover the gamut: new graduates, current librarians who change or assume more responsibilities, administrators, department heads, systems, collection management, technical services, and public services librarians, bibliographers as well as an array of non-MLS library staff. The list is enormous and varied.

Where have they found their skills and knowledge? In the classroom, on-the-job, and through efforts in networking, professional development, and continuing education. Library schools may have fallen a little behind the curve in the development of curricula or curricular elements to meet the requirements of the digital information age, but many practitioners point to the importance of learning in the workplace.

These chapters are framed in the context of the delivery of e-information, but it is hoped that the reader will discover something here about the people who have assumed the responsibility to meet user needs, to be creative and innovative, and to lay the groundwork for future success as the LIS profession moves to meet the expectations of its communities of researchers, scholars, students, and users.

*Mark Jacobs*
*28 October 2006*

# THE POSITION:
# WHO, WHAT, WHERE, AND HOW?

## Preferred Political, Social,
## and Technological Characteristics
## of Electronic Resources (ER) Librarians

Kathy A. Downes
Pal V. Rao

**SUMMARY.** The digital revolution has created a need for a new type of professional called the electronic resources (ER) librarian. This chapter traces the development of this new position in academic libraries, identifies preferred characteristics needed to succeed in this position, and provides a rationale for why some characteristics are essential while others are desirable. Using economic, political, social, and technological factors as determinants, the authors further the discussion and ask the question: has

Kathy A. Downes, MLIS, MPA, is Associate Dean of University Libraries (E-mail: kathy.downes@wichita.edu); and Pal V. Rao, PhD, MS, MSLS, is Dean and Professor of University Libraries (E-mail: pal.rao@wichita.edu), both at Wichita State University, 1845 North Fairmount, Wichita, KS 67260-0068.

[Haworth co-indexing entry note]: "Preferred Political, Social, and Technological Characteristics of Electronic Resources (ER) Librarians." Downes, Kathy A., and Pal V. Rao. Co-published simultaneously in *Collection Management* (The Haworth Information Press, an imprint of The Haworth Press) Vol. 32, No. 1/2, 2007, pp. 3-14; and: *Electronic Resources Librarianship and Management of Digital Information: Emerging Professional Roles* (ed: Mark Jacobs) The Haworth Information Press, an imprint of The Haworth Press, 2007, pp. 3-14. Single or multiple copies of this article are available for a fee from The Haworth Document Delivery Service [1-800-HAWORTH, 9:00 a.m. - 5:00 p.m. (EST). E-mail address: docdelivery@ haworthpress.com].

doi:10.1300/J105v32n01_02

this position become a permanent fixture in the library culture or is it a passing trend? doi:10.1300/J105v32n01_02 *[Article copies available for a fee from The Haworth Document Delivery Service: 1-800-HAWORTH. E-mail address: <docdelivery@haworthpress.com> Website: <http://www.HaworthPress.com> © 2007 by The Haworth Press. All rights reserved.]*

**KEYWORDS.** Economic factors, technical skills, social skills, political skills, position description

## *INTRODUCTION*

As the eminent library scholar S. R. Ranganathan stated, the library is a living organism. It continuously evolves and adapts to the ever-changing world. The purpose of this chapter is to outline one aspect of the modern library's adaptation to the so-called digital revolution. When libraries moved from a manuscript culture to a print culture they faced enormous challenges. As paper publications multiplied by leaps and bounds, the book lists and other forms of organizational methods that were adequate for the manuscript culture became inadequate for the ever-growing volume of the print culture. Hence, individuals like Melvil Dewey and Halsey William Wilson invented new methods to organize information through classification and indexing systems. These new methods called for a new breed of trained professional: the cataloger and the indexer.

Today libraries are again faced with a major transition, the shift from a print-based culture to a digital culture. This shift was described in a 29 October 2003 Reuter's news release that read:

> A study by the University of California at Berkeley shows that during 2002, five billion gigabytes of data was generated around the world. That amount, which is the equivalent of about 800 megabytes per person, is enough to fill 500,000 U.S. Libraries of Congress. The university conducted a similar study in 1999, and the new results indicate a 30 percent rise since the first study in the amount of stored information. The amount of data stored on hard disk drives was up 114 percent from the earlier study.[1]

To address this explosive growth of digital information, libraries found a need to develop new breeds of professionals in possession of new and different skill sets. One of these is the electronic resources (ER) librarian. This chapter draws, primarily, on the authors' experiences to trace the recent, adaptive changes occurring in libraries, especially in academic libraries; the need for such changes; and the preferred characteristics needed to manage the challenges associated with ER. More specifically, we examine how ER librarianship originated within the context of classic organization theory; how it matured within the context of economic, political, social, and technical factors; and what are the preferred characteristics needed, in the current environment, to be a successful ER librarian.

Talcott Parsons, a leading light in the classic theory of organizations and professions, described an organization as "a social system oriented to the attainment of a relatively specific type of goal, which contributes to a major function of a more comprehensive system, usually the society."[2]

Within the organization, Parsons describes the role of professions in terms of *functional specificity* supporting goal attainment. Professions grow through a series of stages called professionalization. In *The System of Professions*, Andrew Abbott expands on Parsons' basic construct and analyzes how new professions develop when a disturbance causes the authority in a specific area to become obsolete or replaced by the need for new expertise. As the professions or subspecialties develop their specific expertise in order to respond to the disturbance, the area develops a consistency in its skills and role and balance is restored.[3]

This role consistency then allows the profession a way to institutionalize its expertise. Organizations identify the new area of expertise and integrate it into their organizations when their decision-makers determine the expertise will assist the organization's goal attainment. Over the last fifteen years, the library as an organization has increasingly demonstrated its need for the expertise found in the ER librarian.

So, what is an ER librarian? The emergence of micro-electronic tools, such as personal computers, and connectivity tools, such as the Internet, has provided many opportunities for all professions to better serve their clientele. Librarianship has also benefited from the capabilities provided by these electronic tools to expand its services to its clients. Just like other professions, librarianship initially used computer technology to automate its traditional functions, such as acquisitions, cataloging, and circulation. During this phase, libraries, especially academic libraries, demonstrated that they recognized the special, professional skills needed for automated activities by the creation of new positions, e.g., automation librarian and systems librarian. This was also the era of librarian-mediated searches of commercial databases, which resulted in the creation in many libraries of positions such as the online search librarian. It was not until the 1990s, as the

Internet began to spread its tentacles around the globe that unmediated searches became popular, publishers began to move into the realm of marketing digital products, and a need became clear for yet another type of library professional. Again, academic libraries were the first to identify this new need and created the ER librarian position to fill it: to coordinate access to the wealth of new ER.

One of the authors of this chapter first encountered the concept of the ER librarian while in service as the Dean of Library Services at Central Missouri State University (CMSU) in 1990. As the local area network (LAN) of the CMSU libraries and its number of ER expanded, its executive council discussed the need for a new type of position. The goal of this new position was to fine-tune CMSU's dynamic, electronic systems on a continuous basis and to make them convenient for use by service-providers and clients.

In subsequent discussions members of the executive council identified the following requirements for the position:

- technical-savvy and the ability to keep up-to-date in a technology environment that continuously changes
- the ability to interact with ease with both technologists and lay-persons
- effective teaching and communication skills

In July 1990, with this somewhat loose definition in place, an electronic services librarian position was advertised and hired; one of the first positions of this type in the country.

From this type of beginning, the ER librarian position has become one of the most critical in academic libraries over the last decade and a half. However, it is still in question whether the position is transitory or whether it has developed the consistency in expertise that will allow it to become a *functional specificity*: a true subspecialty. H. G. Wells, the well-known British author, wrote that consistency in four factors determines whether a trend is passing or permanent: economic, political, social, and technological. Is the ER librarian a passing trend or has it developed the consistent economic, political, social, and technological characteristics/skills necessary to enable it to become a permanent part of the field of librarianship?

For the purpose of this discussion, economic characteristics are defined as skills or aspects of behavior that facilitate the procurement and efficient use of resources. Technological characteristics are defined as those skills or aspects of behavior that are acquired, either by education or experience, that allow a person to successfully complete well-defined and specific tasks. Political characteristics are defined as those skills or aspects of behavior that are used in a deliberate way to influence people or decision-making toward a desired outcome. Social characteristics are defined as those skills or aspects of behavior that enhance the development and maintenance of relationships through successful interaction and communication with others.

A first step to determine if the ER librarian has become an integrated subspecialty in library organizations is to look at how representatives of organizations outline the requirements for the position in position descriptions: are libraries, as a whole, looking for the same characteristics when they search for an ER librarian? In general, organizational representatives will, consciously or subconsciously, use Wells' four factors as they develop a new position description. The economic impact of the position is a crucial factor to determine whether or not to create or fill such a position in the first place. Technical skills for the position are systematically identified and evaluated. The social and political skills needed for a position may not be as systematically identified, but when a position advertisement indicates requirements such as excellent communication skills, strong interpersonal skills, team-orientation, and the ability to work with diverse constituencies, it is an indication of an attempt to recruit social and political skills.

In a 2003 article, William Fisher started to codify the key characteristics of an ER librarian through the use of position requirements listed in job advertisements posted to *American Libraries* between 1985 and 2001.[4] Fisher found that the top ten characteristics fell into three categories: (1) traditional public service responsibilities, (2) technology-related skills, and (3) personal characteristics. Listed under traditional, public services characteristics were reference services, collection development, and bibliographic instruction. The instruction component was more frequently directed towards the instruction of library staff than library patrons. The technology-related functions included computer applications, online searches, and Web applications. The personal attributes included communication skills, professional experience, management/coordination experience, and interpersonal skills. Fisher was surprised to find that the position had a significantly higher public services component than expected and that anticipated responsibilities such as vendor relations and license management were not among the most cited characteristics.

A key component of a mature profession is that the key requirements of a particular position within that profession do not change, dramatically, over time. To see if Fisher's key characteristics have held up since 2001, the authors examined position advertisements found in *American Libraries* from 2002 through March, 2005. Like Fisher, the authors removed from consideration positions with titles that indicated that the activities of the position were extensions of traditional functions, i.e., ER cataloger. The authors also removed from consideration abbreviated advertisements that referred readers to a Web site for full details, if the Web site no longer existed. After all deletions, a total of 25 advertisements were examined.

Although the sample size was considerably smaller than that of Fisher, the three categories still worked well with the new study. Under traditional, public services characteristics, the most frequently mentioned were still reference and instruction. As in Fisher's study, there was a major, internal focus on instruction duties. Missing from this study's public services characteristics was the collection development component replaced by a more, specific emphasis on the selection of ER as part of a team or a consortial effort. In the technology-related area, Web development skills gained the top position. The online searches and non-specific computer application requirements found in Fisher's study disappeared to be replaced by knowledge or experience with library management systems and specific software applications. Excellent communication skills still took the top place in the personal characteristics category of both studies. In a departure from Fisher, general professional experience was replaced by the need for specific, professional experience requirements. Experience with ER was most frequently requested followed by experience in an academic library and project management experience. To be able to work cooperatively also made its way into a top-ten position. One personal attribute, not mentioned by Fisher that appeared in the top-ten list was knowledge of trends in ER. Finally, in a significant departure from the Fisher study, requirements for the ability to handle vendor relations and license management entered the list of top-ten characteristics.

Examined through the prism of Wells' four factors of professional consistency, the current study suggests that they are still applied by the representatives of organizations. The position descriptions examined attempted to include traits or competencies that would enhance the economic value of the person in the position: they advertised for energetic, innovative, dynamic, and motivated persons. To be able to work efficiently was mentioned or implied in various ways and it was common for the economic value of the position to be extended by the inclusion of requirements for skills in or knowledge of library activities such as reference, cataloging, or interlibrary loan (ILL).

In the area of technical skills, a degree from an ALA-accredited program was still a core requirement for all, but four of the institutions. All had requirements that centered, in some fashion, on handling ER. Web development skills topped the list at 72% followed by the ability to implement, use, and provide access to ER and management tools. Knowledge of trends and emergent technologies was also important to almost 50% of the institutions. Other technical competencies mentioned included skills in the facilitation of resource-connectivity (48%) and experience with an integrated library system (ILS) (44%).

Political skills or qualities that would enhance a candidate's effectiveness in the position were also featured prominently in the advertisements. The negotiation of licenses or contracts was mentioned in 48% of the descriptions. The ability to assess, evaluate, and work with vendors as well as products was a requirement of 52% of the descriptions. One-third of the institutions signaled their need for candidates to have prior knowledge of the political landscape by a requirement for previous academic library experience. One-third, also, wanted candidates to have leadership skills.

Social skills were an important part of the position descriptions. The majority of libraries wanted applicants to have excellent communication and interpersonal skills. Possession of excellent communication skills was the fourth highest trait identified overall. The ability to work collaboratively or in teams or to form working relationships was mentioned by almost half of the institutions.

After looking at specific characteristics, the authors attempted to discover the approaches under which this new role for librarians was to be integrated into the parent organization. It is evident that some ambivalence still exists. The reporting lines could be determined in only 13 of the 25 positions advertised. Of those, five reported to the technical services area, four reported to the library's central administration, three were intended to be part of an electronic services unit, and one reported to a coordinator of reference services-collection management. While several of the position advertisements that did not delineate a reporting line described public services responsibilities, which might have suggested the position's placement in the public services area, this could not be verified. Harkening back to Abbott, some of this ambivalence may arise from the origins of the position in the library. For example, if the resources for the position came from the elimination or reconfiguration of another position, e.g., an online search librarian, the library administration might have chosen to keep the ER librarian position in the same unit. Conversely, if the position was developed due to the need for new expertise, i.e., a license negotiator, the administration might have chosen to place the position in the unit where the need for new expertise arose. Despite the ambiguity that surrounds decisions as to where the position belongs in the organizational structure, the descriptions, as a whole, construct a prototype of what a fully matured ER librarian position could be and how those technical, political, social, and economic characteristics could be used to strengthen an organization.

The strong demand for the ALA-accredited degree found in the position advertisements demonstrates that, in the area of technical skills, the prime requirement for any successful ER librarian is competent librarianship on a broad scale. Like all librarians, the ER librarian provides access to information resources, only in a new and different format and with new and different tools. Hence, this librarian needs to have the professional competence and knowledge necessary to analyze client information needs and match those needs with the appropriate information resources. The ER librarian, also, is called upon to have specialized knowledge that facilitates access to digital information resources. The growth of Web-based applications and services has created a need for the ER librarians to develop and make use of specific skills sets to understand and make use of the software and electronic tools already in use by their parent organizations. Many of the position descriptions called for candidates to have knowledge of specific software packages. These requirements are meant to allow the hiring organization to plan for a shortened start-up time for the new hire and give the organization immediate knowledge of and access to the ER librarian's expertise.

The position advertisements also reveal that the successful ER librarian must have a wide-range of political skills in order to influence decision-making towards a desired outcome. Requirements such as leadership, the ability to negotiate, problem-solving skills, and being innovative indicate the need for the ER librarian to have a strong set of political skills. The need for these skills becomes even more apparent with a further examination of the tasks that the ER librarian might be asked to perform.

For example, many of the position descriptions required that the ER librarian provide leadership in the development of the library's ER program; thus, a major political skill that would be required of successful ER librarians would be the ability to anticipate patron needs. While the majority of services provided by the library profession tend to be on-site and face-to-face interactions, ER librarians face the challenge to work with remote clients in a high-technology, virtual environment. This type of service demands that the ER librarian be able to interpret non-traditional, or even vague, input from clients in order to anticipate their various needs. Once these needs are established the ER librarian must develop outcomes that match them.

Once the desired outcome has been determined, steps must then be taken to secure resources to support the project, which is a core, political skill. Thus, ER librarians practice a high degree of diplomacy when they attempt to secure such resources. It is not uncommon for ER librarians to find themselves in situations where they need to communicate highly complex, technological matters to listeners who understand technology at widely varied levels. More often than not, the members of this latter group are decision-makers/funding authorities and may be skeptical when faced with the high degree of ambiguity that is, often, associated with the development of new, electronic information services, which makes diplomacy especially important for the ER librarian who must explain the utility of these new systems. Diplomacy is especially important, also, when representatives of the library work with university administrators who may have a limited view of the benefits of technological enhancements to library users. In this situation, it is important for the ER librarian to gauge the technological-savvy of the audience and present information in a manner the listeners can understand and to which they will respond. To do otherwise may result in failure to gain support.

Once resources have been procured another political skill, the art of negotiation comes into play. Though not every ER librarian will be expected to negotiate vendor/publisher contracts for digital products and services they are relied upon, more and more, to do so. In order to utilize such a negotiation skill, the librarian must have a firm grasp of the needs of the organization and the will to advocate for these in the face of vendor/ publisher reluctance. Effective negotiation work, also, depends upon the technical knowledge previously mentioned. To negotiate for and facilitate new services, ER librarians must be careful/vigilant to comply with applicable legal/license requirements, which means a thorough familiarity with the laws that govern copyright and intellectual property rights.

If the negotiations are successful and all legalities are in place, ER librarians are, once again, called upon to use their diplomatic skills to navigate through uncertain paths in the implementation of new services, which may lead to the utilization of another political skill/characteristic: risk-taking. It will fall upon the ER librarian, sometimes in collaboration with others, to either implement new systems or upgrade extant ones. When the implementation of a new system or service does not proceed as smoothly as the vendor/publishers have indicated it should, the ER librarian must be prepared to address problems that result from interrupted service and the wrath of frustrated users. Hence, successful ER librarians must have the courage and drive to take and accept reasonable risks in order to create an optimum, electronic services environment and the diplomacy to smooth ruffled feathers when upgrades do not go as well as planned.

While political skills are used to get others to buy into organizational goals, well-developed social skills can be used to ensure that participants maintain positive attitudes. The position descriptions examined highlighted the need for strong, social skills by the requirement of excellent communication and interpersonal skills along with the ability to work cooperatively. Libraries are social organizations that rely on social structures to accomplish tasks; thus, the ability to lead and work with teams is a must for ER librarians. To develop and manage major systems involves work with individuals with various skills, backgrounds, personalities, and egos. An ER librarian has to be a skilled consensus-builder in order to develop a team dedicated to a shared vision and goal, to create a productive technological environment, and to meet client needs. Along with the skill to build a team, ER librarians must have the communication skills to explain systems, technical processes, and procedures in a lucid manner and take into consideration the audience's level of technical knowledge. To be able to discern the technical competencies of the members of the team and tailor presentations to the level of team comprehension are important attributes for ER librarians. Other social skills that will be necessary will be the ability to cope with rapid changes as well as to communicate changes to the team members and to help them accept and cope with the changes. Although adaptation to change is a prime requirement for all professions in the information age, it is especially important for ER librarians. While all professions have to deal with some change, the changes faced by librarians and, especially, ER librarians are more fundamental, constant, and rapid. Without the ability to cope with a volatile environment, one should not undertake an ER librarian position.

Beyond the library's walls, ER librarians also need to have social skills that allow them to act as communication bridges when they work with parties who hold different philosophies of access to information. It is often the ER librarian's responsibility to coordinate with librarians the work of information technologists who are responsible to supply the organization's technological infrastructure. The heritage of the technologist is to be concerned with security and control foremost as most of them work in academic computer centers where the primary function is to control access to the organization's computer systems (and the information they contain) according to a set of pre-determined criteria. For example, most non-library organizational systems require a username/password, sign-on process to gain access. Librarians, on the other hand, make their on-line catalogs and resources available to all users with only grudging acceptance of sign-on controls for commercial resources to which there is a subscription. The ER librarian must display tact in order to reconcile the two opposite views so to create a harmonious work environment.

Finally, the position descriptions revealed the economic characteristics library administrators value in a fully matured ER librarian position. It is to an organization's economic advantage to recruit employees who will share the cost of their professional development. The current ER environment is very dynamic and volatile. To be successful, persons who work in this environment must continue to learn and upgrade their professional and technical skills. Given the travel and professional development budgets of many libraries today the parent organization will value an ER librarian who can acquire grants or who will use personal funds to share in the costs of professional development activities. Library administrators will also expect the ER librarian to work within available avenues of professional advancement. Today, this still means that the publication of articles in peer-reviewed journals and conference presentations are the best ways to improve salary, advance in academic ranks, and achieve tenure. Finally, most library administrators will see an economic incentive if they hire an ER librarian who has a skills set that allows the librarian to perform selected, traditional responsibilities beyond ER activities.

In this chapter, the origins of ER librarianship were examined within the context of classic organization theory as well as how the position has developed within the context of economic, political, social, and technical factors. Based on the examination of position advertisements a set of skills that are preferred for the *ideal* ER librarian have been identified. It is unrealistic to expect that all applicants for an ER librarian position will have all of the proposed skills, but the majority of these skills should be in place, if the ER librarian is to be successful. Whether the position of ER librarian will retain its current importance over time is still in question. Although the examination of recent position advertisements document that core characteristics have developed long-term consistency, the jurisdiction of foundation responsibilities such as license negotiation as well as the ER librarian's role within the organization are still to be determined.

## NOTES

1. "More Data, But No Less Paper," *Technology in the Humanities* 11(1) (winter, 2004); http://www.humanities.uci.edu/hirc/humtech/articles.html (viewed September 30, 2005).

2. Talcott Parsons, "Suggestions for a Sociological Approach to the Theory of Organizations–I," *Administrative Science Quarterly* 1(1) (1956): 63.

3. Andrew Abbott, *The System of Professions: An Essay on the Division of Expert Labor* (Chicago: University of Chicago Press, 1988), 215.

4. Andrew Fisher, "The Electronic Resources Librarian Position: A Public Services Phenomenon?" *Library Collections, Acquisitions, & Technical Services* 27(2003): 3-17.

doi:10.1300/J105v32n01_02

# Marian Through the Looking Glass:
## The Unique Evolution
## of the Electronic Resources (ER)
## Librarian Position

Rebecca S. Albitz
Wendy Allen Shelburne

**SUMMARY.** The current responsibilities of an electronic resources (ER) librarian are very different than those of her colleagues. She works between the world of business and libraries–negotiating, haggling, troubleshooting. When academic libraries first offered databases, however, the associated responsibilities were usually attached to another position, such as a reference or systems librarian. As technology developed, allowing more diverse electronic resources (ER) to be made available, the responsibilities of the people managing those products became more complex. This article traces the evolution of the ER librarian, from a part-time position to one completely different than any other found in librarianship. doi:10.1300/J105v32n01_03 *[Article copies available for a fee from The Haworth Document Delivery Service: 1-800-HAWORTH. E-mail address: <docdelivery@haworthpress.com> Website: <http://www.HaworthPress.com> © 2007 by The Haworth Press. All rights reserved.]*

Rebecca S. Albitz is ER and Copyright Librarian, Penn State Shenango. Wendy Allen Shelburne, MS, MA, is ER Librarian, University of Illinois at Urbana-Champaign Library.

[Haworth co-indexing entry note]: "Marian Through the Looking Glass: The Unique Evolution of the Electronic Resources (ER) Librarian Position." Albitz, Rebecca S., and Wendy Allen Shelburne. Co-published simultaneously in *Collection Management* (The Haworth Information Press, an imprint of The Haworth Press) Vol. 32, No. 1/2, 2007, pp. 15-30; and: *Electronic Resources Librarianship and Management of Digital Information: Emerging Professional Roles* (ed: Mark Jacobs) The Haworth Information Press, an imprint of The Haworth Press, 2007, pp. 15-30. Single or multiple copies of this article are available for a fee from The Haworth Document Delivery Service [1-800-HAWORTH, 9:00 a.m. - 5:00 p.m. (EST). E-mail address: docdelivery@haworthpress.com].

doi:10.1300/J105v32n01_03

**KEYWORDS.** ER librarian, database management, ER management, ER staffing, library staffing

## INTRODUCTION

How has the electronic resources (ER) librarian position evolved? One way to document shifting responsibilities for any professional position is to track changes reflected in position announcements in the literature. A number of articles in the library literature have done just this–examined certain positions or responsibilities through a longitudinal study of job announcements and drawn conclusions about changes within these specializations. However, can job postings alone tell the whole story of a specialization, particularly one that is so difficult to define? Because the authors, much like Alice in Wonderland, often find ourselves in a world which is very different from that of our more traditional colleagues–a world filled with pricing models, legalese, technological snafus, and negotiations–we were curious to explore this question. To do so, we chose to examine how ER librarian positions, since they first began to appear, have been defined through position announcements and, then, to compare those results with the current state of ER librarianship as defined through survey results.

In three recent articles which examined job postings for positions in digital or ER management in libraries, the advertised responsibilities for many of these positions look as though little care was taken to delineate the parameters of the position. The list of responsibilities seems to be beyond the capacities of any single individual. The reason for this is that, while library administrators realize the need to address the access and ongoing management of the growing number of electronic and digital information resources, they also understand the need to continue to maintain more traditional library services, such as in-person reference, bibliographic instruction, and print-based acquisitions and cataloging. Without an ER position dedicated to all the issues and tasks which surround the delivery of digital resources, extant library staff will have to take on these additional responsibilities. So, in order to ensure that all ER activities are accomplished, administrators have had to design positions which only a superhuman could perform successfully, or create "kitchen sink" positions which include a variety of disjointed responsibilities that no current employees perform. The initial responsibilities for many niche positions in libraries are defined in this way. As the most significant responsibilities related to the position grow and become more complex, peripheral activities begin to disappear until a core definition for the job has been established. This is the pattern which governs the development of the subject of this chapter, the ER librarian.

## *GROWTH OF ELECTRONIC RESOURCES (ER)*

The role ERs (ER) play in libraries has grown dramatically in the past ten years–a migration from stand-alone CD-ROMs, to networked CD-ROMs, and now to Internet-based services–while the primary surge towards Web access occurred in 1998.[1]

The move to the Web increased the accessibility of electronic materials which, in turn, increased the amount librarians were willing to pay for digital titles. In its 1997-1998 annual report, the Association of Research Libraries (ARL) recorded that the mean expenditure for ER among reporting libraries was 8.85% of their entire collections budgets.[2]

In 2002-2003, the mean had risen to 22.01%.[3]

The growth in electronic collections has exacerbated the difficulties inherent in their management, a challenge which is reflected in the library literature, where current ER management policies and practices are discussed, demonstrated, and questioned. A search of the library literature on the keywords *electronic* and *management* returned articles which focus on issues related to electronic journal or database management. However, ER staffing as the primary focus of an article was absent. A search on the subject heading *information systems/administration* retrieved results which explored issues related to OPACs, networks, and other internal systems, but not ER administration.

There is a strong interest in the non-human side of ER management reflected in the number of library technology companies, e.g., Innovative Interfaces, Inc. (III), which have developed ER management systems (ERMS). These products have responded to the many home-grown and hybrid products that have been developed and implemented by librarians. The introduction of *ER Management: Report of the DLF [Digital Library Federation] Electronic Resource Management Initiative* states:

> most of the responding DLF libraries had found that their existing integrated library systems (ILS) were incapable of supporting these functions and had begun to design and build local automated tools to fill the gaps.[4]

III has developed a module to manage licensing and purchasing information for indexing and abstracting services, electronic journals, and full-text resources. Ex Libris has done the same with its Verde product. According to the Web site *A Web Hub for Developing Administrative Metadata for Electronic Resource Management* (located at: http://www.library.cornell.edu/cts/elicensestudy/home.html), Endeavor, EBSCO, the Colorado Alliance of Research Libraries (CARL), and Visionary Technology in Library Solutions (VTLS) have all pursued the development of similar systems. Both the literature and the marketplace reflect the technical and management issues associated with ER and the importance of these to the profession and its delivery of library services.

## LITERATURE REVIEW

With so much written about ER management and so much money going into product development to support it, one might think that a similar amount of energy would be expended on the consideration of the appropriate staffing which is necessary to manage these resources. But, as mentioned previously, based on the relative dearth of articles found in *Library Literature* which discuss this topic, staffing has not been a high priority. Vicki Grahame and Tim McAdam, authors of the ARL SPEC (Systems and Procedures Exchange Center) Kit 282, titled *Managing ER*, compiled a bibliography of articles that discuss some aspect of ER personnel, two of which are pertinent to this discussion. Croneis and Henderson analyzed position descriptions announced between 1990 and 2000 which contained either the word *electronic* or *digital* in the job title. This broad position description analysis shows "an increasing number of . . . position announcements, a greater diversity of functional areas involved, a wider variety of types of institutions placing advertisements, and the emergence of distinctions between 'electronic' and 'digital' positions in terms of job responsibilities."[5]

William Fisher's article "The Electronic Resources Librarian Position: A Public Services Phenomenon?" reviews more focused position announcements which appeared over a seventeen-year period. Fisher analyzed 298 position advertisements from *American Libraries* and found that reference/information services were the most often cited position responsibilities and concluded that ER positions lean heavily towards public services. Although responsibilities that can be tied to technical services, such as acquisitions and sometimes collection development, are present in these advertisements, Fisher states "the position title of Electronic Resources Librarian has been pre-empted by the public service sector of the profession."[6]

An article Grahame and McAdam did not cite took essentially the same approach as Croneis and Henderson, as well as Fisher, to evaluate ER librarian positions in academic libraries. Albitz analyzed position descriptions published in *College & Research Libraries News* between 1996 and 2001, intentionally omitting those positions that focused more on digital project management and cataloging. The goal of this review was to determine if trends existed in reporting structures, responsibilities, and position requirements. Albitz determined that ER librarians are found in many different departments, may be required to perform almost any task a librarian might perform in an academic library, and are not required to have much professional experience.[7]

Each of these articles analyzed comparable data, but from different publications at different time periods. Thus, it is useful to combine the results in order to trace the changing responsibilities of the ER librarian. The information gleaned covers a breadth of positions and illustrates the changes in responsibilities of the position which have occurred over the past twenty years. For the purposes of this chapter, this information will be compared to the authors' own survey results. The sets of data will be compared to determine what, if any, changes in terms of role, responsibilities, or tasks have occurred for incumbents in ER librarian positions. Do the tasks performed by those currently holding this position still reflect the advertisements published in prior years?

## RESEARCH METHODOLOGY

In order to gather data which concerns the current state of ER librarianship, the authors chose to utilize the ARL membership list. ARL academic libraries in the United States received two surveys: one addressed generically to the ER librarian and the other addressed by name to the library director. Each of these two mailings contained a separate survey (see Appendix A) which requested information concerning the current and past role of this position. More specifically, the requested information reflected the information Fisher, Albitz, and Crome/Henderson compiled in their studies, which allowed for ease in comparison.

## SURVEY RESPONSES

A total of 202 surveys were distributed. The response rate was around 20%–21 ER librarians and 23 library directors returned their surveys. A number of other unusable surveys were returned: three institutions wrote to indicate that they would not participate; four were recruiting to fill a similar position; two addressed positions outside the scope of this project; one was returned undelivered; and eight institutions did not have such a position. It is probable that many more than eight ARL libraries do not employ an ER librarian, and so chose not to respond to the survey. These survey results offer a view of the current state of ER librarianship in ARL libraries as well as the perspective of library directors on the success of the evolution of the position within their institutions.

### A Comparison of Reporting Structures

The three research articles mentioned above all placed the ER librarian primarily in public services. Albitz looked at reporting lines and determined that 42% of the positions were specifically in public services areas, 33% were in technical services areas, and 25% were either split between those areas or their reporting line could not be determined.[8] Croneis and Henderson looked at primary job functions and determined that the majority of positions announced over a ten-year period fell within public services, although the percentage difference between public services and technical services grew smaller each year.[9] Fisher mapped public services, personal, and technological attributes in the positions posted over a seventeen-year period. Of the ten most frequently cited responsibilities, reference/information services was the most common, with bibliographic instruction second.[10]

The ER librarians surveyed for this project, however, told a different story. Fifty-two percent currently work within a technical services department, 15% report through public services, 30% are in collection management, and one respondent is in administration. This discrepancy is not a surprise. Fisher, and Croneis and Henderson were looking at responsibilities, rather than reporting structures. While a position may have a number of public services responsibilities, that would not necessarily preclude the incumbent from being expected to report to an aministrator in technical services. According to Albitz, 26% of the positions reviewed reported to both public and technical services or their reporting lines could not be determined. That figure, added to the technical services figure from her study, more closely reflects the results of the survey discussed in this chapter. Finally, 30% of the survey respondents cited collection management as their administrative area. It depends upon the organization, but a collection management office might be a part of technical or public services, or it might be a unit unto itself.

## *Position Responsibilities*

As stated previously, responsibilities delineated in a position announcement may not, for a number of reasons, translate into the actual responsibilities of the person who assumes the position. The reasons for that might include the incumbent's skills, knowledge, talents, or interests; or changes within the library which, originally, announced the position. A comparison between the Albitz and Fisher studies reveals similarities in the content of the announcements reviewed, although the reviewers chose different publications from which to glean the advertisements which they analyzed (see Table 1). Fisher found that reference responsibilities appeared most often in his group, while Albitz's research showed reference to be the second most frequently cited responsibility after ER coordination which, obviously, might encompass a myriad of tasks.[11]

Each noted that bibliographic instruction was the next most common responsibility.

The results of the survey discussed in this chapter, however, indicate a marked shift away from the responsibilities annotated in position announcements of the past ten years. Public services responsibilities are no longer highlighted. ER librarians are now expected to focus on the management of electronic journals and databases and all of the complexities which accompany this task. The most common activity referred to in the current survey results is the rather vague role of ER coordination, which might include in its long list of responsibilities department management, department liaison, and management of the acquisitions process, as well as other more specific tasks in a variety of functional categories. According to Albitz, the coordination responsibility appeared in 69% of the announcements reviewed. As the second most common activity, three responsibilities appeared with equal frequency: purchase management (acquisitions), renewals, and cancellations of ER; license and pricing negotiations; and troubleshooting technical problems. Fisher's analysis may have grouped activities like purchasing under the general umbrella term of collection development, although he suggests "the collection development function itself, like bibliographic instruction, is often associated with public service oriented positions."[12]

TABLE 1. Position Responsibilities

| Position Responsibility | Fisher Results (percentage) | Albitz Results (percentage) | Survey Results (percentage) |
|---|---|---|---|
| Reference | 77 | 58 | 10 |
| Instruction | 74 | 53 | 19 |
| Collection Development | 53 | 32 | — |
| Computer Applications | 55** | — | — |
| Online Searching | 47 | — | — |
| World Wide Web Applications | 41 | 42 | 24 |
| Manage/Coordinate Program | 34 | 69 | 57 |
| Automation | 28 | 30* | — |
| Purchasing, Reviewing, and Cancellation Coordination | — | 7 | 71 |
| Licensing/Pricing Negotiations | — | 18 | 62 |
| Troubleshooting | — | 30* | 62 |
| User Statistics Management | — | 3 | 33 |
| Link Resolver Management | — | — | 29 |
| Trials/Testing Management | — | — | 29 |

*Automation and troubleshooting were grouped in Albitz's article
**Definition of computer applications is vague; it may include personal computer applications, knowledge of operating systems, experience with word processing or spreadsheet applications, or troubleshooting hardware or software problems.

His list does not include mention of either licensing or troubleshooting. In the Albitz survey, licensing was present in 18% of the position advertisements and technical and automation support appeared in 30%.

Three other activities were grouped together next among the current survey responses: management of a link-resolver or a federated search product; coordination or trials of products; and management of usage data, often referred to as statistics. None of these three activities appeared in any of the previous studies.

In the current survey, reference responsibilities appeared twice only and user education (which includes database-specific instruction) appeared in four responses.

What might account for the differences between position announcements posted during and before 2001 and the daily responsibilities of ER librarians in 2005? As Fisher noted, position announcements published before 1993 focused either on direct-connection searching via BRS or Dialog, or CD-ROM searching.[13] Mediated searching required direct contact between the librarian and the patron as research goals were translated into appropriate search terms. While self-service CD-ROMs offered broader access, they were still fairly new to our users, who needed more instruction in their use than they might now. Selection of these products did not require a lot of time–decisions were based on content, not interface, because so few information providers had ventured into the digital information arena. And, because CD-ROMs were self-contained, librarians did not have to worry about networking issues beyond their own institution. Therefore, selection and management demands on the ER librarian prior to 2001 were less than they are today, allowing time for the reference and instruction activities that came along with these new formats.

As electronic information resources became more common during the 1990s, the number of position announcements increased, as both Albitz and Fisher note, and, as the previously cited ARL data establish, spending on these resources by libraries increased accordingly. In the early 1990s, however, the number of products available through the Internet, as well as vendor/publishers who offered them was few. Complexity in the management of ER began to creep in as different access venues (mediated searching, CD-ROMs, and the Internet) and digital information products began to be simultaneously maintained by libraries. Such complexity takes more time to manage. The increase in the responsibilities categorized as *ER coordination* and the corresponding decrease in reference and instruction responsibilities reflected in Albitz's position description analysis–which focused on a more recent time period–supports this conclusion.

The increased complexity of the position and the need to focus the incumbent's responsibilities on ER management rather than on reference or bibliographic instruction are articulated in the library director responses to the survey. In the libraries of the survey respondents, the positions were established between 1980 and 2005 with the majority created in 2000-2001 (see Table 2). Fourteen directors indicated that the responsibilities of the position had changed since its inception, while four indicated that they had not. More telling, however, are the responsibility changes noted on the survey responses. In almost all cases, the position originally included functions other than ER management which were, subsequently, eliminated. OPAC support, Web management, reference, online searching, instruction, and scholarly communications were all responsibilities which were transferred from the ER librarian to other

TABLE 2. Start Dates of Surveyed ER Librarians

| Date Position Established | Frequency |
|---|---|
| 1980 | 1 |
| 1990 | 1 |
| 1995 | 2 |
| 1999 | 1 |
| 2000 | 6 |
| 2001 | 4 |
| 2002 | 2 |
| 2003 | 1 |
| 2004 | 3 |
| 2005 | 2 |

faculty and staff. And while all but one director said the position currently fulfills their needs, some still indicated that they need to increase staff support in this area.

As the director responses indicate, some of these positions were developed before the advent of Web-based information products, but most of those who now hold these positions were appointed in the past five years. The ER librarians who responded to the survey were hired in 2000-2001, the same years in which, according to the directors who responded, the majority of the positions were established. Only two incumbents were hired prior to 2000–one in 1998 and the other in 1999.

### Prior Professional Experience

The shift in responsibilities attributed to ER librarians over the past ten years reflects the technological changes experienced in library services as well as the acquisition and maintenance of library collections. Rather than a public services focus, these positions incorporate elements of technical services in the traditional sense (acquisitions, serials management), computer-support services, and business and legal services.

No study, until the present one, has traced the professional backgrounds of ER librarians since such positions began to appear. Would such a study show similar shifts in the professional experiences of those who move into these positions? One of the questions we asked of ER librarians was about their professional background. What were all the positions they had held in librarianship? No pattern emerged, but the results reflected a breadth of professional experience.

As Table 3 illustrates, not one of the incumbents held a similar position prior to their current appointment. In fact, none of them had backgrounds which encompassed the responsibilities of the position which they now hold. This also suggests that the creation of ER librarian positions has been in response to the shift in institutional needs brought on by technological change. Because no one in the profession had relevant experience, the selection of qualified people to fill ER librarian positions was yet another challenge for librarians. Sixty-seven percent of the ER librarian survey respondents were internal candidates. Either they were asked to apply for the position or, as in the case of 43% of the respondents, they were reassigned, which suggests that librarians adjusted to the need for ER management through internal reallocations, rather than through the creation of new positions. Whether this is true in a broader sense will require further investigation.

## TRAINING OPPORTUNITIES

Whether internal or external, incumbents entered these positions, as survey results indicate, with little or no experience with ER management.

TABLE 3. Survey Respondents' Prior Positions

| Position | Number of Respondents Who Held This Position |
|---|---|
| Reference/Bibliographer | 9 |
| Serials | 7 |
| Acquisitions | 4 |
| Access Services | 3 |
| Special Projects | 3 |
| Instruction | 2 |
| Electronic Reference Coordinator | 2 |
| Systems | 2 |
| Finance/Administration | 2 |
| Collection Development | 1 |
| Vendor | 1 |
| Web Design/Applications | 1 |
| Media Librarianship | 1 |

One of the biggest hurdles they faced was to gain the knowledge needed to handle the business and legal responsibilities associated with product pricing and licensing. When asked to describe any training they had received, the ER librarians offered no consistent response. Twelve noted that they had taken either one or both of the licensing workshops offered through ARL. Eight respondents indicated that they were self-taught and one specified receiving no formal training. Organizations which offer opportunities for training were mentioned, e.g., American Library Association (ALA), Association of College & Research Libraries (ACRL), North American Serials Interest Group (NASIG), and American Association of Law Libraries (AALL), which offered events like pre-conferences and workshops, training sponsored by information resource providers, and teleconferences. In addition to these learning opportunities, some respondents indicated that they would like to have more training in leadership and management, computer science, database design, statistics, copyright, and budgets. While most respondents had some continuing education opportunities, there are currently no broadly available educational programs for ER librarians. One respondent indicated that to be successful in this position it is important to be willing to take the initiative and learn on your own.

## CONCLUSION

In libraries we speak of evolving information resources, but in the case of ER in the past fifteen years it is more appropriate to discuss a revolution. The changes that have occurred have been fast-paced and the profession's response to these changes has had to be as rapid. The revolution is apparent in a review of job position announcements for those responsible for the management of this change. In the earliest stages of the digital age, a librarian might have been able to handle on-demand database searching, reference work, bibliographic instruction, and collection development. But as the complexity of the digital environment increased, ER librarian position announcements changed as they began to focus more on ER management and less on other activities of librarianship. These days a description of the positions bears little resemblance to those examined by Fisher in 1985. Fisher's study showed us that ER librarian positions changed slowly in the early 1990s, but the position's responsibilities began to shift rapidly as librarians, on behalf of their libraries, invested more money in a broader variety of electronic information resources. Instruction and reference work related to online titles has reverted back to public service librarians, which allows ER librarians to concentrate on the licensing and management of the increasing numbers of digital resources. Many current incumbents are also responsible for the management of new technologies related to electronic information resources, e.g., link-resolvers and federated search products.

Librarians would undoubtedly agree that they have had little or no control over the revolutionary shift in libraries towards ER and have had little time to plan for their management–which has meant, in many cases, internal staffing adjustments where new positions could not be created. But, no one person can know, understand, or keep track of all the intricacies of ER librarianship as they evolve, which makes the development of consistent, systematic, broadly available training opportunities critical.

When Alice looked into the mirror, only to find herself on the other side, she experienced the confusion and inconsistencies of a digital information world where the unexpected becomes the commonplace. Librarians who find themselves in the role of ER manager often experience this same unsettled feeling because of rapid changes in product availability, new technologies, pricing structures, and licensing terms. In direct response to these external forces, librarians have made shifts in reporting structures and position responsibilities. Our inability, as a profession and as a society, to control this environment only adds to the disorientation. Like the products themselves, the ER librarian position still evolves. It plays many roles, e.g., traditional librarianship, Web design, systems management, and accepts many responsibilities, e.g., contract attorney, business manager, technology troubleshooter. Until some or all of these multiple roles are accepted as common within librarianship, and their definitions and responsibilities are more standardized, ER librarians will continue to operate on the other side of the looking glass.

## NOTES

1. Greg R. Notess, "The Year Databases Moved to the Web," *Database* 21, no. 66 (December 1996): 56.

2. *ARL Supplementary Statistics 1997-98* (Washington, DC: Association of College & Research Libraries, 1998), 3.

3. Mark Young and Martha Kyrillidou, eds. and comps., *ARL Supplemental Statistics 2002-03* (Washington, DC: Association of College & Research Libraries, 2004), 12.

4. Timothy D. Jewell et al., *Electronic Resource Management: Report of the DLF Resource Management Initiative* (Washington, DC: Digital Library Federation, 2005), 3.

5. Karen S. Croneis and Pat Henderson, "Electronic and Digital Librarian Positions: A Content Analysis of Announcements from 1990 through 2000," *Journal of Academic Librarianship* 28, no. 4 (July 2002): 233.

6. William Fisher, "The ER Librarian Position: A Public Services Phenomenon?" *Library Collections, Acquisitions, & Technical Service*s 27(11) (2003): 4.

7. Rebecca S. Albitz, "Electronic Resource Librarians in Academic Libraries: A Position Announcement Analysis, 1996-2001," *Portal: Libraries and the Academy* 2, no. 4 (2002): 597.

8. Ibid., 593.

9. Croneis and Henderson, 234.

10. Fisher, 8.

11. Albitz, 595.

12. Fisher, 9.

13. Ibid.

doi:10.1300/J105v32n01_03

# APPENDIX A

## ER Librarian Questionnaire

1. Name (optional):

2. Institutional affiliation:

3. Position title:

4. Please provide a brief position description (please attach a separate sheet if you wish):

5. To whom do you report?–please provide position title and whether this position is considered "public services" or "technical services," or if that distinction cannot be determined:

6. Please provide a brief summary of your career in libraries, as a librarian and, if appropriate, staff member, with institution names and dates of service (please attach a separate sheet if you wish):

7. When were you appointed to your current position?

8. Why did you apply for this position?

9. Have your responsibilities within this position evolved since you were first appointed? If so, how?

10. What kind of training or continuing education have you had in order to learn how to, for example, read a license or negotiate with a vendor? Please provide course/program name, what organization offered the program, where or how was it offered (city or online?).

11. What part of the training was effective? What was not?

12. Do you see gaps in training opportunities available to people in your position? What is missing?

13. Are there changes you would like to see made to your job description so it better reflects your responsibilities? If so, what change(s) would you make?

## Library Director Questionnaire

1. Name (optional):

2. Institutional affiliation:

3. Position title:

4. Please indicate when the ER position was established at your institution:

5. Please provide a brief job description for this position when it was first conceived (please use a separate sheet if you wish).

6. To whom (position title) did this original position report? Would you classify it as being part of public services, technical services, or neither?

7. Has the job description for this position changed since it was first conceived? If so, please provide a current position description (attach a separate sheet if needed). If the position's responsibilities or reporting line have not changed, please skip to question 10.

8. If the position has changed, what was the impetus to make these changes? At whose request?

9. If the reporting line has changed, to whom does this position now report? Why was this change made?

10. As the position is now configured, does it fulfill your organization's needs? Would you change the current responsibilities? If so, how?

# Expanding the Role of the Electronic Resources (ER) Librarian in the Hybrid Library

Lai-Ying Hsiung

**SUMMARY.** As libraries transition rapidly from print to digital, the electronic resources (ER) librarian in technical services has a crucial role to play in the management of the hybrid collection where print-based materials are collected and used alongside the digital. The ER librarian will help integrate and coordinate the hybrid function, improve the information technology infrastructure, populate bibliographic systems with useful data, apply new processes to bibliographic systems, collaborate with external partners, and adopt/adapt new Web technologies. doi:10.1300/J105v32n01_04 *[Article copies available for a fee from The Haworth Document Delivery Service: 1-800-HAWORTH. E-mail address: <docdelivery@haworthpress.com> Website: <http://www.HaworthPress.com> © 2007 by The Haworth Press. All rights reserved.]*

**KEYWORDS.** Hybrid library, print and digital, electronic resources librarian, bibliographic systems, technical services

---

Lai-Ying Hsiung, MLS, is Acting Head of Technical Services, University Library, University of California, Santa Cruz, 1156 High Street, Santa Cruz, CA 95064 (E-mail: lhsiung@ucsc.edu).

[Haworth co-indexing entry note]: "Expanding the Role of the Electronic Resources (ER) Librarian in the Hybrid Library." Hsiung, Lai-Ying. Co-published simultaneously in *Collection Management* (The Haworth Information Press, an imprint of The Haworth Press) Vol. 32, No. 1/2, 2007, pp. 31-47; and: *Electronic Resources Librarianship and Management of Digital Information: Emerging Professional Roles* (ed: Mark Jacobs) The Haworth Information Press, an imprint of The Haworth Press, 2007, pp. 31-47. Single or multiple copies of this article are available for a fee from The Haworth Document Delivery Service [1-800-HAWORTH, 9:00 a.m. - 5:00 p.m. (EST). E-mail address: docdelivery@haworthpress.com].

doi:10.1300/J105v32n01_04

## INTRODUCTION

The library's rapid transition from paper only to a hybrid model that incorporates print and digital resources is a new development of the twenty-first Century. To support this complex environment with its multiple needs as well as to keep up with constant changes in technology is a Herculean task. Librarians use bibliographic systems to manage hybrid collections and capitalize on new, digital opportunities to facilitate information access and interface navigation. This chapter will highlight several trends in the development of technical services in hybrid academic libraries and describe the possible role and responsibilities of the electronic resources (ER) librarian in this environment.

## THE DIGITAL TREND

As recently as a decade ago, print-based resources were the most important format in the provision of academic library services. "The rapid emergence of new forms of digital library collections has suddenly raised fundamental challenges to traditional concepts of building, servicing and preserving library collections."[1]

Four forms of digital information resources were described in an April 2004 report prepared by the Systemwide Library and Scholarly Information Advisory Committee at the University of California. Licensed digital collections, which consist of traditional scholarly publications produced in digital format by for-profit and not-for-profit publishers, are the most common type of digital resources now available in academic libraries. The second most common form is *digital-built content* created internally by academic libraries or from extant academic collections. The fury of rapid, journal digitization has moved into the digitization of monographs, reference materials, and special collections. Recently, Google's ambitious digitization of the world's major research libraries, and the formation of the Open Content Alliance (OCA),[2] a global consortium that provides open access to information, are the preamble of a new era. Today's biggest challenge for librarians comes from the third most common form; free information from the Internet. The Web revolutionizes the way users create and seek information and the way information providers market and present their products. Users *surf the Web* and access their favorite Web sites and do not realize that many of the resources they find and use there have been purchased by their libraries. In addition, they overlook print-based resources because they are under the impression that all the information they need can be found on the Web. The fourth most common form of digital information is datasets created by academic departments and, usually, contained in servers scattered throughout the university.

## Why Does Need for the Print-Based Information Format Still Exist?

There are many reasons for a library collection to remain hybrid despite the exponential rise in the use of the Web and the continual shift of library collections from print to digital. Some materials are still published only in print, especially in the developing world. Crawford pointed out that "several categories of journals remain available both in print and online. These include the core journals in each field (5-10% of the total), well-regarded journals where thematic issues and other forms of context make the print journal more valuable than the sum of individual articles, and journals with more, non-library subscribers than library subscriptions."[3]

Online content is not always perfect and may be incomplete or inadequate: peripheral or complementary materials may not be digitized or the quality of the digitization may not meet the requirements of serious users in fields such as biology, art, or graphic design.

Many users prefer to read a book on paper. Online versions of popular publications, which rely on print advertisements or personal subscriptions, may only offer individual, user registration; not institutional registration, which makes online access cumbersome for library clientele.

The volatile nature of online resources means librarians will not give up on print-based materials entirely. One reason is that they have experienced frequent access instability in the online format. Downtime can be due to technical problems or regular system maintenance. Other causes can be much more problematic. The host site may remove access, if they do not have a record of a library payment. This could result from machine or human error on the part of the publisher, the vendor, or the library. Other denials of access may occur when titles are sold from one publisher to another, when libraries change vendor/publishers, when titles are eliminated from an electronic package, or when a consortium is unable or unwilling to include certain titles at renewal time. Publishers change their policy about whether a subscription to a print journal should continue to include free, online access. Some or all of the articles from open access titles may, without warning, stop being offered in the open access model. If a subscription to a title ends for any reason, access to back issues, previously enjoyed by library users, might be denied by the publisher. For the most part, librarians still have no easy or inexpensive way to track changes to access on a systematic basis. Also, the content and presentation of digital information can be altered. This instability causes some librarians to remain committed to print-based information.

There are other reasons for librarians to retain print collections. Preservation of knowledge has always been a fundamental mission of libraries. Special and archival materials remain valuable even after they are digitized. In addition, there are shelves and shelves of extant, print-based materials that cannot be digitized due to copyright laws or have not been digitized due to limits on funding.

## Librarians Have to Manage Both Print and Digital Resources

There have been studies that confirm the need to retain of print-based information in libraries. A 2001 study by Dilevko and Gottlieb found that "undergraduates across various disciplines do value books and print journals, and they make extensive use of them when confronted with essays and assignments in which they want to excel."[4]

There is a lively debate going on among librarians who, at the same time, consider the need to expand and preserve print collections and the need to expand and support the rapid development of ER.[5]

Perhaps the data supplied by Michelle Wu to support the proposition that a twenty-first Century, academic law library "requires both traditional print materials and ER,"[6] is reflective of the philosophy of librarians in general. Print and online resources often intertwine and complement each other. At least for the foreseeable future, it is unlikely that all libraries will be entirely virtual in nature. "Some single-function, single-mission libraries will be virtual, but the majority of libraries will develop into hybrid, multi-purpose libraries, with multiple access and dissemination processes."[7]

## The Hybrid Library

The concept of the hybrid library was first suggested by Sutton[8] and popularized in the United Kingdom (UK) in the late 1990s by the Higher Education Funding Councils' eLib Phase 3 Programme under the direction of Rusbridge.[9]

Oppenheim and Smithson point out that "a simple way of defining the hybrid library is that it is a means of integrating the traditional library with the digital library . . . The contemporary information-user now has to operate in a hybrid environment where electronic and paper-based sources are used alongside each other."[10] However, "the balance of print and digital meta-information leans increasingly towards the digital."[11] So, the concept of the hybrid library is similar to that of the gateway library to bridge the gap between print-based and online collections.

## THE POSITION OF THE ER (ER) LIBRARIAN

When digital resources were introduced into libraries, ER functions were divided among the collection development, acquisitions, serials, systems, reference, and catalog units. The creation of the ER librarian position was meant to fill a void generated by the need for special skills that were unique in the management of the digital environment, like the legal finesse needed in license and contract negotiations and the technical skills required to handle large data sets from digital packages. So far, the position of the ER librarian has been assigned a wide variety of responsibilities as well as to many, different library units, e.g., technical services (acquisitions, billing, linking issues), collection development (trials, licensing, usage data), or information technology/systems (Web interfaces, hardware/software, systems architecture). The position may also function in public services to work with bibliographic instruction, database-searches, and interface usability. There are job titles like electronic services librarian, digital initiatives librarian, information technologies librarian, multimedia services librarian, Web services librarian, and Internet services librarian; all of which deal with electronic resource components similar to those handled by the ER librarian.

If a library decides to transition a staff member to the position of ER librarian, the serials librarian would be a likely candidate. It is clear that the responsibilities of the position of serials librarian, or its equivalent, can be expanded from management of print-based materials only to include electronic publications like online journal, ebooks, and database subscriptions.

### Role of the ER Librarian

There are several major hybrid library trends that affect the role of the ER librarian. In the print-based, research world, users are instructed to consult multiple information sources. However, the Web has revolutionized user expectations and Google has set a new standard for librarians in the search for acceptable, system solutions to provide a coherent view of the range of library resources. The ER librarian's responsibilities will include the integration and coordination of hybrid functions, the improvement of the information technology infrastructure, the population of bibliographic systems with useful data, the application of new processes in bibliographic systems, collaboration with external partners, and the adoption and adaptation of Web technology to library uses.

## Integrating or Coordinating Distributed Hybrid Functions

Despite tremendous growth in digital collections during the past decade, librarians have found that print-based resources remain essential, and yet, nearly everybody in the library ends up with a role to play in the delivery of digital resources. As a result, some librarians have found that it makes more sense to adopt a distributed support model.[12]

Rather than create, maintain, or retain a separate ER unit, they incorporate the management of digital resources into extant print-based workflow and processes. Catalogers describe digital items, and create and maintain Web links, in addition to the process of print and microform materials. Acquisitions and serials staff place orders; create bibliographic, order, and holdings records; and process payments for both print and digital objects. This hybrid library staff may not have titles that specifically indicate that they are responsible to handle some aspect of the delivery of ER, but ER responsibilities have become an integral part of their daily work.

On the other hand, job postings for ER librarians continue to be announced; especially for larger academic libraries where greater specialization of duties is common. In some libraries where the ER workload is high, there are separate units made up of staff whose responsibilities are specific to the delivery of ER. As library collections shift, more and more, from print to digital and as the responsibility for the performance of ER functions continues to spread and proliferate among various levels of library staff, the ER librarian may assume a more managerial and coordination role. The responsibilities of the ER staff may evolve from the performance of routine tasks to work with complicated and more problematic issues, i.e., special projects.

It is important for the ER librarian to avoid the creation of new silos: workflows, applications, data streams, or systems built autonomously and independently within a library information infrastructure to accommodate the increased demands of the digital environment. If the local situation does not allow or is not ready for the total integration of print-based and online resources functions, bridges that provide opportunities for the creation of hybrid processes may still be envisioned and put in place. The ER staff must work closely with other library units because ER workflow often moves in loops, rather than in a linear fashion.

## To Improve the Information Technology Infrastructure

The integrated library system (ILS) with its Online Public Access Catalog (OPAC) has been *the* bibliographic tool for library users to seek information and for library staff to manage resources and provide access; at least until library collections began to turn digital. "Libraries now manage a patchwork of systems"[13] and their ILS are used by librarians to manage a smaller part of library activity. The OPAC remains a finding tool for print-based items[14] and an access tool for digital items. OpenURL link resolution tools take users from online citations to full-text content. ER management systems (ERMS) manage digital resources. Information portals, subject guides, A-Z lists, and intermediate pages, which contain instructions to access and use digital resources, are maintained on the library's Web site. This proliferation of information tools, technologies, formats, and services in libraries is viewed as a transition towards the eventual integration of the print and the digital. Librarians "must address the need for a new generation of OPAC that offers significantly enhanced functionality, much of which can be based on standard features of Web search engines and online bookstores."[15]

Dietz and Grant write, "Library systems must no longer solely deal with the internal flows of cataloging, circulation, acquisitions, serials, and OPACs, but rather must be compatible with other internal systems and, more important, external systems."[16]

Calhoun adds, "Libraries' traditional methods for producing electronic resource descriptions generally result in suboptimal, fragmented discovery and retrieval systems."[17]

One process meant to address such issues that is currently in use by ER librarians is to make the OPAC a node in the library's network of access tools. Users are directed, in multiple ways, to the OPAC as an access option. Federated searches and Z39.50 tools include the OPAC as one of the search targets. Users are guided by Web-search technology that converges with link resolution tools. ER librarians have begun to exploit link technologies in order to help users navigate the information infrastructure in a seamless way. Ideally, users should be able to start anywhere and link from the Web to citation databases and/or to digital full-text. If need be, they should be re-directed automatically to the library catalogs for the print versions of information as well as other information options, e.g., book reviews, images, or finding aids for primary sources.

The ER librarian must take the next, logical step and participate in or lead the discussion about the integration of the functionality of multiple, electronic tools and processes so that they begin to function as a coherent information system. The development of information technology infrastructures to simplify access to information for library users is a high priority for the ER librarian.

## Populating Bibliographic Systems with Useful Data

A bibliographic system is as useful as the data in it. For ease of use, information resources should be treated in a consistent fashion, if possible, regardless of format. The following are the possible types of data that the ER librarian must handle.

### A Vendor's Table of Contents for a Print-Based Resource

The search for print resources relies on surrogate bibliographic records with no direct or immediate access to full-text. The ER librarian may help improve the situation by adding a vendor's table of contents into bibliographic records in the OPAC and indexing that data. The new emphasis on access over description in the bibliographic control of the digital resource has been carried over to the traditional, library collection.

### An Increased Number of Bibliographic Data Sources and Types

The billions of carefully, tagged records in library catalogs are recognized and affirmed in educational circles and beyond as a unique, effective, and uniform retrieval tool, but in-house creation can no longer keep up with the demand. Libraries have been resourceful to acquire MARC bibliographic records from various sources, e.g., vendors, publishers, and consortia. Calhoun proposes new models for resource description that incorporate various record types created by librarians in collection development, reference, cataloging, and information technology. In her proposed system resource descriptions could also come from vendors, publishers, or authors themselves. Data will also flow in from resource description databases (e.g., CORC), from metadata knowledge-bases (e.g., Dublin Core, EAD, and MARC/AACR2), and from the Internet resources themselves. The process ends with the output of metadata and its integration into the library information discovery and retrieval system.[18]

When these records come to the library, one of the responsibilities of the ER librarian may be to ensure that their sources are identified for future maintenance and manipulation and that their content and structure are compatible to the standards of the library system for incorporation into the information infrastructure.

## Classification Data for Digital Objects

Cataloging and classification have been the trusted avenues to make print-based resources available to library users. The power of the keyword search has created an erroneous impression among some library administrators that there is no longer a need to undertake what are, admittedly, expensive and time-consuming tasks. But, according to Wilson, "more than a century of classification in libraries should not be suspended just when research begins to show how applicable classification is for knowledge organization of electronic and Internet resources."[19] The utility of classification for collection development purposes, to integrate materials in all formats in a virtual shelf-list, and to support subject-browsing of both print and online resources, is well-known. Newer applications include the creation of discipline-based, scholarly portals where the *MyLibrary* concept has been adopted. These Web site portals allow the delivery of content-specific information to a targeted audience. Another recent application is found in library catalogs, like that of North Carolina State University http://www.lib.ncsu.edu/catalog/ that exploits the hierarchical nature of classification with the ability to broaden or narrow a search. Even if the library's current policy is not to assign call numbers to electronic publications, librarians should consider the storage of class number data from bibliographic records in the library's bibliographic system. Such data could be useful for purposes like subject-mapping and collection statistics. Then, if librarians decide, at a future date, to classify online titles, the stored data will be available.

## Historical Acquisitions and Holdings Data for Digital Resources

Acquisitions and holdings data are other, useful types of information found in bibliographic systems that librarians rely upon to manage access to the library's collections. The order history of a print-based title can be archived after a number of years as long as there is a record that indicates that the title has been received. Non-receipt is, normally, limited to specific issues and they are claimed by library staff within a certain time-frame. The order history of a digital title is a different story. Vendor/ publishers require an accurate account of who is eligible to access the resource and for how long. Libraries require a record of titles available to users; under what terms and conditions; and from which sources. This information must be retained permanently in order to guarantee perpetual e-access for library users to past issues of the title (an online archive), if the current subscription (and access) to the current issues of the title (usually the most recent year) has been cancelled. This necessity, to retain subscription records indefinitely for cancelled titles with online components, is a new exigency of the digital age for librarians. It is also necessary to track:

- titles under consideration for purchase, i.e., in trial, pending cancellation, and
- titles that are and were included in a digital package.

It is the responsibility of the ER librarian to ensure that comprehensive and accurate acquisitions data, historical as well as current, is maintained for online resources.

This interest in the management of acquisitions records for online titles and the new generation of the ILS that can be used by librarians to retrieve and manipulate data in batches have led to a need for the standardization of acquisitions data elements.

If the past few decades were a period for the standardization of bibliographic data, then the coming decades will be a period for the standardization of acquisitions data. There are few discussions in the professional literature about the standardization of acquisitions data elements. Acquisitions data is local data (it is created in libraries by library personnel for internal use). There is no standardized structure for acquisitions records; so the data is, often, not portable (able to be moved from one system to another). As a result, ILS migrations can result in data loss. A role for the ER librarian might be to promote the use of standardized data elements for online information management. Standards are, currently, under development by organizations like the Digital Library Federation (DLF).[20]

## Digital Resources Acquisitions Data for ERMS

The library's ILS can be used to manage the acquisition of print-based materials quite well, but it is not adequate for digital resources. Sets of bibliographic records that are loaded into an ILS do not always come with acquisitions data. Further, it is difficult to use the ILS to accept or manipulate acquisitions data for individual titles that are contained in e-journal packages. However, there is intense competition among information vendors to develop a digital resources management tool for libraries. ERMS are new and relatively immature tools, especially in the areas of consortial services. An ERMS must support selection, negotiation, rights management, preservation, and many other management needs, i.e., to compare content among digital packages in order to avoid redundancy. Eventually, an ERMS might be used to manage print-based materials also, which would reduce the need to consult multiple, bibliographic sources. A responsibility of the ER librarian might be to participate in the set-up of an ERMS, which could be used to accommodate the current and future needs of the hybrid library in the management of its multi-format collections.

## Acquisitions Data in Bibliographic Records for Digital Resources

In the print world, there never was a need for the global manipulation of data in bibliographic systems as that produced by the age of the digital information resource. ER have made manual record-keeping close to impossible due to their volatile nature and the sheer number of titles involved. The single-record approach to cataloging, which mandates the bibliographic description of the print version of a title while the existence of the digital version is noted on the same record, further complicates matters.

In lieu of or before the implementation of an ERMS, the bibliographic record may be used to store acquisitions data like:

- subscription status, i.e., active, inactive, moving wall, etc.
- the title is part of an aggregator package
- the name of the publisher of the online version of the title, if different from the publisher of the print version

This practice would complement the acquisitions data in the order record for the print version of the title. A prelude to the implementation of an ERMS might be a project to clean up ILS records in order to facilitate mapping and migration.

## Unique Identifiers

Even though identifier numbers like the ISSN or the ISBN are not always unique, they have become vital to link or map from Internet search results or database citations to library holdings at the title level. However, some serials that have never been assigned an ISSN have been indexed by abstracting and indexing services and included in online databases. Librarians have asked the U.S. ISSN Center to assign identifier numbers retrospectively to those titles. Other types of identifier numbers, like SFX object identifiers or OCLC record numbers, are also used to link to resources at the title level.

## THE APPLICATION OF NEW PROCESSES
## TO BIBLIOGRAPHIC SYSTEMS

Librarians must rethink their inflexible, exacting technical services processes that are too slow to handle the volume and complexity of digital resources management. Manual operations are common with print titles and one-by-one checking is the norm, but the influx of the volatile digital resource has provided a great incentive for librarians to reconsider and revamp conventional assumptions.

For example, when librarians purchase 20,000 e-books as a package or receive 10,000 bibliographic records from a shared-cataloging program in one file, the best that can be done, in terms of quality control, is to ensure that the correct number of items has been delivered. It is not an option to check in titles or review records one-by-one. Librarians must trust that the vendor or other outsourcing agency has sent the correct titles or records. In some libraries vendors, like SerialsSolutions and EBSCOhost, have taken over the maintenance of both print and electronic serials holdings.

Batch-processing by machine is the most efficient way to handle large volumes of data and those ER librarians who make full use of automatic tools to facilitate setup, upgrades, and maintenance will be able to manage both the print and the digital formats in an effective manner. Tasks that require interpretation are best handled by human intellect, but tasks that require consistency and repetition are best handled by machine. The ER librarian must identify tasks or portions of a task that should be handled by machine-processing, i.e., the creation of large record sets by batch-cloning, batch-insertion, updates of constant data, and global updates of data. Task-oriented user interfaces and service standards are helpful. In the past, print backlogs have been tolerated in libraries, but user expectations for prompt information and technological advances in the delivery of that information have pointed librarians in new directions.

A great wealth of data resides in the bibliographic systems of libraries. ER librarians must play an active part in the extraction, manipulation, and interpretation of this data and employ a variety of software applications, e.g., Java, Perl, Excel, FileMaker Pro, etc., to provide the management information required by collection development, public services, and library administration.

### Collaborating with External Partners

In order to guarantee access to online publications, librarians have entered into unprecedented collaborations with external partners, i.e., publishers, vendors, bibliographic utilities, and consortia. An ILS has an elaborate structure designed to aid library staff as they receive, check-in, claim, bind, print items, and many other tasks as well. Due to the time that elapses between the order and the reception of print-based materials, on-order records are placed in the library's ILS. In the digital age, many of these types of procedures can be curtailed because more and more purchased items are digital and come in great bulk. What alternate mechanisms should be put in place to ensure that users are guaranteed ready access to a library's print and ER? Instead of each library binding identical, print issues for storage and preservation, librarians have negotiated with publishers and consortia to build shared print collections. The expansion of electronic access and the continued need to house print resources within finite library spaces have stimulated collaboration in the development of print archives. For example, JSTOR has cooperated with many libraries to archive the journals they have digitized.[21] Other examples include the Five-College Library Depository's collaborative storage plan[22] and the Committee on Institutional Cooperation's (CIC) coordinated, preservation-sensitive archiving of print journals.[23] The LOCKSS (Lots of Copies Keep Stuff Safe) Alliance,[24] announced in late 2004, is a membership organization dedicated to the support and growth of the LOCKSS system to the preservation of a wide variety of materials (scholarly electronic journals, government documents, electronic theses and dissertations, and special and archival materials). This LOCKSS system is open-source software created and implemented to provide libraries with a way to preserve and provide access to their own, local copy of digital content they have purchased. To help safeguard library collections in all formats, the ER librarian must assume an active role in the development and implementation of such projects.

## *ADOPTING AND ADAPTING WEB TECHNOLOGY*

"The hybrid library takes the Web as its delivery mechanism and, from this one access point, users should be able to have direct access to the electronic information to which they are entitled and be able to reach for and also locate relevant physical resources."[25] The ER librarian must use Web technology to develop an integrated, online environment for the user of the library's hybrid collection based on a simple, rich, and efficient system of bibliographic control.

The future of technical services is a future made up, in large part, of Web technology, applications, and resources. Bibliographic utilities, integrated library systems, and vendor/publisher databases are almost exclusively Web-based. ER librarians must help other library personnel employ Web technologies in their daily work. For example, Google search technology might be adopted for the library intranet where management data or reports might be posted.

Although, to many, Google is representative of an information culture that believes libraries have become irrelevant because of the Web, the company has progressed in its relationship with librarians to the point that it has become an industry buzzword. Librarians incorporate references to Google Scholar on their Web pages and promote it as a tool to locate full-text information at the library; a citation index. Librarians send their library's holdings information and IP addresses to Google Scholar so that OpenURL *emphasized links* to the library's full-text may be included in search results. In this way, Google Scholar users will be directed to a library's full-text resources or to the library's catalog, if no full-text is available. There are many Web-based products and tools that librarians may adapt in innovative ways. An example is a Web-based, trouble-ticketing system like Request Tracker,[26] which is used in IT departments to manage tasks, issues, and requests. The ER librarian might lead library personnel in the implementation of such a system to track problems and their resolutions, i.e., broken links, bibliographic errors, etc., and to manage communication with library users, library staff, and vendor/publishers.

With the overall goal to be the effective management of the library's hybrid collection, these are among the services and technological innovations that the ER librarian might be called upon to identify and make available in the library in order to streamline staff operations.

## Skills Needed

ER librarians in technical services departments or elsewhere in the library should be able to combine a basic understanding of traditional library operations, originally conceived and implemented to manage print-based materials, with a forward-looking appreciation of emergent standards, trends, and technologies for the management of online materials. Different sets of skills are required for the management of different format types in a hybrid library. To assume an effective role in the ER area requires the possession of technical, technological, interpersonal, analytical, and evaluative skills. ER professionals must have a vision, be able to think *outside the box*, and be able to integrate new ideas into the current, library environment. Similarly, they need good organizational skills in order to work on projects as well as the ability to learn quickly to meet the challenges of a rapidly changing environment. Sensitivity to the needs of and pressures experienced by other library personnel must be a basic requirement for ER librarians as, frankly, it should be for all librarians in the high-stress LIS world. The hybrid library requires continual development in all aspects of the management of all formats and the ER librarian has a valuable role to play here.

In-line with these challenges and opportunities, strategies are needed to encourage the professional development of ER librarians. There should be funds available for such purposes as there should be for the development of all librarians. In addition, these skills must be emphasized in library school curricula whose instructors have a responsibility to ensure that they are addressed in every class.

## CONCLUSION

The academic library is first and foremost a service organization. The primary mission of librarians is to support the learning, teaching, and research activities of the library's parent institution. One of the ways they do this is to provide deep and seamless integrated access to information, regardless of format. Bibliographic systems are used to help library patrons discover, identify, and retrieve the most appropriate information resources for their needs as well as to help library employees manage print and digital collections. The ER librarian has a crucial responsibility to facilitate this process through a coherent view of the information technology infrastructure and apply it to the management of the hybrid library.

## NOTES

1. *Systemwide Strategic Directions for Libraries and Scholarly Information at the University of California* (Oakland, Calif.: Systemwide Library and Scholarly Information Advisory Committee, Office of Systemwide Library Planning, University of California, April 2004), 5.

2. "Open Content Alliance," http://www.opencontentalliance.org/OCARelease. pdf (viewed Nov. 6, 2005).

3. Walt Crawford, "Journals Revisited: A Survivable Future," *American Libraries* 35(5) (May 2004): 56-57.

4. Juris Dilevko and Lisa Gottlieb, "Print Sources in an Electronic Age: A Vital Part of the Research Process for Undergraduate Students," *Journal of Academic Librarianship* 28(6) (Nov.-Dec. 2002): 381-392.

5. Thomas H. Teper, "Current and Emerging Challenges for the Future of Library and Archival Preservation," *Library Resources & Technical Services* 49(1) (Jan. 2005): 32-39.

6. Michelle M. Wu, "Why Print and Electronic Resources are Essential to the Academic Law Library," *Law Library Journal* 97 (spring 2005): 233.

7. John Fenner and Audrey Fenner, "The Future in Context: How Librarians Can Think Like Futurists," *Library Philosophy and Practice* 7(1) (fall 2004); http://libr. unl.edu:2001/LPP/fenner2.htm (viewed April 23, 2005).

8. S. Sutton, "Future Service Models and the Convergence of Functions: The Reference Librarian and Technician, Author and Consultant," chapter in K. Low, ed., *The Roles of the Reference Librarians, Today and Tomorrow* (New York: The Haworth Press, Inc., 1996), 125-243.

9. C. Rusbridge, "Towards the Hybrid Library," *D-Lib Magazine* (July/August 1998); http://dlib.org/dlib/july98/rusbridge/07rusbridge.html (viewed November 17, 2005).

10. Charles Oppenheim and Daniel Smithson, "What is the Hybrid Library?" *Journal of Information Science* 25(2) (1999): 97-112.

11. Ibid.

12. Mori Lou Higa et al., "Redesigning a Library's Organizational Structure," *College & Research Libraries* 66(1) (January 2005): 41-58.

13. L. Dempsey, "The Integrated Library That Isn't," http://orweblog.oclc.org/ archives/000585.html (viewed November 25, 2005).

14. Martha M. Yee, "FRBRization: A Method for Turning Online Public Findings Lists into Online Public Catalogs," *Information Technology and Libraries* 24(2) (June 2005): 77-95.

15. John D. Byrum, Jr., "Recommendations for Urgently Needed Improvement of OPAC and the Role of the National Bibliographic Agency in Achieving It," presentation at World Library and Information Congress, 7th IFLA General Conference and Council, August 14-18, 2005, Oslo, Norway.

16. R. Dietz and C. Grant, "The Dis-Integrating World of Library Automation," *Library Journal* 130(11) (June 15, 2005): 38-40.

17. Karen Calhoun, "Redesign of Library Workflows: Experimental Models for Electronic Resource Description," http://dlist.sir.arizona.edu/591/01/calhoun_paper. html (viewed November 17, 2005).

18. Ibid.

19. Mary Dabney Wilson, "Flying First Class or Economy? Classification of Electronic Titles in ARL Libraries," *Portal: Libraries and the Academy* 1(3) (2001): 225-240.

20. Kimberly Parker et al., "DLF Electronic Resource Management Initiative," http://www.diglib.org/pubs/dlfermi0408appb.htm (viewed April 27, 2005).

21. "About JSTOR," http://www.jstor.org/about/ (viewed December 1, 2005).

22. Willis E. Bridegam, *A Collaborative Approach to Collection Storage: The Five-College Library Depository* (Washington, DC: Council on Library and Information Resources, 2001); http://www.clir.org/pubs/reports/pub97/contents.html (viewed January 31, 2004).

23. "Committee on Institutional Cooperation," http://www.cic.uiuc.edu/ (viewed December 1, 2005).

24. "LOCKSS Alliance," http://lockss.stanford.edu/ (viewed December 1, 2005).

25. Michael Breaks, "Building the Hybrid Library: A Review of UK Activities," *Learned Publishing* 15(2) (2002): 99-107.

26. "RT: Request Tracker," http://www.bestpractical.com/rt/ (viewed December 1, 2005).

doi:10.1300/J105v32n01_04

# Education and Electronic Resources (ER) Librarianship: How Library School Programs Are Meeting the Needs of the ER Librarian Position

Michael L. Bradford

Mark Dehmlow

Anastasia Guimaraes

M. Ladd

Pat Loghry

Marcy Simons

**SUMMARY.** The authors of this chapter undertook a study to determine how well library school education is preparing students for electronic resources (ER) librarianship. The study provides an analysis of 100 ER librarian position descriptions to determine the requisite skills, training, and knowledge, and then an analysis of how well those skills

---

Michael L. Bradford, MLS, is Serials and ER Librarian, Andover-Harvard Theological Library, Harvard Divinity School, 45 Francis Avenue, Cambridge, MA 02138 (E-mail: michael_bradford@harvard.edu). Mark Dehmlow, MSLIS, is Electronic Services Librarian (E-mail: mdehmlow@nd.edu); Anastasia Guimaraes is Supervisor, Catalog and Database Maintenance Unit (E-mail: aguimara@nd.edu); M. Ladd is Overseer, Music Collections Office (E-mail: ladd.3@nd.edu); Pat Loghry, MLIS, is Audio-Visual Catalog and Licensing Librarian (E-mail: ploghry@nd.edu); and Marcy Simons is a supervisor within Access Services, all at the Theodore M. Hesburgh Library, University of Notre Dame du Lac, Notre Dame, IN 46556. Both Ms. Guimaraes and Ms. Simons are Graduate Students, School of Library and Information Science, IUPUI.

[Haworth co-indexing entry note]: "Education and Electronic Resources (ER) Librarianship: How Library School Programs Are Meeting the Needs of the ER Librarian Position." Bradford, Michael L. et al. Co-published simultaneously in *Collection Management* (The Haworth Information Press, an imprint of The Haworth Press) Vol. 32, No. 1/2, 2007, pp. 49-69; and: *Electronic Resources Librarianship and Management of Digital Information: Emerging Professional Roles* (ed: Mark Jacobs) The Haworth Information Press, an imprint of The Haworth Press, 2007, pp. 49-69. Single or multiple copies of this article are available for a fee from The Haworth Document Delivery Service [1-800-HAWORTH, 9:00 a.m. - 5:00 p.m. (EST). E-mail address: docdelivery@haworthpress.com].

are covered in the ALA-accredited Master's level library programs
through their course descriptions. The authors also examine ways to define, explore, and bridge the gap between the practical issues of the job
and the theoretical approach to such issues as provided by library
schools. doi:10.1300/J105v32n01_05 *[Article copies available for a fee from The
Haworth Document Delivery Service: 1-800-HAWORTH. E-mail address:
<docdelivery@haworthpress.com> Website: <http://www.HaworthPress.com>
© 2007 by The Haworth Press. All rights reserved.]*

**KEYWORDS.** Graduate education, electronic resources, skills and training, position description, library education, library school, MLIS, MIS,
MLS, library jobs, library employment

## INTRODUCTION:
## EVOLUTION OF ELECTRONIC RESOURCES (ER)
## LIBRARIANSHIP AND LIBRARY SCHOOL PROGRAMS

With the current rapid development and ubiquity of online collections
and resources, it is clear that library acquisition, organization, and provision of access to materials is changing, growing, and evolving faster
than anyone could have imagined just ten years ago. Library employees
of all kinds will need flexibility and the constant development of new
skills to meet the emerging needs created by the growing online environment. Renewal, revival, and risk will be key words to describe the requisite skills employees will have to possess to address the requirements of
today's information consumer. We know that we are still at the preci-
pice of this transformation and libraries are struggling to re-think the
way they manage resources and develop the skills that will be needed to
keep up with patron demands. By extension, the graduate schools
which offer masters degrees in library and information science (LIS),
hitherto identified as *library schools*, are also under pressure to evolve
their programs in order to grow with the ever-changing services that
patrons are demanding and libraries are developing. Because it is with
education that the path to librarianship starts, it is especially crucial for
the courses offered by library school programs to reflect this evolution.

There may be consolation in the fact that the curricula of library
school programs are not the only ones which need review and redesign
in order to meet the demands of a changing information environment. In a
May 2005 article in the *Harvard Business Review*, Bennis and O'Toole
discuss the need for business schools to "strike a new balance between

scientific rigor and practical relevance," if business schools are going to continue to be pertinent.[1] Bennis and O'Toole advocate that the "best classroom experiences are those in which professors with broad perspectives and diverse skills analyze cases that have seemingly straightforward technical challenges and then gradually peel away the layers to reveal hidden strategic, economic, competitive, human, and political complexities."[2]

Library education as well must strike a balance between the theoretical knowledge taught in the classroom and the practical hands-on experience that is gained on the job. Library schools need professors who have the "broad perspectives and diverse skills" which librarians will need to confront the technical challenges of the present and the future.[3]

The changes that librarians are encountering in the workplace are the same ones that are causing library schools to rethink and adjust their curricula. These transformations have provided the impetus for graduates to request new online continuing education opportunities so that they can develop the latest skills to deal with emerging trends and technologies. Positions within libraries, like the ER librarian, are at the cutting edge of, if not the catalyst for, these changes. In 1998, Andrew Abbott began to consider the way libraries would change in the future:

> There will always be a need for information brokers. They may look very different soon, but they will still exist.
>
> However, one result of heavy commodification in librarianship is quite likely an increased distance between a core professional elite that is concerned with maintaining and upgrading the increasingly centralized knowledge and physical resources of the profession–algorithms, databases, indexing systems, repositories–and a larger peripheral group that provides actual client access to those resources.[4]

The changes in libraries have been anticipated for a while. In 1993, the results of a survey of library administrators about new trends anticipated the need for libraries to make adjustments by calling upon them to be ready for, cause to happen, and take advantage of:

- advances in telecommunications and computer technology
- changes in curricula that recognize the inter-relationship of disciplines
- increases in demand for prompt, responsive information service
- a sense of information overload for faculty members and students

- a corresponding need for greater discretion and selectivity amid the glut of information
- funding and spatial constraints that limit acquisitions, storage, access, and service options.[5]

Now, more than a decade later, what was anticipated has become a reality. It is the culmination of changes within the information landscape that sets the table for our analysis of how well library school education addresses the age of the electronic resource.

So, how well *is* library school education preparing students for careers in ER librarianship? When posed with this question, we decided to evaluate current library school programs in the context of position descriptions for ER librarians. At the outset of our examination, we thought there might be a gap between what students learned about the management of digital resources in the classroom and what employers looked for in prospective employees as outlined in position descriptions. We decided to try to answer the following questions:

- What are the most important skills required for ER librarians?
- Are these skills taught in American Library Association (ALA)-accredited library school programs?
- What needs are being met in libraries, where are the deficiencies, and are there areas in which library schools can compensate?
- Should internships and residency programs be required in order to provide necessary experience?
- What skills and knowledge should be required, preferred, enhanced?
- Are there educational opportunities available to help practicing professionals enhance their skills and develop new ones?

We chose a two-channel research approach to answer these questions. First, we amassed 100 recent ER librarian job descriptions in order to determine just what it is libraries look for in candidates for the position. Then, we evaluated the descriptions of courses offered in 55 of the 57 ALA-accredited library school programs. The analysis was surprising and dispelled some misconceptions while, at the same time, confirming some suspicions. In general, library school education provides training for many of the skills needed by ER librarians, but there are also some key components that are missing. There may be some ways in which library schools can correct these deficiencies, but sometimes only real world, on-the-job experience can provide the necessary credentials. The gaps between the theoretical training provided by library schools and the practical requirements of libraries suggest the need to teach applied skill sets with on-the-job training, internships, and research projects. But, before presenting an evaluation of the results, it is useful to consider the nature of the ER librarian position.

ER librarianship has evolved organically in the library profession. The specific divisions of labor in libraries (acquisitions, access services, etc.) were not designed to address the needs created by the emergence of electronic materials. Thus, each library division/department/unit/office faces its own specific obstacles in managing ER. Because their prevalence and the mechanisms for their delivery have changed over the last ten years, e-resource management has become more complicated. Even so, libraries have continued to utilize traditional workflows and organization as they respond to changes and this approach is no longer adequate. The growing complexities in the management of ER have revealed the need to create electronic specialist positions.

The distinctive issues created by the management of ER in libraries are varied and widespread and, consequently, ER librarianship has become an amalgamation of many disparate jobs within the traditional library. In a recent article, Jasper and Sheble analyze the evolutionary approach that Wayne State University has taken towards ER management.[6] The university assembled an outstanding team of individuals who possess unique strengths in order to mitigate "the challenges associated with acquiring, paying for, setting up, and maintaining access to" ER.[7] This team has representation from "traditional technical services functional areas, including cataloging, acquisitions, database management, and serials" as well as new and emerging positions like ER librarians and web management experts.[8] This management model supports our analysis of position descriptions; the desired skills of ER librarians have been spread, traditionally, all over the library. In addition, the management of ER is grounded in both traditional and emerging library specializations and the requirements are changing continuously.

The ER librarian position has been evolving for over ten years. In 1998, Roy Tennant began writing about the "skills, experience, and qualifications" which would benefit foreseeable and pending changes in the profession for the "new millennium."[9]

He suggested the following qualities would be necessary to address the proliferation of electronic materials and collections:

- a capacity to learn quickly
- flexibility
- "innate skepticism"

- risk-taking
- a public service perspective
- an appreciation of diversity
- the ability to enable change
- the capacity to work independently.[10]

A year later, he listed the technological skills that would be necessary to "create and manage digital library collections and services."[11]
These included:

- imaging technologies
- optical character recognition
- mark-up languages
- cataloging and metadata
- indexing and database technology
- user interface design
- programming
- web technology
- project management experience.[12]

William Fisher published a study in 2003 that analyzed ER position descriptions from *American Libraries* dating back to the mid-1980s. He found that the top ten most important attributes requested were, in order of the most desired:

1. reference skills
2. bibliographic instruction skills
3. communication skills
4. collection development skills
5. computer applications skills
6. online searching skills
7. professional experience
8. experience with worldwide web applications
9. experience with program management
10. interpersonal skills.[13]

In order to establish what general types of skills libraries demanded for these positions, Fisher grouped the attributes into three categories: public service, personal, and technical.[14]

In his study, public service experience and personal attributes showed up more often as desired traits in position descriptions than did technical attributes.

What has been the library school response to these requirements? Historically, library schools have taught traditional skills. Irwin's 2002 article, "Characterizing the Core: What Catalog Descriptions of Mandatory Courses Reveal about LIS Schools and Librarianship," is valuable in documenting the history of library school programs.[15] Early programs focused on basic coursework in cataloging, reference work, book selection, bibliography, management, library administration, etc. The results of the research allow us to suggest that, even today, much of the core curriculum in library school programs remains consistent with this model. On the other hand, library schools have also introduced many courses on emerging topics that teach skills and knowledge that libraries look for in ER librarians; however, the presence of these courses fluctuates widely among programs, ranging from one or two courses per library school to entire concentrations.

## RESEARCH METHODOLOGY

In our effort to answer the questions we laid out at the beginning of the chapter, we analyzed two sets of data. To ascertain which skills are desired by libraries that advertise for ER librarian positions, we analyzed 100 job descriptions and then categorized the requisite skills listed. To ascertain how well library schools are providing the necessary skills for those positions, we evaluated course descriptions from 55 of 57 ALA-accredited library school programs in the context of the skills taken from the position descriptions.

The research group consisted of five individuals:

- one seasoned librarian and two who have entered the field within the last two years, and
- one library school student at the beginning and another at the middle of her studies.

### Position Descriptions

The first data set for our study came from 100 position descriptions advertised in *American Libraries*; on the Association of College & Research Libraries (ACRL) Web site;[16] and on the LISJobs Web site for the time period 2000-2005.[17]

We gathered position descriptions that mentioned ER and were advertising for librarians, specialists, or coordinators. Only position descriptions which required an ALA-accredited graduate degree were considered for the study.

The typical position description for a librarian or professional in any field describes the job duties, the qualifications a successful candidate should possess, and a short description of the library and its parent institution. For the purpose of this study we reviewed each job advertisement for position title, duties/responsibilities, and qualifications. Each member of the group analyzed approximately 20 position descriptions. After a list of the qualifications and skills mentioned in the reviewed advertisements was compiled, parallel phrasings were collocated and organized into 38 logical categories, which represented specific skills: web-mastering, cataloging, experience with integrated library systems (ILS), ER management, instruction, supervision, programming, etc. (Figure 1).

Placing the 38 skills noted in this study into the same categories as the Fisher study (public service, personal, and technical) reveals how ER librarian positions have become more dependent on technical rather than on public service or personal attributes (Figure 2).

The next step was to determine the five types of libraries which offered ER librarian positions. Of 100 total advertisements, 86 were from academic libraries, 6 were from corporate libraries, 4 were from public libraries, 3 were from consortia, and 1 was from a state library (Figure 3).

## *Library School Programs*

The second part of our research consisted of evaluating course description from ALA-accredited library schools in order to determine how well the courses offered address the requisite skills listed in the position descriptions. Each member of the group analyzed eleven programs. At the time of the study, there were 57 ALA-accredited programs. However, programs at the universities of Montreal and Puerto Rico are taught in French and Spanish respectively and were not included in this study.

The analysis of library schools was complicated by the fact that four programs listed only course titles without accompanying descriptions. A further complication was that the process turned out to be more subjective than we had originally imagined. The group came to the realization that each of us had our own personal biases and this would likely impact

FIGURE 1. Requisite Skills Indicated in Position Descriptions

| Category | Rank | Total PD Representation |
|---|---|---|
| Web-mastering (1) | 1 | 58 |
| Cataloging (2) | 2 | 35 |
| ILS (3) | 3 | 35 |
| eResource Management (4) | 4 | 31 |
| Instruction (5) | 5 | 28 |
| Supervision (6) | 6 | 26 |
| Programming (7) | 7 | 24 |
| ER Knowledge (8) | 8 | 24 |
| Licensing (9) | 9 | 23 |
| Acquisitions (10) | 10 | 23 |
| Hardware (11) | 11 | 22 |
| Reference (12) | 12 | 19 |
| Databases (13) | 13 | 19 |
| Cur & Em Tech (14) | 14 | 17 |
| Metadata (15) | 15 | 17 |
| IT Background (16) | 16 | 17 |
| DRM/CR (17) | 17 | 14 |
| MS Office (18) | 18 | 13 |
| Linking Soft (19) | 19 | 12 |
| Subject (20) | 20 | 11 |
| Specific Field (21) | 21 | 11 |
| Staff Train (22) | 22 | 10 |
| Public Rel (23) | 23 | 10 |
| Com Prot (24) | 24 | 9 |
| Prof Dev (25) | 25 | 9 |
| Elc Ref and CW (26) | 26 | 8 |
| 2nd Masters (27) | 27 | 8 |
| Dist Ed (28) | 28 | 6 |
| Windows (29) | 29 | 5 |
| Usability & Acc (30) | 30 | 5 |
| Coll Dev (31) | 31 | 4 |
| Foreign Lang (32) | 32 | 4 |
| ERMS (33) | 33 | 3 |
| Intel Freedom (34) | 34 | 3 |
| Fac St (35) | 35 | 3 |
| Proxy (36) | 36 | 2 |
| Metasearching (37) | 37 | 1 |
| Consortia (38) | 38 | 1 |

FIGURE 2. Three Skill-Set Categories

| Technology | Public Service | Personal |
|---|---|---|
| 276 | 129 | 14 |

FIGURE 3. Types of Libraries Found in Job Ads

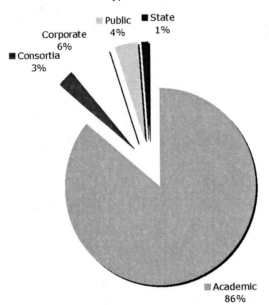

how we each interpreted whether a particular course addressed a particular skill. We decided to defer the analysis of ambiguous descriptions to practicing ER librarians and, if there was no description available for a course, to count only the skills specifically mentioned in the course title, e.g., cataloging, reference, collection development.

While course descriptions provide a glimpse into what a class may cover, they do not comprehensively reveal every topic that an instructor might give treatment. Therefore, in the future, a more complete study might be called for to analyze course syllabi in order to gather more in-depth information about them. Another approach might be to survey library school students, professors, and program directors on the subject of how library programs are training students to meet the professional requirements for ER librarian jobs.

## DATA ANALYSIS

Next, we analyzed the two sets data. Section 3.1 contains an analysis of the skills extracted from ER librarian position descriptions and section 3.2 reports how often those skills appear in the course descriptions that we reviewed.

## Position Descriptions

We grouped the desired skills from position descriptions into 38 categories (Figure 1). For the purposes of this report, we evaluate only the top twelve most desired skills in order to highlight those which are most important to employers (Figure 4). In order of most occurrences in position descriptions, the top twelve skills are:

1. Web-mastering
2. cataloging
3. ILS experience
4. e-resources management
5. instruction
6. supervision
7. programming
8. e-resources knowledge
9. licensing
10. acquisitions
11. hardware administration
12. reference.

The data confirms that multiple units of the library, e.g., cataloging, acquisitions, systems, etc., represent the diversity of the most sought-after skills. The data shows an even split (six to six) between traditional library skills such as cataloging and bibliographic instruction, and emerging skills like Web-mastering and hardware administration, affirming the continued importance of fundamental library skills even in the context of a changing information environment. Some of these emerging skills are still evolving and we can all expect them to grow in importance in the coming years, particularly in the areas of metasearching, licensing, and digital rights management/copyright.

Notably, the most important discovery in the study centers on core principles of librarianship and traditional services which libraries have always provided:

- the acquisition of (acquisition, licensing)
- organization of (cataloging), and
- assistance in the access of (reference and instruction)

library materials. These skills are, perhaps, even more relevant in the electronic age. In fact, the ubiquity of misinformation and the short life-span of Web sites are factors which make traditional library skills the most effective tools librarians can use to help patrons navigate the cyberspace information morass. As more and more library materials enter the digital realm, locating authoritative information and gaining access to it will become more difficult; libraries will continue to address those needs by acquiring quality information resources, organizing them, and providing patrons with assistance in finding and utilizing them.

While traditional skills remain essential to provide access to ER, the study reveals that there is also a need for an equal representation and application of new and emerging library skills. The top technological skills can be grouped into two categories:

- understanding how to use, implement, and manage ER (e-resources management, e-resources knowledge), and
- providing access to ER by supporting the systems and environments in which they exist (Web-mastering, ILS experience, programming, and hardware administration).

The first step towards effective management of ER is to understand what they are, how they work, and how to access them. While many ER

FIGURE 4. Top 12 Skills for eResources Librarian Position Descriptions (Listed by Rank and Number of Occurrences)

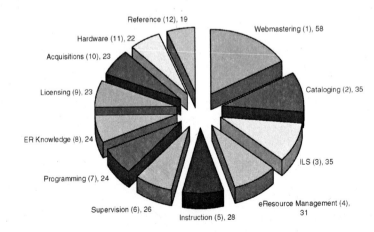

Reference (12), 19
Hardware (11), 22
Acquisitions (10), 23
Webmastering (1), 58
Licensing (9), 23
Cataloging (2), 35
ER Knowledge (8), 24
Programming (7), 24
ILS (3), 35
Supervision (6), 26
eResource Management (4), 31
Instruction (5), 28

are online versions of printed resources, perhaps their greatest strength lies in the flexibility with which they can be searched.

To effectively manage the technical aspects of ER is to understand the systems that host them. Vendors have accelerated their development of online administrative tools so that librarians can take a do-it-yourself approach to the management of the digital resources to which they subscribe. As more resources become available on the Web, to provide access will mean to design and publish Web pages, manage the servers on which those pages are displayed, program Web forms and other scripts to provide seamless access to those materials, and manage the integration of the materials into the online catalog.

In essence, ER librarianship is the nexus at which the traditional meets the contemporary in the delivery of information, where the needs for core traditional skills and emerging technological skills are perfectly in balance. In the maintenance of this equilibrium, information policy, organization, and education are equally as important as implementation and provision of access. It is at this crossroads that one can see the need for a unique and diverse set of skills to manage ER effectively and efficiently.

### Library School Programs

The second data set represents an analysis of course descriptions from ALA-accredited library schools. Figure 5 shows the number of courses per program, on average, that taught the specific skills mentioned in the reviewed job descriptions. To neatly categorize these skills from course descriptions often required us to extrapolate from a related concept or term. For example, supervision, while not specifically mentioned in many course descriptions, is often referred to in courses that include discussion on personnel or human resources topics. These tend to be library management courses.

The top twelve skills which show up, on average, in the greatest number of library school courses per program (Figure 6) are:

1. specific field (knowledge of specialized libraries, e.g., science, law, art)
2. supervision
3. information technology (IT) background
4. reference
5. cataloging

6. knowledge of ER
7. collection development (including selection, de-selection, and licensing of resources)
8. subjects (knowledge of resources pertaining to a specific subject, e.g., engineering, business)
9. database management
10. electronic reference and courseware
11. integrated library systems
12. metadata.

We were not surprised to see that seven of the top twelve skills that appeared most often in course descriptions are traditional library skills. Notably, four of these seven, i.e., cataloging, reference, collection development, and supervision, have been cornerstone components of library education since the 1920s, if not earlier.[18]

On the other hand, there are numerous classes devoted to non-traditional emerging skills such as information technology infrastructure, ER use, and database management. These skills are either taught in courses which are completely devoted to the emerging skill or, as often was the case, in traditional courses that have incorporated less-traditional elements. As an obvious example, reference courses emphasize the use of electronic databases in anticipation of the transition from print-based reference sources to electronic, e.g., abstracting and indexing tools. In general, library school programs have integrated many timely and emerging topics into their curricula, including classes on database management, electronic publishing, digital collection-building, object-oriented programming, software engineering, and Web-mastering. However, the availability of technology-based courses varies widely across programs and ranges from no technology classes in some programs to curricula which are almost exclusively technology-based. On average, though, there is a solid and growing presence of technology-rich courses available in library education.

## *Comparison*

After we evaluated ER librarian position descriptions and determined the requisite skills needed to compete for those positions; and then evaluated library school program course descriptions in order to determine which of these skills might be acquired through library school education, we chose to compare how often a skill appeared in po-

FIGURE 5. Skill Categories Indicated in Course Descriptons

| Category | # of Courses per School Ave | Ranking by Category as Found in Courses |
|---|---|---|
| Specific Field (21) | 5.47 | 1 |
| Supervision (6) | 4.85 | 2 |
| IT Background (16) | 4.32 | 3 |
| Reference (12) | 3.70 | 4 |
| Cataloging (2) | 3.51 | 5 |
| ER Knowledge (8) | 3.30 | 6 |
| Subject (20) | 3.21 | 7 |
| Coll Dev (31) | 3.17 | 8 |
| Databases (13) | 2.83 | 9 |
| Elc Ref and CW (26) | 2.60 | 10 |
| ILS (3) | 2.45 | 11 |
| Metadata (15) | 2.19 | 12 |
| Programming (7) | 1.98 | 13 |
| Acquisitions (10) | 1.94 | 14 |
| Web-mastering (1) | 1.75 | 15 |
| Instruction (5) | 1.72 | 16 |
| Cur & Em Tech (14) | 1.68 | 17 |
| Com Prot (24) | 1.68 | 18 |
| Usability & Acc (30) | 1.25 | 19 |
| Hardware (11) | 1.15 | 20 |
| Public Rel (23) | 1.13 | 21 |
| DRM/CR (17) | 1.11 | 22 |
| Intel Freedom (34) | 0.96 | 23 |
| Metasearching (37) | 0.77 | 24 |
| Consortia (38) | 0.58 | 25 |
| eResource Management (4) | 0.55 | 26 |
| Dist Ed (28) | 0.43 | 27 |
| Prof Dev (25) | 0.38 | 28 |
| Staff Train (22) | 0.34 | 29 |
| MS Office (18) | 0.26 | 30 |
| Windows (29) | 0.26 | 31 |
| Linking Soft (19) | 0.25 | 32 |
| Licensing (9) | 0.17 | 33 |
| ERMS (33) | 0.17 | 34 |
| Proxy (36) | 0.11 | 35 |
| Fac St (35) | 0.09 | 36 |
| Foreign Lang (32) | 0.04 | 37 |
| 2nd Masters (27) | 0.00 | 38 |

FIGURE 6. Top 12 Skills as Taught in LIS School Courses (Average Number of Courses per School)

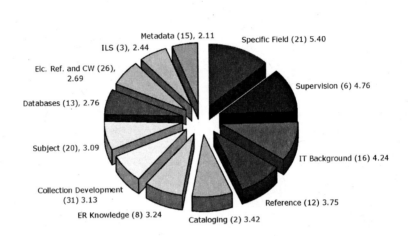

Categories include PD ranking in parentheses and average courses per school that cover that category

Metadata (15), 2.11
ILS (3), 2.44
Elc. Ref. and CW (26), 2.69
Databases (13), 2.76
Subject (20), 3.09
Collection Development (31) 3.13
ER Knowledge (8) 3.24
Cataloging (2) 3.42
Reference (12) 3.75
IT Background (16) 4.24
Supervision (6) 4.76
Specific Field (21) 5.40

sition descriptions with how often it seemed to be taught in library courses. The results of this comparison provide a sense of how well library schools are preparing students for positions like ER librarian.

The evaluation of skills in position descriptions measures something different than the evaluation of course descriptions, e.g., how many times a particular skill appears as a requirement in position descriptions vs. how many courses, on average, per library school program provide training in specific skills. Because of this difference, we determined that the best appraisal would result from comparing the relative ranking of each skill in both data sets. The goal of this study is to determine how well library school education meets the needs of the ER librarian position. As mentioned above, we chose the top twelve of the thirty-eight skills mentioned in position descriptions for analysis. We then compared a skill's ranking in position descriptions to its ranking in terms of coverage in library school program course descriptions (Figure 7).

By measuring the difference between the rankings of a specific skill in both data sets it is possible to determine how the priorities of library education, as exemplified by those who design courses and write course descriptions, compares to the priorities of libraries, as exemplified by those who write course descriptions for ER librarian positions.

The first tier, the well-matched level, includes cataloging, acquisitions, knowledge of ER, and supervision. This tier's ranking difference (the difference between its rank in importance to a job description and its rank in average coverage per program) ranges from ± 2 to ± 4 ranking levels. These skills are covered on average in three to five courses per program (see Figure 5). Since the qualifications in this tier are among the top five requested by employers, this is a good indication of how well education is meeting the needs of the profession. It is interesting that with the exception of knowledge of ER, these are all traditional library skills.

The second tier, those skills whose ranking difference falls between ±7 and ±15, includes integrated library systems, hardware, programming, reference, instruction, and Web-mastering. These skills are covered in library courses at a reasonable level, i.e., approximately two courses per program (Figure 5).

Instruction and Web-mastering are high on the list of desired skills mentioned in position descriptions. Although well-represented in course descriptions, they are still significant skills in the minds of those who write ER librarian job descriptions. Taking heed of the results from our study, we would recommend that library schools increase their emphasis in these areas. The Internet is the primary environment in which us-

FIGURE 7. Comparison of Occurrences in Position Description Ranking and Occurrences in Classes Ranking

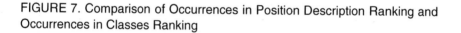
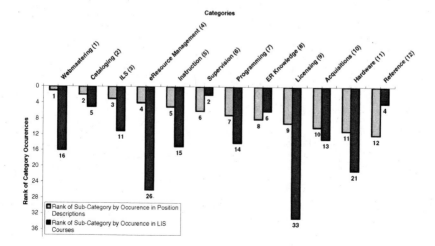

ers interact with ER and the development of these resources for the Web will continue to grow. ER librarians who understand how to manage the Web will play a significant role in the libraries of the future. As well, a significant aspect of bibliographic instruction now and in the future will be to train users to find the most authoritative and valuable online information.

The third tier represents the most substantial deficiencies in library school education. The ranking difference for these skills, e-resources management experience and licensing, ranges from ±22 to ±26 and represents, on average, one or fewer courses per program (see Figure 5).

ER management is a recent development in libraries, which may help explain its lack of coverage in library school curricula. Librarians are struggling to determine how best to manage ER and have drawn few absolute conclusions on how it should be accomplished other than that it requires a diverse team of skilled employees to do it effectively. ER librarian positions and ER departments are being imagined, designed, implemented, and assessed in the wake of, and as a reaction to, this ambiguity. ER management systems (ERMS) are the hot new library automation technology, and new data management and interchange standards are in development. In libraries, this area is the one most deeply mired in transformation as well as the one most likely to see considerable change in the years to come. Obviously, this is a significant topic for teaching and one library school educators should consider adding to their curricula.

Licensing is, if not the most important aspect of ER management, certainly the most complicated. Licenses from the same vendor will differ across institutions and they are often dense with complex, legal language. Licensing is a specialty that requires substantial attention because a license controls a library's legal rights, bound up in copyright and the principle of fair use, to deliver subscribed-to and paid-for digital information to users. Licensing is extremely important in the electronic age because vendors/publishers have begun to rethink and redesign their business models in ways that will have significant repercussions for librarians and library users. Licensing is such a critical component to the management of ER that library school educators should make it a high priority to add it to library school curricula. As a result, library school programs will begin graduating ER librarians who possess some legal knowledge and negotiating savvy, and who will, in turn, enable the libraries they serve to get the best deal they can in their negotiations for digital resources.

## OTHER OBSERVATIONS FROM THE STUDY

In addition to the data that we gathered, there were some other conclusions we drew from the information that we encountered. While the results of this study support the assertion that library school programs are covering many skill areas needed for ER librarianship, it is still important to consider the gap between practical needs, as expressed in position descriptions, and the theoretical way in which library school courses address those needs. For example, any manager who has ever taken a management course will confirm that while a course can give proficient grounding in the concepts of management, there is nothing like on-the-job experience to solidify an individual's understanding for how to supervise people. There may be a correlation between the desire of employers for people with supervisory experience and the efforts of library schools to teach managerial theory, but the coursework on a resume is not likely to get a new graduate hired. Supervision is one of the skills that require real-life experience for one to be truly effective at it. The trend for library schools has been to move away from trade schools for librarians and toward more respected academic frameworks. While practical, hands-on courses may be difficult to find, they are considerably valuable in providing real experience in a skill.

Students need not despair if they cannot find hands-on courses or classes that cover specific topics required to pursue a specialization in the library profession. Library schools often offer many alternatives to conventional classes that may provide the necessary supplementary experience. Internships and other hands-on training are ideal ways to acquire experience in an actual work environment. We are not sure that it is necessary yet to require either one or even both of library school students, but we highly recommend students enroll in them if they are offered within their chosen program. Independent studies offer an excellent opportunity to explore under-represented topics in some depth, and they may include the possibility for hands-on experience. Library school students should consider independent studies as valuable resources for attaining skills that could give them a competitive advantage in the job market. Some institutions also offer the ability to take classes in other departments. Universities with business schools or computer science departments may offer interesting possibilities for acquiring knowledge that is not available directly in their library school program.

Many schools offer courses such as "hot topics," "issues in," and "current topics in" which are much more adaptable when it comes to meeting the rapidly changing environments in modern libraries. They allow students to tailor their programs to individual specialization. In addition to library course offerings, students can gain new skills and supplement their knowledge through continuing education workshops, some of which are available online. Lesley Ellen Harris, a well-known copyright and licensing consultant, offers a series on copyright, licensing, and digital rights management that can be used to develop or enhance licensing and copyright skills (lesley@copyrightlaws.com). In addition, regional opportunities such as Ball State's annual copyright workshop offer great ways to learn about current issues or developing trends in licensing and copyright (http://www.bsu.edu/library/conference/copyright).

Given that library school programs may require supplemental education to prepare students for specific kinds of library jobs; prospective students should have a clear idea of their intended library specialization before picking a library school. There are many courses and programs available for those interested in ER librarianship, but these courses alone may not be enough to gain the necessary experience to compete in the job market.

## CONCLUSION

We set out to determine how well library school education meets the needs created by ER librarian positions. Overall, our research findings support that, generally, library schools are offering curricula in areas that address these needs, such as cataloging, supervision, e-resources knowledge, and acquisitions. It looks as though basic needs are being met, but there are deficiencies, particularly in the areas of e-resource management and licensing. Based on our findings, one way of compensating for a lack of structured programming in these areas is to look for independent studies and internships which most of the library school programs offer.

It is important to keep in mind that librarianship as a profession is always changing. These changes should be manifested in the education provided by ALA-accredited graduate-level programs. Just because a course was required twenty or even ten years ago does not mean we should automatically assume today that it will have relevance. Programming should be reviewed frequently for enhancements in light of our constant state of flux. What is preferred today may disappear tomorrow when the latest technology causes yesterday's databases to become obsolete. Librarianship should be dependent on a love of lifelong learning; therefore continuing education opportunities for practicing professionals should be developed and renewed by looking ahead to the future of the profession. Overall, the education of future librarians who will be managing our ER appears to be in good hands. The fact remains that traditional reference, public service, and management skills will be necessary for a long time to come, and it is good to know that library schools have shown that they are willing to adjust and accommodate emerging trends as needed.

## NOTES

1. Warren G. Bennis and James O'Toole, "How Business Schools Lost Their Way," *Harvard Business Review* 83, no. 5 (2005): 98.

2. Ibid., 101.

3. Ibid.

4. Andrew Delano Abbott, "Professionalism and the Future of Librarianship," *Library Trends* 46, no. 3 (1998): 440.

5. Ann DeKlerk and Peter V. Deekle, "Perceptions of Library Leadership in a Time of Change," *Liberal Education* 79, no. 1 (1993): 42.

6. Richard P. Jasper and Laura Sheble, "Evolutionary Approach to Managing E-Resources," *The Serials Librarian* 47, no. 4 (2005): 55-70.

7. Ibid., 68.

8. Ibid., 66.

9. Roy Tennant, "The Most Important Management Decision: Hiring Staff for the New Millennium," *Library Journal* 123, no. 3 (1998): 102.

10. Ibid.

11. Roy Tennant, "Skills for the New Millennium," *Library Journal* 124, no. 1 (1999): 39.

12. Ibid.

13. William Fisher, "The Electronic Resources Librarian Position: A Public Services Phenomenon?" *Library Collections, Acquisitions, & Technical Services* 27, no. 1 (2003): 8.

14. Ibid., 10.

15. Ray Irwin, "Characterizing the Core: What Catalog Descriptions of Mandatory Courses Reveal About LIS Schools and Librarianship," *Journal of Education for Library and Information Science* 43, no. 3 (2002): 175-84.

16. "Association of College & Research Libraries (ACRL)," http://www.ala.org/ACRL (accessed October 18, 2006)

17. LISjobs.com, "E-mail Discussion Lists for Job-seeking Librarians," http://www.lisjobs.com/mail.htm (accessed October 18, 2006)

18. Irwin, "Characterizing the Core," 176.

doi:10.1300/J105v32n01_05

# The Electronic Resources (ER) Librarian As Teacher: Bibliographic Instruction and Information Literacy

Cheryl Goldenstein

**SUMMARY.** The transition to electronic resources (ER) creates opportunities and challenges for library instruction. Users have access to abundant information even without consultation with librarians. Instruction must address not only the mechanics of finding information, but also how to evaluate and ethically use information from any medium. *Information literacy* has been used to describe these competencies. Schools and postsecondary institutions are integrating information literacy (IL) into curricula, giving librarians a more prominent role in the educational process. doi:10.1300/J105v32n01_06 *[Article copies available for a fee from The Haworth Document Delivery Service: 1-800-HAWORTH. E-mail address: <docdelivery@haworthpress.com> Website: <http://www.HaworthPress.com> © 2007 by The Haworth Press. All rights reserved.]*

**KEYWORDS.** Information literacy, library instruction, marketing

---

Cheryl Goldenstein, MLIS, is Reference/Instruction/Collection Development Librarian, University of Wyoming Libraries, Department 3334, 1000 East University Avenue, Laramie, WY 82070 (E-mail: cgold@uwyo.edu).

[Haworth co-indexing entry note]: "The Electronic Resources (ER) Librarian As Teacher: Bibliographic Instruction and Information Literacy." Goldenstein, Cheryl. Co-published simultaneously in *Collection Management* (The Haworth Information Press, an imprint of The Haworth Press) Vol. 32, No. 1/2, 2007, pp. 71-82; and: *Electronic Resources Librarianship and Management of Digital Information: Emerging Professional Roles* (ed: Mark Jacobs) The Haworth Information Press, an imprint of The Haworth Press, 2007, pp. 71-82. Single or multiple copies of this article are available for a fee from The Haworth Document Delivery Service [1-800-HAWORTH, 9:00 a.m. - 5:00 p.m. (EST). E-mail address: docdelivery@haworthpress.com].

## *INTRODUCTION*

Libraries, by their very nature, are catalysts for lifelong learning. From the toddler story hour at the local branch library through elementary and secondary schools and then on to the academic, and special collections at colleges and universities that offer the foundation for discoveries and innovations and back to the public library with services for the growing population of senior citizens, librarians provide resources, expertise, programming, and collaborative spaces where learning can flourish at all stages of life. Electronic resources (ER) expand these learning opportunities beyond library walls to homes, offices, classrooms, Internet cafés, automobiles, and anywhere with an Internet connection.

Much of the learning that takes place as a result of libraries is self-directed. Librarians provide guidance through readers' advisory and reference services or they may host programs that feature outside experts who can address the needs of specific groups of users.

Librarians also teach skills that facilitate lifelong learning. In 2000, 17% of public library outlets offered basic literacy instruction, English as a second language, GED, and other adult literacy programs and 56% offered computer or Internet instruction.[1] Academic libraries sponsored 432,451 cultural, recreational, and educational presentations to over 7.5 million users in 2000.[2] Of 770 school library media specialists who responded to a 2002 *School Library Journal* survey, 70% reported teaching classes in the library that averaged 13.6 sessions per week.[3]

The transition from print-based to digital research tools and collections has changed library instruction, but not to the extent that our users' experiences with technology, media, and, particularly, the Internet have impacted what and how we teach. Because users can easily access an overwhelming amount of information from sources of varied quality library-focused instruction has, necessarily, evolved to address competencies for interaction with information in any setting. Educators and accreditation agencies integrate information literacy (IL) into higher education standards to address our society's need for citizens and workers who can effectively find and use information to solve problems.[4]

Academic librarians teach for-credit courses in IL, co-teach with classroom faculty, and provide curriculum support for faculty who teach IL concepts integrated into engineering, accounting, nursing, anthropology, and a variety of other courses. However, the predominant model for instruction is still the *on-demand* session requested by faculty to introduce students to library resources, which allows for limited reference to IL concepts.[5]

Librarians must take an increased interest in the education of library users, especially in academic libraries whose mission includes the support of the educational mission of the colleges or universities of which they are a part. If we align our collections and services to the educational needs of library users, we increase the relevance of the library for faculty and students alike. As a result, even librarians whose job descriptions do not include instruction responsibilities will find opportunities to support teaching and learning of information competencies in the academic community.

## *DEFINITIONS:*
## *BIBLIOGRAPHIC INSTRUCTION*
## *AND INFORMATION LITERACY*

In her historical overview of IL, Shirley Behrens points to a speech by Paul Zurkowski about workplace issues as the first appearance of the term "information literacy."[6] The discussion of IL gained momentum among librarians by the mid-1980s when Patricia Senn Breivik from the University of Colorado-Auraria shared a working definition for IL.[7] In 1989, Breivik and Gee suggested previous efforts to reform higher education had experienced limited success because institutions had overlooked the potential role of librarians to transform learning.[8] In an increasingly information-dependent society, they said, libraries modeled a real-world environment of multidisciplinary information in various formats where students could develop problem-solving skills.[9] Consequently, librarians can help students master IL skills that will serve them in the classroom, in the workplace, and in a democratic society.[10]

That same year the American Library Association (ALA) Presidential Committee on Information Literacy released its final report, which included this description:

> To be information literate, a person must be able to recognize when information is needed and have the ability to locate, evaluate, and use effectively the needed information . . . Ultimately, information literate people are those who have learned how to learn. They know how to learn because they know how knowledge is organized, how to find information and how to use information in such a way that others can learn from them. They are people prepared for lifelong learning, because they can always find the information needed for any task or decision at hand.[11]

One of the goals of a 1992 study sponsored by the National Forum on Information Literacy was to "create a comprehensive definition of information literacy."[12] Doyle's Delphi study resulted in these attributes of an information literate individual:

- Recognizes the need for information
- Recognizes that accurate and complete information is the basis for intelligent decision-making
- Formulates questions based on information needs
- Identifies potential sources of information
- Develops successful search strategies
- Accesses sources of information, including computer-based and other technologies
- Evaluates information
- Organizes information for practical application
- Integrates new information into an existing body of knowledge
- Uses information in critical-thinking and problem-solving.[13]

Christine Bruce has advocated a relational model of information literacy more in line with constructivist practices in education. Bruce identified seven interrelated conceptions of how information literacy is experienced in her phenomenographical study of higher educators whom she assumed to be information literate. According to her study, information literacy might be described as:

- Using information technology for retrieval and communication
- Finding information in information sources
- Executing a process to fill an information needs
- Gathering and storing information
- Critically reflecting on information to develop a knowledge base in a new area of interest
- Relying on personal experience or insight to extend knowledge
- Using information wisely to benefit others.[14]

How does IL differ from bibliographic instruction (BI)? Bruce outlines a continuum from library instruction through bibliographic instruction to information literacy education. Library instruction introduces individuals or groups to library resources. BI is more discipline-focused and teaches processes for formal library research. IL education teaches "skills, knowledge and attitudes which are required for learning from information sources of all kinds" and the application of those skills in a variety of contexts not limited to libraries. BI encompasses library instruction and is a subset of IL education.[15]

Whether information literacy is the best term to use as well as how we should define information and literacy have been ongoing matters for debate.[16] Regardless, many educators outside the library world see IL as a desired outcome of a liberal education.[17] Librarians are in a position to play a crucial role to promote this outcome.

## THE CHALLENGES AND OPPORTUNITIES FOR TEACHING INFORMATION LITERACY

The expertise of librarians in the selection, organization, and retrieval of information makes them the likely choice to teach these skills to others. Many academic librarians are unprepared for the role of teacher. As Library and Information Science (LIS) students prepare for a career in academic librarianship they would do well to take a course in library instruction or information literacy. There are resources available for those already on-the-job to develop and improve their teaching skills, i.e., texts devoted to learning theories, learning styles, instructional design, and assessment. Many campuses have centers for teaching excellence that host workshops for instructional improvement.[18]

Professional library associations offer guidelines for IL programs, continuing education opportunities at conferences or workshops, and electronic discussion forums to share practical ideas in regard to IL.[19]

Another source of practical information is the LOEX Clearinghouse for Library Instruction. LOEX offers low-cost memberships to libraries that allow library employees to access publications and attend conferences at a discounted rate.[20]

IL instruction need not be limited to the classroom setting. One-on-one live or remote assistance at the reference desk or in research consultations provides point-of-need instruction to users. Librarians can create general or course-specific guides for distribution in print, on the library's Web site, and through courseware. Library displays that feature a range of viewpoints about a topic and multiple-media to use to find information can demonstrate IL concepts. A more challenging activity in terms of time and technical expertise is the development of streaming audio/video orientations to library resources or online interactive tutorials that cover IL topics.[21]

The combination of a variety of modes for IL instruction addresses differences in learning styles and allows the librarian to place instruction in proximity to where students carry out research activities.

ER facilitate access to scholarly materials for distance learners. The delivery of IL instruction to distance users is a challenge, but librarians who work with outreach students must take their special and specific needs into consideration.[22]

Librarians do not bear sole responsibility for teaching IL concepts. They, typically, have a limited influence over the academic activities of students whereas classroom faculty assign and evaluate projects, convey subject knowledge, explain and enforce expectations for scholarly behavior, demonstrate multiple approaches to the presentation of information, and share information within the context of a discipline. The encouragement of IL practices across the curriculum reinforces learning and carries the message that IL is important.

Curzon identifies nine models for IL instruction that necessitate different levels of collaboration on the part of librarians and classroom faculty. In one model, librarians work with faculty to introduce students to IL concepts in first-year courses or programs. A second model holds IL as a general education requirement and faculty develop courses that meet criteria recommended by librarians. IL is written into the intended learning outcomes of academic departments in a third model. Librarians have responsibility to teach credit courses on IL in a fourth model.[23]

Curzon's fifth model requires students to pass an IL test before they can graduate. Librarians provide behind-the-scenes support to interested faculty in the sixth model through guidance on research assignments or the development of instructional materials for individual courses. The next model partners academic librarians with faculty, school librarians, and teachers as part of a college-readiness program. Such a program prepares students for success in the eighth model: an IL test required before high school or transfer students may enter college. The last model is the on-demand model mentioned previously.[24]

Partnerships benefit librarians, faculty, and students alike. Librarians gain additional insight into the research needs of students and faculty to advance collections, reference, and instructional services. Faculty build familiarity with the library, improving course assignments and enhancing their own research. Students practice IL competencies within the context of coursework, which makes library exercises more relevant. Faculty and librarians work together to identify specific IL skills, knowledge, and resources that will be useful to students as they begin their careers.

Guidelines as regard the skills, concepts, and attitudes that should be developed in IL instruction are available from professional organizations. The Association of College and Research Libraries (ACRL) approved *Information Literacy Competency Standards for Higher Education* in 2000. The standards have been endorsed by the American Association for Higher Education (AAHE) and the Council of Independent Colleges (CIC). Twenty-two performance indicators accompany the five standards. Learning outcomes for each indicator reflect lower or higher order thinking skills based on Bloom's Taxonomy of Educational Objectives.[25] ACRL has, also, compiled a list of resources related to discipline-specific standards and curricula in IL as well as a document that highlights best practices of IL programs.[26]

The Australian and New Zealand Institute for Information Literacy offers its *Information Literacy Framework* as a guide for educators. The recently revised *Framework* draws from the ACRL standards and places them in the context of Bruce's relational model of IL. Nineteen outcomes accompany the six standards.[27]

For elementary and secondary education levels, the American Association of School Librarians (AASL) and the Association for Educational Communications and Technology (AECT) developed nine *Information Literacy Standards for Student Learning*. Three levels of proficiency, based on Bloom's Taxonomy, are associated with multiple indicators.[28] Nearly half of school library media specialists who participated in a *School Library Journal* survey reported teaching IL competencies through the use of the Big Six Skills approach to information problem-solving created by Eisenberg and Berkowitz.[29]

The six steps are:

- task definition
- information-seeking strategies
- location and access
- use of information
- synthesis
- evaluation

The authors offer resources for the implementation of a Big Six curriculum.[30]

Any of these frameworks would be useful as a foundation for IL instruction, program planning, and assessment. How IL develops at a given institution will vary in terms of what is taught and what collaborative models are used.

## THE CHALLENGES POSED BY ER

The adaptation of print indices and catalogs to the electronic format has expedited the process required to locate and access information. Current students likely have a different perspective on the search for information from those experienced with print-based finding aids. Many students come to college now with experience in the use of the Internet, i.e., communication with friends, online games, shopping, news, and entertainment.[31] They may have also used the Internet for school-related work, and their parents and teachers may agree with them that the Internet is a teaching tool.[32] However, even though students may feel the Web is a repository of knowledge that they have already mastered, the library's more structured search tools may be unfamiliar or even intimidating.

Bowen has used the term "serial failure" to describe the "failure of academic libraries to facilitate students' access to articles."[33]

Librarians *should* simplify access to ER through user-centered Web design, federated searches, improved links, and enhanced displays of related items in search results.[34]

However, a simplification of access does not, necessarily, create information-literate users. IL instruction–or some counterpart–is still necessary if we want students who

- think critically about whether information is appropriate for a given task
- successfully adjust search strategies to find relevant information
- use information ethically and legally

Rather than replace IL instruction, the simplification of access allows librarians and classroom faculty to spend less time teaching the mechanics of database searches in favor of a focus on the development of higher-level thinking about information.

Another issue to consider is that graduates, when they enter the work force, may no longer have access to the subscription databases they used for coursework. The information skills and concepts they develop should transfer to other library and work settings as well as to information technologies that have yet to be developed.

Through IL instruction it can be demonstrate that library search systems are, actually, more efficient than Web search engines for many research tasks. Students must be made aware of the shortcomings inherent in Web search engines. Much of the world's knowledge is not available on the Internet and Web search engines do not index all information that *is* available online. Search results may not be as random as users might expect given the commercial nature of the Internet and Web search engines as well as the ability of Web designers to manipulate the order of search results.[35]

Rather than ignore these search engines entirely, however, librarians in library instruction classes might remind students that these tools are more appropriate for some research tasks than for others.

The line between free Web and library-subscribed resources has blurred. Librarians have incorporated Web sites into federated searches and Web search engines crawl scholarly literature. Publishers have begun to move towards open access models in many cases and cultural institutions have made digitized collections available to the world. Users must be able to identify and evaluate what they have found through a search whether it is a scholarly article, census data, a wiki entry, a personal diary, an infomercial, a hoax Web site, or an e-book. Even as librarians pull together, in a single access point, quality sources that students may not have thought to consult these items have been, in many instances, taken out of context. IL instruction gives students experience to recognize and determine the credibility and relevance of different types of information.

Librarians are well aware of the pitfalls of the Internet, which range from the publication of uninformed opinion presented as fact to the expansion of the arena for illegal activities like identity-theft and child-exploitation. The Internet has also created opportunities to hear voices less-heard in mainstream media or scholarly circles. It facilitates communication among those with shared interests and allows one to view ideas and events from multiple perspectives. The Internet expands the library's collections and provides openings for librarians to teach users about IL.

In addition to their responsibility to teach others how to use these resources, subscribed ER pose other challenges for instruction librarians. Search interfaces evolve, access to electronic subscriptions require continuous maintenance, and technical problems occur at any time. Instruction librarians must keep up with changes to resources and the technology used to access, organize, and share information. Ongoing training provided by vendors or by knowledgeable colleagues is essential to prepare librarians to teach.

Teachers also learn from students; not only from typical mistakes they make, but how they successfully use their own strategies or new technologies for information tasks. Most users have already successfully navigated online information without librarian intervention. IL asks users to reflect on that information and whether it really is adequate for course assignments or personal needs. IL instruction, like higher education in general, challenges students to step out of an information comfort-zone and try new tools to make more efficient searches with higher quality results.

## FINAL THOUGHTS

Hannelore Rader found over 5,000 reviewed publications relating to instruction in libraries between 1973 and 2002 with over 300 in 2002 alone.[36] Given the abundance of information related to IL this chapter can serve only as an introduction. To select a set of IL standards and design instruction and assessment around those standards is a starting point for a librarian called on to teach. Building relationships with classroom faculty is also important. If IL is not part of the local lexicon, librarians may want to direct discussions toward related topics like critical thinking and academic integrity.

The goal of IL instruction is not to create mini-librarians. Library catalogs and indexes should not require users to have librarian-level skills to navigate them. Nor is the overarching goal of IL instruction to promote libraries, though we would hope IL students would be lifelong library users. Librarians are experts at finding information and we provide needed services in an evolving information age. If we make our users feel inadequate because our systems are complicated and our interactions with them are condescending they will use libraries only as a last resort–if at all. If we, along with classroom faculty, demonstrate that libraries offer value for them we will remain a source for learning in their professional and private lives.

## NOTES

1. Laurie Lewis and Elizabeth Farris, *Programs for Adults in Public Library Outlets,* NCES 2003-010 (Washington, DC: U.S. Department of Education, National Center for Education Statistics, 2002): 9-13; http://nces.ed.gov/pubs2003/2003010.pdf (viewed January 3, 2006).

2. Nancy Carey and Natalie M. Justh, *Academic Libraries 2000,* NCES 2004-317 (Washington, DC: U.S. Department of Education, National Center for Education Statistics, 2003): 24; http://nces.ed.gov/pubs2004/2004317.pdf (viewed January 3, 2006).

3. Debra Lau, "Got Clout?" *School Library Journal* 48(5) (May 2002): 44.

4. Ilene Rockman, ed., *Integrating Information Literacy into the Higher Education Curriculum: Practical Models for Transformation* (San Francisco: Jossey-Bass, 2004), 9-16.

5. Susan Carol Curzon, "Developing Faculty-Librarian Partnerships in Information Literacy," in Rockman, ed., *Integrating Information Literacy*, 43.

6. Shirley J. Behrens, "A Conceptual Analysis and Historical Overview of Information Literacy," *College and Research Libraries* 55(4) (July 1994): 310.

7. Ibid., 312.

8. Patricia Senn Breivik and E. Gordon Gee. *Information Literacy: Revolution in the Library* (New York: Macmillan, 1989), 2-10.

9. Ibid., 3-28.

10. Ibid., 47.

11. "Presidential Committee on Information Literacy Final Report," http://www.ala.org/acrl/legalis.html (viewed January 3, 2006).

12. Christina S. Doyle, *Outcome Measures for Information Literacy with the National Education Goals of 1990.* Final Report to the National Forum on Information Literacy. Summary of Findings. ED 351 033 (ERIC, 1992): 1; http://www.eric.ed.gov/contentdelivery/servlet/ERICServlet?accno=ED351033 (viewed January 3, 2006).

13. Ibid., 2.

14. Christine Bruce, *The Seven Faces of Information Literacy* (Adelaide: Auslib Press, 1997), 110-151.

15. Ibid., 42-48.

16. Loanne Snavely and Natasha Cooper, "The Information Literacy Debate," *Journal of Academic Librarianship, 23*(1) (January 1997): 9-14; Edward K. Owusu-Ansah, "Information Literacy and the Academic Library: A Critical Look at a Concept and the Controversies Surrounding It," *Journal of Academic Librarianship* 29(4) (July 2003): 219-230.

17. *Liberal Education Outcomes: A Preliminary Report on Student Achievement in College* (Washington, DC: AACU, 2005); http://www.aacu-edu.org/advocacy/pdfs/LEAP_Report_FINAL.pdf (viewed January 3, 2006).

18. Scott Walter, "Improving Instruction: What Librarians Can Learn from the Study of College Teaching," presentation at the Association of College and Research Libraries 9th National Conference, Minneapolis, Minn., April 7-10, 2005); http://kuscholarworks.ku.edu/dspace/bitstream/1808/262/1/Walter_ACRL_05.pdf (viewed January 3, 2006); Steven J. Bell and John Shank, "The Blended Librarian: A Blueprint for Redefining the Teaching and Learning Role of Academic Librarians," *College and Research Libraries News* 65(7) (July/August 2004): 372-375.

19. "ACRL Information Literacy," http://www.acrl.org/ala/acrl/acrlissues/acrlinfolit/informationliteracy.htm (viewed January 3, 2006); "Library Instruction Roundtable," http://www3.baylor.edu/LIRT/ (viewed January 3, 2006); "American Association of School Librarians," http://www.ala.org/ala/aasl/aaslindex.htm (viewed January 3, 2006); "Information Literacy Section," http://www.ifla.org/VII/s42/ (viewed January 3, 2006).

20. "LOEX," http://www.emich.edu/public/loex/loex.html (viewed January 3, 2006).

21. Examples: "Research 101," http://www.lib.washington.edu/uwill/research101/ (viewed January 3, 2006); "Libraries, in Texas and around the world, provide access to a variety of resources including the Internet," http://tilt.lib.utsystem.edu/ (viewed January 3, 2006); "Bruin Success with Less Stress," http://www.library.ucla.edu/bruinsuccess/ (viewed January 3, 2006); "TIP: Tutorial for Info Power," http://tip.uwyo.edu (viewed

January 3, 2006); "University of San Francisco, Gleeson Library Geschke Center," http://www.usfca.edu/library/movies/tourbbhi.html (viewed January 3, 2006).

22. "Guidelines for Distance Learning Library Services," http://www.ala.org/acrl/resjune02.html (viewed January 3, 2006).

23. Curzon, 38-45.

24. Ibid.

25. *Information Literacy Competency Standards for Higher Education* (Chicago: ACRL, 2005); http://www.ala.org/acrl/ilcomstan.html (viewed January 3, 2006).

26. "Information Literacy in the Disciplines," http://www.ala.org/ala/acrlbucket/is/projectsacrl/infolitdisciplines/index.htm (viewed February 17, 2006); "Characteristics of Programs of Information Literacy that Illustrate Best Practices: A Guideline," http://www.ala.org/ala/acrl/acrlstandards/characteristics.htm (viewed February 17, 2006).

27. Alan Bundy, ed., *Australian and New Zealand Information Literacy Framework: Principles, Standards and Practice*, 2nd ed. (Adelaide: Australian: New Zealand Institute for Information Literacy, 2004); http://www.anziil.org/resources/Info%20lit%202nd%20edition.pdf (viewed January 3, 2006).

28. "Information Literacy Standards for Student Learning," in *Information Power: Building Partnerships for Learning* (Chicago: American Library Association, 1998), 8-44.

29. Lau, 45.

30. Michael B. Eisenberg and Robert E. Berkowitz, *Information Problem-solving: the Big Six Skills Approach to Library and Information Skills Instruction* (Norwood, NJ: Ablex, 1990); "Big6: An Information Problem-Solving Process," http://www.big6.org/ (viewed January 5, 2006).

31. Amanda Lenhart, Mary Madden, and Paul Hitlin, *Teens & Technology* (Washington, DC: Pew Internet & American Life Project, 2005): 35-43; http://www.pewinternet.org/pdfs/PIP_Teens_Tech_July2005web.pdf (viewed January 3, 2006).

32. Amanda Lenhart, Maya Simon, and Mike Graziano, *The Internet and Education: Findings of the Pew Internet and American Life Project* (Washington, DC: Pew Internet and American Life Project, 2001), 3-4; http://www.pewinternet.org/pdfs/PIP_Schools_Report.pdf (viewed January 3, 2006).

33. Jennifer Bowen et al., "Serial Failure (Advisor Op-Ed),"*Charleston Advisor* 5(3) (January 2004); http://www.charlestonco.com/features.cfm?id=146&type=ed (viewed January 3, 2006).

34. Ibid.; Judy Luther, "Trumping Google? Metasearching's Promise," *Library Journal*, *128*(16) (1 October 2003): 36-39.

35. Stephen E. Arnold, "Relevance and the End of Objective Hits," *Online*, *29*(5) (September/October 2005): 16-21.

36. Hannelore Rader, "Information Literacy 1973-2002: A Selected Literature Review," *Library Trends* 51(2) (fall 2002): 242-259.

doi:10.1300/J105v32n01_06

# The Electronic Resources (ER) Librarian and Patrons with Disabilities

## Cheryl Riley

**SUMMARY.** The Electronic Resource (ER) librarian must be familiar with Web technology. Central to the electronic resource position is access. A critical aspect of ensuring access is providing access to users with disabilities. Laws requiring accessible resources and libraries are briefly discussed. Guidelines for accessible Web pages are discussed in detail, as are the elements that comprise accessible Web page design. Studies reviewing the general accessibility of Web resources in higher education, Web pages of college and university libraries, and the Web pages of library schools indicate that approximately 50% are accessible. A study at Oregon State University indicated that 95% of all subscription databases were accessible in 2002 whereas in 1995, 95% were inaccessible. Assistive technologies and additional resources to help ER Librarians better serve users with disabilities are identified. doi:10.1300/J105v32n01_07 *[Article copies available for a fee from The Haworth Document Delivery Service: 1-800-HAWORTH. E-mail address: <docdelivery@haworthpress.com> Website: <http://www.HaworthPress.com> © 2007 by The Haworth Press. All rights reserved.]*

---

Cheryl Riley, MBA, MLS, is Professor and Librarian, James C. Kirkpatrick Library, Central Missouri State University, Room 2254, 601 South Missouri Street, Warrensburg, MO 64093 (E-mail: riley@libserv.cmsu.edu).

[Haworth co-indexing entry note]: "The Electronic Resources (ER) Librarian and Patrons with Disabilities." Riley, Cheryl. Co-published simultaneously in *Collection Management* (The Haworth Information Press, an imprint of The Haworth Press) Vol. 32, No. 1/2, 2007, pp. 83-98; and: *Electronic Resources Librarianship and Management of Digital Information: Emerging Professional Roles* (ed: Mark Jacobs) The Haworth Information Press, an imprint of The Haworth Press, 2007, pp. 83-98. Single or multiple copies of this article are available for a fee from The Haworth Document Delivery Service [1-800-HAWORTH, 9:00 a.m. - 5:00 p.m. (EST). E-mail address: docdelivery@haworthpress.com].

**KEYWORDS.** Accessible Web pages, accessible electronic resources, accessible catalogs, accessible course management software, HTML standards

## BACKGROUND

In addition to understanding the hardware, software, and programming requirements which surround the electronic information resources used in libraries today, the electronic resources (ER) librarian must possess a basic knowledge of the needs of library users with disabilities. The world of disabilities is large–there are print disabilities, speech disabilities, · hearing disabilities, orthopedic disabilities, learning disabilities, and other cognitive disabilities–the list is long. As a simple illustration of the size of the disability universe, consider that there are twelve internationally recognized disability access symbols.[1]

Each type of disability may require a different type of accommodation. United States census data from 2002 indicates that 19.3 percent of the population (almost 50 million people) had a disability. The data further reveals that 9.3 million people reported a sensory disability involving sight or hearing; 21.2 million reported a condition limiting basic physical activities; and 12. 4 million reported a physical, mental, or emotional condition.[2]

The Heath Resource Center reports that "the proportion of full-time college freshmen reporting disabilities remained stable (6 to 8 percent) between 1998 and 2000."[3]

Given these two measurements, librarians can expect library clients with disabilities to include between six and twenty percent of the total service population.

A person with a disability is anyone who:

1. has a physical or mental impairment which substantially limits one or more of the person's major life activities,
2. has a record of such impairment, and
3. is regarded as having such an impairment.[4]

The library profession has always been the long-time champion to make library materials readily and easily available to all, but the electronic information age has brought new attention to the service of persons with disabilities in the library because, historically, they were not as visible. In the past, travel to the library was one of the primary barriers that people with disabilities faced in accessing library information. Not only has the digital age made information available from almost everywhere, but public transportation is now more accessible to those with disabilities. This progress in accessibility, as with most change, presents particular challenges for librarians. Andrew K. Pace cautions librarians, "Be careful what you wish for."[5]

Pace claims "whether you're talking about people with disabilities or the digital divide, reaching *everyone* with electronic information represents the next major challenge for libraries."[6]

Although the job description of an ER librarian varies from institution to institution and position to position, one consistent requirement is familiarity with Web resources. This familiarity may or may not include the design of Web pages, work with OpenURL technology, the implementation of federated searching, the negotiation of licenses for e-resources, and tracking online journals. One underlying concept, however, that is central to the electronic resource position is that of access. It is the job of the ER librarian to provide and ensure access to a library's ER. A critical aspect of that job is to provide access to users with disabilities.

One way to ensure access for all users is to focus on universal design. Universal design is the practice of designing products, buildings, public spaces, and programs to be usable by the greatest number of people. In the fifteen years since the passage of the *Americans with Disabilities Act of 1990* [7] (ADA), curb cuts, wheelchair ramps, accessible parking, and public transportation with accommodations for the disabled have become a part of the American landscape. These accommodations do not only benefit the disabled. Curb cuts and wheelchair ramps are used by those pushing a stroller, those making deliveries, and those who find steps unpleasant; curb cuts are just as likely to be used by someone on a bicycle, skateboard, or roller-blades as by someone in a wheelchair. Providing accessible information is one more step to the realization of a completely accessible society. As the baby-boomer generation moves into their senior years, the need for an accessible society will increase; the incidence of disability rises as individuals reach the sixth and seventh decades of life. The "graying of America" will increase the need for information which is accessible to all.

## DISABILITY LAW–BRIEFLY

No discussion of accessible information is complete without examining the key legislation and policies that mandate the provision of accessible information by libraries. Specific laws include the *Architectural Barriers Act of 1968*;[8] the *Rehabilitation Act of 1973*,[9] amended 1986, and 1992; the *Individuals with Disabilities Education Act*;[10] and the *ADA*.[11]

Taken together, these laws provide a powerful imperative not to discriminate against the disabled. Disability law is civil rights law and is all about equal opportunity.

The *Architectural Barriers Act of 1968* required buildings financed with federal funds to be accessible to the physically handicapped. Buildings remodeled after this time must also be accessible, if financed with federal funds.[12]

Section 504 of the *Rehabilitation Act of 1973* protects qualified individuals from discrimination based on their disability, if an employer or organization receives funds from any federal agency or department.[13]

The concept of reasonable accommodation originates from this law. For employment purposes, a qualified individual with a disability is one who, through a reasonable accommodation, can perform the essential functions of the job for which he or she has applied or been hired. Specific language in Section 504 states:

> No otherwise qualified individual with a disability in the United States, as defined in section 706 (20) of this title, shall, solely by reason of her of his disability, be excluded from participating in, be denied the benefits of, or be subjected to discrimination under any program or activity receiving Federal financial assistance.[14]

Section 504 defines a "program or activity" to include "a college, university, or other postsecondary institution, or a public system of higher education."[15] Section 508, a 1986 amendment to the *Rehabilitation Act*, provides standards for accessible information technology, including Web pages, computer operating systems and software, self-contained products, and information kiosks.[16] The *Individuals with Disabilities Education Act* mandates a free public education for all children with disabilities and requires that such education focus attention on future education, employment, and independent living.[17] Obviously, most libraries are required to provide information accessible to those with disabilities.

Although the legal basis is well-established in civil rights law, perhaps a better barometer for librarians is the action taken by the American Library Association (ALA). The ALA issued a policy statement in January 2001 which states that libraries are expected to comply with the

ADA and, in most cases, with Section 504 of the *Rehabilitation Act of 1973*.[18]

Some libraries have additional responsibilities under Section 508. Part two of the policy requires equal access to library resources for the disabled. Specific services referenced in this section include "extended loan periods, waived late fines, extended reserve periods, library cards for proxies, books by mail, reference services by fax or email, home delivery service, remote access to the OPAC, remote electronic access to library resources, volunteer readers in the library, volunteer technology assistants in the library, an American Sign Language (ASL) interpreter or real-time captioning at library programs, and radio reading services."[19]

## ACCESSIBLE WEB PAGES AND THE W3C

Creating an accessible Web page requires an understanding of the elements of good Web page design and adherence to established standards. Accessible Web page design allows for alternate ways to access information. It may include a text-only version and a large-print version. It may allow the user to control the color, contrast, font, and font size used on the screen. It may allow the user to turn certain elements on or off. At the very least, a page must include alt-text tags for any buttons or images. Utilizing the elements necessary to make an accessible Web page may be simple or complicated–it depends on the complexity of the information available on the site. Sandstrum discusses several simple exercises which demonstrate the barriers which individuals with disabilities encounter using the Web.[20]

The World Wide Web Consortium (W3C) was formed in 1994 by Tim Berners-Lee, an individual instrumental in the development of the Web. The W3C is an international consortium that allows member organizations, staff, and the public to work together to develop Web standards. The official mission of the W3C is "to lead the World Wide Web to its full potential by developing protocols and guidelines that ensure the long-term growth for the Web."[21] To date, more than eighty standards have been developed, which help to ensure that fundamental, Web technologies are compatible and work together. "W3C also engages in education and outreach, develops software, and serves as an open forum for discussion about the Web."[22]

The Web Accessibility Initiative (WAI) was created in 1997 and is one of the four domains of the W3C. The WAI develops "guidelines . . . resources . . . and support materials"[23] to help make the Web accessible to people with disabilities. The WAI has developed three standards that detail what is necessary to provide accessible Web pages. The standards are Web Content Accessibility Guidelines, Authoring Tool Accessibility Guidelines, and User Agent Accessibility Guidelines. A working draft of a fourth standard, Evaluation and Report Language, was published in September 2005. A draft of Version 2.0 of the Guidelines for Web Content was distributed for comments in late 2005. The guidelines are expected to be agreed upon and distributed in 2006.[24]

The organization also publishes the ten "quick tips to make accessible Web sites."[25] The quick tips include:

- using the alt attribute to describe the function of each visual;
- using client-side image map elements;
- providing captioning and transcripts of audio and descriptions of video;
- using text that makes sense when read out of context;
- using cascading style sheets (a formatting mechanism) for layout and style;
- summarizing graphs and charts;
- providing alternative content in case active features are unsupported or inaccessible;
- using well-designed, sensible frames;
- having tables that include summaries and meaningful titles; and
- validating or otherwise checking the design.

The consensus process which involves different stakeholders in Web accessibility has resulted in the accessibility options available for standard authoring products.

### Web Content Accessibility Guidelines

WAI has published fourteen guidelines for Web content accessibility. Each guideline includes three levels of priority for compliance. The most accessible resource is one that complies with all three priority levels. Priority one items are those design elements that must be satisfied or one or more groups will find it *impossible* to access the information. Priority two items must be satisfied or one or more groups will find it *difficult* to access the information. Priority three items must be satisfied or one or more groups will find it *somewhat difficult* to access the information. The fourteen guidelines for WAI are:

1. Provide equivalent alternatives to auditory and visual content.
2. Do not rely on color alone.
3. Use mark-up and style sheets and do so properly.
4. Clarify natural language use.
5. Create tables that transform gracefully.
6. Ensure that pages with new technology transform gracefully.
7. Ensure user-control of time sensitive content changes.
8. Ensure direct accessibility of embedded user interfaces.
9. Design for device independence.
10. Use interim solutions.
11. Use W3C technologies and guidelines.
12. Provide context and orientation information.
13. Provide clear navigation mechanisms.
14. Ensure that documents are clear and simple.[26]

The WAI site provides definitions for each guideline along with examples of accessible coding and detailed examples of both accessible and inaccessible pages.[27]

Each guideline includes several checkpoints to use to determine priority levels. The information at this site is very technical and may be overwhelming to the novice Web designer, but examples for every element in the Web Content Accessibility Guidelines are provided. There are other resources which include less technical and detailed examples of accessible coding. Providenti lists coding examples for three common Section 508 errors (alt-text tags; labels for frames; and labels for all input elements).[28]

He first lists the source code for the inaccessible version; then provides the code for the accessible solution.

Another important resource to use to write accessible HTML is *Web Accessibility for People with Disabilities* by Michael G. Paciello.[29]

Many of the standard Web development tools have accessibility modules (either integrated into the tool or freely available as add-ons) that will check for compliance and highlight problem areas. As awareness of the problems Web-based resources pose for the disabled population grows, more tools are being developed to automate accessible design.

### Tools to Assist in Evaluating Resource Accessibility

A number of validation programs can help the Web developer understand a site's level of accessibility; other programs are useful for keeping up-to-date with currently accepted HTML conventions by validating the HTML on a given page or site. The WAI maintains a list of over 80 tools[30] which can help with evaluation, but no tool is sophisticated enough to do the entire job: knowledgeable human interaction is always required. The librarian will, eventually, have to make a judgment on whether or not the Web page is accessible.

The need to make a judgment about the level of accessibility of a page or site may be the most difficult aspect of providing accessible Web pages. The librarian needs the technical skills to develop a Web page and a practical understanding of how different users can be affected by those decisions. In addition to the technical expertise, a basic understanding of design and visual elements is important. Ultimately, the librarian needs to have sufficient confidence to reach a logical and well-considered decision about the accessibility of a Web page or Web-based product. This is the type of skill and knowledge which is not, routinely, acquired in library school, but is one which is learned on-the-job, through continuing education, and through professional development activities. There are a number of national conferences that address the needs of the disabled consumer, and workshops which focus on specific techniques may be available at some of these conferences. Online courses which have been designed to train providers of information to make that information accessible are growing in number. Librarians who work with large populations of disabled clients as well as library school students may also pursue a certificate or degree in assistive technology or accessible design. The most well-known of these programs is the *Assistive Technology Applications Certificate Program* from the Center on Disabilities at California State University, Northridge. As the needs of disabled clientele are more fully understood by librarians and in libraries, there will be more courses dedicated to the needs of special users which will and should be developed. In the future, LIS graduates will arrive at libraries with this knowledge and these skills and will continue their development on-the- job. One of the first steps for librarians responsible for the design of Web pages is to be aware and make use of the tools which are available to be used in the evaluation of the accessibility of Web pages and sites.

Bobby™, a tool developed by the Center for Applied Special Technology[31] (CAST), has been widely used in libraries, and reviewed in the professional literature. Although developed by CAST, Bobby™ was acquired by Watchfire in July 2002; Watchfire is responsible for all continued development, marketing, and distribution. Users submit the Uniform or Universal Resource Locator (URL) for an individual site which they own. Bobby™ analyzes the tagging in the document by re-displaying the page with an accompanying picture of the hat of a bobby (a London policeman) along with the disability access symbol, if an access problem is identified. Bobby™ performs over 90 accessibility checks, including such things as alternative text descriptions for images, alternative text descriptions for image maps, inaccessible links, problems with HTML tagging, tagging which cannot be read by screen-readers, adjacent links which are not separated, audio files without descriptive text, and frames without alternative text.[32] Sites in compliance with all Priority 1 checkpoints receive an "A" approval rating; those which comply with all Priority 2 checkpoints receive a "AA" approval rating; and those which comply with all three priority levels are awarded a "AAA" approval rating. Bobby™ also reports on Section 508 compliance.

### Electronic Resource Accessibility

Rowland[33] reported on Web page accessibility in higher education. Other studies (Lilly and Van Fleet,[34] Spindler,[35] Schmetzke,[36] and Providenti[37]) have reported on Web page accessibility at libraries and library schools. In toto, their findings indicated that approximately 50% of the Web pages they surveyed were accessible. Lewis (a blind librarian) and Klauber[38] presented real-life examples of inaccessible Web pages for those with print disabilities. Kirkpatrick and Morgan discussed insights gained after listening to Web sites with a screen-reader[39] and working with a blind professional.[40]

In an attempt to provide information about specific resources which are available to librarians, Axel Schmetzke served as the guest editor for two issues of *Library Hi-Tech*[41] and reviewed databases, integrated library systems (ILS), and course management products, e.g., Voyager 2000,[42] iPac 2.0,[43] Lexis-Nexis, ProQuest, EBSCO Academic Search Premier, Expanded Academic Index ASAP, Business & Company ProFile ASAP, Electronic Collections Online (ECO),[44] PubMed, OVID MEDLINE, MEDLINEplus, CANCERLIT,[45] Electric Library Plus, Encyclopedia Britannica Online,[46] Blackboard 4 and 5, Prometheus 3, and WebCT 3.[47] These studies document approaches to assess the accessibility of online resources. Results varied from "with some effort it can be successfully navigated by experienced users of assistive technology"[48] or "able to complete a basic search, navigate search results, display an article and access help without difficulty"[49] to "does not provide easy access for a student using a screen reader."[50] In 2002, after reviewing the accessibility of all research databases available at Oregon State University, Ron Stewart, Director of the Northwest Center for Technology Access, found that 95% of the databases were accessible, whereas, in 1999, 95% of the databases reviewed were inaccessible.[51] One possible reason for the results reported by the *Library Hi-Tech* reviewers and those reported by Stewart might be the level of familiarity each of the reviewers had with the assistive technology used for the evaluation. Stewart has a long history with adaptive technology and has evaluated databases for accessibility since 1997; many of the *Library Hi-Tech* reviewers were careful to point out that they were not experts in using a particular screen-reader.[52]

Another factor, obviously, might be the subjectivity of the analysis which would reflect differences in the individual evaluators. It is logical to assume that some had higher standards or were harder to please. One obvious conclusion for the complete change in the accessibility of databases at Oregon State University is that the products were simply more accessible in 2002 than in 1999. Another impact might be the influence and knowledge that comes from affiliation with a disability center. Regardless of the reasons for the differences in results, the fact that there are still differences in individual evaluations illustrates the challenges faced by any librarian who works with digital resources to provide accessible information for disabled users.

The complexity of the content of a Web page or information from an electronic database available via the Web impacts the level of complexity required to provide accessible information. The ER librarians should be aware of the accessibility level of each resource even if they cannot guarantee that every electronic journal or Web-based resource is accessible to all patrons. Stated another way, the ER librarian should recognize the impediments to access which a particular group of users might encounter when using a specific product; alternate resources should be available for these clients.

The ER librarian must work with providers of hardware, software, and ER to guarantee accessible content and to inform them of areas that have proven problematic for specific users. In addition, as leaders in the use of electronic information, librarians must utilize proactive measures to encourage providers of information to embrace the concept of universal design. Just as universal design concepts have made physical structures friendlier for everyone, providing universally accessible content will make the information superhighway available to a wider range of users.

Although to provide accessible content is a huge step forward in order to serve the disabled, the responsibilities and concerns of the ER librarian do not stop with providing accessible content. Usability is another important component to maintain accessible ER. Usability is the expectation that the design of an interface will not impede the use of a technology.[53]

Research by User Interface Engineering, Inc. shows that "people cannot find the information they seek on Web sites about 60% of the time."[54]

The ER librarian and the vendor/publishers who supply ER should collaborate to provide usable environments for information delivery. Usability studies are designed to help librarians understand the difficulties library users encounter when they attempt to use library interfaces to access information. A usability study does not have to be difficult, time-consuming, or expensive. A simple approach is to ask questions of a focus group–ask disabled users to share the unique challenges they face when they use library resources.

## ASSISTIVE TECHNOLOGY

Librarians may utilize many different approaches/techniques in their efforts to ensure access to information for the disabled population. One approach is to fulfill requests as they are received. A second approach is to proactively provide assistive technology devices which are often, prohibitively expensive for individuals to purchase. For those persons, the library may serve the dual purpose to provide accessible information as well as the mechanisms for its use.

The first step in serving any community is to understand its needs. Every library should survey its community of users in order to identify the kinds of accommodations which users might require. These accommodations vary from library to library and with the type of library.

Academic libraries might develop a partnership with the university office which serves the needs of students with disabilities. This office should be able to provide both a census of persons with disabilities on the campus and insights into the types of assistive technologies which might serve the needs of the greatest number of users.

A public library should have a community assessment document to use for planning purposes.

A screen-reader or magnifying program will serve those with print disabilities, learning disabilities, and some of those with other cognitive disabilities. A flat-bed scanner and speakers, in addition to a computer, are usually required to use this software. Some screen-readers are complex and require a significant investment of time to utilize; others are simpler and quickly mastered. Many program vendors offer trial periods so that librarians may evaluate different readers and select the best tool for the patrons of their libraries.

For librarians who serve users with physical impairments, alternative input devices such as large track balls, larger monitors, or special keyboards may be required. A one-button, automatic, adjustable table, although expensive, will allow maximum flexibility for the library and the most autonomy for the client. For patrons with good speech, but poor physical dexterity, dictation software might be a useful tool.

But, not all assistive devices are expensive. A hand-held magnifying glass may be sufficient for some users of print-based materials. An inexpensive reacher (a pole with claws on one end which allows the user to pick up materials) may provide some patrons with the ability to reach items on top or bottom shelves.

## ADDITIONAL RESOURCES

No one librarian knows and remembers how to use every reference book in the library and no one librarian is able to remember which digital resources are more or less accessible to disabled patrons. But, just as the job of the reference librarian is to know where to go to find the information the patron requires, the ER librarian must know where to go to find the resources which will help determine the accessibility of an online resource. In the years since the passage of the ADA, a number of monographs directed at the subject of accessibility of information in libraries have been published. In 2000, Barbara T. Mates, Regional Librarian for the Blind and Physically Handicapped, at the Cleveland Public Library published an excellent overview, *Adaptive Technology for the Internet: Making ER Accessible to All*,[55] which includes an extensive list of resources for disability rights advocates as an appendix. Courtney Deines-Jones and Connie Van Fleet's 1995 publication, *Preparing Staff to Serve Patrons with Disabilities: A How-To-Do-It Manual for Librarians*,[56] also provides an overview. The Association of Specialized and Cooperative Library Agencies (ASCLA), a division of the ALA, published *Guidelines for Library and Information Services to* the American Deaf Community[57] in 1996; *Guidelines for Library Services for People with Mental Retardation*[58] in 1999; and Rhea Joyce Rubin's *Planning for Library Services to People with Disabilities*[59] in 2001. ASCLA's newest publication is *Revised Standards and Guidelines of Service for the Library of Congress Network of Libraries for the Blind and Physically Handicapped.*[60] Two older, but still valuable, documents produced by the Trace Research and Development Center are *Checklists for Making Library Automation Accessible to Patrons with Disabilities*[61] and *Checklists for Implementing Accessibility in Computer Labs and Colleges and Universities.*[62]

## CONTINUING EDUCATION

There are many opportunities for interested professionals to increase their knowledge of barriers faced by library users with disabilities. Many disability-related organizations host local, regional, and national conferences. In addition to a number of workshop and training opportunities, many conferences include a vendor display area which allows participants to observe how a specific product works to resolves a specific issue. Two national conferences that might be of interest are *Closing the Gap* in Minneapolis, MN and the *Annual International Technology and Persons with Disabilities Conference*, sponsored by the California State University, Northridge Center on Disabilities. The Association on Higher Education and Disability (AHEAD) and many other disability organizations host annual conferences. The Internet has several sites that maintain calendars of disability-related conferences.[63]

Organizations such as *EASI*;[64] *WebAim*;[65] and *DO-IT: Disabilities, Opportunities, Internetworking, and Technology*[66] offer workshops and training materials.

## CONCLUSION

A popular saying affirms that it takes a village to raise a child. Providing a usable and accessible environment for library patrons with disabilities takes a committed, library community and the hard work of ER librarians who work with vendor/publishers to proactively advocate for ER which are accessible to all. For those who work with digital resources now and in the future, an awareness of the law, a sensitivity to the issues, and an understanding of the opportunities and challenges provided by e-resources is paramount. The first step to resolve a problem is to admit that the problem exists; the first step to provide accessible information for all users is to acknowledge that some users with disabilities will not be able to use some types of information without special help. The ER librarian must be one of the individuals who play a primary role in ensuring that electronic information is used by all library customers.

## NOTES

1. "Disability Access Symbols," http://www.gag.org/resources/das.php (viewed September 19, 2005).
2. Judith Waldrop and Sharon M. Stern, "Disability Status: 2000," http://www.census.gov/prod/2003pubs/c2kbr-17.pdf (viewed September 19, 2005).
3. Cathy Henderson, *2001 College Freshmen with Disabilities: A Biennial Statistical Profile* (Washington, D.C.: HEATH Resource Center/American Council on Education, 2001).
4. *Americans with Disabilities Act of 1990*, Public Law 101-336, 104 STAT 327, 42 USC § 12102(2) Sec. 3(2)(A)(B)(C).
5. Andrew K. Pace, "Be Careful What You Wish For," *Computers in Libraries* 21(9) (Oct. 2001): 64.
6. Ibid., 66.
7. *Americans with Disabilities Act of 1990*, Public Law 101-336, 42 USC §§ 12101-12213.
8. *Architectural Barriers Act of 1968*, Public Law 90-480, 82 STAT 718, 42 USC §§ 4151-4157.
9. *Rehabilitation Act of 1973*, Public Law 93-112, 87 STAT 355, 29 USC §§ 701-725.
10. *Individuals with Disabilities Education Act*, Public Law 109-63, 20 USC § 1400-1487.
11. *Americans with Disabilities Act of 1990*.
12. *Architectural Barriers Act of 1968*, 42 USC § 4151, § 4155.
13. *Rehabilitation Act of 1973*, Public Law 93-112, 87 STAT 394 § 504,
14. Ibid., 29 USC § 794(a).
15. Ibid., 29 USC § 794(b)(2)(A).
16. *Rehabilitation Act of 1973*, as amended by Public Law 102-569, 106 STAT 4430 § 508(a).
17. *Individuals with Disabilities Education Act,* 20 USC § 1400(d)(1)(a).
18. "Library Services for People with Disabilities Policy Press," http://ala.org/ascla/asclaissues/libraryservices.html (viewed September 27, 2005).
19. Ibid.
20. Jim Sandstrum, "Accessible Libraries: Providing Barrier Free Access to the Web for Library Patrons with Disabilities," *Colorado Libraries* 28(4) (winter 2002): 5-6.
21. Ian Jacobs, "About the World Wide Web Consortium (W3C)," http://www.w3.org/consortium/ (viewed September 15, 2005).
22. Ibid.
23. "WAI Mission and Organization," http://www.w3.org/WAI/about.html (viewed September 27, 2005).

24. "Web Accessibility Initiative (WAI)," http://www.w3.org/WAI/ (viewed September 23, 2005).

25. "Quick Tips to Make Accessible Web Sites," http://www.w3.org/WAI/References/QuickTips/Overview.php (viewed September 23, 2005).

26. "Web Content Accessibility Guidelines 1.0," http://www.w3.org/TR/WCAG10/ (viewed September 23, 2005).

27. Ibid.

28. Michael Providenti, "Library Web Accessibility at Kentucky's 4-Year Degree Granting Colleges and Universities," *D-Lib Magazine* 10(9) (September 2004), doi:10.1045/september2004-providenti.

29. Michael G. Paciello, *Web Accessibility for People with Disabilities.* (Lawrence, Kans.: CMP Books, c2000).

30. "Evaluation, Repair, and Transformation Tools for Web Content Accessibility," http://www.w3.org/WAI/ER/existingtools.html (viewed September 23, 2005).

31. "Bobby™ 5.0 Factsheet: Web Accessibility Testing," http://www.watchfire.com/resources/bobby-overview.pdf (viewed September 23, 2005).

32. Ibid.

33. Cyndi Rowland," Accessibility of the Internet in Postsecondary Education: Meeting the Challenge," http://www.webaim.org/coordination/articles/meetchallenge (viewed September 23, 2005).

34. Erica B. Lilly and Connie Van Fleet, "Wired But Not Connected: Accessibility of Academic Library Home Pages," *The Reference Librarian* 34(67/68) (1999): 5-28.

35. Tim Spindler, "The Accessibility of Web Pages for Mid-Sized College and University Libraries," *Reference & User Services Quarterly* 42(2) (2002): 149-154.

36. Axel Schmetzke, "Web Accessibility at University Libraries and Library Schools," *Library Hi Tech* 19(1) (2001): 35-49.

37. Providenti, "Library Web Accessibility."

38. Valerie Lewis and Julie Klauber, "[Image] [Image] [Image] [Link] [Link] [Link]: Inaccessible Web Design from the Perspective of a Blind Librarian," *Library Hi Tech* 20(2) (2002): 137-140.

39. Cheryl H. Kirkpatrick and Catherine Buck Morgan, "How We Renovated Our Library, Physically and Electronically, for Handicapped Patrons," *Computers in Libraries* 21(9) (Oct. 2001): 27.

40. Ibid., 28-29.

41. Axel Schmetzke, "Accessibility of Web-Based Information Resources for People with Disabilities, *Library Hi Tech* 20(2) (2002); Axel Schmetzke, "Accessibility of Web-Based Information Resources for People with Disabilities (Part Two), *Library Hi Tech* 20(4) (2002).

42. Robert Axtell and Judith M. Dixon, "Voyager 2000: A Review of Accessibility for Persons with Visual Disabilities," *Library Hi Tech* 20(2) (2002): 141-147.

43. Susan M. Johns, "Viewing the Sunrise: iPac 2.0 Accessibility," *Library Hi Tech* 20(2): 148-161.

44. Vibiana Bowman, "Reading Between the Lines: An Evaluation of WindowEyes Screen Reader as a Reference Tool for Teaching and Learning," *Library Hi Tech* 20(2): 162-178; Suzanne Byerley, "Usability Testing and Students with Visual Disabilities: Building Electronic Curb Cuts into a Library Web Site," *Colorado Libraries* 27(3) (fall 2001): 22-24; Cheryl A. Riley, "Libraries, Aggregator Databases, Screen Readers and Clients with Disabilities," *Library Hi Tech* 20(2) (2002): 179-187.

45. Sarah K. McCord, Linda Frederiksen, and Nicole Campbell, "An Accessibility Assessment of Selected Web-Based Health Information Resources," *Library Hi Tech* 20(2) (2002): 188-198.

46. Jennifer Horwath, "Evaluating Opportunities for Expanded Information Access: A Study of the Accessibility of Four Online Databases," *Library Hi Tech* 20(2) (2002): 199-206.

47. AnnMarie Johnson and Sean Ruppert, "An Evaluation of Accessibility in Online Learning Management Systems," *Library Hi Tech* 20(4) (2002): 441-451.

48. Axtell and Dixon, 146.

49. Howarth, 202.

50. Bowman, 164.

51. Ron Stewart, "Accessibility of Online Databases: A Usability Study of Research Databases," http://tap.oregonstate.edu/research/ahg.htm (viewed September 19, 2005).

52. Johnson and Rupert, 446.

53. Joan E. Conger, *Collaborative Electronic Resource Management* (Westport, Conn.: Libraries Unlimited, 2004), 221.

54. "Why Is Usability Important?" http://usability.gov/basics/index.html (viewed September 22, 2005).

55. Barbara T. Mates, *Adaptive Technology for the Internet: Making Electronic Resources Accessible to All* (Chicago: American Library Association, 2000).

56. Courtney Deines-Jones and Connie Van Fleet, *Preparing Staff to Serve Patrons with Disabilities: A How-To-Do-It Manual for Librarians* (New York: Neal-Schuman, 1995).

57. Association of Specialized and Cooperative Library Agencies, *Guidelines for Library and Information Services to the American Deaf Community* (Chicago: American Library Association, c1995).

58. *Guidelines for Library Services for People with Mental Retardation* (Chicago: American Library Association, 1999).

59. Rhea Joyce Rubin, *Planning for Library Services to People with Disabilities* (Chicago: American Library Association, 2001).

60. Association of Specialized and Cooperative Library Agencies, *Revised Standards and Guidelines for the Library of Congress Network of Libraries for the Blind and Physically Handicapped* (Chicago: American Library Association, 2005).

61. Jane R. Berliss, *Checklists for Making Library Automation Accessible to Disabled Patrons* (Madison, Wisc.: Trace Research and Development Center, 1992).

62. Jane R. Berliss, *Checklists for Implementing Accessibility in Computer Labs at Colleges and Universities* (Madison, Wisc.: Trace Research and Development Center, 1991), http://trace.wisc.edu/docs/accessible_labs/campus.htm (viewed September 27, 2005).

63. "Calendar of Events in Disability, Rehabilitation, and Assistive Technology: List of Conferences 2006 and Beyond," http://www.starlingweb.com/adp/as00028e.htm (viewed January 11, 2006).

64. "EASI: Equal Access to Software and Information," http://www.starlingweb.com/adp/as00028e.htm (viewed January 11, 2006).

65. "WebAIM," http://www.webaim.org/ (viewed January 11, 2006).

66. "DO-IT: Disabilities, Opportunities, Internetworking, and Technology," http://www.washington.edu/doit/ (viewed January 11, 2006).

doi:10.1300/J105v32n01_07

# The Electronic Resources (ER) Librarian and Special/Corporate Libraries

Stephen C. Boss
Glenn S. Cook

**SUMMARY.** Like all librarians, special/corporate libraries face change everyday. Many of them are very different in many ways than they were ten years ago. Many have moved from the delivery of information in books and print-based journals to that in virtual resources. These resources may be accessed online through subscription services or may be created and stored in-house. Corporate libraries publish in-house standards, specifications, policies/procedures, and work instructions that document and support their processes. Library personnel in these types of environments must be flexible and innovative and must be able to work collaboratively with a variety of professionals with different backgrounds. doi:10.1300/J105v32n01_08 *[Article copies available for a fee from The Haworth Document Delivery Service: 1-800-HAWORTH. E-mail address: <docdelivery@haworthpress.com> Website: <http://www.HaworthPress.com> © 2007 by The Haworth Press. All rights reserved.]*

---

Stephen C. Boss, MA, is Systems Librarian, University of Wyoming Libraries. Glenn S. Cook, MLIS, is Quality Content Systems Administrator, Coors Brewing Company, P.O. Box 4030, BC620, Golden, CO 80401 (E-mail: glenn.cook@coors.com).

Address correspondence to: Stephen C. Boss, University of Wyoming Libraries, Department 3334-1000 East University Avenue, Laramie, WY 82070 (E-mail: sboss@uwyo.edu).

[Haworth co-indexing entry note]: "The Electronic Resources (ER) Librarian and Special/Corporate Libraries." Boss, Stephen C., and Glenn S. Cook. Co-published simultaneously in *Collection Management* (The Haworth Information Press, an imprint of The Haworth Press) Vol. 32, No. 1/2, 2007, pp. 99-116; and: *Electronic Resources Librarianship and Management of Digital Information: Emerging Professional Roles* (ed: Mark Jacobs) The Haworth Information Press, an imprint of The Haworth Press, 2007, pp. 99-116. Single or multiple copies of this article are available for a fee from The Haworth Document Delivery Service [1-800-HAWORTH, 9:00 a.m. - 5:00 p.m. (EST). E-mail address: docdelivery@haworthpress.com].

Available online at http://col.haworthpress.com
© 2007 by The Haworth Press. All rights reserved.
doi:10.1300/J105v32n01_08

**KEYWORDS.** Special library, electronic resources, internal documentation, intranet, portal

## INTRODUCTION

Special libraries are in a constant state of change. Corporate libraries of old were showcases. Often located at a prime location in a corporate building these libraries consisted of large, book collections and long runs of industry journals as well as other material in hard-copy formats, e.g., microform. Today, after corporate downsizing and mergers as well as a refocus on primary, business objectives and the financial bottom-line many contemporary corporate libraries bear little resemblance to the past. As Stephanie Boyd points out

> Now the same library is flourishing, but we don't give tours of our space, which has been reduced to regular office cubicles. The extensive paper collection has been carefully allocated to other institutions, and our documents are electronic, housed on an intranet Website.[1]

Librarians who work in special libraries now have a diverse role to play in the selection and purchase of electronic resources (ER) and in the development of internal digital resources. As they work with stakeholders librarians ensure that the information that is delivered is up-to-date and relevant and they provide instruction for end-users on how best to use internal and external resources efficiently and effectively.

The work of librarians in the corporate library environment is tied to the business process that is supported by their activities and their libraries' collections may change in order to meet new business needs. Corporate libraries and the businesses that they support are diverse and there is no single model of library support.

In the 1970s, commercial databases indexed the content of journal articles and books, but the bulk of library collections were purchased and stored on shelves. Online databases became commonplace in the 1980s as online public access catalogs (OPACs) replaced card catalogs as a means to store bibliographic data and library holdings. In the late-1980s, digital full-text became available and storage of information in the library became less of a concern. As technologies have advanced the Internet has become a major conduit for both commercial and private digital information. Recent times have seen the development of databases with user-friendly, Web-based, public interfaces, which librarians use to track and document their company's critical internal documentation, projects, and policies/procedures.

Rather than act only in a support role the corporate librarian often has the opportunity to work and contribute as a partner, with researchers. The authors gained experience and insight as corporate librarians at a water-engineering firm, mining company, and brewery. While the commercial ER that were purchased by these libraries were utilized and highly valued by end-users the most valuable use of electronic documents was in the collection and delivery of internal/consulting reports and the supporting documentation that went into their creation; best practice resources; process work instructions; product/packaging quality standards and specifications; and industry procedures.

Information specialists at corporate libraries often support the following business functions:

- Research for internal clients
- Production of value-added materials, either from the library itself or in collaboration with content experts outside the library, e.g., technical writers or documentation specialists
- Proactive distribution of information to subject or project-specific client teams
- Selection of Web site content
- Design, maintenance, and enhancement of Web sites
- User-training
- Vendor-relations and content[2]

Libraries with a wholly digital focus that supports disparate business functions have a number of characteristics that are shared by all successful digital libraries:

- A single interface for users that delivers externally based and internally created information from a portal or a Web-based launch point
- Digital content that can be accessed from desktops
- Staff who possess competencies in the procurement and license of e-content
- Professional training, support, and referral for users
- Interactive online communications, i.e., e-mail, chat, cell phone, intranet, etc.
- Staff who possess competencies in user needs assessment, marketing, and product selection

- Secondary content relative to specific job functions, i.e., news/trade sources; scientific/technical journals and standards; financial databases; market research reports; legal/regulatory materials; patents; distance-learning or online training materials; e-books; as well as online explanations, training, and password applications for this content
- Secondary reference content pertinent to a corporate audience (general interest publications, encyclopedias, statistical sources, dictionaries; distance-learning/online-training materials); and online explanations, training, and password applications for this content
- Web directories (relative to organizational needs, categorized listings, with links to general and application-specific Web sites) and other types of referral resources
- Online access to internally generated knowledge (staff directories, departmental listings, employee handbooks) and knowledge-bases (intellectual capital, laboratory notebooks, presentations, reports, vendor/publisher lists, client/competitor information, expert networks)
- Online catalogs of library holdings, e-journals, and general information about the information center.[3]

## WRIGHT WATER ENGINEERS

Most areas of the Colorado Front Range urban corridor have benefited from the work of the professionals at Wright Water Engineers (WWE), which is one of the premier water-engineering firms in Denver. Some clients of WWE have been with the firm since it was founded in 1961 by Kenneth Wright, an expert in urban drainage/flood control and water supply, treatment, and rights. WWE subscribes to databases like WaterNet and Engineering Index. However, most WWE library projects focus on internal resources; materials that support WWE business functions, i.e., the production of technical reports that address specific problems and recommend solutions.

Librarians at WWE are required to write these technical reports as well as to track/organize them so that they can be used as reference materials. Much of the current work at WWE is built upon the knowledge gained/reported in past studies.

### Work Product at WWE

Engineering drawings and technical reports organized into sets are the primary products of a consultant engineering firm. During the course of the investigation/design phase of a project, a great deal of technical information, physical and/or virtual in nature, is amassed. A librarian is responsible for the organization and the management of these materials, e.g., procedures, standards, progress reports, etc., that support/document the processes. In a print-based environment this information is difficult to retrieve; the effort is time-consuming, costly, and reliant upon the indexing skill of the librarian.

The problem has been addressed, partially, in the digital age. At WWE materials that once were archived in their original formats are now stored digitally, which makes them more readily accessible. While some firms digitize all of their engineering files soon after they are produced, at WWE they are digitized as needed.

Some WWE publications are distributed to clients electronically, e.g., technical reports. PDF files can be locked-down with read-only permission so that they cannot be changed, which is critical for the integrity of the information.

The handling and delivery of government publications is made easier because of the online revolution. Government information produced by state and federal agencies is an important resource for the engineers. In the past, it had to be collected by hand. Large amounts of time were spent to research and copy files. Digitized data can now be discovered and delivered online. Digital resources meet the needs of modern corporate library users who expect to find much of the information they need online.

### Marketing Efforts

Another area where WWE takes advantage of the expertise of its librarians is collaboration with engineering and marketing personnel to produce public Web sites. The goal is to make a memorable impression on potential customers, i.e., name-recognition, through the capture of their interest and imagination.

As another example of public outreach, the WWE News, an online newsletter, gives insights into current WWE projects, some of an historical nature, as well as projects that appeal to a diverse audience with an emphasis on cultural heritage.

WWE Web sites give users access to richly detailed digital resources that feature related information and online documents, i.e., an impressive series of studies conducted by WWE engineers of ancient site locations, e.g., the Incan City of Machu Picchu and the Indian ruins at Mesa Verde, where scholars learn of the engineering efforts of these ancient cultures to manage their most precious resource: water. These ancient water-use projects are outlined at the Wright Paleohydrological Institute Web site: http://www.wrightwater.com/wpi/wpihome.html[4] (see Figure 1).

Engineering surveys, photographs, lectures, interviews, and analyses of Machu Picchu hydrology reports are available on the site, which hosts a number of virtual field trips conducted by engineers and contributing scholars.

Finally, the WWE librarian has built a public portal of engineering *best practices* documents to serve the public. The site also serves the interests of WWE as a marketing device where prospective clients can see the high-quality work and special services that the company offers.[5]

## THE LIBRARY AT COORS BREWING COMPANY

In 1991, the Coors Library was a traditional library with a collection made up of books and print journals. To use the library's resources patrons walked to where it was located at the brewing company's office complex in Golden, Colorado.

### Reengineering/Focus on Process

Change had begun in the library in the 1980s with its expansion to a multi-room facility and the introduction of an integrated library system (ILS). Vast amounts of brewing literature were indexed at the article-level.

The library had a built-in collection development system with subject experts from the research and development unit at service as bibliographers; the engineering department was more reliant on the librarian to act as the bibliographer in that subject area. As a result, the engineering collection was more broad-based.

In the 1990s an organizational shift moved the company from a fairly standard top-down, paternalistic organization to a more customer-focused, process-driven, team-centered, project-grounded, results-oriented company. These changes began to be reflected in the library as well.

As has already been mentioned, corporate libraries often collect large amounts of internally produced information. In "Competencies for Special Librarians of the 21st Century" it is stated

FIGURE 1. Wright Paleohydrological Institute

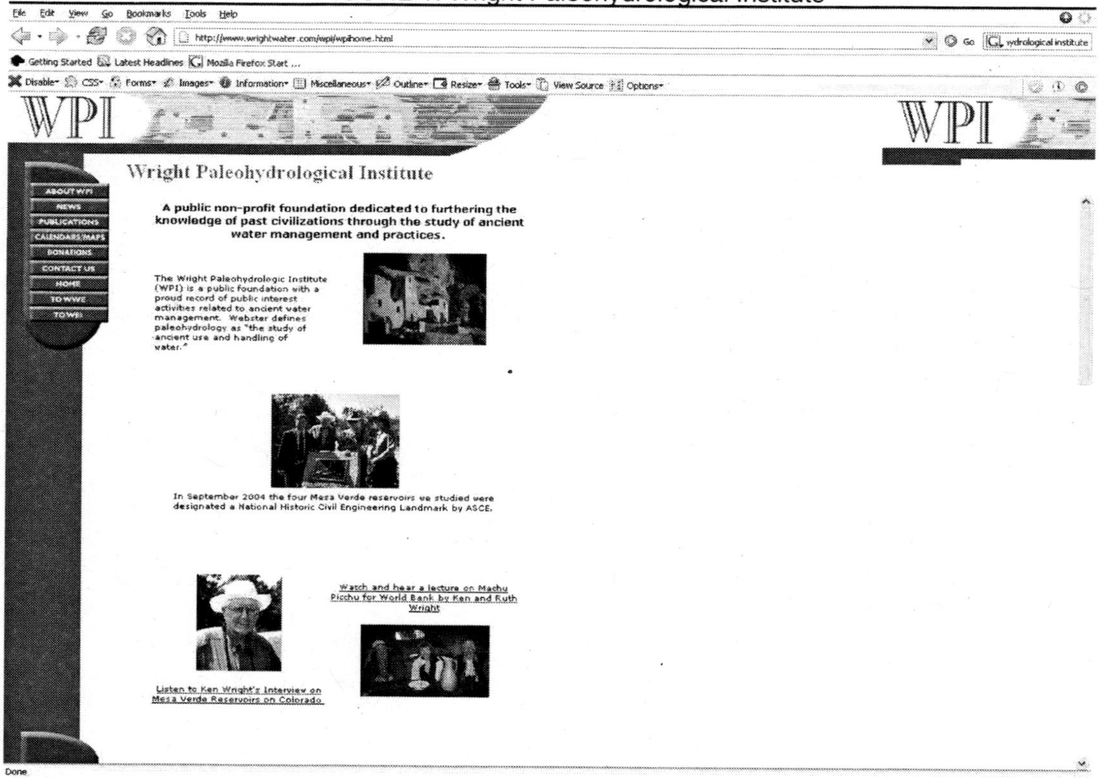


Used with permission.

In the information age, specialists in information service are essential–they provide the competitive edge for the knowledge-based organization responding with a sense of urgency to critical information needs. Information, both internally and externally produced is the lifeblood of the knowledge-based organization that is attempting to understand and manage its intellectual capital, often in a global context. Library and information professionals play a unique role in gathering, organizing and coordinating access to the best information sources for the organization as a whole.[6]

Although librarians at Coors had always focused on the delivery of internally produced information resources, the emphasis placed on their management, preservation, and delivery has greatly increased in the last ten years as they have been converted to the digital format and as the audience for their use has increased. This movement from a library that initially served a small highly specialized user group to one that serves a much wider patronage is the story of the Coors Library.

### Organizational Change

A change in an organizational structure, which had been static for some time, resulted in a closer alignment of the work of library personnel and corporate technical writers. The technical writing group was a discrete department; technical writers were assigned to various company units with specialized functions. Technical manuals were updated by the manual owner's hand, which resulted in problems, i.e., manuals were not updated, their organization was not consistent, and if the manual writer was not in the office to troubleshoot problems for manual users the work in that subject area halted.

The library had been positioned to work in collaboration with the technical writing group. Library personnel were expected to answer questions in all subject areas. But, questions that pertained to technical specifications to make, pack, and ship malted beverage products had to be answered by the technical writer who was the expert in the process in question. A problem would arise if, for instance, one of the technical writers left the company and was not replaced. An unexpected benefit was that the writers and library personnel in the company, by necessity, began to collaborate on the creation of the E-Docs system. They used the library's ILS software and some technical-writing templates to create documents and manuals that were uniform in format; and easy to access, distribute, and update.

Libraries and librarians, clearly, have expertise and provide a number of advantages in the organization and dissemination of information, which is especially apparent in a corporate environment in the digital age.

### World Wide Web

With the advent of the World Wide Web, a new expert in the library profession, the Web-design librarian, digital librarian, cybrarian, or, most recently, the ER (ER) librarian, arose to introduce a cataloged collection of digital resources to the end-users in the company. As previously stated, in the corporate library environment a librarian can wear many hats. The ER librarian developed Web interfaces that either queried the ILS or locally developed databases that were tied to *pre-canned* search pages, which led to internally/externally developed digital content. This dynamic search interface is a combination of aesthetic design, computer code, and electronic documents designed for the computer screen, which was introduced as a bridge between the keepers of the database, the library's knowledge-workers, and the information-seekers, the end-users. Through the use of descriptive metadata and Web-design the ER librarian in a corporate library helps users find the information that is critical to business functions, i.e., a corporate portal to enhance user access to digital information at Coors.

## DESIGNING AND BUILDING THE PORTAL

A portal provides users with a common interface to use to access information. NetBar, the portal developed at Coors for the corporate intranet, was designed to interface seamlessly with the library ILS through a functional series of search screens (see Figures 2 and 3). The portion of the portal for the delivery of digital information was called E-Docs, now the Coors Quality Management System (CQMS). The CQMS colors match classic Coors red, gray, and blue and the icons are based on those designed by the Coors Information Technology Department for the NetBar Web site.

### Portal Subject Specific Search Screens

One of the promises of a portal is the ability to plug end-users directly into information and give them the option to conduct interactive searches or to use canned, or pre-designed, searches (see Figures 4 and 5).

FIGURE 2. Coors NetBar Portal Login Page

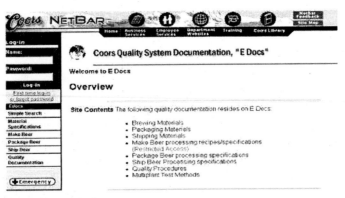

Used with permission.

FIGURE 3. Coors NetBar Portal–The Gateway to E-Docs

Used with permission.

A canned search for "glass bottles" returns a result list (see Figures 6 and 7).

### Managing ER

Large amounts of time and effort are expended at Coors in the management of information. Company employees produce most of the policies/procedures, standards/specifications, defect manuals, and internal

FIGURE 4. E Docs–Coors Quality Management System–Documentation Gateway

Used with permission.

technical reports. The user community is a large, highly specialized group of subject experts; thus, the librarian works with a variety of people with varied backgrounds.

## THE DEVELOPMENT
## OF AN INTERNAL INSTITUTIONAL REPOSITORY

The E-Docs system at Coors is very much like an academic institutional repository where librarians develop and contribute to in-house, electronic publishing, software systems. The move towards electronic publication of materials formerly held in hardcopy format is a major change for the Coors Library. The change began due to the tightening of the beer market. Coors had to become more competitive and eliminate waste; thus, workflows that did not contribute to the company's fiscal bottom-line had to be reconsidered. These changes made their way to the library, which became a virtual service point for a much larger user community. One change that occurred was that the librarian became involved in the creation, implementation, and maintenance of the CQMS; thus, the responsibilities of the position have grown beyond the acquisition and description of books and journals.

FIGURE 5. Coors E Docs–Bottle Specifications–Canned Searches

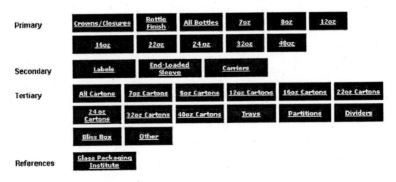

Used with permission.

FIGURE 6. E Docs–Canned Search Return List

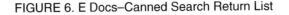

Used with permission.

Coors sells a high quality packaged product and the packages must also be of a high quality; stable and safe for consumers to use; and attractive as marketing devices. The packages represent the company and if they are of a poor quality this negative image reflects on the company and impacts the fiscal bottom-line.

The library ILS is used to digitally deliver the standards and specifications that define the quality of the product and its packaging. Taken from a quality packaging manual, two examples of electronic standards and specifications illustrate poor quality packaging. Figure 8 shows a can with a missing pull-tab and two cans with poor color definition. Fig-

FIGURE 7. E Docs–Bibliographic Detail Showing Links to the Electronic Documentation

*12 oz Convenience Bottle*

**Linked Resources:** Connect to the Specification
Connect to the Master Specification
Connect to the Finish Specification
Connect to the Qualification

**Call Number:** PKMS010
**Title:** 12 oz Convenience *Bottle*
**Publisher:** Coors Brewing Company Golden, Colorado **Effective Date:** 02/11/2002
**Main Author:** Moghadamnia, Shahram

Used with permission.

FIGURE 8. E Docs–Packaging Quality Defect Manual

Used with permission.

ure 9 shows packages with illegible date codes and water damage on the cartons.

## Purchased ER

The Coors librarian has subscribed to a number of ER over the years. One of the first was BrewInfo published by the Institute of Brewing and Distilling, a bibliographic database that indexes and abstracts brewing literature. Two other early resources in the library abstracting and indexing portfolio were services from Lexis-Nexis and Dialog, which were used, primarily, to research bibliographic information, rather than as full-text surrogates for print-based information.

As journal prices increased and the journal budget stayed the same, print-based journal cancellations increased. At first this was easy because the scope of the R & D Department became more limited. Online access to full-text articles became more commonplace and the cost decreased. The library uses EBSCOhost for access to about 4,000 full-text journals while print subscriptions have dropped from over 120 in 2002 to 24 currently.

FIGURE 9. E Docs–Packaging Quality Defect Manual

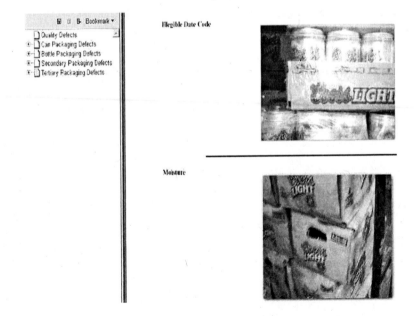

Specifications and standards as they relate to e-resources are under investigation. An informal group has met to determine which specifications and standards would best meet company needs. It is anticipated that by 2006 the library will have portal access to a vendor that provides this type of information.

### Current State

The current state of the library is that it is significantly smaller; back to a one-room facility with fewer books and journals. All books related to business, computers, and human resources have been removed from the holdings and dispersed to appropriate departments. It is now a technical library with a focus on the products used in brewing, brewing processes, quality, and the history of the industry. The librarian assists with the internal purchase of books by individuals.

The role of the librarian is much more centered on the delivery of e-information, i.e., the management of the EBSCO account along with a number of new responsibilities. One of these new tasks is Web page design in order to develop access, metadata, and canned searches to internal documents. Another new role is the publication of internal specifications as well as the provision of access to these documents. The library now publishes and provides access to work instructions to all Coors manufacturing sites in the United States.

There are over 30,000 published documents in the library catalog; the new work instructions will add over 10,000 documents, many of which must be revised from time to time, which requires additional support from the librarian. Under consideration by the company is to provide the same level of support for library services to all worldwide corporate sites.

Special libraries are in a constant state of flux. As companies merge or spin-off portions of their businesses, their libraries add and subtract user constituencies, which means that the librarians who manage them must be nimble in order to deal with the changes. Corporate library collections are geared to what the corporation's identity is and as the corporate organization changes focus, so must its library focus. Desktop delivery of ER now offers the corporate librarian a great medium for change with a constant need to reengineer innovate in order to meet customer expectations.

## FUTURE STATE:
## LIBRARIAN AND LIBRARIES
## IN THE SPECIAL LIBRARY ENVIRONMENT

In *The Future of the Special Library: One Person's Perspective*, R. James King states "In order to better understand the potential future, we must first understand the rich past on which we are built as well as the current environment. Also helpful is remembering that every library is different because every user community is different."[7]

No two corporate libraries are mirror-images of each other. Each company has differing justifications for the support of library programs and expectations vary greatly. Some companies provide a traditional library setting with books, journals, and research assistance contained within a physical structure while others have moved towards a more virtual environment. In either case, the librarian must work in a setting with few or no colleagues who understand libraries or library issues and requirements. Corporate libraries must change as the corporation it supports changes. Many special librarians find that they need to add additional skill sets over time. Some questions that must be asked are:

1. How much do librarians need to know about business management?
2. What skill sets do they need to work with computer programs or systems administration?
3. Are the major roles to be played in corporate libraries concerned with responsibilities in public services and technical services?
4. Are a focused education and specific skill sets preferable or is it better to have a diverse background and a holistic approach?

What skills do corporations look for when a librarian is hired? Planning skills may be paramount. The focus has moved from reference, technical skills, and online searching to "how you plan to position your library services in two to five years."[8]

Because of directives from upper-management to cut costs and increase access to research materials, many corporate libraries have moved from the traditional to the virtual library model, which necessitates a shift in library services from the traditional print-based books and journals approach to training users how to access the ER. Among the new responsibilities entailed by these changes for the corporate librarian are:

- work with corporate legal staff on contracts
- work with corporate finance staff to pay for online services

- an understanding of how to set up Web pages with links to online resources

Another area to consider is to identify the corporate library user group. Is it, primarily, members of business administration, legal, technical, or R & D units, or a combination? In any case, it benefits a librarian who works in this kind of environment to have public services skills, e.g., knowledge of how to conduct a reference interview. Such a skill may be more important than subject expertise. Reference interviews may be conducted in-person, over the telephone, via e-mail, or through chat. "Good virtual reference does not replace other reference services. Rather it is an important part of the full-service modern library,"[9] which includes the corporate library.

## CONCLUSION

It is multi-varied and the role of the special/corporate librarian continues to evolve in order to keep up with technological advances. This role is now centered on the provision of virtual access to both internal and external sources of information. Some library users may never step into the library in order to use its resources as they can now be accessed through web interfaces; they may include e-books, e-journals, and internal/external documentation. There is still a need for the traditional services, though on a much more selective basis.

The skills necessary for success include the administration of library systems, the ability to design and maintain Web pages, contract negotiation skills, the creativity to develop ideas into products/processes, and a wide array of so-called traditional library skills and knowledge. In addition, the corporate librarian must have the ability to work with a diverse group of professionals from many areas of expertise, e.g., I/T, law, marketing, science, engineering, etc. The challenges have increased but so have the opportunities expand the role of the librarian within the corporate setting.

Finally, in the context of this monograph on ER (ER) librarianship, it must be recognized that the corporate librarian and the corporate library staff are, by necessity, practitioners of ER librarianship. They must be technically savvy, innovative, flexible, and exceptional communicators. Not only must they speak the reference, technical services, and systems languages of the library world, but the finance, marketing, and R & D languages of the business world. How far away then are these individuals from the status of the modern renaissance professional? With no end in sight to technological advance and the challenges/opportunities it poses, the answer lies in the day-to-day work, the professional development activities, and the vision/imagination of the MLS graduates of today and tomorrow: the ER librarians.

## NOTES

1. Stephanie Boyd, "A Traditional Library Goes Virtual," Online 26(2) (March/April 2002): 41.

2. Stephanie Boyd, "What's Next for Corporate Virtual Libraries: The Elimination of a Paper Collection and the Need for a Walk-in Library Space Frees the Information Specialist to Choose Their Optimal Work Space," Online 28(6) (November/December 2004): 16.

3. Anthea Stratigos and Roger Strouse, "Going Virtual With the Corporate Library," Online 25(2) (March/April 2001): 66-67.

4. "Wright Palehydrological Institute," http://www.wrightwater.com/wpi/wpihome.html (viewed October 2, 2005).

5. "WWE Publications," http://www.wrightwater.com/wwe/wwepubs/wwepubs.html (viewed October 2, 2005).

6. "Competencies for Information Professionals of the 21st Century, Revised edition (June 2003), http://www.sla.org/content/learn/comp2003/index.cfm (viewed October 2, 2005).

7. R. James King, "The Future of the Special Library: One Person's Perspective," *Serials Review 30*(3) (2004): 171-175.

8. Debbie Schachter, "Building Your Team With Hiring Practices," *Information Outlook 9*(11) (November 2005): 12-13.

9. Carol Tenopir, "Chat's Positive Side," *Library Journal* 129(20) (2004): 42.

doi:10.1300/J105v32n01_08

# THE DIGITAL RESOURCE
# AND ITS MANAGEMENT

## Electronic Resources (ER)
## Management in the Academic Library:
## Process vs. Function

Stephen C. Boss
Lawrence O. Schmidt

**SUMMARY.** Academic Libraries, like all types of libraries, are in transition as they move from books on shelves to bytes on computers. Academic libraries, limited by space and staff to cover their hours of operation, have created 24-hour, digital information commons. The librarian focus on the millennial undergraduate features a virtual library that highlights extensive software suites and modules with computers where students can work collaboratively 24 hours a day, an expanded center for writing instruction, and a center for computer training, technical assistance, and

Stephen C. Boss, MA, is Systems Librarian (E-mail: sboss@uwyo.edu); and Lawrence O. Schmidt is Science Reference Librarian, Coe Library Reference (E-mail: lschmidt@uwyo.edu), both at the University of Wyoming Libraries, Department 3334, 1000 East University Avenue, Laramie, WY 82071.

[Haworth co-indexing entry note]: "Electronic Resources (ER) Management in the Academic Library: Process vs. Function." Boss, Stephen C., and Lawrence O. Schmidt. Co-published simultaneously in *Collection Management* (The Haworth Information Press, an imprint of The Haworth Press) Vol. 32, No. 1/2, 2007, pp. 117-140; and: *Electronic Resources Librarianship and Management of Digital Information: Emerging Professional Roles* (ed: Mark Jacobs) The Haworth Information Press, an imprint of The Haworth Press, 2007, pp. 117-140. Single or multiple copies of this article are available for a fee from The Haworth Document Delivery Service [1-800-HAWORTH, 9:00 a.m. - 5:00 p.m. (EST). E-mail address: docdelivery@haworthpress.com].

repair. To transition to this type of library can be a challenge for a profession not noted for the embrace of dynamic change initiatives and paradigms. This chapter looks at a number of change-management initiatives and models taken from private industry, looks at how digital resources impact and challenge traditional library workflows, and focuses on new ways these workflows can be altered to accommodate the new electronic information format in the academic library that has rapidly become the norm. doi:10.1300/J105v32n01_09 *[Article copies available for a fee from The Haworth Document Delivery Service: 1-800-HAWORTH. E-mail address: <docdelivery@haworthpress.com> Website: <http://www.HaworthPress.com> © 2007 by The Haworth Press. All rights reserved.]*

**KEYWORDS.** Academic libraries, electronic resources, workflows, process, function, process reengineering, learning organizations, total quality management, continuous improvement, changing customer needs and expectations

Change should be a friend. It should happen by plan, not by accident.

–Philip Crosby, *Reflections on Quality*

## INTRODUCTION

In recent years, libraries and librarians have experienced a great deal of change. Universities are under pressure to contain their budgets, which affects the ability of librarians to purchase new materials and maintain their collections, facilities, and operations. Funding of libraries has been, at best, static and many universities have cut library budgets. On top of this, the cost of serials has increased at a rate higher than inflation. Librarians have increased their holdings of born digital content as paper-based offerings have been transitioned to the digital format. Price structures have changed from individual title purchases and access via the print-based medium to the purchase of package deals that cluster digital content together. These packages include electronic databases, e-journals, and e-books.This will not be the end of change as a new generation of born digital or converted to digital information resources enters the realm of important collections. Other formats such as MP3 files, pod casts, and digital movies will be available in libraries in the near future. These new formats have impacted and will continue to impact libraries from top to bottom, from administration to collection development to reference, from systems to cataloging to access services. Another factor that cannot be overlooked is the change in the patrons of the academic library. Users are familiar with and have rapidly become experts with computers, software, and Internet search engines. The search engines themselves have become more sophisticated and user-friendly than the online public access catalog (OPAC) of the library. As the technical expertise of users has increased, so have their expectations. These changes demand that librarians take a fresh look at how they manage their traditional and digital content as well as how human resources are allocated to manage existing, evolving, and future library resources. New material types, especially digital ones have an impact on library workflows that evolved over vast periods of time and were designed to handle books and hardcopy journals rather than digital content. Since the management of digital materials impacts those who handle them, a new paradigm in management, organization, and workflow is required. Therefore, library managers must utilize change-management models that are already in use in the private sector as well as encourage reorganization in libraries to alter the way materials and personnel are managed in extant departmental structures or as they evolve towards completely new organizational structures.

## *CHANGING CUSTOMERS*
## *AND CHANGING CUSTOMER EXPECTATIONS*

Librarians have, traditionally, met the needs of their customers by listening to what they have to say. In academic libraries, collection development officers and subject bibliographers work with classroom faculty to acquire relevant content for the collections. While the majority of library materials will continue to be offered in print-based formats for now, increasingly, dynamic journal content is published in the digital format. Publishers put a greater emphasis on their digital publications and offer bundled electronic journal packages to their customers. They know their audience. As publishers of scientific journals they know researchers prefer new content in their subject areas to be published digitally and that the students who attend academic institutions prefer materials that are digital and available at their fingertips. Increasingly the students who use libraries have been exposed to and prefer to use electronic resources ER).

The students who enter college today are very different in their attitudes to technology from those who preceded them.[1]

Unlike previous generations who may have been introduced to computers and the Web after they became adults, many students who enter college now have never known a world without personal computers, video games, and the Internet. This generation likes results fast and old methods of research like paper indexes and writing down citations with a pencil are looked upon with disfavor. For the most part this is because this traditional approach takes too much time. While some researchers still use a combination of electronic and print resources, most undergraduates as well as the general public prefer ER because they are easier to use and provide the instant gratification desired. Fewer and fewer library patrons enjoy the thrill of the hunt. In their article, "Public Services and ER: Perspectives from the Science and Engineering Libraries at Duke University," Gray and Langley write:

> Like most people, our users prefer to follow the path of least resistance. If given the choice between searching for and downloading articles electronically, or physically locating journals in the stacks and then photocopying the articles, most patrons will resoundingly choose the former.[2]

The rapid rate at which older journal articles are digitized, the production of online full-text databases and digital journals coupled with the increase in customer acceptance and expectations that digital content will be available are all clear indications of the future path of scholarly communication. ER is a highly convenient and rapidly evolving material type that has dramatically changed library collections, policies, and workflows. The need to adapt to the requirements of the digital format is the new reality in information management.

## CHANGING MEDIUMS, CHANGING ROLES FOR LIBRARIANS

One of the greatest challenges for librarians these days is the management of ER. Patrons, as mentioned earlier, prefer ER to hardcopy ones. In many libraries a new position has been created to help manage ER. The ER Librarian is a cross between a reference librarian, a collection development officer, an acquisitions manager, a cataloger, and an information technology specialist. An ER librarian also has to be familiar with contracts and be a skilled negotiator.

The nature of e-resources has not only made necessary the creation of a new position to cope with the challenges brought on by the digital age, but it has also changed the way formerly vertically integrated library departments are organized. In many cases, new departments, cross-functional teams, or working groups are created to address these challenges. More than ever before, librarians view the selection, acquisition, description, and delivery of ER as a process made up of a number of interrelated functions that are contributed by employees from various units in the library organization. The advantage of this process approach is that the management of digital resources becomes a well-designed, coordinated process that enables the effective delivery of ER to library patrons and increases customer satisfaction.

## CONSUMER AND LIBRARY MARKETS: PAST AND PRESENT

Customer expectations are not the only things that have changed with the advent of the electronic age. Consumers are more diverse and the Internet has shifted them to a global market rather than localized economies. Reflect for a moment on the role of the product designer in consumer markets. In the past, the United States consumer market was fairly straightforward:

> The U.S. was a mass market and people acted in concert. They bought similar things, they watched similar movies, and they even praised similar gods. If a designer understood a small group of people–perhaps neighbors, friends or family–then he or she could design for them and still be relevant to millions of others.[3]

Most academic libraries fit this model. They were designed for a certain segment of the population, which came to the library and used the collection according to its rules and situations. So, for example, when an item was checked-out by a user it could not be used by another patron until it was physically returned to the library. This may have been accepted by consumers in the past, but with consideration of the current expectations of library patrons librarians must adopt new technologies for the management and delivery of digital information to meet their needs.

## THE MOVE FROM REACTION TO PRO-ACTION

Today, the attitudes of U.S. consumers are very much like those of new college freshmen. They are a very diverse group of people and have been exposed to many more life experiences and consumer products than were their parents or grandparents. The nature of the consumer market and the expectations of consumers require constant change and innovation in product design. Newspaper business sections are full of reports of business failures that can be attributed to a lack of research and design innovations. For today's product designer and academic librarian, "knowing what the end-user wants or needs requires an understanding of people, cultures and belief systems that may seem completely foreign and unintelligible."[4]

How should libraries and librarians react to these changes? The answer is, they should not react to change, but should lead change and make it proactive. Librarians lead as they constantly challenge and improve the way users are provided access to information in libraries. Librarians must embrace change and lead as they turn libraries into high-tech access hubs; a physical and a virtual presence where students and faculty can quickly gain access to a world of information regardless of its format.

## *HOW DO ACADEMIC LIBRARIANS LEAD CHANGE?*

The impact of technology on librarians and their relationships with their customer-base as the result of the rise of personal computers and powerful information networks creates a peer-to-peer communication that is a modern day revolution. In "Peer to PeER librarianship: Mirroring the Network," Anne Buck and Kimberly Douglas reflect on this revolutionary change:

> We do know that the agent of change is the network: a result, perhaps unintended, of inventing the computer. The digital network links personal computers and creates a killer communication conduit for the whole world. All new mechanisms for human contact ultimately drive huge societal changes. The printing press made it possible for an individual author's works to be quickly and reliably copied for distribution. This technology was the foundation for new businesses that allowed authors to reach untold strangers over great distances and over time. It changed the world. It is critical to comprehend that the network is more than a means of distributing objects such as printed text or audio files. It is about sharing and it is about wide, fast, immediate distribution. It is fundamentally about human-to-human communication.[5]

Where, then, are examples for librarians of persons who act as role models as they embrace and implement proactive change? How can librarians become better at the anticipation of change, deal with the challenges of an information revolution, and lead change within their libraries as opposed to a reaction to change? The answer is that they can look to business models that are used in private industry that focus on change and how to effectively deal with change management. Examples of these models include:

- Total Quality Management and Continuous Improvement
- Process Reengineering: Radical Steps to Approach Process Redesign
- Learning Organizations

In order to affect these models, librarians must gather data/information through surveys, focus groups, scorecards, and customer-focused literature. They might also use statistical methods to find out what their customers want and expect.[6]

### *Organizational Change*

To address these issues, librarians have begun to change the way they do business as they look at a variety of private business sector initiatives and organizational models. Businesses in the private sector have long been under pressure to improve their bottom lines and customer satisfaction. In their article, "Five Business Trends Every Human Service Organization Should Understand," representatives of Social Entrepreneurs, Inc. stated:

> A phenomenon of the past two decades has been that management innovations in the business world have permeated the human services world in the nonprofit, for-profit, and governmental sectors alike.[7]

### ARIZONA STATE UNIVERSITY

Some academic librarians have taken these organizational development methods, conducted thorough evaluations of library workflows, and have changed how libraries are organized. An example of this is the process of organizational change process at the University of Arizona Libraries. Before any organizational change at this library is implemented, library personnel conduct an environmental scan that includes a review of the university's mission, strategic plan, and other critical local and documented traditions. They do this to ensure that any changes they make in the library conform to the goals and objectives of the university.[8]

## LOS ALAMOS NATIONAL LABORATORY (LANL) AND THE LIBRARY WITHOUT WALLS (LWW)

The library at Los Alamos National Laboratory (LANL) is a model of change. The director of the library, Rick Luce, was one of the first to recognize the dawn of the digital information age.[9]

He made a name for himself as a leader in the field of digital librarianship. As librarians know, information comes in a wide variety of types and formats called media. The number of media and containers that hold the information has rapidly expanded. Some formats such as books and bound or unbound journals are viewed as traditional materials while non-traditional formats, i.e., ER, continue to proliferate. The printed book is one of the most efficient and compact ways information can be presented to a user. Today, however, information can be packaged in numerous physical or digital formats. Due to the innovations of publishers, librarians, and archivists, the concept of libraries without walls has become for many special libraries a reality. At LANL, Luce was the architect of a virtual research project called the Library Without Walls (LWW). The Los Alamos campus is a series of separate buildings spread across a large mesa and digital information is provided across the campus and throughout the United States; a paramount concern of the institution. "The first-generation goal of the LWW program was to acquire and deliver e-content."[10]

This digital information is delivered to LANL's distance research customers in the same way in which academic institutions deliver information to distance education students. For Luce, however, the first-generation goal, reached in 1999, was just the beginning. The second-generation goal was to make the digital information collected at LANL more usable. To that end, Luce has worked to assist scientists by "developing new ways to exploit our information repositories, and promote scientific collaboration."[11]

Academic librarians may not ever experience the unpredictable and ongoing change that special librarians face in the governmental or private sector; rather they may face change that is more constant and ongoing. Regardless, librarians in academe must be nimble and assume a leadership role to face change. To help them in this effort, there are several business management models available, which focus on the needs of the customer and encourage organizations to change the way they operate. These organizational business models can be easily adapted to libraries and may help librarians to adapt more effectively to the multiple pressures they experience as they work in an environment that is dramatically altered. They include: Total Quality Management (TQM), Process Reengineering, and developing Learning Organizations.

## MODEL FOR CHANGE–TOTAL QUALITY MANAGEMENT

After the Second World War, Japan emerged as a major economic power. Japanese products used to be viewed with disdain due to their low quality. That perception changed in the 1970s when Japanese automobiles began to be viewed as superior in quality to those produced in the United States and elsewhere. One of the major reasons for this change in quality was the Japanese acceptance and implementation of the Total Quality Management (TQM) systems that were based on the ideas and recommendations of TQM architect, W. Edward Demming. "TQM is a system of continuous improvement, employing participative management centered on the needs of the customers."[12]

Key components of TQM include active employee involvement and participation, problem-solving teams, statistical methods, long-term thought processes, goal-setting, and the recognition that systems, not people, produce inefficiencies. Steps in the application of TQM to the improvement of library patron satisfaction with the delivery of ER include:

- reduce departmental barriers
- know who are the customers
- strive to reach a state of continuous improvement

### Know Who the Customers Are

When they use TQM strategies library administrators and others on the process improvement team should strive to know their customers, which means make every attempt to find out the wants and needs of the library's users.

In the case of academic libraries, users comprise two separate groups. University faculty and staff are internal customers since they receive ongoing library services and support for their academic research and teaching curricula. On the other hand, students are external customers. They are a temporary audience because they are at the university for a fixed period of time. Most will not become a permanent part of the university community, but will take what they have learned elsewhere. In order to best serve their customers, librarians must constantly consider the questions: What does the customer need and how can that need best be met?

Among the reasons both internal and external customers come to the library are:

- to seek subject expertise
- to use library materials
- to collaborate, work, and visit with their friends
- to use the library's technological assets
- to use electronic databases and software
- to learn how to use or access library resources

### Reduce Departmental Barriers and Strive to Reach a State of Continuous Improvement

The next step is to address and reduce barriers that stand in the way of the provision of effective customer service. The best way to do this is to rework internal processes to better accommodate the customer's needs. Demming and others outlined steps to implement TQM. Some of the steps most applicable to libraries include:

- Improve constantly and forever the system of products and/or services. Improvement is not a one-time effort; management is responsible to lead the organization into the practice of continual improvement in quality and productivity.
- Institute an ongoing and aggressive program of education and retraining. Workers need to know how to do their jobs correctly, especially if they are required to learn new skills.
- Break down barriers between staff areas. Managers should promote teamwork as they help staff in different areas/departments work together. When management fosters interrelationships among functional departments, it results in better quality decision-making.
- Encourage teams. Faculty and staff in libraries must collaborate with one another.[13]

Change management does not happen overnight. A TQM program must have strong and consistent support from the library administration. Those impacted by workflow changes must buy-in to the concept of change management and let go of sacred cows and traditions, i.e., work processes that have been done a certain way for years. A true analysis of workflow may reveal tasks that are no longer necessary or tasks that can be transitioned to students or other lower-paid workers. Redesigned workflows and policies that support the changes must be given time to prove effective. A successful change management program might take several years to implement. By the time a program has been implemented, i.e., workflows accepted and institutionalized, and functional work units redesigned to fit the new processes, enough change outside the walls of the library may have taken place that the TQM process must begin again.

For example, librarians may expend great time, effort, and expense to move from an older, ASCII-based to a new Web-based integrated library system (ILS); an effort in which changes in processes and workflows would be inevitable, only to find that the new ILS has serious workflow and resource-discovery flaws in attempts to deal with ER. An online library management system, although computer-based, that was designed to manage print-based collections and traditional departmental workflows often does not adequately address the challenges of electronic resource management.

## *Model for Change–Process Reengineering*

In 1993, Michael Hammer and James Champy wrote the landmark book, *Reengineering the Corporation*. This work inspired management personnel at numerous for-profit and, ultimately, non-profit institutions to take a hard look at the way work was done as well as the reasons it was done in certain ways. The authors examined the purposes of businesses and institutions in terms of the provision of goods and services and refocused attention on the most important purpose: to offer value and service to the customer. The authors make the case for fundamental changes, demonstrate how process redesign can yield breakthroughs in performance, and identify the key elements needed for reengineering success.[14]

Reengineering is not a new concept; nor should its potential benefits be limited to the private sector. The leaders of all organizations must examine the way they do business, recognize the changes that go on, make adjustments, and rework the way things get done. Reengineering uses information and information technology to invent a better way to accomplish tasks. To implement changes in organizations that are accustomed to doing things in a traditional manner requires leaders with vision who see the big picture, make use of information technology, and empower employees to become decision-makers, which results in decision-making that becomes a part of the daily work.

One of the central components of reengineering is the concept of process redesign or improvement. Often the leaders of organizations are not experienced to think in terms of processes. For example, in organizations such as libraries, leaders often set up the management structure of the library in a strict hierarchical manner built around traditional functional departments. Those who manage the departments tend to be experts within the specific functions the departments are tasked to accomplish. Personnel in departments such as cataloging, acquisitions, interlibrary loan, reference, circulation, and collection development are wholly focused on their specific roles. Under this strict task and management hierarchy, those who work in these functional departments have very little contact or interaction with employees in other units.

Hammer and Champy define a "process as a collection of activities that takes one or more kinds of input and creates an output that is of value to the customer."[15] The output is often called a product. The product is either a physical object or a service. They go on to state that an example of a valuable conclusion to a manufacturing process is that of order fulfillment, which is when the customer pays and takes possession of the product. If the process fails to deliver the product to the customer, profit cannot come into the organization. All the work done prior to the delivery of the product is incidental unless the customer gets the product, the product is of high quality, and the customer believes that the product is something that he/she needs or enjoys. If that is the case, the customer will be attracted to the product as well as the producing organization. If a library's main product is service in the form of the delivery of information, library patrons should, as a result of the library's process of information delivery, get the information they look for, be impressed with the quality of the information they receive, and feel that the information is something they need or desire.

Libraries are service organizations that have undergone a lot of change. The transition from print to ER represents the biggest change. Journal prices have escalated far beyond the Consumer Price Index rate of inflation. The publishing industry has consolidated into larger and more profit-driven entities, which have been very aggressive with their pricing policies. Scholarly publishing models have changed as libraries spend more money than ever to purchase and manage access to digital content. Workflow issues in libraries have also changed as librarians transition to their new roles as purchasers of access to digital content, rather than as collectors and caretakers of books and journals. In many cases, librarians now lease access to scholarly content and, as a result, the processes inherent to workflow management have changed as well.

As stated earlier, libraries have very traditional workflows and entrenched divisions of labor. Technical services and public services personnel rarely cross each other's paths. Karen Calhoun, in an article entitled "Redesign of Library Workflows: Experimental Models for Electronic Resource Description," discusses some of the basic differences between past and current bibliographic control in libraries.[16]

In the past, collections were mostly print-based and the library catalog guided users to the print copy in the library. The description of the materials in the catalog was separate from the items themselves. No matter the format, librarians use highly standardized schemas to describe and organize library materials. The current model includes collections of data sets that are held locally or remotely as well as access to commercial full-text ER. The catalog and the items described have, in more and more cases, converged and indices have less structure; mixed representations of data and metadata are prescribed by various rules or the description can be freeform.

## *Model for Change–Learning Organizations*

Peter Senge has authored a number of books that have appeared on the shelves of Fortune 500 companies as well as in the collections of academic libraries. Senge has focused his work on organizational development in the specific area of the development of learning organizations. His landmark book in this area was *The Fifth Discipline: The Art and Practice of the Learning Organization.*[17] He has also written or coauthored works such as *The Fifth Discipline Field Book: Strategies and Tools for Building a Learning Organization,* and *The Dance of Change: The Challenges to Sustaining Momentum in Learning Organizations and Schools That Learn.*

In *The Fifth Discipline,* Senge describes concepts that are the pillars upon which a learning organization rests: shared vision, personal mastery, mental models, group learning, and systems thinking. A number of his ideas mirror TQM and process reengineering. Systems-thinking is, perhaps, the most important of the five pillars[18] and serves as the cornerstone of the learning organization foundation. Systems-thinking is the ability to see the big picture in a work process, rather than a scope-limiting view of smaller, isolated tasks or functions. Someone who employs systems thinking will be in a position to understand how ER are selected and acquired; how they are organized and described; where they are located; and how they are used by patrons. If the systems thinking approach is applied, employees in any department along the digital delivery process would now be able to jump into any part of the process to offer perspectives for improvements because they would no longer see themselves as just an individual who performs an isolated task or function that is only peripherally related to the successful realization of the library's mission, but as an agent for change and improvement in the organization.

In a 2004 *Library Trends* article, Joan Giesecke and Beth McNeil write about the benefits to libraries if they become learning organizations. "To survive in the constantly changing information environment libraries must find ways to become agile, flexible organizations. Rigid rules, entrenched bureaucracies, and stable hierarchies will not help these organizations survive new technologies, tight budgets, competition, and changing expectations of patrons and users."[19]

Management of ER is a perfect laboratory to develop skill sets based on the concepts of the learning organization.

The University of Arizona has used Senge's concepts as they go through a process of organizational change intended to put them in a position to become a learning organization. One of their primary goals is to become a highly successful digital library that will provide 80% of its services and resources electronically by the year 2008. This is an aggressive goal and it has been articulated throughout the organization. UA librarians do everything according to the processes outlined in *The Fifth Discipline*. Customers are the focus of the goal and competition with other academic institutions is a high priority. How often do librarians and staff inside academic libraries ever stop to think of other institutions as competitors, i.e., for grants and scholarships, or as students as paying customers?[20]

Libraries need to be fashioned into learning organizations in order to adapt to additional technological changes that are on the horizon, e.g., digital images/sounds and media formats that are yet uncreated. Learning organizations provide a structure that allows for the prediction of and adaptation to future trends through a communication network that incorporates every part of the organization. No matter where employees are stationed along the process, no matter what their specific tasks or functions, if they notice problems in the process that need to be addressed or opportunities for improvement at any point they will understand the significance of what they have witnessed in the larger context of the library's mission. (See Figure 1.)

## *The Management of ER–To Transform Functions into a Process*

Academic libraries have retained the functional model, which uses the "selection, acquisition, and dissemination of library materials as the basis for logically grouping people and work. The main departments in academic research libraries continue to be collection development, technical services, and public services." While this structure has worked well for the acquisition of physical materials, ER require a new organizational approach to accommodate end-user expectations as well as the reality of work with non-physical information objects.[21] Employees in function-oriented departments are at a disadvantage when they attempt to deal with digital resources, which tend to cut across departmental lines. Because departmental needs tend to come first in the thought processes of employees, it is often difficult for them to focus on the library's users or work well with one another in a collaborative manner.

Obviously, on initial observation the model is complex. On the unit-level, however, its success relies on communication and a broad understanding of the processes that underlie the delivery of digital information and, for that matter, all library services. To that end, what follows are brief descriptions of the processes-in-play in library units. These

FIGURE 1. The Electronic Resources Management Process

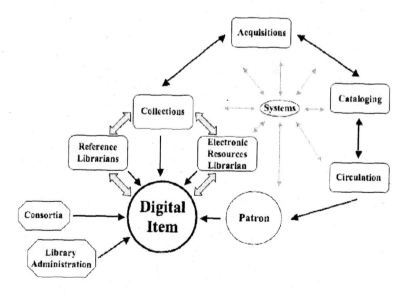

descriptions will highlight the necessary interrelationships in a process-oriented approach.

## REFERENCE AND ACCESS SERVICES

A process for the management of ER begins with those librarians who usually have first contact with the library's customers. Reference and access services librarians and staff are in the best position to be aware of changes in the needs and expectations of library patrons as they answer patron questions, direct them to the library's resources, and instruct them in the use of digital resources. The skills required for adaptation to a digital environment flow naturally out of the reference and access services environments.

Reference librarians liaise with academic personnel; act as bibliographers, subject specialists, and fund managers; staff the reference desk where they provide directional, ready-reference, and intensive, detail-oriented, research assistance to users; teach classes; design Web pages and guides; and work to develop and maintain collections. In other words, they are already consummate multi-taskers who have an appreciation for and who participate in a variety of library processes. They are also in a position to analyze the impact of new information resources on diverse user groups; the connection of users to information is what reference is all about. In the ER management process, reference librarian subject expertise cuts across library departments. As material selectors and liaisons with teaching faculty, they have close contact with the collection development department. The cross-departmental nature of the selection process that involves reference personnel and collection development staff lends itself to the ER management process. With a bit of formalization, workflow improvement, and assistance from library systems the work already done by these separate departments can be transitioned into a process.

All workers in all library units must proactively seek to understand the entire information delivery process. It is to the benefit of users that the lines of communication are open and flow in all directions, i.e., how e-resources are selected, acquired, organized, described, delivered, and assessed. At any moment, any library employee might be asked for such information by a user. The key elements here in a process-orientation are that all staff be knowledgeable and interested; to be informed and communicative; to be helpful, effective, and service-oriented.

Students who work at points of sale in the library, e.g., access services, can be important communicators of information that pertains to the delivery of e-information, i.e., where it is in the interface, contact information for librarians who work with e-resources, general interface navigation, etc. Access services managers can be proactive and make their own contribution to the process as they instruct students there to check e-resource links and report problems. Such a task exemplifies communication among units and the process-orientation as it requires collaboration among persons in access services, reference, systems, and collection development.

## COLLECTION DEVELOPMENT

The collection development office (CDO) has been responsible, traditionally, for the purchase of materials for the library. With the advent of online resources these librarians have found themselves in unfamiliar territory. "Acquisitions librarians still select and purchase books and traditional journals, but they must also deal with many 'access without ownership' issues involving leased electronic databases, full-text journal article access services and other services that are acquired only virtually."[22]

Collection development librarians work with subject specialists or bibliographers who, in turn, liaise with academic departments to take advantage of teaching faculty knowledge in order to build a library collection that meets the education/research needs of the university community. Digital resources are often interdisciplinary in nature and represent a formidable challenge for selectors. One way to convert these activities into an overall process might include reengineering the department so liaison work is done digitally via a peer-to-peer network. Librarians and staff could meet virtually or in-person with the faculty they serve.

## COLLECTION DEVELOPMENT AND TECHNICAL SERVICES

Large interdisciplinary e-journal packages pose opportunities and requirements for accounting/organization processes in acquisitions departments. The functional requirements of the work must give way to the process as acquisitions staff communicates with collection development staff to learn what has been purchased and how those purchases might best be reflected in ILS modules. Inter-departmental cooperation and decision-making is essential when purchasing large electronic journal packages. Collection development must decide how to deal with new accounting requirements, i.e., fund names and numbers, allocation of funds, and assignment of purchase order numbers. Acquisitions staff must align publisher accounting templates with those in their ILS and decide how to track packages as well as the individual journal titles of which the packages are comprised. The business office must pay the bill in a fashion that complements the accounting module template of the ILS while at the same time satisfies the accounting exigencies of the vendor/publisher. Everyone else in the library that might have need of the account information must be made aware of and trained in the processes that are necessary to take information from the system. Consortia group purchases of packages that might even cross state lines require flexible organization and administration. Process and communication are the keys.

### Systems

A major characteristic of working in systems is that things never become static or predictable. Technology constantly changes. The systems group is an essential part of a cross-functional library management team that works to improve library services.

In a process-orientation, systems personnel introduce new technologies and their benefits to library employees and users. Systems employees make sure that everyone in the library understands the benefits associated with the new technologies, enable those who teach to make informed decisions about the integration of new technologies into their daily tasks, and create an awareness of new ER that are available so that they can be shared with library customers.

What are some examples of the systems department contributing to the ER management process? Examples are:

- Enable customer access to ER by the placement of them in a prominent location on the library's Web site
- Provide ongoing trouble-shooting when users encounter difficulties with access to the resources
- Research software solutions for the management of e-resources
- Set-up internal Web sites and locally produced databases that facilitate the management of ER
- Set-up OpenURL resolutions that link citation index databases with full-text content
- Work with technical services staff to set-up and deploy cross-walked metadata schemas
- Set-up and implement a federated search tool

## Digital Librarianship Collaborative

An option for library administrators who work on the issue of e-resource management from a process as opposed to a function orientation might be the creation of a digital librarianship collaborative. This would be a cross-functional set-up with employees from various library units called upon to contribute to the management of e-resources, local digital projects, digital archives, and other value-added efforts. An office of digital librarianship would include librarians with functional expertise in the following areas:

- *Electronic Resource Librarian:* Collection development, descriptive metadata creation, use-data management, systems expertise, project management/planning, programming, Web site development, server management, OpenURL resolution management
- *Reference Librarian:* Subject bibliographer expertise, conducts ongoing end-user use studies, tracks Web search behaviors, human/computer interaction studies, evaluation of information retrieval systems

Other potential members of this office might be a technical services specialist, an e-resources cataloger, a systems/Web site expert, or an ILL professional.

## *ER LIBRARIAN AND COMMUNICATION*

The ER librarian is involved in selection, contract negotiation, acquisitions, organization, description, delivery, assessment, and coordination of use of e-resources. The position is often a part of the technical services/collection development departments and communication among the three is essential. The ER librarian facilitates this communication through coordination and leadership as the library is moved towards a process oriented approach to digital resources management. To be effective, the ER librarian must communicate selection opportunities with subject bibliographers, be aware of fund and budget requirements, and be aware of the organization of electronic content displayed on the library Web site. ER librarians must stay in contact with systems librarians to be informed of the latest technology that, for example, helps maintain, organize, and gather use data on electronic content. If changes are authorized in content, platform, interface, or software/hardware, the ER librarian works with systems personnel for implementation.

These examples highlight the communication and facilitation roles that the ER librarian undertakes to work with:

- vendor/publishers to establish trials of digital resources
- subject specialists to identify resources of interest for trial
- reference head to determine best time for trial
- vendor, publisher, or consortium to set up trial
- systems and administration to gather facts necessary for implementation of the trial, e.g., FTE counts and IP ranges
- Web site maintenance to ensure visibility of trial
- bibliographers, reference librarians, and bibliographic instructors to make sure classroom faculty, students, and other users know a trial is in place
- all library staff to gather comments on the trial for vendor/publishers, library administration, and fund managers

If a decision is made to purchase, the ER librarian becomes the lead negotiator with the vendor/publisher for the purchase and the license. Once the purchase is made, the ER librarian works with CDO personnel to organize and document the purchase, with the vendor/publisher to enable access, with acquisitions to organize access and describe the item purchased, and with the systems to display the resource to users and troubleshoot any problems with access that may arise. After implementation of the resource, the ER librarian collects and compiles use data and assesses the value of the resource to the user.

## NEW DIRECTIONS FOR E-RESOURCES LIBRARIANSHIP–INSTITUTIONAL REPOSITORIES

A functional management orientation is often informed by and, in turn, perpetuates a business-as-usual attitude in the thought processes of librarians whereas a process approach is dependent upon and encourages thinking that is innovative. As a result of the digital revolution, library innovators, who may or may not appreciate the process orientation of their efforts, have tackled the important issue of institutional repositories. Mention of it here is to provide an example of a move in academia toward a paradigmatic shift in scholarly communication. Issues like copyright transfer, digitization, and shared collections cannot be and will not be resolved in an atmosphere of resource management based on function and task orientations and business-as-usual practices. The market relationship between those who create scholarly content and those who publish it has been established over time and is engrained in academic circles. The rapid rise in information technology innovations has empowered content providers to take a more active and direct role in the publication of their work. An excellent example of library resource management through an orientation to process is for everyone in the library to be familiar with the realities of the exchange of scholarly communication. The tasks and functions that each employee performs have a bearing on the promotion of good will between the library and the university community. Everyone has a role to play in the creation and realization of a digital institutional repository.

The development of software to meet the needs of the scholarly publishing market and other initiatives that surround the advent of institutional repository initiatives have pushed academic librarians into new roles and the development of new skills. In his article, "The Repository Adventure," H. Frank Cervone states:

> The librarians leading this charge work in innovative ways, as part of collaborative teams that can include information technologists, archivists, records managers, faculty and university administrator, as well as local government officials and community members.[23]

The development and implementation of an institutional repository will change what some librarians do and how they conduct library business. The price of technology has fallen to the point that a well-organized and process-oriented effort in this regard is sustainable.

## CONCLUSION:
## THE UBIQUITOUS LIBRARY
## AND THE LIBRARY AS PLACE

Libraries in recent years have witnessed a great deal of change brought on by the new information format, the digital resource. Academic libraries continue to purchase and maintain large, tangible collections of traditional materials like books and journals, but will also be in the forefront of technological change as they continue to innovate with electronic tools and deliver digital content. The ubiquitous library is a new term used to describe libraries that contain information in many different formats. According to Lowry, the use of the term ubiquitous is meant to convey that the libraries will be available to the campus community in a pervasive fashion, basically at their fingertips.[24]

Of course this does not mean every print volume will be put online. The ER management process is a way to deal with the new challenges brought on by the rise of information as it transitions from the print-based type of container to the digital. While the traditional library was focused on print-based media, the ubiquitous library "will have a number of characteristics that relate to the way we deliver information and the way library faculty and staff will be engaged in the teaching and research mission."[25]

Other characteristics of the "ubiquitous library" are:

- More scholarly information will be accessible online in full-text. Although the shift to networked ER has accelerated for journals the publication of books will persist in print for some time until peripherals can mimic their high usability.
- Use of federated search tools will create single points of access in library interfaces.
- Librarians will be consulted 24 hours a day through virtual reference services. Some reference work will be outsourced to other time zones, perhaps in other countries. Such outsourcing is a way to extend the hours of reference availability without an over-taxation of an in-house reference staff.
- The roles of librarians will continue to change as they become more directly engaged in classroom teaching and research in collaboration with faculty, particularly with respect to information literacy.
- The notion of the library as place will be resilient, characterized by high demand. Better access provided by the ubiquitous library will produce a strong demand on facilities for use of the library in-person.
- Large retrospective print-based collections will be required at research universities, but libraries will enter into shared-use agreements and will organize consortia in order to eliminate duplication in the collection of low-use materials.
- Digital library initiatives will makes special collections/archives available to a wider audience, including high impact on the K-12 educational community. This will serve to broaden and strengthen the role of libraries and universities.
- Libraries that have carved out a strong place, nationally, in organizational development will become examples of learning organizations as they respond quickly and effectively to the changing landscape of scholarly information and communication.

- Due to tight finances in libraries, librarians will investigate cost-recovery and entrepreneurial programs that generate income.
- Librarians will become institutional leaders as they advance access to scholarly research. The use of institutional repositories will increase.[26]

This is an exciting time in the library and information science profession despite speculation on the future of libraries. But, while the look and feel of libraries might change over time, information output and organization of information resources, no matter what their container, will continue to be needed. The concept of the ubiquitous library and the idea of information delivered in a variety of containers drive the need for the purchase, implementation, description, and delivery of library resources to be process, not function-based. Rigid hierarchies formed when print was the reigning media format, when libraries only managed vast, print-based collections, must transition to a more team-based, collaborative, fluid, adaptable, and process-driven approach. There are a number of business models available for librarians to follow. But, these models are only the blueprint for change. For it to happen and be effective, for librarians to continue to deliver the information needs of library users in an effective manner, the concepts of the process-orientation, the ubiquitous library, and the business model of change management must be embraced and applied.

## NOTES

1. Susan Gardner and Susanna Eng, "What Students Want: Generation Y and the Changing Function of the Academic Library," *portal: Libraries and the Academy* 5(3) (2005): 405-420.

2. Edward Gray and Anne Langley, "Public Services and Electronic Resources: Perspectives from the Science and Engineering Libraries at Duke University," http://www.istl.org/02-summer/article2.html (viewed October 15, 2005).

3. Brenda Laurel, "Design Research Methods and Perspectives," introduction to Christopher Ireland, *The Changing Role of Research* (Cambridge, Mass.: MIT Press, 2003), 22.

4. Ibid., 22.

5. Anne Buck and Kimberly Douglas, "Peer to Peer Librarianship: Mirroring the Network," http://caltechlib.library.caltech.edu/30/00/Peer-to-peer_1-08-02.pdf/ (viewed October 15, 2005).

6. Shelly E. Phipps, "The System Design Approach to Organizational Development: The University of Arizona Model," *Library Trends* 53(1) (summer 2004): 93.

7. "Five Business Trends Every Human Service Organization Should Understand," http://socialent.aztechcs.com/resources/articles/five_business/ (viewed October 15, 2005).

8. Shelly E. Phipps. "The System Design Approach to Organizational Development: The University of Arizona Model," *Library Trends* 53(1) (2004): p. 70.

9. Rick Luce, "Los Alamos Takes 'Library Without Walls' to the Second Generation," *LibraryZone Newsletter* 7(1) (November 2004): 6.

10. Ibid., 6.

11. Ibid.

12. Denise G. Masters, "Total Quality Management in Libraries," http://www.ericdigests.org/ 1997-1/tqm.html (viewed October 15, 2005).

13. Ibid.

14. Michael Hammer and James Champy, *Reengineering the Corporation: A Manifesto for Business Revolution* (New York: HarperBusiness, 1993), 1.

15. Ibid., 35.

16. Karen Calhoun, "Redesign of Library Workflows: Experimental Models for Electronic Resource Description," http://www.loc.gov/catdir/bibcontrol/calhoun_paper.html (viewed October 10, 2005).

17. Peter M. Senge, *The Fifth Discipline: The Art and Practice of the Learning Organization* (New York: Currency Doubleday, 1990), 4-5.

18. Ibid., 6-16.

19. Joan Giesecke and Beth McNeil, "Transitioning to the Learning Organization," *Library Trends* 53(1) (summer 2004), 54.

20. Peter M. Senge, *The Fifth Discipline: The Art and Practice of the Learning Organization* (New York: Currency Doubleday, 1990), 6-16.

21. Calhoun, http://www.loc_gov/catdir/bibcontrol/calhoun_paper.html (viewed October 10, 2005).

22. Daryl C. Youngman, "Library Staffing Considerations in the Age of Technology," http://www.library.ucsb.edu/istl/99-fall/article5.html (viewed October 10, 2005).

23. Cervone, H. Frank. "The Repository Adventure: On the Way to Changing Scholarly Communication, Libraries May End Up Changing Themselves," *Library Journal*, 129 Number 10 (June 1, 2004): http://www.libraryjournal.com/article/CA421033.html, (viewed October 9, 2005).

24. Charles B. Lowry. "The Ubiquitous Library: University of Maryland Libraries in the Next Five Years–New Directions & Continuing Legacy," http://www.lib.umd.edu/deans/ublibreport.html (viewed October 10, 2005).

25. Ibid.

26. Ibid.

doi:10.1300/J105v32n01_09

# The Nature of the Digital Resource: How the Process for the Management of Digital Resources Differs From (and Is the Same As) That of Other Formats

Jian Wang

Althea Pribyl

**SUMMARY.** The transition from print-based to digital format has profoundly influenced the way knowledge is organized, delivered, accessed, and archived. There are fundamental differences in the natures of print-based and online resources that have, in the short years of the digital information age, made necessary the advent of library professionals who possess skills and knowledge particular to the requirements of the digital information format. This chapter explores those differences in the context of digital resources management within the realm of the academic

---

Jian Wang, MLIS, MA, is Serials Catalog Librarian and Serials/Documents Cataloging Coordinator (E-mail: jian@pdx.edu); and Althea Pribyl, MLS, is ER Cataloging and Database Maintenance Assistant (E-mail: apribyl@pdx.edu), both at the Portland State University Library, P.O. Box 1151, Portland, OR 97207.

[Haworth co-indexing entry note]: "The Nature of the Digital Resource: How the Process for the Management of Digital Resources Differs From (and Is the Same As) That of Other Formats." Wang, Jian, and Althea Pribyl. Co-published simultaneously in *Collection Management* (The Haworth Information Press, an imprint of The Haworth Press) Vol. 32, No. 1/2, 2007, pp. 141-153; and: *Electronic Resources Librarianship and Management of Digital Information: Emerging Professional Roles* (ed: Mark Jacobs) The Haworth Information Press, an imprint of The Haworth Press, 2007, pp. 141-153. Single or multiple copies of this article are available for a fee from The Haworth Document Delivery Service [1-800-HAWORTH, 9:00 a.m. - 5:00 p.m. (EST). E-mail address: docdelivery@haworthpress.com].

library. Issues that concern cataloging, maintenance, access, and archives are discussed. The impact of the new format on library staff and workflows is examined as well. doi:10.1300/J105v32n01_10 *[Article copies available for a fee from The Haworth Document Delivery Service: 1-800-HAWORTH. E-mail address: <docdelivery@haworthpress.com> Website: <http://www.HaworthPress.com> © 2007 by The Haworth Press. All rights reserved.]*

**KEYWORDS.** Digital resources, electronic journals, cataloging, link maintenance, Electronic Resources Management, staffing

## INTRODUCTION

The number of digital resources delivered to academic library patrons has grown explosively over the past decade and has prompted a reassessment of various aspects of library operations in view of the challenges posed in the digital age. Should these resources be integrated into the library's catalog or should they be organized into a separate database? If they are added to the catalog, should they have a separate bibliographic record or should a hyperlink and a descriptive note be added to an existing record? How should the uniform resource locator (URL) and coverage/holdings changes be managed? What about the long-term stability of digital content, if the subscription is cancelled?

Numerous articles have been published in the library literature that discuss the challenges of the management of digital collections. In titles like "Toward Better Access to Full-Text Aggregator Collections,"[1] "Harmonizing Bibliographic Control of Serials in the Digital Age,"[2] and "Which Route Do I take? A Viewpoint on Locally Developed versus Commercially Available Journal Management Solutions"[3] librarians have illustrated how they and their colleagues have approached the spectrum of problems they have encountered while they attempt to provide improved access to electronic resources (ER).

There are fundamental differences in the natures of print-based and digital resources, i.e., their manifestation (tangible/intangible), the way they are delivered (off-the-shelf/via the desktop), and the way they are organized and located (to classify or not to classify). But, digital resources have also meant, most importantly to librarians, a necessary re-evaluation of time-honored approaches to workflow and staff. In some cases, the more things change, the more they stay the same. However, in many other instances, change, and significant change, has been the rule, not the exception.

This chapter examines how, in response to the requirements of their nature, librarian management of digital resources differs from (and is similar to) that of other formats within the realm of the academic library. Issues that concern description and organization; access; and delivery of digital information are the focal points. For the purpose of this chapter, digital (electronic) resources include electronic serials/journals, databases, and Web sites.

The nature of print-based materials begins with their tangibility. Library resources have been, traditionally, housed and accessed in and from a physical structure; a building. Library users expect to find what they need on a shelf and physically carry it away with them. This concept has been challenged with the introduction of digital resources that are licensed, distributed, and accessed virtually. Users can find and retrieve what they need via networked computers from any place and at any time. As they do not pertain to digital resources in the changing information landscape, ownership, place, control, and permanence, all aspects of the nature and management of print-based materials are no longer the sole determinants of the academic library's collection management scope. A new concept of a hybrid collection is warranted, one which reflects the mix of analog (i.e., print-based) and digital resources, as well as the dynamism of digital information.[4]

The transformation of library collections from analog to hybrid underscores the need to effectively manage digital information and develop new ways to organize, describe, and maintain the accessibility of its volatile content.

## INTEGRATED ACCESS THROUGH THE OPAC

Since librarians began to integrate digital resources into their collections, their online public access catalogs (OPACs) began to take on a new look and became more inclusive, sophisticated, and versatile. In many libraries, the OPAC now functions as a gateway to an online information universe. Links/URLs offer direct remote access to full-text content, a virtual information commons to a variety of digitized books, journals, newspapers, manuscript collections, CD-ROMs, databases, Web sites, and consortia catalogs.[5]

Other advantages of the virtual OPAC include the allowance of simultaneous users, the provision of timely access, the support of search capabilities, no requirement for a physical process, and the saving of storage space. Users may not know what has been done behind the scenes to deliver online information to them, but they certainly enjoy the benefits of those efforts. This transformation from an online version of the card catalog to a complex, ever-changing digital environment was inevitable and is now a critical component of library services.

When academic librarians started to purchase electronic packages in the late-1990s, they questioned whether to catalog them as many librarians assumed that the library did not really own digital resources and cataloging had always been a way to reflect ownership. However, "resistance to adding new types of information to the catalog [would] almost certainly be seen as inadequacy, inflexibility, or obstructionism" by many members of the library community.[6]

Besides, the advantages of the integration of ER into the library catalog were so compelling that librarians were forced to reevaluate the role of the OPAC in order to be able to keep up with user demands.

## CATALOGING ISSUES

### Single or Separate Records

One of the issues that, initially, confront librarians when they catalog ER is whether to follow a single or separate record approach. Both methods present advantages as well as challenges that depend upon the size of the library, the collections, and the staff. Separate records allow better identification and description of the bibliographic universe, and ease the tasks of batch-processing and database maintenance. The single record approach seems to be preferred when librarians have not yet built a large collection of ER and/or have not purchased vendor-supplied records. In addition, public services staff seem to favor single records because they allow for a coherent single display of the library's holdings for a title regardless of the format. As the amount of electronic information grows, this issue of a single or separate record as well as what impact each approach has on the library's OPAC display will continue to receive much attention in the library literature. Perhaps the issue will grow even more intricate with the implementation, in the near future, of Functional Requirements for Bibliographic Records (FRBR).

### Link Maintenance

As the digital collection grows, problems associated with online access pose new challenges for librarians. Internet addresses change and Web sites, suddenly, become unavailable for any number of reasons. For example, publishers have regularly redesigned and reorganize their Web sites, especially with the acquisition or sale of journal titles. Free online access associated with print subscriptions may disappear with little warning or the conditions for the maintenance of paid online access may change. In recent years, this instability has become less of an issue since most large vendor/publishers redirect users, who click on old links, to the new Web site where the content can be found; at least; this is the case for a time. But, network breakdowns due to weather or other unforeseen events; technical difficulties; and scheduled/unscheduled upgrades may still hinder online access.

The maintenance of active links to digital resources in the OPAC has become an essential and demanding aspect of library work. Unfortunately, this task is still perceived by many librarians as a routine extension of cataloger responsibilities. As Cohen observed in an address of issues of URL management for digital collections, discussions in the library literature pay little attention to this new enterprise.[7]

The nature of digital resources requires the acquisition and implementation of new skills. The maintenance of links, especially the management of URLs that connect users to licensed digital resources, requires not only a good understanding of the relationship between the URL and the technological infrastructure, but the development of new skills and the exertion of substantial effort to find or construct correct links, create proxy server access, and solve access problems.

Often, access to licensed resources is restricted by IP (Internet Protocol) authentication. Computerized workstations on the campus from which users access digital resources have unique Internet addresses that are registered with vendor/publishers in order to restrict access to the resources for members of the university community. However, off-campus users, also, need to access online resources licensed by the library for their use; they will use computers at home or elsewhere that have Internet addresses that do not fall within the university's assigned and registered IP range. To register all the different Internet addresses, perhaps in the thousands, would be an onerous and inefficient process. To solve this problem, the proxy server is used. The address of the server falls within the IP range of the university's registered/authenticated range and off-campus users are channeled through it in order to give them access to licensed resources. The proxy server, which acts as an intermediary between the campus local area network (LAN) and the vendor/publisher's Web site, sends the user's page request to the vendor/publisher whose server recognizes the campus IP address and permits access. This process allows users with valid accounts to access the library's licensed resources from any location at any time.[8]

Online resources are linked in the resource's surrogate MARC record in the OPAC. The record includes a URL in the 856 field with a prefix that points to the proxy server that, in turn, points to the online content, as shown in the following example:

http://proxy.lib.pdx.edu:2048/login?url=http://www.jstor.org/

A lack of URL standardization among vendor/publishers makes the management of different types of URLs problematic. To identify starting point URLs is another difficulty that catalogers of ER face when they perform original cataloging. "A starting point URL is a persistent durable URL that connects a browser to a resource"[9] and is the URL that is entered in the 856 field of the bibliographic record. This URL is accessed through the OPAC and connects a user to a desired resource on the Internet. There are four types of starting point URLs: static URLs, dynamic URLs, directory URLs, and formula URLs.[10]

What follows are examples of each type of URL:

- A static URL connects to a destination without calling a script; i.e., the destination URL is identical to the starting point. This is the URL that catalogers can use in the MARC record. An example is a Project Muse title, the *Journal of Democracy* at: http://muse.jhu.edu/journals/journal_of_democracy/
- A dynamic URL processes a script to connect to a destination and is transformed at the destination. Therefore, the destination URL should not be used as a starting point URL in the catalog. For example, *Advances in Computational Mathematics* via SpringerLink has a starting point URL of: http://www.springerlink.com/openurl.asp?genre=journal&issn=1019-7168
  but is transformed at the destination to: http://proxy.lib.pdx.edu:2120/app/home/journal.asp?wasp=a1e32224db2045719a1cab5c5f5cc64e&referrer=parent&backto=linkingpublicationresults,1:101738,1
- A directory URL without a filename points to a directory's default file. Catalogers should always append a trailing forward slash "/" to static URLs to conserve the vendor/publisher's server resources and to omit ending default file names such as index.html, default.asp, etc.
- Finally, a formula URL is a required structure that adheres to a specific format and must be used to connect to a destination. Catalogers should check the vendor/publisher's Web site for instructions

to construct formula URLs, which may be either static or dynamic. Here are a couple of examples:

1. http://www.bioone.org/bioone/?request=get-journals-list&issn= 0002-7685 (unchanged at the destination)
2. http://www.springerlink.com/openurl.asp?genre=journal&issn= 1019-7168, changed at the destination to: http://proxy.lib.pdx. edu:2120/app/home/journal.asp?wasp=a1e32224db2045719a1cab 5c5f5cc64c&referrer=parent&backto=linkingpublicationresults, 1:101738,1

The URL Clearinghouse (http://library.albany.edu/clearinghouse/) for licensed resources has been developed to serve as a centralized repository of strategies to use to create vendor/publisher URLs and is, currently, maintained by Laura B. Cohen, Library Web Administrator at the State University of New York (SUNY) at Albany. The clearinghouse also offers time-saving suggestions for use to construct vendor/publisher URLs.

Broken links provoke user frustration and diminish the library's service-oriented reputation. Many librarians employ link-checking software to identify bad or inactive links. Some integrated library system (ILS) vendors offer a link-checking feature that may help to make link maintenance less labor-intensive. Despite the assistance of such software, much work still has to be done by library staff, e.g., correct and/or update links and identify and/or verify the cause of access problems. When a slow connection causes the requested linking session to time-out, a false report of a link error may be generated. A slow link, as opposed to an inaccurate link, may mislead users to think that the link they requested is dead. These and other link issues are aspects of the nature of digital resources. Part of the librarian's reaction to the requirements of that nature is to acquire and refine new skills to meet the continued challenge not only of link maintenance, but to help to create a *Web-educated* community of users; even though they may already be *Web-savvy*. Once again, this is an example of the difference between the natures of print-based and online resources; the necessity for the advent of new library professionals who possess skills and knowledge particular to the requirements of the information format.

## *Coverage Maintenance*

It is in the nature of serials, regardless of format, to change title, split into two or more new publications, merge two or more titles into one, or cease publication altogether. Unique to their nature though, the use of ER is governed by the conditions described in a license agreement that defines the terms of access, including coverage. Upon cancellation, this access may remain, in the form of an online archive, for a limited time, in perpetuity, or, access may disappear altogether.

This aspect of the nature of digital resources has meant that those who work with them are required to spend a lot of time as they attempt to keep journal coverage dates accurate in the catalog. To augment the efficiency and accuracy of this process and to maintain an overview of online journal coverage from multiple vendors, many libraries make use of simple and flexible spreadsheets or flat-file databases. Typically, a file created, by the use of one of these tools, for this purpose will include: title, ISSN, online coverage dates, library holdings (in all formats), URL, and title continuations. Additional information, e.g., call number, subscription price, and subjects, may be added as well. The data in these files can then be applied to a variety of tasks: the creation of brief records for the catalog, the facilitation of coverage analysis, as an aid to bibliographers, to make reports to administrators, etc., and when combined with data from other departments may offer an overview of the current collection that may, also, be useful in collection management.

In the last several years, the rise of open access publishing has added another dimension to journal maintenance. While most online journals in a library's collection require a paid subscription and are restricted to institutional use, there has been an increase in the number of publishers that offer free access to some or all of the content of selected journals. There are many different open access models. For example, on the HighWire Press platform a paid subscription is needed to access recent issues (often the last 12 months) while the rest of the digitized content is freely available. As of Dec. 2005, the entire content of 31 journals was available free on the platform and a portion of the content of 207 journals was free without registration; not including trial journals.[11]

Many academic libraries catalog individual open access journals and offer access to large and frequently updated online collections, e.g., the Directory of Open Access Journals (DOAJ) and PubMed Central. Open access is, of course, a concept that has arisen as a result of the very nature of digital resources as the Web-based expertise of ER (ER) librarians grows in reaction to the exigencies of that nature, which has meant and continues to mean the consideration, practically and philosophically, of a wide variety of issues and ideas that never came up in the print-based world.

## ER Management Systems (ERMS)

As licensed collections of digital resources proliferate, there has been a growth in the demand for tools and systems to manage them effectively. Efforts have been made to create such management tools both at the library-level and through partnerships with vendor/publishers. The staff of some libraries have developed their own management systems in order to save money, preserve local control, and provide customization; other librarians have favor vendor-based solutions because of "convenience and added value (e.g., by integrating OpenURL services for citation linking)"[12] as well as to lower long-term costs with a wider applicability to libraries.[13] Other reasons to choose a vendor-supplied service include cost-effectiveness, long-term sustainability, and immediate integration into a library's existing ILS. SerialsSolutions, for example, tracks electronic journals from various aggregator databases and provides an A-Z list of these journals. Innovative Interface's (III) ER Management Module (ERM), also, integrates with extant library systems to help streamline workflows in the management of ER.

The ERMS was originally designed with these goals:

- to integrate the license and purchase details of e-resources into a single interface
- to streamline workflows and eliminate the need to maintain separate spreadsheets or databases
- to store and selectively display information in the OPAC for staff and patrons
- to load holdings data in batch mode
- to track vendor contracts.[14]

All of these features help librarians deal with ER and improve user access. As ERMS gain popularity, more librarians have opted for the commercial solution. ERMS improve the efficiency of the catalog unit as well as many others. librarians are now able to add or update current holdings for electronic journals via batch loads as an alternative to the daunting task of the manual maintenance of electronic holdings.

Tools like ERMS have proven applicable, in some instances, to print-based materials as well. However, their development and implementation by librarians has been in direct reaction to the nature of digital resources, i.e., complexity, expense, and volatility. Librarians have, by necessity, addressed this nature as they have learned to use these tools.

## ARCHIVE ISSUES

Archive issues have always been of concern in the print-based world. The nature of the online format, e.g., intangibility, has not meant that the topic may be overlooked by librarians who work in the digital format. Unlike print publications, which a library owns and can access permanently, there is no guarantee of permanence in the archive of digital resources. Access to electronic journals on the publisher Web site is often terminated when the library subscription is cancelled. As Neavill and Sheble note, the long-term stability of digital resources has always been a concern in the library community:

> Libraries are responsible for preserving and providing continuing access to a society's accumulated stock of recorded knowledge. The electronic information industry is concerned primarily with current preservation of information. The library emphasis on mediating access to current information as well as the preservation of information is unique . . .[15]

Barnes urged all parties, including publishers, libraries, and information system providers, to get involved to address the electronic archive issue. Publishers incorporate archival and ownership rights in their license agreements; librarians evaluate the necessity of permanently holding online materials locally in an environment where the technical, economic, and logistical requirements can be met; and information systems providers supply the tools and services that allow librarians to maintain their fundamental role as preservationists and that of the library as an information repository.[16]

To address this paramount need, the LOCKSS (Lots of Copies Keep Stuff Safe) program was initiated at the Stanford University Libraries to enable librarians to collect, store, preserve, and archive authorized electronic content in an easy and affordable way. "Using their own computers and network connections, librarians can obtain, preserve and provide access to a purchased copy of an e-journal, [which] is analogous to libraries' use of their own buildings, shelves and staff to obtain, preserve and provide access to paper journals."[17]

Through the LOCKSS program, librarians are able to provide long-term preservation and perpetual access to digital information and, thus, retain local control of electronic content and restore, somewhat, the traditional idea of the ownership of library collections.

## STAFF ISSUES

### Workloads

Traditional practice has been to build physical collections and the services to support them. However, traditional approaches to staff and budget allocation do not provide the flexibility and speed that libraries need to build or manage the hybrid collection effectively; nor do they, necessarily, reflect the relative importance of digital resources to end-users. As they incorporate the more dynamic and volatile digital resources into both their collections and workflows, librarians will need to reconsider not only their approaches to selection and process, but the related fiscal and staff resources that are devoted to the maintenance of digital collections.[18]

Montgomery and Sparks examined the organizational impact of the transition from the print-based to the electronic format. According to them, libraries will experience a decrease in staff needs and the operational costs associated with the maintenance of print journal collections, such as check-in, claims, repair, replacement of pages, and binding, and a correspondent increase in the areas of selection and acquisitions; database and Web site maintenance; and systems.[19]

Therefore, one aspect of the nature of digital resources, i.e., their instability, means an increase in workload in database maintenance. Broken links, coverage changes, the appearance and disappearance of journals and aggregators, and the need for constant vigilance for the appearance of new journals require many staff hours. In many cases, it has been necessary to reexamine/reconfigure existing positions as well as to create new positions in response to a change in needs.

### Training

The activities associated with the maintenance of digital resources require a higher-level of knowledge and skills than those associated with the maintenance of print-based collections. Librarians are faced with the need to retrain, re-deploy, or even reduce existing staff.[20]

Training and retraining has become an integral part the success of library services. It is essential that library staffs who work with online resources are kept up-to-date with developments in cataloging, acquisitions, and other technical aspects of e-resource maintenance as well as with aspects of collection management, systems, and public services work in order to take advantage of new tools and approaches for the management of the digital format.

Another aspect of the nature of the online resource is its pervasive quality, its ubiquitousness. Whether we like it or not, the fact is that it enjoins upon every task, every process, and every decision by every employee in the library. To describe the role of serials/ER catalogers in today's digital age, Steve Shadle states that they have become workflow managers and trainers and play a key role as content experts in their institutions. This new trend is highlighted in the library literature by a number of authors, e.g., Chervinko, El-Sherbini and Klim, and Boydston and Leysen.[21]

For librarians involved in the management of ER, training is continuous, especially when new tools are implemented, new systems are installed, new catalog standards are established, or new procedures are adopted.

## CONCLUSION

In the print-based environment, the management process for a format with a static nature has been fairly stable and routine. But, today's rapid shift towards digitization has led to the development of much more sophisticated practices due to the idiosyncratic nature of digital resources. Compared to their print counterparts, digital publications are expensive, volatile, intangible, and require constant maintenance. Other aspects of their nature that have meant the reassessment of basic library management approaches are their computerized delivery, the lack of a need to classify them in order to help users locate them, and their ambiguous status in relation to traditional librarian concepts of ownership, place, control, and permanence. All of these characteristics have dramatically impacted the ways in which librarians collect, store, provide access to, and preserve them. The fundamental roles of librarians are unchanged, i.e., to organize knowledge, provide equal access to information, and preserve scholarly work. However, the profession has reached a milestone and prepares to turn an important corner because of the essential nature of its newest format. Librarians and all who work in libraries with digital information meet the challenges of the digital age as they learn and develop new skills and knowledge, make innovative and effective use of electronic tools and technological systems, and increase the timeliness and effectiveness of the services they provide to library users.

# NOTES

1. Lynda S. Kresge, "Toward Better Access to Full-Tex Aggregator Collections," *The Serials Librarian* 38(3/4) (2000): 291-297.
2. Regina Romano Reynold, "Harmonizing Bibliographic Control of Serials in the Digital Age," *Cataloging & Classification Quarterly* 28(1) (1999): 3-19.
3. Steve Oberg, "Which Route Do I Take? A Viewpoint on Locally Developed versus Commercially Available Journal Management Solutions," *Serials Review* 30(2) (2004): 122-126.
4. Mary Frances Casserly, "Developing a Concept of Collection for the Digital Age," *portal: Libraries and the Academy* 2(4) (2002): 577-587.
5. Donald Beagle, "Conceptualizing an Information Commons," *Journal of Academic Librarianship* 25(2) (March 1999): 82-89.
6. Jane Swan Hill, "The Elephant in the Catalog: Cataloging Animals You Can't See or Touch," *Cataloging & Classification Quarterly* 23(1) (1969): 5-25.
7. Laura Cohen, "Issues in URL Management for Digital Collections," *Information Technology and Libraries* 23(2) (2004): 43-49.
8. "EZproxy by Useful Utilities," http://www.usefulutilities.com/ (viewed September 4, 2005).
9. "The URL Clearinghouse," http://library.albany.edu/clearinghouse/types.htm (viewed September 4, 2005).
10. Ibid.
11. "Free Online Full-Text Articles," http://highwire.stanford.edu/lists/freeart.dtl, accessed Dec. 14, 2005.
12. Oberg, 123.
13. Diane Grover and Theodore Fons, "The Innovative Electronic Resource Management System: A Development Partnership," *Serials Review* 30(2) (2004): 110-116.
14. Ibid.
15. B. Neavill and M. A. Sheble, "Archiving Electronic Journals," *Serials Review* 21(4) (1995): 13-21.
16. J. Barnes, "Electronic Archives: An Essential Element in Complete Electronic Journals Solutions," *Information Services and Use* 17(1) (1997): 37-48.
17. "LOCKSS," http://lockss.stanford.edu/about/about.htm (viewed September 4, 2005).
18. Stephen R. Lawrence, Lynee Silipigni Connaway, and Keith H. Brigham, "Life Cycle Costs of Library Collections: Creation of Effective Performance and Cost Metrics for Library Resources," *College and Research Libraries* 62(6) (2001): 541-551.
19. Carol Hansen Montgomery and JoAnne L. Sparks, "The Transition to an Electronic Journal Collection," *Serials Review* 26(3) (2000): 4-18.
20. Ibid.
21. Steve Shadle, "Cataloging for the 21st Century Training Program," workshop conducted at the 2005 Annual Conference of the American Library Association, Chicago, IL; Jeanne M. K. Boydston and Joan M. Leysen, "Internet Resources Cataloging in ARL Libraries: Staffing and Access Issues," *Serials Librarian* 41(3/4) (2002): 27-145; James S. Cervinko, "The Changing State of Original Cataloging: Who's Going to Do It Now?," *Illinois Libraries* 74(5) (Nov. 1992): 493-495; Magda El-Sherbini and George Klim, "Changes in Technical Services and Their Effect on the Role of Catalogers and Staff Education: An Overview," *Cataloging & Classification Quarterly* 24(1/2) (1997): 23-33.

DOI:10.1300/J105v32n01_10

# Standards for the Management of Electronic Resources (ER)

## Paoshan W. Yue

**SUMMARY.** The increasingly networked, scholarly information environment requires librarians to use more and different standards in order to manage electronic resources (ER) well. Many key activities associated with the various stages in the life-cycle of ER will benefit from the development and adherence to standards. This chapter will review a number of major standardization initiatives that have emerged to address those needs. doi:10.1300/J105v32n01_11 *[Article copies available for a fee from The Haworth Document Delivery Service: 1-800-HAWORTH. E-mail address: <docdelivery@haworthpress.com> Website: <http://www.HaworthPress.com> © 2007 by The Haworth Press. All rights reserved.]*

**KEYWORDS.** Electronic resource management, electronic journals, standards

---

Paoshan W. Yue, MLS, is ER Access Librarian, University of Nevada, Reno Libraries, Getchell Library/MS 322, University of Nevada, 1664 North Virginia Street, Reno, NV 89557-0044 (E-mail: yue@unr.edu).

[Haworth co-indexing entry note]: "Standards for the Management of Electronic Resources (ER)." Yue, Paoshan W. Co-published simultaneously in *Collection Management* (The Haworth Information Press, an imprint of The Haworth Press) Vol. 32, No. 1/2, 2007, pp. 155-171; and: *Electronic Resources Librarianship and Management of Digital Information: Emerging Professional Roles* (ed: Mark Jacobs) The Haworth Information Press, an imprint of The Haworth Press, 2007, pp. 155-171. Single or multiple copies of this article are available for a fee from The Haworth Document Delivery Service [1-800-HAWORTH, 9:00 a.m. - 5:00 p.m. (EST). E-mail address: docdelivery@haworthpress.com].

Available online at http://col.haworthpress.com
© 2007 by The Haworth Press. All rights reserved.
doi:10.1300/J105v32n01_11

## *INTRODUCTION*

Standards have everything to do with interoperability, efficiency, and quality. In an ever-more digital and networked environment, the need for new standards and the revision of existing standards for the management of information has never been greater. Such a need is especially evident in the area of electronic resources (ER). Many initiatives have emerged to address standardization needs at various stages in the life-cycle of ER. Some of them have become national standards while others have been widely accepted and are already bearing fruit. Still others are under development or revision, but promise improvements in the management of ER once completed.

The life-cycle of ER, generally, includes these stages: selection, acquisition, administration, bibliographic/access control, and assessment. Each stage has its own set of challenges as well as a need for standards. It depends upon the libraries where they work, but ER (ER) librarians may be called upon to manage any number of those stages. As a result, they will need to collaborate with their colleagues from other library units in order to manage the complete life-cycle. Librarians who are involved in the management of this cycle may be found in various library units, e.g., technical services, public services, systems, and administration. No matter where they are on the library's organizational chart, the players in each of those stages must pay close attention to the standards that apply in their areas as well as possess a basic awareness of all standardization initiatives that are applicable in the library in order to help make all management activities as effective as possible.

Many key activities associated with the management of the e-resource life-cycle will benefit from the development and adherence to standards. This chapter will review a number of major standardization initiatives that have emerged to address those needs:

- Digital Library Federation Electronic Resource Management Initiative (DLF ERMI)
- NISO/EDItEUR: ONIX for Serials
- Library of Congress XML-based metadata schemas and RDA: Resource Description and Access
- OpenURL Framework for Context-Sensitive Services: ANSI/NISO Z39.88-2004
- National Information Standards Organization (NISO) Metasearch Initiative
- International Standard Serial Number (ISSN) revision
- Project COUNTER (Counting Online Usage of Networked ER).

## DIGITAL LIBRARY FEDERATION ELECTRONIC RESOURCE MANAGEMENT INITIATIVE (DLF ERMI)

ER call for a new set of management activities many of which have not been present in the management of the traditional print-based format. Librarians who have attempted to incorporate digital resources into their libraries' collections, services, and operations have found their extant integrated library systems (ILS) insufficient to support the complexity of e-resource management. As observed by Tim Jewell of the University of Washington in his 2001 study for the Digital Library Federation (DLF), librarians, because they lacked available software solutions, began to develop local automated tools to provide needed functionality.[1]

Prompted by the growth in interest among librarians in comprehensive electronic resource management systems (ERMS), Jewell and Adam Chandler at Cornell University created a *Web hub* in 2001 in order to highlight locally developed solutions and promote communication among interested librarians.[2]

Soon after the Web hub began, an informal meeting on e-resource management was held at the 2001 American Library Association (ALA) annual conference in San Francisco. The meeting attracted more than forty librarians and resulted in the establishment of an informal steering group to begin discussions of possible standards. The work of this group, ultimately, led to a workshop on ERMS standards in May 2002 sponsored by the DLF and National Information Standards Organization (NISO). The participants, approximately fifty librarians, and representatives from publishers, subscription agents, library systems vendors, and publication access management services (PAMS) reached a consensus that standards were desirable as a guide to facilitate the development of ERMS. To achieve the goal of the development of ERMS standards the workshop steering group decided that a more formal and collaborative approach should be adopted. As a result, the Digital Library Federation Electronic Resource Management Initiative (DLF ERMI) was established in October 2002. Two advisory panels that consisted of librarians, library systems vendors, and representatives of related service providers were also organized to provide ongoing expert advice.

The aim of the DLF ERMI was to aid the rapid development of ERMS by the production of a series of interrelated documents in order to define functional requirements and to establish data standards upon which libraries, consortia, and vendors could base their work.[3]

A number of deliverables were produced as a result of the initiative:

- A specification of forty-seven functional requirements for electronic resource management
- A workflow diagram that provided an overview of the processes associated with the management of the life-cycle of ER
- An entity-relationship diagram (ERD) that illustrated the major concepts or entities and the relationships between those entities for ERMS design
- A data element dictionary that identified and defined over 300 individual data elements for ERMS
- A data structure that mapped data elements to the entities and relationships defined in the ERD
- A report on the investigation to apply Extensible Markup Language (XML) technology to exchange selected ERM data elements between systems

The initiative has received very positive responses from librarians and vendors. Most importantly, it has provided the impetus needed for the development of commercial ERMS of which several, vendor-developed, are already available while some others are under development. Much of the system development work has drawn heavily upon the initiative's deliverables, especially the functional requirements and the data element dictionary.

The DLF ERMI final report identified several development areas that needed to be addressed further in order to improve the management of e-resources; among these are consortium support and functionality, usage data, and data standards. In recognition that some of these issues were to be addressed by other emergent initiatives, the ERMI steering committee decided not to duplicate those efforts.

To build on its initial success a second phase of ERMI was proposed to the DLF in November 2005 in order to help propel additional developments that are needed in e-resource management. The proposed ERMI Phase 2 will focus on data standards, issues related to license expression, and usage data.

## NISO/EDItEUR: ONIX FOR SERIALS

The greatest area of growth in ER has been in serials. As electronic serials grow exponentially, so grows the need for the exchange of serials subscription information among librarians, publishers, content aggregators, library systems vendors, and other, third-party service providers. For example, publishers must supply librarians with price and title lists for a specific product. Content aggregators must provide title lists and holdings data to librarians and PAMS. Librarians must supply subscription data to PAMS, while PAMS must provide librarians with coverage data for A-Z lists. Librarians, also, must populate the knowledge databases for their link resolution servers and ERMS with coverage data, which may be provided by publishers, content aggregators, or other, third-party service providers.

Because it has lacked a uniform standard, serials data has been exchanged in many formats without consistency in data elements or message structure. Librarians have had to massage and manipulate the data that comes from different parties in order to meet the data format requirements of their in-house tools. Likewise, publishers, PAMS, and other parties, also, must reconcile external and internal data. A standard for the exchange of serial subscription data would benefit all parties involved and significant savings and efficiencies would be gained.

In early 2002, the National Information Standards Organization (NISO) commissioned Ed Jones of National University to do a study on the exchange of serial subscription information, which resulted in a white paper published in September of the same year.[4] Jones recommended that EDItEUR's Online Information Exchange (ONIX) for Serials be assessed for use in the development of such a standard and, also, pointed out that it is important to find a solution to the problem of identifiers in data exchanges. He proposed that all interested parties be encouraged to participate in the development of the standard.

Soon after Jones' white paper was published, NISO and EDItEUR established the Joint Working Party (JWP) to look into the potential of ONIX for Serials as a basis for a standard. This international group has 35 official members who represent libraries, library systems vendors, publishers, PAMS, subscription agents, and online content providers from the United States and the United Kingdom.[5]

The JWP's initial charge was threefold:

1. To recommend modifications to the existing ONIX for Serials specifications to allow their use in this context;
2. To pilot the use of the format(s); and
3. To investigate a transaction-based (i.e., query/response) exchange.[6]

Later, the JWP decided not to pursue the third element of the charge. They proposed three sets of message formats that could be used in a variety of applications: Serials Online Holdings (SOH), Serials Products and Subscriptions (SPS), and Serials Release Notification (SRN). The proposed formats would share the same data elements and permitted code values for each element.[7]

The SOH format is designed for content-suppliers or service-providers to use to deliver online serials holdings information to libraries that subscribe. This information is necessary for librarians to populate knowledge databases which support A-Z lists and link resolution servers. After a series of pilot projects based on Release 0.9, the SOH Release 1.0 was published in July 2005 and, subsequently, revised in September 2005 for general use.[8]

The SPS format is designed for vendor/publishers to convey product catalog and price information as well as the specific subscriptions held by one or more libraries that subscribe. Librarians may, also, use this format to list the products and titles to which they subscribe from a specific vendor/publisher.[9]

The SPS subgroup intends to finalize a Version 0.9.1 for a second trial exchange.[10]

The SRN format is intended to support information exchange about serials resources at the article, issue, or, more generally, the *release-level*. This format can be used for tables of contents alerts, automated library check-in, notification of pattern changes, and registration of Digital Object Identifiers (DOI).[11]

The SRN subgroup intends to finalize the first draft, Version 0.9, to pilot test.[12]

In order for the ONIX for Serials standard to work, it is essential to have unambiguous identifiers for serial titles, serial works, and parties such as vendor/publishers and libraries. Unfortunately, the JWP found that there are problems with each of the above and decided that identifier issues are beyond the scope and power of the group. They will call attention to the problems and try to encourage the development of solutions.[13]

## LIBRARY OF CONGRESS XML-BASED METADATA SCHEMAS AND RDA: RESOURCE DESCRIPTION AND ACCESS

In order for a user to access an electronic resource, the resource must be identified. In order to identify a resource, it must be described. However, the use of the Machine-Readable Cataloging (MARC) bibliographic standard and the Anglo-American Cataloguing Rules, Second Edition (AACR2) cataloging rules to describe ER has been likened to putting a square peg into a round hole. There are many attributes of ER that cannot be adequately accommodated by MARC standards and AACR2 rules, which were developed in the 1960s and the 1970s, respectively, for the description of print-based formats. Additionally, in the highly networked, scholarly information environment there is an increased need to produce bibliographic metadata in a format that is compatible with other metadata formats, e.g., Dublin Core and Encoded Archival Description (EAD), which have been used in digitization projects. It is clear that MARC and AACR2 will have to change in order to meet the challenges.

In response to these needs, the Library of Congress' Network Development and MARC Standards Office launched several initiatives meant to transform the MARC record structure into a variety of Extensible Markup Language (XML) formats. The purpose of the transformations is to allow greater extensibility in the record structure and better integration with mainstream computing. The Library of Congress initiatives have produced three format standards for resource description: MARCXML, Metadata Object Description Schema (MODS), and Metadata Authority Description Schema (MADS).

MARCXML provides a framework to work with MARC data in an XML environment. It allows a lossless conversion of MARC data into an XML structure where MARC data can then be used in ways that accommodate specific needs. It is also possible to convert a MARCXML record back into a MARC record. The Library of Congress provides schemas, style sheets, and software tools for the framework.[14]

MODS, a derivative of MARC, is designed to carry a subset of MARC elements as well as to enable the creation of original resource description records in XML. MODS is simpler than full MARC, but richer than Dublin Core. Its main features include language-based tags, rather than numeric ones; the ability to share element definitions with their equivalents in MARC; and a repackage of some redundant MARC elements.[15]

MADS is designed to carry selected authority data from MARC records as well as to enable the creation of original authority data. Intended as a companion to MODS, MADS has a relationship to the MARC 21 Authority format in the same way as MODS has to the MARC 21 Bibliographic format. It is an XML schema for an authority element set that may be used for descriptions of agents, events, and terms.[16]

As a response to the increasingly digital and networked environment, the drafters of the 2002 revision of AACR2 incorporated a new perspective on ER, serials, and integrating resources. But, more changes are needed. As part of its strategic plan, the Joint Steering Committee (JSC) for Revision of AACR works on a new edition of the most widely used cataloging rules. Originally called AACR3, the new edition was renamed RDA: Resource Description and Access in April 2005 when the JSC decided to take a different approach to cataloging, which emphasizes more principle-based rules whose application will build and augment cataloger judgment. It also encourages the application of the Functional Requirements for Bibliographic Records (FRBR) model. RDA is envisioned as a new content standard for resource description and access designed for the digital environment and is meant to be independent of any data communication format and metadata standard. It consists of three parts: resource description, relationships, and access point control and is scheduled for publication in 2008.[17]

## *OPENURL FRAMEWORK FOR CONTEXT-SENSITIVE SERVICES: ANSI/NISO Z39.88-2004*

The explosive growth of ER has created all sorts of new challenges for librarians. One of these is the appropriate copy problem. When multiple, online copies of a resource exist, librarians want to direct their patrons to the copy for which the library has established user access privileges. A typical scenario is that librarians want to direct their patrons from a citation in an abstracting and indexing database to its full-text counterpart that is available in an electronic journal subscribed to by the library, or via an aggregator database. Vendors of citation databases could build the links by means of embedded, static URLs. However, those hard-coded URLs may change frequently due to the fluid nature of the e-journal publishing environment. In addition, the static link method would require the vendors or information service providers to know all resources to be interlinked at the time when the citation records are created. Though quite straightforward, this approach cannot be easily scaled-up in order to deal with large numbers of resources. To address the limitations of static links some vendors adopted a dynamic link method where the links are calculated at the time when the user makes a request of a link. But, neither of those two link methods places the control of the link in the hands of librarians who need something better in order to maximize the use of varied resources to which the library has subscribed as well as to address increased demands for more comprehensive access services.[18]

It was in such an environment where the concept of OpenURL was envisioned and developed.

An OpenURL is an actionable URL that transports bibliographic metadata and resource identifiers between information services. In order to make open links in the Web-based scholarly information environment possible the construct of the URL must conform to a standard syntax. The initial concept for OpenURL was developed by Herbert Van de Sompel in 1999 at Belgium's Ghent University.[19]

Van de Sompel, Patrick Hochstenback (Ghent University), and Oren Beit-Arie (Ex Libris) developed an OpenURL resolution system. Special Effects (SFX) was designed to perform context-sensitive linking that consists of three main components: sources, targets, and the link resolver that connects them. The user initiates a search in a source, typically an online abstracting and indexing database, and requests a specific article by sending an OpenURL, which contains descriptive metadata about the article, to the link resolver. The resolver parses the metadata and compares them with its internal knowledgebase of titles and holdings in order to determine which target, typically an online journal package or a full-text database, can provide the article for the user. The link resolver then produces a service menu that the user can use to link to the identified full-text article as well as other extended services pre-configured by librarians to appear in the menu window, e.g., a check pf the library catalog, or to find additional information about the journal in *Ulrich's Periodicals Directory*. Sources and targets must be OpenURL-compliant in order to exchange metadata in a context-sensitive link system.

Van de Sompel and Beit-Arie submitted the OpenURL proposal to NISO for standard accreditation. NISO approved it as a fast-track work item in December 2000 and formed the Committee AX in 2001 to prepare the standard. The committee's charge was to develop an extensible mechanism for the transportation of packages of metadata and identifiers about an information object.[20]

Its work based on the OpenURL as developed for SFX, also known as OpenURL 0.1, the committee developed OpenURL 1.0 and published the new standard, *The OpenURL Framework for Context-Sensitive Services: ANSI/NISO Z39.88-2004*, in 2004.

The OpenURL Framework has a much broader scope than OpenURL 0.1 because it is designed to cover all scholarly information, textual or non-textual. In addition, its extensibility allows future application into other non-scholarly information domains. At a conference about the OpenURL Framework held in October 2003, Van de Sompel was reported to have remarked, "The OpenURL Framework has the potential to change the linking experience on the web."[21]

## NATIONAL INFORMATION STANDARDS ORGANIZATION (NISO) METASEARCH INITIATIVE

Today's library user, accustomed to the single search box model common in Web-based services like Google, expects the same type of *one-stop shopping* experience at the library. More often than not, however, users become frustrated when they have to repeat the same search in every relevant resource in order not to miss potentially useful information. To make matters worse, users often have to deal with different search interfaces and results displays for different online resources. In response to the need for a single point of access to the world of knowledge, metasearch products have emerged, which allow library users to issue a single search request across several heterogeneous databases and receive results in a single unified list.

Librarians who were early adopters of metasearch products report positive responses and strong support for the concept from users. However, as is the case in many situations the simpler the solution looks from the outside the more complex is the internal work reality. Behind the simple metasearch box of the public interface lie a myriad of joint configuration efforts between librarians, metasearch service providers, and content providers. In the absence of widely supported standards it is a challenge to provide an efficient metasearch service. There are three main considerations:

1. A metasearch service must offer access to many database targets, which provide many types of content and are tied to different access requirements.
2. Protocols that govern search and retrieve vary among content providers. The most common protocols are NISO's Z39.50, proprietary application program interfaces (API), and screen-scrapes.
3. Descriptions of resources from different content providers do not include the same data elements, which makes it difficult for users to compare resources and to select the appropriate ones for their research needs.

As a consequence of increased metasearch activities database providers began to notice server load problems. In 2003, at the ALA Midwinter Conference, several stakeholders met to discuss the problem. NISO representatives volunteered to lead a concerted effort to find a solution.[22]

In May 2003, NISO convened a strategy meeting in Denver to identify problems and issues, to review extant standards and approaches, and to define NISO activities in support of the metasearch process. A broad range of problems were identified in six key functional areas that support metasearching: access management, statistics, searching options, metasearch identification, resource description, and result set management.[23] In October 2003, a follow-up workshop was held in Washington, DC in order to inform librarians, content providers, and aggregator vendors about the metasearch process.

As a result, in January 2004 NISO established the Metasearch Initiative with the goals to enable:

- Metasearch service providers to offer more effective and responsive services
- Content providers to deliver enhanced content and protect their intellectual property
- Librarians to deliver services that are distinguishable from those provided by Google and other free Web services[24]

With over 60 members to represent metasearch service providers, content providers, and libraries the Metasearch Initiative conducts its work through three Task Groups. Each Task Group focuses on one of these areas: access management, collection description, and search/retrieve. Final versions of Task Group recommendations are available for public use on the NISO Metasearch Initiative Web site at: http://www.niso.org/committees/MS_initiative.html

Ongoing activities and working copies of documents from the Task Groups can be found in the NISO Metasearch Initiative wiki at: http://www.lib.ncsu.edu/niso-mi/index.php/Main_Page.

## INTERNATIONAL STANDARD SERIAL NUMBER (ISSN) REVISION

Unique identifiers play a vital role in the ever-linking world of ER. As the most important identifier in the serials world the International Standard Serial Number (ISSN) in its current state (ISO 3297, 3rd ed.) does not meet the challenges encountered by ER managers across the information supply chain.

Originally designed in the 1970s to serve as the numerical equivalent of the serial title and to help users distinguish between the same or similar titles the ISSN is now used in many e-resource management activities, i.e., search, identification, file-matches, de-dupes, and link resolution. But, the application of the ISSN to those activities is problematic for four reasons:

1. Serial publications do not always have ISSNs.
2. Publishers do not always assign separate ISSNs to different formats (e.g., print, online, CD-ROM) of a serial as is recommended in the current Cooperative Online Serials (CONSER) policy.
3. Library database systems do not always have a mechanism to use to store multiple ISSNs.
4. The current policy of multiple ISSNs for different formats does not support the need to connect users with serial content, regardless of format.

In May 2003, in response to changes in the serials world and the current digital environment the International Organization for Standardization (ISO) established a work group to revise the ISSN standard. The ISO Working Group was made up of twenty experts who were either nominated for membership by national standards organizations or were invited to join the group because of their expertise. The membership includes representatives from ISSN international and national centers, CrossRef, OpenURL, DOI, journal publishers, subscription agencies, rights management groups, and other organizations that use or might potentially use the ISSN.[25]

The ISO Working Group began its work in January 2004 with a focus on major issues such as the scope of the ISSN, concerns about the policy of assigning a separate ISSN to different versions of a serial, and the procedures that ISSN centers follow to assign the numbers. As Reynolds pointed out, "The aim of these goals is supporting or extending the use of the ISSN in publishing, distribution, and library applications."[26]

In February 2005, at its 4th meeting the group reached a consensus on the major issues:

- The scope of the standard will be all serials and other continuing resources, including selected integrating resources.
- There will be product-level (or manifestation-level) and title-level (or work-level) identification. Separate ISSNs will continue to be assigned to different versions of a serial while a collocating number (CN) will be used for title-level identification. The CN is not to

be mistaken as a new identifier, but rather a new function of the ISSN. The first-assigned product-level ISSN will also be used for the CN. The ISSN International Centre will assign the CN retrospectively. As such, every serial will retain its regular ISSN along with the CN, which will be recorded in the 024 field of the MARC record.

- An ISSN User Group was established to provide ongoing input to the ISSN Governing Board from the user communities. It will also serve as a sounding board for governing board proposals.
- The ISSN International Centre will provide new services to meet the needs of various ISSN users for information about relationships among ISSNs. The new services to be developed are ISSN data distribution (subscription) and look-up (online access) services.[27,28]

Publication of the revised standard is projected for 2007.

## PROJECT COUNTER
### (COUNTING ONLINE USAGE OF NETWORKED ER)

Usage data are an essential metric to determine the value of ER. librarians need data to assess the value of different online products, to support collection development, and to justify increased expenditures on ER. Publishers and third-party service providers need data to assess the relative importance of different delivery channels, to experiment with new price models, and to plan future infrastructure. Accurate and reliable usage data helps both information consumers and providers to better manage their ER and services.

The early efforts in the collection and analysis online usage data met two major obstacles: no data element definitions and inconsistencies in the data received from publishers. For example, publishers have different opinions on what constitutes a *search* or a *hit*. Additionally, publishers differ in the usage events they count and in the report formats that they provide. These stumbling blocks make it impossible for librarians to measure online usage effectively or to compare, in a meaningful way, similar electronic products, or services.[29]

Launched in March 2002 in the UK, COUNTER is an international effort to track online usage. Its foundation is the work of a number of important ongoing initiatives and standards relevant to usage data:

- The Association of Research Libraries (ARL) E-Metrics Project
- The International Coalition of Library Consortia (ICOLC) Guidelines for Statistical Measures of Usage of Web-Based Information Resources
- The National Information Standards Organization (NISO) Standard Z39.7.[30]

COUNTER quickly gained support from many publishers and library organizations, including the ARL. In January 2003, its developers launched Release 1 of its Code of Practice for Journals and Databases with the stated purpose to facilitate the recording, exchange, and interpretation of online usage data through the establishment of open international standards and protocols for the provision of vendor-generated usage data that are consistent, credible, and compatible.[31]

COUNTER specifies requirements that vendor/publishers must meet in order for their usage reports to be designated COUNTER-compliant.

The Code of Practice includes the following:

- A glossary of terms with definitions and examples
- Specifications for usage report type, content, format, frequency, and delivery method
- Data processing requirements; basic principles are that only intended use is recorded and that all requests that are not intended by the user are removed
- Audit requirements for vendor/publisher use reports and processes

The Code of Practice urges librarians to ask for a clause to be included in license agreements that would require vendor/publishers to provide COUNTER-compliant usage reports.

Vendor/publishers have responded positively and have begun to work towards COUNTER-compliant status; by September 2004, over thirty major vendor/publishers had achieved it.[32]

Fifteen months later, as of this writing, 46 vendor/publishers were listed in the official Register of COUNTER-compliance, which is available on the COUNTER Web site.

In continuation of its efforts, COUNTER released, in July 2004, an Extensible Markup Language Document Type Definition (XML DTD) for use reports that added to the previous format options of CSV and Excel. In April 2005, COUNTER published Release 2 of its Code of Practice for Journals and Databases that incorporated input from various sources and provided some highly sought enhancements.[33]

On 1 January 2006, Release 2 became the definitive version of the Code of Practice.

To expand COUNTER's coverage beyond journals and databases, a Draft Release 1 of the COUNTER Code of Practice for Books and Reference Works was published in January 2005. Publication of the final version of the Code is projected in 2006.[34]

## CONCLUSION

Standards are crucial for librarians to manage ER well. In fact, the highly networked environment requires librarians to use more and different kinds of standards than they ever needed in the pre-Internet era. As investments in ER grow and innovative technologies and business models evolve development of new standards and revisions of extant ones is an ongoing effort. ER librarians and other e-resources managers must understand standardization issues and stay abreast of the development of the latest standards. Relevant workshops, conferences, Webinars, and standardization initiative Web sites are excellent resources to use to learn and train. If they support, adopt, and integrate standards in the management of ER, librarians will be better positioned to provide services that will meet user needs and expectations.

## NOTES

1. Timothy D. Jewell, *Selection and Presentation of Commercially Available Electronic Resources: Issues and Practices* (Washington, DC: Digital Library Federation and Council on Library and Information Resources, 2001); http://www.clir.org/pubs/reports/pub99/pub99.pdf (viewed February 26, 2006).

2. "Web Hub for Developing Administrative Metadata for Electronic Resource Management," http://www.library.cornell.edu/cts/elicensestudy/webhubarchive.html (viewed February 26, 2006).

3. *Electronic Resource Management: Report of the DLF ERMI Initiative* (Washington, DC: Digital Library Federation, 2004); http://www.diglib.org/pubs/dlfermi0408/ (viewed February 26, 2006).

4. Ed Jones, *The Exchange of Serials Subscription Information: A White Paper Prepared for the National Information Standards Organization, with Support from the Digital Library Federation* (Bethesda, MD: NISO Press, 2002); http://www.niso.org/Serials-WP.pdf (viewed February 26, 2006).

5. Priscilla Caplan, "Stretching ONIX for Serials: The Joint Working Party on the Exchange of Serials Subscription Information," *Against the Grain* 15(6) (December 2003/January 2004): 88-89.

6. Priscilla Caplan, "NISO EDItEUR Joint Working Party on the Exchange of Serials Subscription Information (JWP)," paper presented at the CONSER Summit on Serials in the Digital Environment in Alexandria, VA (March 18-19, 2004); http://www.loc.gov/acq/conser/ONIX-summit.html (viewed February 26, 2006).

7. "NISO/EDItEUR ONIX for Serials," http://www.editeur.org/onixserials.html (viewed February 26, 2006).

8. "ONIX for Serials, SOH: Serials Online Holdings–Release 1.0," http://www.editeur.org/onixserials/ONIX_SOH1.0.html (viewed February 26, 2006).

9. "ONIX for Serials, SPS: Serials Products and Subscriptions–Release 0.9," http://www.editeur.org/onixserials/ONIX_SPS09.html (viewed February 26, 2006).

10. "JWP Conference Call Notes for June 2, July 12, August 8, September 20, and October 27, 2005," http://www.fcla.edu/~pcaplan/jwp/confCall35.pdf, http://www.fcla.edu/~pcaplan/jwp/confCall36.pdf, http://www.fcla.edu/~pcaplan/jwp/confCall37.pdf, http://www.fcla.edu/~pcaplan/jwp/confCall38.pdf, http://www.fcla.edu/~pcaplan/jwp/confCall39.pdf (viewed February 26, 2006).

11. "ONIX for Serials, SRN: Serials Release Notification," http://www.editeur.org/onixserials/ONIX_SRN01.html (viewed February 26, 2006).

12. "JWP Conference Call Notes."

13. Caplan, "NISO EDItEUR Joint Working Party."

14. "MARCXML: MARC 21 XML Schema Official Web Site," http://www.loc.gov/standards/marcxml/ (viewed February 26, 2006).

15. "MODS: Metadata Object Description Schema Official Web Site," http://www.loc.gov/standards/mods/ (viewed February 26, 2006).

16. "MADS: Metadata Authority Description Schema Official Web Site," http://www.loc.gov/standards/mads/ (viewed February 26, 2006).

17. "RDA: Resource Description and Access," http://www.collectionscanada.ca/jsc/rda.html (viewed February 26, 2006).

18. Jenny Walker, "OpenURL and SFX Linking," *Serials Librarian* 45(3) (2003): 87-100.

19. Herbert Van de Sompel and Patrick Hochstenbach, "Reference Linking in a Hybrid Library Environment. Part 2: SFX; a Generic Linking Solution," *D-Lib Magazine* 5(4) (April 1999); http://www.dlib.org/dlib/april99/van_de_sompel/04van_de_sompel-pt2.html (viewed February 26, 2006).

20. "The OpenURL Framework for Context-Sensitive Services. Standards Committee AX-Charge," http://www.niso.org/committees/committee_ax.html (viewed February 26, 2006).

21. Ann Apps, "The OpenURL and OpenURL Framework: Demystifying Link Resolution," *Ariadne* 38 (January 2004); http://www.ariadne.ac.uk/issue38/appsrpt/intro.html (viewed February 26, 2006).

22. Andrew K. Pace, "Much Ado about Metasearch," *American Libraries* 35(6) (June/July 2004): 92-93.

23. Mark Needleman, "The NISO Metasearch Workshop," *Serials Review* 29(3) (Autumn 2003): 256-57.

24. "NISO Metasearch Initiative," http://www.niso.org/committees/MS_initiative.html (viewed February 26, 2006).

25. Regina Romano Reynolds, "Revision of the ISSN Standard: The Challenge of Change," *Against the Grain* 16(2) (April 2004): 84-86.

26. Ibid.

27. Regina Romano Reynolds, "Revision of the ISSN Standard Moves Forward," *CONSERline: Newsletter of the CONSER Program* 26 (Spring 2005); http://www.loc.gov/acq/conser/consln26.html (viewed February 26, 2006).

28. Regina Romano Reynolds, "Unique Identifiers in Libraries: ISSN Revision," program presented at the NASIG Annual Conference, Minneapolis, MN, May 19-22, 2005).

29. Peter Shepherd, "Keeping Count," *Library Journal* 128(2) (February 1, 2003): 46-48.

30. "Project COUNTER-About COUNTER," http://www.projectcounter.org/about.html (viewed February 26, 2006).

31. "The COUNTER Code of Practice Release 1: December 2002," http://www.projectcounter.org/codeofpractice.pdf (viewed February 26, 2006).

32. "Compliance with the COUNTER Code of Practice," *COUNTER News Release* (August 9, 2004); http://www.projectcounter.org/Modifications_to_compliance_process_August_2004.doc (viewed February 26, 2006).

33. "The COUNTER Code of Practice Release 2: April 2005," http://www.projectcounter.org/r2/COUNTER_COP_Release_2.pdf (viewed February 26, 2006).

34. "Draft Release 1 of the COUNTER Code of Practice for Books and Reference Works," http://www.projectcounter.org/cop_books.ref.html (viewed February 26, 2006).

doi:10.1300/J105v32n01_11

# Acts of Vision:
# The Practice of Licensing

## Rachel Miller

**SUMMARY.** This chapter provides an overview of licensing practices in the realm of electronic information. The role of licensing in current library organizational structures is described. The resources and tools that license practitioners use to perform effectively are reviewed. In addition, licensing issues and challenges are discussed, and attention is drawn to the ways in which the practice of licensing shapes the library and information science (LIS) profession. doi:10.1300/J105v32n01_12 *[Article copies available for a fee from The Haworth Document Delivery Service: 1-800-HAWORTH. E-mail address: <docdelivery@haworthpress.com> Website: <http:// www.HaworthPress.com> © 2007 by The Haworth Press. All rights reserved.]*

**KEYWORDS.** Licensing, electronic resource licenses, license negotiation

Rachel Miller, MA, is Head, Acquisitions/Serials Department, University of Kansas Libraries, 1425 Jayhawk Boulevard, Lawrence, KS 66045-7544 (E-mail: rmiller@ku.edu).

The author wishes to thank Gaele Gillespie, Serials Librarian, University of Kansas, for her helpful comments on this paper.

[Haworth co-indexing entry note]: "Acts of Vision: The Practice of Licensing." Miller, Rachel. Co-published simultaneously in *Collection Management* (The Haworth Information Press, an imprint of The Haworth Press) Vol. 32, No. 1/2, 2007, pp. 173-190; and: *Electronic Resources Librarianship and Management of Digital Information: Emerging Professional Roles* (ed: Mark Jacobs) The Haworth Information Press, an imprint of The Haworth Press, 2007, pp. 173-190. Single or multiple copies of this article are available for a fee from The Haworth Document Delivery Service [1-800-HAWORTH, 9:00 a.m. - 5:00 p.m. (EST). E-mail address: docdelivery@haworthpress.com].

Practice means to perform, over and over again in the face of all obstacles, some act of vision, of faith, of desire. Practice is a means of inviting the perfection desired.

                                        –Martha Graham[1]


## INTRODUCTION

Over the past fifteen years, electronic resources have increased in their significance as a component of library collections. With license agreements as the standard mechanism for acquiring these resources, licensing is now a key activity in libraries. As a specialization, it has advanced and matured. Across the profession, librarians recognize that the issues dealt with in licensing are fundamentally important to libraries and to scholarly communication.

Not long after license agreements first appeared on the scene, in the late 1980s and early 1990s, libraries began to recognize their legal and administrative significance, and moved to design and put in place institutional policies and procedures to govern the licensing process. In the beginning, collection development, serials, and acquisitions librarians assumed the day-to-day responsibility for licenses. In recognition that contract terms could and should be negotiated rather than just accepted, they began to seek the new knowledge and skills required to interpret, negotiate, and administer license agreements.

As the number of electronic resources grew, librarians responded by restructuring their organizations to provide better support for the entire electronic resources management (ERM) process, including licensing. Existing print-based workflows were streamlined so that staff could be freed up to focus on the new digital workflows. A common response was to create an electronic resources (ER) librarian position, either through internal reallocation or external recruitment, and give the holder of the position the responsibility for licenses as well all other aspects of the ERM process.

The assignment of license management to a "single resident expert coordinator" emerged as a best practice.[2] At the same time, librarians recognized that effective license management required "a well-developed team process" with representation from several areas of the library and the university.[3]

## STAFFING AND ORGANIZING THE LICENSING FUNCTION

After much experimentation, organizational models for ERM still vary considerably. Staff configurations are fluid and continue to change as tasks and workflows become better defined and best practices emerge. ER librarian positions have proliferated, and their responsibilities range from bibliographic control and metadata, to reference and outreach, instruction, Web technology, acquisitions, serials, and collection development.[4]

How license functions are staffed varies from one library to the next and depends upon the institution's size and type, the volume of licenses, and the consortial context. A library that lacks access to consortial licenses and must license electronic resources on its own requires much more in-house license expertise than a library that can license consortially most or all of its electronic resources.

Although there is diversity as to where in the library organization licenses are negotiated and signed, usually the license function resides in the division that is responsible for collection development and scholarly communication issues. Day-to-day license responsibilities typically form part of a broader professional assignment that involves acquisitions, collection development, serials, and other aspects of the ERM process.[5]

A master's degree in library and information science (LIS) is a requirement for positions that have responsibility for the license process, although, on occasion, contract experience and/or legal knowledge may be substituted. Entry-level librarian positions may provide the opportunity to assist with licenses under the guidance of a more experienced professional. At least one institution has experimented with combining responsibility for the management of content and software licenses into one position.[6] As the volume of licenses grows, some libraries rely on support staff for the initial review of licenses and on student employees to assist with the management of files.[7]

Because of the specialized knowledge that is required to negotiate licenses and the legal implications of signing a contract, most libraries centralize licensing responsibilities. Although in some libraries a single individual handles all aspects of license review and negotiation, including signing the license, it is more typical to divide the functions. Signature authority is delegated by the parent institution to a high-level administrator in the library, usually the director, or an assistant director. Negotiations with providers by collection development staff often occur as part of the selection process. A collection development librarian or a bibliographer negotiates business terms with the e-content provider; after agreement on the price, the remainder of the negotiation–including review of legal language as well as the terms and conditions of use–is turned over to licensing staff. When the negotiation is completed, the individual with signature authority conducts a final review of the contract and signs it.

A legal or purchasing office outside the library often plays a role in the review of the license, and in some cases retains final approval and signature authority.[8] Library staff can benefit from a legal counsel's assistance with the general terms of the contract and, in turn, help the counsel to better understand the issues important to librarians in these agreements. A license has implications for the entire institution, and effective licensing is a highly collaborative and consultative process.[9]

### Education and Training for Licensing

The specific knowledge, skills, and abilities that license practitioners need to be effective are recognized in statements of professional competency.[10] These competencies can be gained through library school coursework, continuing education/professional development, and on-the-job experience.

LIS programs provide students with a basic foundation for license work, with coursework on copyright issues and scholarly communication as well as collection management, acquisitions, and serials management. Such courses, at a minimum, address the basic concepts of the license process. The Association of Research Libraries (ARL) has offered license workshops at sites in the United States and Canada, and online workshops through its Online Lyceum.[11]

American Library Association (ALA) pre-conferences, conference programs, and discussion groups address license topics. Regional, state, and special interest conferences focus on e-resource issues, including licensing. The body of professional literature ranges from practical guidebooks[12] to edited collections on particular aspects of licensing,[13] original research,[14] conference reports,[15] and articles on practical matters.[16]

Another important resource is the model license. Model and standard licenses have been developed by associations, consortia, vendor/publishers, and libraries.[17] Also useful are checklists of terms and conditions that include examples of acceptable and prohibited language.[18]

Practitioners who need help with specific license issues or wish to participate in discussions of hot topics may subscribe to two discussion lists, LibLicense-L and ERIL-L (Electronic Resources in Libraries). LibLicense-L addresses a range of license, copyright, and scholarly communication issues. ERIL-L discussions tend to deal with the more practical aspects of managing electronic resources.

As valuable as all these resources are, it is impossible to become an effective license practitioner without on-the-job experience. This is especially true for learning negotiation skills. Effective negotiators depend on judgment and confidence; these are best developed through practice in an organizational situation that encourages experimentation, flexibility, and learning from mistakes.[19]

Effective negotiation requires both "a knowledge about the specific deal [and] a skill set specific to the negotiation process."[20] The negotiator must understand the particular resource: its pricing structure, its place in the library's collection, how it will be used, and how specific license terms will affect user behavior or staff workflow. Every detail of the contract must be carefully read and discussed with the licensor. Negotiation skills include the ability to be patient, to treat the opposite negotiator with respect, and to work towards long-term relationships. Negotiation is an art, not a science with hard and fast rules. Each license situation is unique, "in shades of gray–without much black and white."[21]

Another way to view negotiation is as a process to assess risk, accepting that some risk is unavoidable. Negotiators learn to decide when to press, when to accept less-than-ideal terms, and when to walk away from an offer. A basic negotiation skill is to be able "to state in layman's language–not library or legal language–the reason for a desired change. The most common reason for a failed negotiation . . . is being unable to articulate the reason behind one's requests."[22] In their interactions with vendor/publishers, licensing librarians represent not just their individual institutions, but the profession as a whole. They have the opportunity to educate vendor/publishers about the LIS world and to advocate on behalf of information consumers.

Beyond the review of licenses and negotiations with providers, licensing librarians have operational responsibilities as managers of a workflow. An effective license manager must have organizational skills and develop techniques to manage more than one contract at once. A production-oriented mindset is important. To review an individual license agreement and communicate requests for changes to the licensor may not take long, but the negotiation that follows may be protracted. The license may move from the library to the parent institution's legal counsel, to the licensor and back again, with discussion of specific points and revisions required at each stage. Consultation with the original selector of the item for the collection may be necessary. Licensing librarians learn how long to wait for a response and what techniques to employ in an effort to avoid delay and keep the process on track. As librarians with multiple competing responsibilities, license practitioners must be able to focus their attention; one way to do this is by "taking licenses and deep-thinking projects into quiet rooms to read."[23]

Above all, license practitioners must develop effective communication skills to manage a complex structure of relationships with information providers, colleagues, and consortial partners.

### Components of the Licensing Function

License practice varies across libraries and continues to evolve, but certain basic functions form part of the process: [24]

- *Development and maintenance of an institutional policy.* The library's first task is to prepare a statement of principles, philosophy, and strategy to guide its license activities, supplemented by a practical outline of the local process that defines the institutional context and the roles of various players, including the institution's legal counsel and purchasing office. The statement identifies the positions with negotiation, final review, and signature authority. Consortial memberships and library policies concerned with consortial participation are defined here. Also included is an explanation of the institutional license compliance system, with procedures outlined for handling claims of infringement.[25]

  These principles are not only meant to guide license staff, but should also be understood by all library employees, especially selectors/bibliographers who must appreciate how digital content licenses impact the marketplace and the scholarly communications system. By documenting the policy, the library establishes a basic foundation to ensure that license practice remains aligned with the strategic goals of the library despite changes in individuals or organizational structures.

- *Preparation of standard contract language.* Librarians recognize that the use of standard license terms will help achieve efficiencies, and by "signaling" acceptable language to vendor/publishers, lead to better licenses.[26]

  Most librarians have used model licenses as the basis for establishing local standard language of required/preferred terms and conditions.[27] These local documents include definitions of authorized users and required/preferred terms of use for various types of resources. Any institutional requirements, e.g., mandatory state

provisions, are also included. As standards evolve, local requirements must be updated. Use of standard definitions makes compliance straightforward and feasible; without consistent definitions,
compliance may be difficult or impossible.[28]

 License review is never just a mechanical substitution of words
and phrases from a standard license or checklist. However, such
tools simplify the review process, make editing licenses faster and
easier, and, most importantly, ensure consistency.

- *License review and negotiation.* Before finalizing a commitment
  to acquire a resource, designated library staff review the license
  agreement, identify terms and conditions that fail to meet the library's policy, and negotiate changes with the licensor, suggesting
  wording that, ultimately, will be acceptable to both parties. The
  price may also be negotiated, especially if the resource is expensive, or the basis for the price is unclear, or when the negotiations
  are on behalf of a consortium.[29] Some libraries have convinced
  vendor/publishers to use a license crafted in the library as a start
  point for negotiations, but libraries usually work from the ven-
  dor/publisher's license.[30]

 Compared with the early days of licensing, current licenses have
become more standardized and most negotiations are simpler.
Some of the more contentious issues have been resolved.[31] Many
licenses to be reviewed are for renewals, rather than new resources,
and can be dealt with through addenda to existing licenses.[32]

- *Additional licensing issues.* Some of the most difficult licenses are
  those for Web resources that have been designed for individuals,
  rather than institutions; usually these are the products of companies that are unfamiliar with the library market. Another issue for
  librarians is the sheer volume of licenses to be negotiated when a
  library attempts to activate online access to journals from small
  publishers. Often, the publisher posts a statement of terms and
  conditions online, but if any of the posted terms are not in accordance with library policy, the vendor/publisher may have to be
  persuaded to work with the library to produce a contract. Finally,
  there is the challenge of renegotiating old licenses to bring their
  language up to current standards.

- *Maintenance of documentation on license agreements/negotiations.*
  An essential requirement for effective license management is to
  record centrally all information about the digital resource, its terms
  and conditions of use, access details, and technical requirements.[33]

 Sharing information with other staff is important from the beginning of the process through all stages of the negotiations. As the number of licenses that has been negotiated grows, assuring that current, accurate data is accessible to all staff who need it has become an enormous challenge. To address the need for standard solutions, the Digital Library Federation (DLF) sponsored work by the Electronic Resources Management Initiative (ERMI) to establish functional requirements for improved tools to manage electronic resources.[34]

This led to the development of commercial ERM (Electronic Resource Management) systems now marketed by integrated library systems (ILS) vendors, serial agents, and serial data providers. These systems provide access to license terms and include other features to assist with the management of license activities.[35]

- *Interpretation and explanation of license agreements to library staff and education of users in their rights/responsibilities.* License practitioners must educate staff about the library's obligations as articulated in a license agreement. The most basic concept that must be communicated is that access to electronic resources is governed by licenses whose terms take precedence over copyright. Collection development librarians must familiarize themselves with the license terms and conditions of the resources they have selected. Librarians should teach staff members so that they can easily determine whether or not an e-resource can be used in electronic reserves or to fill an ILL request.

  Libraries cannot agree to police user behavior, but should undertake "reasonable efforts" to communicate with users as regards appropriate use of a resource. [36] The best practice is to inform patrons about the allowed/prohibited use by means of mechanisms that do not present barriers and to express terms of use in plain language. Librarians must be proactive, educating patrons about responsible use through reference interviews, bibliographic instruction, and outreach sessions,[37] as well as through involvement in campus-wide efforts to teach educate students about "ethical behavior, computer viruses, campus network bandwidth, and intellectual property."[38]

## CHALLENGES AND OPPORTUNITIES IN LICENSING TODAY

The issues that elicit the most discussion fall into two interconnected categories: issues of license workflow management and issues related to license terms.

## Licensing Workflow Issues

License management may be the biggest bottleneck in ERM workflow. The volume of transactions–number of licenses processed in a year, for example–is very low compared with other processes. Library staff and users, accustomed to rapid turnaround times, are often mystified at how long it can take to negotiate a license. Clearly, one of the biggest challenges in licensing today is to find ways to streamline the process. For ideas on how to do this, it may be useful to turn to the key principles that librarians have used successfully in redesigns of print-based workflows over the past decade. The principles listed here are drawn from the work of R2 Consulting.[39]

The first principle, *Incorporate systems thinking*, draws attention to the need to understand patterns and interrelationships and to develop a shared big picture of the process. This concept was integral to the development of ERM systems. When information on licenses is viewable by all staff, time is saved and communication improved.[40] ERM systems record information on the license process, e.g., the status of negotiations, and issue automatic e-mail alerts to keep the process on track.[41] ERMs can even be used to build automated look-up processes to check ILL and e-reserves requests against license terms.[42]

A greater openness and availability of information will lead to a wider understanding of licensing within the institution and pave the way for work on another workflow redesign principle, *Disallow the expert mentality*. Although only a few staff may need to know how to interpret legal terminology in licenses, a solid understanding of license concepts and processes must become widespread in libraries.

The workflow concepts *Simplify and standardize* and *Take full advantage of existing resources* are evident in the use of model licenses and standard terminology. Such approaches ease review and negotiation up front and simplify the entire management process, including license compliance and staff/user education. Librarians may also save time/money by reliance on consortial licenses, if they accept the terms negotiated by the consortium.[43]

Through the use of consortial licenses with major vendor/publishers, libraries obtained access to thousands of e-journals. Now, as librarians turn their attention to the "long tail" of small publishers–those who publish the remainder of journals for which online access is available–they face a large number of different licenses. Because the issue is the non-scalability of the one-on-one bilateral negotiation process, the use of standard licenses does not solve the entire problem.[44] An alternate approach is to use a "best practice service level agreement" instead of a license. This agreement would address the issues of: authorized users; standard uses, i.e., fair use, ILL, and reserves; system performance expectations; guidelines for the resolution of unauthorized use; the privacy of use data; the library responsibility for user education on copyright issues; and perpetual access rights. Legal language would be omitted altogether and business terms relegated to a separate purchase agreement.[45]

Another workflow principle from the print-based world, *Outsource sometimes*, has been proposed for licensing over the years, but not often adopted.[46] Initially, librarians felt that they must gain direct experience with licenses before they could turn the licensing process over to intermediaries. Conflict of interest might be another concern in cases where the agent hired to conduct the outsourced license negotiation is also a resource provider.[47] In the meantime, serials agents have supported the license process by notifying librarians when online access to a resource requires a license and by maintaining licenses for "big deal" e-journal packages. At least two serial agents provide a license negotiation service to libraries. The agent either incorporates library requirements into the vendor/publisher's license or harmonizes differences between them, but, so far, there has not been a reported case of an agent granted power of attorney or signature authority. A third agent has conducted trials of such a service, but is not currently involved in the negotiation of licenses because of vendor/publisher desire to work directly with libraries.[48]

Two more workflow redesign concepts are *Create a mainstream* and *Automate the mainstream*. As librarians populate their ERM systems with license terms they find this to be the most time-consuming aspect of implementation. License data must be tracked down in paper and online files. Because of the complexity and ambiguity of license wording, decisions as to what to enter into the ERM are not easy or straightforward. To address this problem, the ARL and the DLF offer workshops to teach participants how to analyze and map license language according to the DLF/ERMI Data Elements and Data Dictionary.[49]

The DLF/ERMI project envisions that loading key license terms, expressed in machine-readable format, into ERM systems will reduce costs for libraries and vendor/publishers. To develop new standards for communication of license terms is the role of the License Expression Working Group, whose members represent libraries, publishers, and standards organizations.[50] However, while everyone agrees that the time spent in the review, interpretation, and negotiation of licenses must be reduced, and that inconsistency among licenses is the major reason why license work takes so much time, librarians disagree on the impact of standards for license expression. Some librarians, while they recognize the potential of standards to increase efficiency, argue that license language that is too clear and "locked down" in contracts might lead to technological enforcement, and that librarians, to retain the rights permitted by copyright and fair use, should preserve ambiguities in licenses.[51]

## License Term Issues

The issue of enduring access to licensed content has become a major concern as journal publishers increasingly abandon the print format altogether, as the online versions become the version of record, and as librarians cancel print subscriptions and rely on electronic access only.

Enduring access poses two separate issues. The first is the right of libraries to permanent access to licensed content paid for during the life of a license agreement. Librarians request this right but do not consider it a deal-breaker in most cases, if the request is refused.[52] Even if a license provides for perpetual access rights, these are largely theoretical, as contractual assurances may be expressed too vaguely to stand up in court.[53]

The second issue is the right to copy journal content for preservation purposes. Many license agreements explicitly prohibit the creation of an archival copy.[54] The extent to which publishers have made adequate archive arrangements in order to protect information consumer rights to the purchased content in the event of a publisher business failure or the loss of content is an area of great uncertainty. The situation is complicated by the transfer of journal titles from one publisher to another, as recognized by Project Transfer, which works under the United Kingdom Serials Group (UKSG) to develop standards and best practices in this area.[55]

If librarians abdicate their stewardship responsibilities for creating the archive of the scholarly record, and yield that responsibility to publishers instead, universities risk losing control over that record. In recognition of the implications of this, a group of university administrators and librarians has issued a widely endorsed call for action.[56]

Librarians have started to develop robust and specific license language, e.g., citing archive initiatives such as LOCKSS and Portico in licenses. However, libraries still face uncertain costs to maintain perpetual access to e-content.[57] They may need to divert any savings achieved by the cancellation of print resources–savings accrued in the operational costs to receive, bind, shelve, and circulate print-based items–to the creation and support of reliable archive systems for digital information.[58]

Another major issue is price terms. Librarians are concerned about the complexity of price models, but, ultimately, the overriding issue is the sheer cost of electronic resources.[59] Consortia have economic leverage and have had some success in negotiations on price as well as other terms.[60] They have increased their influence and strengthened their bargaining positions through the communication of librarian expectations to vendor/publishers, the formalization of processes, and the establishment of negotiation criteria/objectives.[61]

However, prices that steadily increase remain the "flash point" in discussions about scholarly publishing, especially prices for scholarly journals in publisher bundles.[62] These "big deal" packages, usually licensed through consortia, have grown as a portion of library budgets, especially as large publishers acquire the journals of scholarly societies and non-profit organizations. Cancellation restrictions are the biggest issue because they hamper the ability of the library to manage its budgets. When these bundles are protected from cancellation by multi-year contracts, libraries that need to cut back on ongoing commitments or add new subscriptions have little budget flexibility and tend to disproportionately cancel titles from smaller publishers. With serials costs escalating faster than their budgets grow, some libraries have begun to cancel big deal packages and return to individual subscriptions chosen on the basis of use data.[63]

Pricing and access models for e-books are also an issue, especially in light of the fading distinction between e-books and e-journals. Although publishers offer a range of license options, the trend is toward marketing e-books in packages, either on a subscription or purchase model. Librarians have also found that e-book licenses present new license problems not confronted before.[64]

The Janus Conference on Research Library Collections issued a statement of Licensing Principles that advocates collective action to address pricing and other issues. According to these principles, librarians should create a library market by challenging the divide-and-conquer approach used by publishers and stipulate to publishers acceptable conditions for e-content licenses. As a part of this strategy, librarians should cease to accept licenses that contain non-disclosure requirements, since they put libraries in competition with each other for the best deals. Instead, libraries should share publicly the terms of their licenses.[65]

Unquestionably, sharing information on licenses helps libraries with negotiations, as has been demonstrated by the increased acceptance by vendor/publishers of clauses that permit ILL and electronic reserves.[66] However, a recent ARL survey on e-journal bundles found that contract terms–non-disclosure requirements, long-term access to content, and length of contracts–varied considerably from library to library. Some libraries and consortia, perhaps through more aggressive negotiations or greater market power, obtained vendor/publisher concessions, but many others accepted unfavorable terms.[67]

The question remains: Will libraries continue to accept contracts with unfavorable terms or will they refuse to do so in greater numbers, and with what effect?

## CONCLUSION

The practice of licensing in libraries has had a significant impact on the shape of the license agreements that vendor/publishers offer. Librarians are active in the open access movement and continue their efforts to influence the scholarly publications market, addressing broad scholarly communication issues as well as the viability of specific open access options. More than ever, librarians pay attention to vendor/publisher behavior in the marketplace. In license negotiations, they engage e-information suppliers in discussions on price models, archive rights, e-journal acquisition practices, author agreements/copyright transfer, institutional repositories, and other issues that affect the scholarly communication system.

The license expertise that librarians have developed is relevant in other arenas as well, e.g., licensing additional types of digital content. The Penn State Libraries, for example, have participated in licensing a campus-wide online music service, integrated it into the library's array of services, and helped to resolve technical implementation issues.[68] Librarians have also taken their license expertise into the realm of campus-wide intellectual rights management, as they lead outreach and education efforts on copyright, author rights, intellectual property, and scholarly communication issues.[69] When librarians license digitization rights to commercial agencies, they rely on their license experience to craft contracts that follow established best practices, stipulate fair subscription terms, assure that archival access responsibilities are addressed, and provide for open access to the digitized works.[70]

Since the first appearance of licenses in libraries, librarians have speculated about the possibility that licenses might, eventually, become obsolete. A decade ago Ann Okerson suggested that "by working very hard to create comprehensive and effective electronic content licenses" and by increasing copyright protections in these licenses librarians could create a future in which the license would "seem less and less relevant and necessary."[71]

Although licenses still persist, the positive impact that librarians have had through their license work cannot be denied. They have improved the terms of licenses and taken steps to streamline licensing workflows. Serious challenges remain to be addressed, but license librarians can be expected to continue as they have, practicing "acts of vision" to promote the widest possible access to digital information.

## NOTES

1. "This I Believe: An Athlete of God," http://www.npr.org/templates/story/story.php?storyId=5065006 (viewed August 14, 2006).

2. George J. Soete and Trisha Davis, *Managing the Licensing of Electronic Products* (Washington, DC: Association of Research Libraries, 1999); http://www.arl.org/spec/248fly.html (viewed August 14, 2006).

3. "Licensing Electronic Resources: Strategic and Practical Considerations for Signing Electronic Information Delivery Agreements," http://www.arl.org/scomm/licensing/licbooklet.html (viewed August 15, 2006).

4. Rebecca S. Albitz, "Electronic Resource Librarians in Academic Libraries: A Position Announcement Analysis, 1996-2001," *portal: Libraries and the Academy* 2(4) (2002): 589-600.

5. Susan Gardner, "Impact of Electronic Journals on Library Staff at ARL Member Institutions: A Survey," *Serials Review* 27(3/4) (2001): 19, 21-22. The author observed similar patterns in vacancy announcements that appeared in *College & Research Libraries News* from mid-2004 to mid-2006.

6. "Vacancy Announcement: Univ of Kansas," http://www.library.yale.edu/~llicense/ListArchives/0406/msg00041.html (viewed August 14, 2006).

7. Ellen Finnie Duranceau and Cindy Hepfer, "Staffing for Electronic Resource Management: The Results of a Survey," *Serials Review* 28(4) (2002): 316-320.

8. Ann Okerson, "The Transition to Electronic Content Licensing: The Institutional Context in 1997," chapter in Richard Ekman and Richard E. Quandt, eds., *Technology and Scholarly Communication* (Berkeley, CA: University of California Press, 1999): 64.

9. "Licensing Electronic Resources," http://www.arl.org/scomm/licensing/licbooklet.html (viewed August 15, 2006).

10. For example: "Shaping The Future: ASERL's Competencies for Research Librarians," http://www.aserl.org/statements/competencies/competencies.htm (viewed August 14, 2006); "The Future of Librarians: IMLS Future of Librarians in the Workforce" Study Update (June 13, 2006), http://libraryworkforce.org/tiki-index.php?page= Presentations (viewed August 14, 2006); "Competencies for Information Professionals," http://www.sla.org/content/learn/comp2003/index.cfm (viewed August 14, 2006).

11. For example: "Licensing Review & Negotiation," http://www.arl.org/arl/pr/lyceum_licensing05.html (viewed August 14, 2006).

12. For example: Lesley Ellen Harris, *Licensing Digital Content: A Practical Guide for Librarians* (Chicago: American Library Association, 2002).

13. For example: Karen Rupp-Serrano, ed., *Licensing in Libraries: Practical and Ethical Aspects* (Binghamton, NY: Haworth Information Press, 2005).

14. For example: Jim Stemper and Susan Barribeau, "Perpetual Access to Electronic Journals: A Survey of One Academic Research Library's Licenses," *Library Resources & Technical Services* 50(2) (April 2006): 91-109.

15. For example: Ellen Finnie Duranceau, Deanna Graham, and Stephen Martin, "After the License is Signed: Collaboration to Resolve License Breaches," *Serials Librarian* 48(3/4) (2005): 339-342.

16. For example: Ellen Finnie Duranceau, "License Tracking," *Serials Review* 26(3) (2000): 69-73.

17. "Welcome to Licensingmodels.com: Model Standard Licenses for Use by Publishers, Librarians and Subscription Agents for Electronic Resources," http://www.licensingmodels.com (viewed August 14, 2006); "CLIR/DLF Model License," http://www.library.yale.edu/~llicense/modlic.shtml (viewed August 14, 2006); "International Coalition of Library Consortia (ICOLC): Statement of Current Perspective and Preferred Practices for the Selection and Purchase of Electronic Information (Update No. 1: New Developments in E-Journal Licensing), http://www.library.yale.edu/consortia/2001currentpractices.htm (viewed August 14, 2006); "Principles for Licensing Electronic Resources," http://www.arl.org/scomm/licensing/principles.html (viewed August 14, 2006).

18. "Checklist of Points to Be Addressed in a CDL License Agreement," http://www.cdlib.org/vendors/checklist.html (viewed August 16, 2006).

19. Ellen Finnie Duranceau, "Why You Can't Learn License Negotiation in Three Easy Lessons: A Conversation with Georgia Harper, Office of General Counsel, University of Texas," *Serials Review* 23(3) (1997): 71.

20. Kristin H. Gerhard, "Pricing Models for Electronic Journals and Other Electronic Academic Materials: The State of the Art," chapter in Karen Rupp-Serrano, ed., *Licensing in Libraries: Practical and Ethical Aspects* (Binghamton, NY: Haworth Information Press, 2005): 15.

21. Duranceau, "Why You Can't Learn License Negotiation," 69-70.

22. Ibid., 70.

23. Ellen Finnie Duranceau, "Zen and the Art of ERM," *Against the Grain* 18(2) (April 2006): 61.

24. Soete and Davis, http://www.arl.org/spec/248fly.html (viewed August 14, 2006).

25. Ellen Finnie Duranceau, "License Compliance," *Serials Review* 26(1) (2000): 58.

26. Ann Okerson, "What Academic Libraries Need in Electronic Content Licenses: Presentation to the STM Library Relations Committee (STM Annual General Meeting, October 1, 1996)," http://www.library.yale.edu/~okerson/stm.html (viewed August 14, 2006).

27. Stephen Bosch, "Using Model Licenses," chapter in Karen Rupp-Serrano, ed., *Licensing in Libraries: Practical and Ethical Aspects* (Binghamton, NY: Haworth Information Press, 2005): 66.

28. Duranceau, "License Compliance," 54.

29. Ann Okerson, "Licensing Perspectives: The Library View (ARL/CNI Licensing Symposium, San Francisco, December 8, 1996)," http://www.library.yale.edu/~okerson/cni-license.html (viewed August 14, 2006).

30. Bosch, "Using Model Licenses," 76.

31. David C. Fowler, "Licensing: An Historical Perspective," chapter in Karen Rupp-Serrano, ed., *Licensing in Libraries: Practical and Ethical Aspects* (Binghamton, NY: Haworth Information Press, 2005): 177-197.

32. Norm Medeiros, "On the Road Again: A Conversation with Jill Emery," *OCLC Systems & Services* 22(1) (2006): 13.

33. Yem S. Fong and Heather Wicht, "Software for Managing Licenses and Compliance," chapter in Karen Rupp-Serrano, ed., *Licensing in Libraries: Practical and Ethical Aspects* (Binghamton, NY: Haworth Information Press, 2005): 143-161.

34. Timothy Jewell et al., *Electronic Resource Management: Report of the DLF ERM Initiative* (Washington, DC: Digital Library Federation, 2004); http://www.diglib.org/publs/dlfermi0408/ (viewed August 14, 2006).

35. Ibid.; Ellen Finnie Duranceau, "Electronic Resource Management Systems from ILS Vendors," *Against the Grain* 16(4) (September 2004): 91; http://hdl.handle.net/1721.1/18191 (viewed August 16, 2006); Ellen Duranceau, "Electronic Resource Management Systems, Part II: Offerings from Serials Vendors and Serial Data Vendors," *Against the Grain* 17(3) (June 2005): 59; http://hdl.handle.net/1721.1/18190 (viewed August 16, 2006).

36. Duranceau, "License Compliance," 55.

37. Jill Emery, "Is Our Best Good Enough? Educating End Users About Licensing Terms," chapter in Karen Rupp-Serrano, ed., *Licensing in Libraries: Practical and Ethical Aspects* (Binghamton, NY: Haworth Information Press, 2005): 27-39.

38. Amanda Maple, "Online Music Services and Academic Libraries," *ARL Bimonthly Report* 244 (February 2006); http:www.arl.org/newsltr/244/music.html (viewed August 15, 2006).

39. Ruth Fischer and Rick Lugg, "From Selection to Access: Optimizing the Collections and Technical Services Workflow," PowerPoint presentation, http://www.ebookmap.net/ppnts/Missouri Seminar 2006.ppt (viewed August 15, 2006).

40. Celeste Feather, "Toward Greater Satisfaction: An Electronic Resources Communication Audit," summary, http://www.electroniclibrarian.org/moodle/course/info.php?id=19 (viewed July 24, 2006).

41. Fong and Wicht, 149.

42. Janet Brennan Croft, "Interlibrary Loan and Licensing: Tools for Proactive Contract Management," chapter in Karen Rupp-Serrano, ed., *Licensing in Libraries: Practical and Ethical Aspects* (Binghamton, NY: Haworth Information Press, 2005): 41-53.

43. Okerson, "The Transition to Electronic Content Licensing," 63.

44. Ibid., 60.

45. Judy Luther and Selden Burgom Lamoureux, "Alternatives to Licensing: Re-Imagining Agreement," http://smartech.gatech.edu/handle/1853/10071 (viewed August 16, 2006).

46. David R. Fritsch, Marilyn Geller, and Adam Chesler, "Outsourcing Electronic Journal Licensing and Negotiation; or, How to Make E-Journal Acquisitions and Licensing Processes as Boring as Ordering Print Journals," *Serials Librarian* 42(3/4) (2002): 183-189.

47. "Agents in Place: Intermediaries in E-Journal Management," http://www.ebookmap.net/pdfs/AgentsInPlace.pdf (viewed August 15, 2006).

48. Dena J. Schoen, Director of Sales, Otto Harrassowitz, July 28, 2006 (personal communication); Lori Soulliere, E-Resources Account Development Manager, EBSCO Information Services, July 28, 2006 (personal communication); Christine Stamison,

Academic Sales Manager, SWETS Information Services, August 4, 2006 (personal communication).

49. "Reading and Mapping License Language for Electronic Resource Management: A Pilot ARL/DLF Workshop," http://www.arl.org/stats/work/mapping.html (viewed August 16, 2006).

50. Nathan D. M. Robertson, "Managing Our E-Resource Licenses: License Expression Standards," http://hdl.handle.net/1853/10407 (viewed August 15, 2006).

51. Richard Fyffe, "Copyright, Contracts, and Fair Use," paper presented at the Publisher-Vendor-Library Relations Forum (Standardized License Expression: Clarity, Control and Fair Use) at the American Library Association Midwinter Conference, January 23, 2006, San Antonio, Texas.

52. Karla Hahn, "The State of the Large Publisher Bundle: Findings from an ARL Member Survey," *ARL Bimonthly Report* 245 (April 2006); http://www.arl.org/newsltr/245/bundle.html (viewed August 16, 2006).

53. Jim Stemper and Susan Barribeau, "Perpetual Access to Electronic Journals: A Survey of One Academic Research Library's Licenses," *Library Resources & Technical Services* 50(2) (April 2006): 102.

54. Sharon Farb, "Libraries, Licensing and the Challenge of Stewardship," *First Monday* 11(7) (July 2006); http://www.firstmonday.org/issues/issue11_7/farb/index.html (viewed August 6, 2006).

55. "Transfer," http://www.uksg.org/transfer.asp (viewed August 16, 2006).

56. "Urgent Action Needed to Preserve Scholarly Electronic Journals," http://www.diglib.org/pubs/waters051015.htm (viewed August 16, 2006).

57 Stemper and Barribeau, 99-100.

58. Roger Schonfeld et al., *The Nonsubscription Side of Periodicals: Changes in Library Operations and Costs Between Print and Electronic Formats* (Washington, DC: Council on Library and Information Resources, 2004); http://www.clir.org/pubs/reports/pub127/pub127.pdf (viewed August 14, 2006).

59. Donald J. Waters, "Managing Digital Assets in Higher Education: An Overview of Strategic Issues," *ARL Bimonthly Report* 244 (February 2006); http://www.arl.org/newsltr/244/assets.html (viewed August 15, 2006).

60. Anne E. McKee, "Consortial Licensing Issues: One Consortium's Viewpoint," chapter in Karen Rupp-Serrano, ed., *Licensing in Libraries: Practical and Ethical Aspects* (Binghamton, NY: Haworth Information Press, 2005): 129-141.

61. For example: "Vendors & Content Providers," http://www.cdlib.org/vendors/ (viewed August 15, 2006); Lorraine Estelle, "NESLI2: A Report on Progress," *Serials: The Journal of the Serials Community* 17(2) (July 2004): 149.

62. Waters, http://www.arl.org/newsltr/244/assets.html (viewed August 15, 2006); Jeffrey N. Gatten and Tom Sanville, "An Orderly Retreat from the Big Deal: Is It Possible for Consortia?" *D-Lib Magazine* 10(10) (October 2004); http://www.dlib.org/dlib/october04/gatten/10gatten.html (viewed August 14, 2006).

63. Nancy J. Gibbs, "Walking Away from the 'Big Deal': Consequences and Achievements." *Serials: The Journal for the Serials Community* 18(2) (July 2005): 89-94.

64. Emilie Algenio and Alexia Thompson-Young, "Licensing E-books: The Good, the Bad, and the Ugly," chapter in Karen Rupp-Serrano, ed., *Licensing in Libraries: Practical and Ethical Aspects* (Binghamton, NY: Haworth Information Press, 2005): 113-128; "Introduction for the Break-Out Sessions: Six Key Challenges for the Future of Collection Development," http://dspace.library.cornell.edu/bitstream/1813/2608/1/Atkinson_Talk.pdf (viewed August 14, 2006).

65. "Revision to Action for Challenge 4 Licensing Principles (formerly Publisher Relations)," http://janusconference.library.cornell.edu/?p=52 (viewed August 14, 2006).

66. Mary Case, "A Snapshot in Time: ARL Libraries and Electronic Journal Resources," *ARL Bimonthly Report* 235 (August 2004); http://www.arl.org/newsltr/235/snapshot.html (viewed August 15, 2006).

67. Hahn, http://www.arl.org/newsltr/245/bundle.html (viewed August 16, 2006).

68. Maple, http:www.arl.org/newsltr/244/music.html (viewed August 15, 2006).

69. For example: "Ohio State University Libraries (June 2006), ALA Midwinter Round Robin, ALCTS Technical Services Directors of Large Research Libraries Group: New Responsibilities and Opportunities for Technical Services," http://www.loc.gov/library/bigheads/source/osu-rr-jun06.pdf (viewed August 16, 2006).

70. Richard Fyffe and Beth Forrest Warner, "Where the Giants Stand: Protecting the Public Domain in Digitization Contracts with Commercial Partners," chapter in Karen Rupp-Serrano, ed., *Licensing in Libraries: Practical and Ethical Aspects* (Binghamton, NY: Haworth Information Press, 2005): 83-102.

71. Ann Okerson, "Licensing Perspectives," http://www.library.yale.edu/~okerson/cni-license.html (viewed August 14, 2006).

doi:10.1300/J105v32n01_12

# Skills for Effective Participation in Consortia: Preparing for Collaborating and Collaboration

Susanne Clement

**SUMMARY.** Consortial participation provides opportunities and challenges for libraries. The intellectual and financial benefits are readily apparent–if libraries work together, they gain access to more content at a lower price. However, consortial participation also provides challenges with regard to coordination and communication. Though library directors/deans often provide initial leadership, especially in the selection of the type and range of consortial participation, collection development and electronic resources (ER) librarians tend to lead the way in work on the more detailed tasks that are involved. It is, primarily, more experienced librarians who are assigned to work with consortial representatives; there is a lot of on-the-job learning. doi:10.1300/J105v32n01_13 *[Article copies available for a fee from The Haworth Document Delivery Service: 1-800-HAWORTH. E-mail address: <docdelivery@haworthpress.com> Website: <http://www.HaworthPress.com> © 2007 by The Haworth Press. All rights reserved.]*

Susanne Clement, MA, MLS, is Head of Collection Development, University of Kansas, Watson Library, 1425 Jayhawk Boulevard, Lawrence, KS 66045-7544 (E-mail: sclement@ku.edu).

[Haworth co-indexing entry note]: "Skills for Effective Participation in Consortia: Preparing for Collaborating and Collaboration." Clement, Susanne. Co-published simultaneously in *Collection Management* (The Haworth Information Press, an imprint of The Haworth Press) Vol. 32, No. 1/2, 2007, pp. 191-204; and: *Electronic Resources Librarianship and Management of Digital Information: Emerging Professional Roles* (ed: Mark Jacobs) The Haworth Information Press, an imprint of The Haworth Press, 2007, pp. 191-204. Single or multiple copies of this article are available for a fee from The Haworth Document Delivery Service [1-800-HAWORTH, 9:00 a.m. - 5:00 p.m. (EST). E-mail address: docdelivery@haworthpress.com].

doi:10.1300/J105v32n01_13

**KEYWORDS.** Library cooperation, consortia, shared collection development, library school curriculum, library skills, consortia–electronic content

## INTRODUCTION

Limited resources are nothing new to libraries, nor are responses to the problem like collaborative work. Librarians have shared their collections for decades through formal agreements–most notably through interlibrary loan (ILL). However, as Web-accessible content has become the norm and users, increasingly, expect that this information will be accessible through their institution's library, "the option of not providing electronic resources is no longer available to most libraries however cash-strapped their budgets."[1]

User expectations have, therefore, increased the need for library collaboration and librarians now view consortial arrangements as a means to obtain essential electronic content. Consortia no longer just serve libraries that are in close geographical proximity of one other, i.e., in the same state or region. Libraries often are members of several different consortia–from state-mandated consortia to those based on opportunities and specific transactions. Librarians have been able to work creatively with publisher/vendors to create many different permutations of consortial relationships among libraries across the nation and beyond.

The purpose of this chapter is not to assess the benefits of consortial participation. The literature includes several good reports of large-scale assessments of consortia, including Borsch et al. who analyzed the impact of collaborative collection development through consortia through the measurement of financial benefits; increased access to and use of content; and user satisfaction.[2]

The literature is, likewise, rich with examples and suggestions of best practices on the role consortia play in collaborations to acquire e-resources. As Allen and Hirshon stated, a consortium provides the means for collaborative survival as compared to the more traditional organizational model of self-sufficiency.[3]

Instead, this discussion is a consideration of the players and their place within the library structure and the skills and training that are required to be successful.[4]

The interdependence of libraries for the effective delivery of user services as well as resource-sharing and material organization means that librarians must spend more time on internal and external cooperation and coordination.[5]

Katsirikou maintains that "trans-organizational sharing and exchange of knowledge serve as the foundation for the development of trust, which in turn leads to successful co-operative relationships."[6]

Librarians who work with each other within a consortium must communicate effectively and efficiently, build trust among and between their institutions, adhere to agreements, and follow through on issues in a timely manner.

As mentioned, libraries often belong to several different consortia at the same time–from state-mandated groups to those concerned with a single product to broad-based networks and peer-institutional organizations. The management of these diverse cooperative agreements can place a strain on librarians, library volunteers, and consortial staff.[7] The paradox is that e-content has made library collaborations easier and more complicated–they are, certainly, less-tangible than traditional print-based sharing has been.

Collaboration doesn't just happen–library professionals make it happen. The path to a successful collaboration will vary widely from library to library and from consortium to consortium. McKee outlined the broad process issues related to collaborative collection development of electronic content–from the determination of what to pursue as a consortial product to the review of potential consortial proposals from vendor/ publishers to the negotiation of price and license terms to the communication of these terms to consortial partners to the receipt of feedback by the negotiator to either finalize or reject the offer to the final determination of how the process to invoice and bill the partners will take place– this is a highly time-consuming and very complex undertaking.[8]

Conversations are rarely linear and require a lot of back and forth among all parties involved; there is potential for failure at many steps along the way due to miscommunication and missed deadlines. Whereas McKee describes a consortium that works within a highly formalized structure that includes an office and professional staff, Bucknall describes how the Carolina Consortium came into existence; an ad hoc "virtual" group that, currently, consists of 38 libraries.[9]

Without benefit of a formal structure, participant universities banded together through both virtual and in-person meetings to realize purchase agreements with three separate publishers. Though not stated in Bucknall's account, I suspect that one person, or perhaps a small core of key librarians, were influential in the coordination of the communication among the participants and publishers. The key to the completion of a successful consortial deal, regardless of organizational structure, is a mutual trust that everyone involved will accomplish their assigned tasks.

Are newly minted librarians prepared to work within this new collaborative environment? Do library school programs incorporate issues of library collaboration and consortial relationship into their curricula? Is this something that can be taught or is it something that is learned on-the-job? How do librarians prepare to work collaboratively, not only within their institution, but with librarians throughout the state, region, country, or world? Missingham questions, do new librarians have the knowledge-base needed to work in a rapidly changing library environment,[10] and is it possible, as Myborg suggests, that new LIS graduates have "a collection of rapidly dated skills."[11]

These are some of the questions that informed the development of the following survey.

## SURVEY

In July 2006, a Web-based survey to find out about the practical issues related to work within consortia was sent to several mailing lists that are used, primarily, by collection development and ER librarians.[12]

The questionnaire had two distinct purposes:

1. To determine the level of consortial involvement, the unique work challenges consortial participation presents, and the identification of the position within the institution that is responsible for various tasks related to consortial participation.
2. To determine what skills are most useful to the librarians who are engaged with a consortium; and where and how those skills were obtained.

The survey consisted of four categories:

1. Level of consortial participation
2. Demographics and job responsibility for various functions related to consortial participation
3. Challenges and opportunities represented by consortial participation
4. How the skills were obtained to deal with these issues

Each category had a main question with several sub-questions or statements that the respondents were asked to evaluate or select. A comment field was also provided to capture any variation to the choices provided.

## *RESULTS*

### Participation

A total of 92 surveys were completed by librarians or consortial staff from 18 states and nine countries or territories. Of these, 49 represented research libraries, 21 represented 4-year colleges/universities, 11 represented 2-year colleges and community colleges, two came from state libraries, and four came from consortia. Five did not indicate an affiliation. No public library participated in the survey.[13] (See Table 1.)

Sixteen libraries belonged to one consortium, 18 belonged to two consortia, 23 belonged to three consortia, 13 belonged to four consortia, five belonged to five consortia, two to six consortia, and one respondent worked at a library that belonged to eight consortia. Fifteen respondents did not indicate how many consortial relationships their libraries have; some of these were respondents from consortia and others who indicated that their libraries have informal relationships with other libraries that could not be considered consortial. Eleven responded that their library's only consortial activity was through a state-sponsored group. More than 60 reported that their libraries had consortial relationships with libraries from more than one state (72%). More than half of the respondents reported that their library has provided leadership within a consortium (51%) and 24% reported that their library provides managerial or clerical support to a consortium.

The greatest benefit noted for consortial participants is the ability to deliver to users more information content than any library is able to do on its own (77%). The second most important benefit reported by respondents is the ability to negotiate lower annual price increases–getting the "biggest bang for the buck" in the words of one of the survey respondents. The benefit of the negotiation of a multi-year contract was reported as less important as was the convenience of the enlistment of a third-party to handle negotiations with vendor/publishers, billing, and technical support. A couple of respondents noted that consortia are not only useful for group purchases of e-content, but can enable libraries to divide up responsibilities for the collection of materials in any format by language, region, subject, etc. Table 2 summarizes all survey replies.

In addition to the measurable benefits of consortial participation, some survey respondents indicated that participation in a consortium provides opportunities for librarians to network with their peers and share information. Respondents reported a benefit from interactions with librarians with similar interests as well as the collegiality of shared information

## TABLE 1. Consortial Involvement

Please indicate the level of your library's involvement in consortia.

| | Yes | No | NA | Respondent Total |
|---|---|---|---|---|
| Library participates in one or more library consortia. | 93% (83) | 1% (1) | 6% (5) | 89 |
| Consortia participation is solely through a state sponsored consortium. | 13% (11) | 81% (70) | 6% (5) | 86 |
| Consortia participation is with institutions within the same state but is not managed by the state library. | 68% (57) | 19% (16) | 13% (11) | 84 |
| Consortia participation is with libraries in several surrounding states. | 72% (62) | 20% (17) | 8% (7) | 86 |
| Consortia participation is with libraries in states throughout the United States. | 51% (43) | 42% (35) | 8% (7) | 84 |
| Consortial participation is with libraries outside the United States. | 15% (13) | 80% (70) | 6% (5) | 88 |
| Library provides leadership role within a consortium (library influential in starting a consortium). | 51% (44) | 40% (35) | 9% (8) | 87 |
| If your institution provides leadership for a consortium, is the consortium incorporated? | 14% (11) | 51% (41) | 35% (28) | 80 |
| Library provides managerial or clerical support of a consortium. | 24% (21) | 67% (58) | 8% (7) | 86 |
| | | | **Total Respondents** | **92** |

## TABLE 2. Benefits of Consortial Participation

What is the determining factor for participating in a consortium?

| | Greatest factor | Lesser factor | Not a factor | Other | Respondent Total |
|---|---|---|---|---|---|
| Access to content | 77% | 16% (15) | 3% (3) | 4% (4) | 92 |
| Multi-year contract | 10% (9) | 53% (49) | 30% (28) | 7% (6) | 92 |
| Participation benefits other libraries | 27% (25) | 5% (52) | 14% (13) | 2% (2) | 92 |
| Lower annual price increases | 58% (53) | 34% (31) | 3% (3) | 5% (5) | 92 |
| Predictable annual prices | 43% (40) | 37% (34) | 12% (11) | 8% (7) | 92 |
| "Convenience"–having a 3rd party negotiate with publisher, billing and technical support. | 32.5% (30) | 47% (43) | 14% (13) | 6.5% (6) | 92 |
| | | | | **Total Respondents** | **92** |

and multiple perspectives provided by other participants. One respondent indicated that, for smaller libraries, the benefits of participation in a consortium were like having additional staff available who could evaluate the variables of various electronic products. Several respondents said that a consortium allows librarians to negotiate more effectively with vendor/publishers for the best prices and for archival rights; and further that, as a group, consortia members receive greater attention from funding sources such as state governments and institutional boards.

## DEMOGRAPHICS AND JOB RESPONSIBILITIES

Participation in a consortium requires many different skill sets, from communication with consortial partners to the review and sign of licenses to decisions as to what products should be included in a consortial package to consolidation of title lists for e-journal packages to the collection and interpretation of use data. The results of the survey indicate that it is rare that the same person is responsible for all the components of collaborative work with other libraries as part of a consortium. The role of the ER librarian is the closest any library comes to having one position that is responsible for most or all of the operations that surround the delivery of digital information. The results of the survey indicate that someone from the upper library administration–a dean or director and/or an assistant dean or director–ultimately decide which consortium the library will join and who will be responsible to sign licenses.[14]

However, survey respondents indicated that committees/subcommittees made up of ER, collection development, and/or acquisitions librarians were involved at a more practical level of consortial operations and were responsible for such tasks as the evaluation of content, the consolidation of titles, and the collection and interpretation of use data. But the involvement in the process of administrators is also indicated by the fact that 25% of the respondents were either deans or assistant deans; another 25% were collection development librarians; 20% were ER librarians; and 23% reported that they had some other title–such as digital librarian, access services librarian, or systems librarian. (See Table 3.)

## CHALLENGES AND OPPORTUNITIES

There was significant agreement among the survey participants that consortial participation benefits their institutions both financially and intellectually (97% and 93%, respectively, strongly agreed).[15]

## TABLE 3. Responsibilities and Tasks

As a consortium participant, please indicate for each question who the primary person responsible for each task is within your library (if necessary, select more than one person per question):

| | Dean/ Assistant Dean | Electronic Resources Librarian | Collection Development Librarian and/or CD Committee | Acquisitions/ Serial Librarian | Subject Librarian | Clerical staff | Other | Respondent Total |
|---|---|---|---|---|---|---|---|---|
| Who is the primary liaison to a consortium? | 44% (36) | 31% (25) | 36% (29) | 7% (6) | 4% (3) | 0% (0) | 10% (8) | 81 |
| Who makes the decision to join a consortium for a particular product or package? | 46% (37) | 25% (20) | 51% (41) | 4% (3) | 7% (6) | 1% (1) | 12% (10) | 81 |
| Who reviews licenses? | 22% (18) | 44% (36) | 28% (23) | 11% (9) | 1% (1) | 4% (3) | 21% (17) | 81 |
| Who signs a license? | 45% (37) | 9% (7) | 10% (8) | 5% (4) | 0% (0) | 2% (2) | 38% (31) | 82 |
| Who confirms your institution's title lists with consortia or publisher? | 5% (4) | 38% (29) | 25% (19) | 36% (28) | 1% (1) | 12% (9) | 9% (7) | 77 |
| Who resolves problems with access? | 4% (3) | 62% (51) | 12% (10) | 18% (15) | 2% (2) | 13% (11) | 16% (13) | 82 |
| Who collects usage statistics on consortial packages? | 6% (5) | 58% (47) | 16% (13) | 4% (3) | 4% (3) | 9% (7) | 19% (15) | 81 |
| Who interprets usage statistics of consortial packages? | 15% (12) | 54% (44) | 37% (30) | 9% (7) | 10% (8) | 2% (2) | 13% (11) | 82 |
| My primary job responsibility or title is … | 25% (20) | 20% (16) | 25% (20) | 5% (4) | 7% (6) | 0% (0) | 23% (19) | 81 |

Total Respondents 83

(skipped this question) 9

The value of consortial participation is, obviously, not in doubt, but there was some variation in the responses as to how easy the process is, internally or externally, to increase of access to digital content through consortial participation (See Table 4). Though a majority of the respondents indicated that they perceived that some convenience would accrue to them and their libraries through participation in a consortium (67%), there was an even split between those who indicated

TABLE 4. Opportunities and Challenges

Participating in consortial arrangements presents opportunities and challenges. From the perspective of a membership library, please indicate your level of agreement with the following statements:

| | Strongly agree | Agree | Somewhat agree | Disagree | Strongly disagree | Respondent Total |
|---|---|---|---|---|---|---|
| Consortial participation benefits my institution financially. | 78% (62) | 19% (15) | 4% (3) | 0% (0) | 0% (0) | 80 |
| Consortial participation benefits my institution intellectually. | 63% (51) | 30% (24) | 7% (6) | 0% (0) | 0% (0) | 81 |
| Consortial participation saves time— "convenience" factor. | 37% (30) | 30% (24) | 22% (18) | 11% (9) | 0% (0) | 81 |
| Member libraries are easy to work with. | 26% (21) | 44% (36) | 25% (20) | 5% (4) | 0% (0) | 81 |
| Member libraries respond in a timely manner to proposals and terms. | 12% (10) | 49% (40) | 29% (24) | 10% (8) | 0% (0) | 82 |
| Negotiating with publishers through consortia is quicker and easier than doing so individually and directly. | 32% (26) | 22% (18) | 28% (22) | 18% (14) | 0% (0) | 80 |
| Getting feedback on consortial packages and deals from colleagues at my institution is easy and timely. | 15% (12) | 35% (28) | 31% (25) | 19% (15) | 1% (1) | 81 |
| My library degree prepared me for working within a consortium. | 4% (3) | 10% (8) | 16% (13) | 52% (42) | 18% (14) | 80 |
| | | | | Total Respondents | | 82 |
| | | | | (skipped this question) | | 10 |

that it was easier and quicker to negotiate with vendor/publishers through a consortium and those who preferred to do it individually and directly (54% to 46% respectively). Seventy percent of the respondents agreed that member libraries are easy to work with and 61% indicated that they found that their colleagues in member institutions responded to proposals and terms in a timely manner. However, the respondents were, once again, evenly split as to how easy it was to work with units within their own libraries. Half indicated that their colleagues provided timely feedback on proposed consortial deals and half that their colleagues were less than prompt.

## SKILLS AND TRAINING

The majority of the survey respondents has worked in libraries for more than 16 years (71%), but has only worked with consortia for six years or less (64%), which is not a surprise. What is somewhat of a surprise is that most of the respondents were senior librarians. (See Table 5.) Several of the respondents indicated that the library's dean or director is the primary liaison to a consortium, but that collection development, ER, or subject specialist librarians were usually a part of committees/ subcommittees within the consortium that were charged with specific tasks. Among the reasons why senior librarians lead a library's consortial participation are:

- Consortial interaction requires a broad understanding of library operations
- It affects library material budgets for the duration of consortial contracts
- It requires a level of internal and external coordination that less-experienced librarians may not have

Some of the skill sets that the participants indicated are very important for successful consortial participation were:

- Evaluating databases (60%)
- Negotiation skills (57%)
- Attention to details (57%)
- Familiarity with licensing terms (52%)
- Communication skills (50%)
- Familiarity with copyright issues (43%)

## TABLE 5. Demographics

Please tell us how long you have been doing the following:

|  | 1-3 years | 4-6 years | 7-10 years | 11-15 years | 16-20 years | 21 + years | Respondent Total |
|---|---|---|---|---|---|---|---|
| Professional librarian (post MLS) | 1% (1) | 9% (7) | 5% (4) | 14% (11) | 16% (13) | **55% (44)** | 80 |
| Responsibility for library's consortial participation | 24% (19) | **40% (32)** | 16% (13) | 11% (9) | 4% (3) | 5% (4) | 80 |
|  |  |  |  |  | **Total Respondents** |  | 83 |
|  |  |  |  |  | (skipped this question) |  | 9 |

If one considers the career longevity of the respondents, it is not a surprise that a large majority (80%) indicated that their library degrees had not prepared them for the skills needed for consortial participation; rather, they had learned the skills on-the-job. (See Table 6). More than 80% of the respondents completed their professional library degrees more than eleven years ago, which was well before the advent of any significant consortial activity with regard to e-resources; so it is unrealistic to expect that such skills would have been part of library school curricula at that time. However, an analysis of the survey responses indicates that even survey participants who had graduated from library programs within the last six years also felt that their professional education had done little to prepare them for consortial participation. They had, however, received more information about copyright issues and had more experience in the evaluation of databases than their more experienced colleagues. The surveys contained a couple of comments that requirements for collaborative class projects had been a good preparation for the collaborative work required for consortial participation.

## *CONCLUSION*

The results of the survey indicate that even though libraries do participate in more than one consortium most activity is within a library's own state or with libraries in close geographical proximity. The demand for more e-content drives most consortial activity along with the lower annual price increase that are negotiated through consortial agreements. It takes good communication skills, an ability to evaluate the value of electronic content, and an understanding of budgets, copyright, and li-

## TABLE 6. Skills and Training

Please indicate how important the following skills are for you to represent your library within a consortium AND indicate whether these skills were taught in your library school program or if you learned these on the job (two answers per row).

| | Very Important | Important | Somewhat Important | Not Important | Library School | On the Job Training | Respondent Total |
|---|---|---|---|---|---|---|---|
| Evaluating databases | 60% (49) | 26% (21) | 10% (8) | 1% (1) | 12% (10) | 78% (63) | 81 |
| Manage serial lists | 34% (28) | 37% (30) | 20% (16) | 10% (8) | 4% (3) | 82% (67) | 82 |
| Familiarity with legal terminology | 29% (24) | 38% (31) | 24% (20) | 7% (6) | 2% (2) | 88% (72) | 82 |
| Familiarity with copyright issues | 43% (35) | 39% (32) | 13% (11) | 2% (2) | 15% (12) | 80% (66) | 82 |
| Familiarity with licensing terms | 52% (43) | 34% (28) | 11% (9) | 1% (1) | 2% (2) | 89% (73) | 82 |
| Budget planning, development and interpretation | 52% (43) | 34% (28) | 12% (10) | 1% (1) | 12% (10) | 78% (64) | 82 |
| Manipulating spreadsheets | 37% (30) | 44% (36) | 15% (12) | 4% (3) | 2% (2) | 85% (70) | 82 |
| Interpreting data elements | 34% (27) | 49% (39) | 15% (12) | 2% (2) | 10% (8) | 80% (64) | 80 |
| Negotiation skills | 57% (47) | 27% (22) | 15% (12) | 1% (1) | 2% (2) | 87% (71) | 82 |
| Attention to details | 57% (47) | 38% (31) | 5% (4) | 0% (0) | 22% (18) | 68% (56) | 82 |
| Written communication skills | 50% (41) | 41% (34) | 9% (7) | 0% (0) | 20% (16) | 72% (59) | 82 |
| Verbal communication skills | 49% (40) | 46% (38) | 5% (4) | 0% (0) | 15% (12) | 74% (61) | 82 |

Total Respondents 82

(skipped this question) 10

censing terms to operate successfully within a consortium. Most of the training for these skills was not included in library school curricula, but learned through years of professional work. A topic for research might be a thorough analysis of library school courses to assess the extent to which library consortial participation is included. One person is seldom responsible for the performance of all of the tasks required for consortial participation. The results of the survey indicate that library deans/directors are often involved in a library's consortial decisions, but, not unexpectedly, they delegate the more practical tasks to other librarians. Consortial participation has become an important component of a library's collection management strategy and has implications for long-term library budgets. Therefore, it is not a surprise to find senior staff involved.

## NOTES

1. Uma Hiremath, "Electronic Consortia: Resource Sharing in the Digital Age," *Collection Building* 20(2) (2001): 81.

2. Stephen Borsch et al., "Measuring Success of Cooperative Collection Development: Report of the Center for Research Libraries/Greater Western Library Alliance Working Group for Quantitative Evaluation of Cooperative Collection Development Projects," *Collection Management* 28(3) (2003): 223-239; Several other good articles have analyzed the benefits of consortial participations such as David F. Kohl and Tom Sanville, "More Bang for the Buck: Increasing the Effectiveness of Library Expenditures Through Cooperation," *Library Trends* 53(3) (2006): 394-411 and Bernie Sloan, "Testing Common Assumptions About Resource Sharing," *Information Technology and Libraries* 17(1) (1998): 18-29.

3. B. M. Allen and A. Hirshon, "Hanging Together to Avoid Hanging Separately: Opportunities for Academic Libraries and Consortia," *Information Technology and Libraries* 17(1) (1998): 36.

4. Though this chapter will primarily focus on consortial involvement in collaborations to purchase electronic content and how this may manifest itself in academic libraries in North America, consortial activity has a rich history throughout the world. See the special issue of *Information Technology and Libraries* (September 1999) for examples of consortia outside North America.

5. Anthi Katsirikou, "Consortia and Knowledge Management: The Functional Context and an Organizational Model," *Library Management* 24(6/7) (2003): 339-340.

6. Ibid., 339.

7. Anne McKee, "Consortial Licensing Issues: One Consortium's Viewpoint," *Journal of Library Administration* 42(3/4) (2005): 132.

8. Ibid., 133-136.

9. Tim Bucknall, "The Virtual Consortium," *Library Journal* 130(7) (2005): 16-19.

10. Roxanne Missingham, "Library and Information Science: Skills for Twenty-First Century Professionals," *Library Management* 27(4/5) (2006): 257-58.

11. S. Myborg, "Education Directions for New Information Professionals," *Australian Library Journal* 52(3) (2003): 223.

12. All the tables presented in this chapter were created through the use of a Web-based analysis tool found at SurveyMonkey.com.

13. Though library collaboration is more pronounced among academic libraries many public libraries are now also engaged in consortial purchases (primarily through state libraries) and they have begun to explore consortium-building in an effort to meet user needs. See Barbara Hoffert, "The United Way: Will Public Libraries Follow Academics as They Take Collaborative Collection Development One Step Further," *Library Journal* 131(8) (2006): 38-41.

14. Most respondents reported that their university's legal counsel reviewed licenses after the library had completed its review; several also reported that, depending on the price and length of a consortial deal, the university's chief financial officer (CFO) was required to sign the license.

15. More than one respondent questioned whether the benefits of consortial participation are as great as perceived. One hypothesized that the benefit of lower prices might be offset by the energy spent in participation.

doi:10.1300/J105v32n01_13

# Challenges of Sharing Online Information Through Traditional and Non-Traditional ILL

## Cyril Oberlander

**SUMMARY.** In response to the challenges with resource-sharing of electronic resources (ER), librarians have developed new strategies to resolve user needs and library information services. While emergent consumer technology radically changed the nature of libraries as places to seek information services, the transformation in resource-sharing has been shaped by librarians and interlibrary loan (ILL) specialists who create workflow procedures, in order to supply requested information, that recognize the exigencies of the transformed information landscape. New strategies include alternative sources and Web services; context sensitive workflow; new partnerships; education and training programs; and efforts to adopt new communication and other emergent technologies. doi:10.1300/J105v32n01_14 *[Article copies available for a fee from The Haworth Document Delivery Service: 1-800-HAWORTH. E-mail address: <docdelivery@haworthpress.com> Website: <http://www.HaworthPress.com> © 2007 by The Haworth Press. All rights reserved.]*

Cyril Oberlander, MS, is Director of Interlibrary Services, University of Virginia Libraries, University of Virginia, Alderman Library, P.O. BOX 400100, Charlottesville, VA 22903 (E-mail: cwo4n@virginia.edu).

[Haworth co-indexing entry note]: "Challenges of Sharing Online Information Through Traditional and Non-Traditional ILL." Oberlander, Cyril. Co-published simultaneously in *Collection Management* (The Haworth Information Press, an imprint of The Haworth Press) Vol. 32, No. 1/2, 2007, pp. 205-223; and: *Electronic Resources Librarianship and Management of Digital Information: Emerging Professional Roles* (ed: Mark Jacobs) The Haworth Information Press, an imprint of The Haworth Press, 2007, pp. 205-223. Single or multiple copies of this article are available for a fee from The Haworth Document Delivery Service [1-800-HAWORTH, 9:00 a.m. - 5:00 p.m. (EST). E-mail address: docdelivery@haworthpress.com].

**KEYWORDS.** Interlibrary loan, resource sharing, online or electronic resources, grey literature and repositories, academic library, education and training

## INTRODUCTION

The challenges presented by online information to traditional and non-traditional ILL parallels many of the challenges faced by information-seekers. Ubiquitous information has made even clear pathways at times inconvenient or obscure. The resolution of discovery options is a primary concern for both user and ILL staff; however, the online information environment also makes transformation of resource-sharing and the library a collaborative process with many partners and competitors. Resource-sharing, as a strategy, is a fundamental library practice that promotes opportunities to cooperate on new workflow approaches as well as the adoption of new services and technologies some of which may lead to new organizational designs. The challenges to locate and handle online resources for the purpose of resource-sharing present opportunities to develop new connections between library resources.

## ENVIRONMENTAL CHANGES

The evolution of the online information environment presents contradictions for resource-sharing, document delivery, and ILL. While search engines and full-text sources mean fast and easy access to information, electronic resources (ER), also, present challenges to that access. Resource-sharing staff are challenged to provide traditional services to users who want information (and ILL request forms) in paper-based formats as well as to provide service to users who ask for content from sources in new formats, e.g., online full-text, color images, and new services, e.g., delivery options and digitization on demands. Since the introduction of online resources and services the information environment has changed radically. The most dramatic changes have been:

- Ubiquitous Information: According to the Pew Internet & American Life Project, there are 84 million subscribers to home broadband, which represents about 42% of all American adults, and 31 million broadband users have posted content to the Web.[1] An OCLC Office of Research study of Web sites found that in 1998 there were about 1.5 million public Web sites, and by June 2002 the publicly accessible

Web had grown to 3.08 million Web sites with about 1.4 billion Web pages.[2]

- Information-sharing based, primarily, on social or peer networks: According to OCLC, in 2004 the daily information exchange of email with attachments was about 16.5 million while the number of United States ILL transactions was 51 thousand.[3]

Because the information-sharing environment has changed so much, part of the challenge for resource-sharing professionals is to shift from a library-centric focus, i.e., streamline library-to-library request and delivery systems, to a chart of new information pathways that make sense of ubiquitous information in a socially networked environment where multiple stakeholders all cooperate to meet user needs.

## USER EXPECTATIONS

As users increase their use of free Web services to discover and work with information, librarians have increased the ER in their libraries' collections and yet the shift by users away from a start of their information-discovery process in libraries has been significant.

- OCLC provides insights into the changes to the information environment; in particular, how users perceive libraries, what has happened to information, and what patterns help predict the future. A startling finding for academic libraries is that 89% of electronic information searches by college students begin with an Internet-based search engine while only 2% start at a library Web site.[4]
- The Pew Project highlights similar changes to the user's environment. For example, in *The Internet Goes to College 2002*, 73% of college students said they used the Internet more than the library.[5]

While the information environment has changed, tremendously, for users the impact on how libraries function is uncertain. One surprising outcome is a parallelism between information-seekers and ILL workers: both have increased and overlapping opportunities to locate information on the free Web. Whether the search is for free or fee-based information services, both users and ILL staff have the opportunity to seek alternatives to information content traditionally found at libraries or obtained through standard resource-sharing. However, the parallelism also extends to service expectations; the more experience users have with Web services the more they expect libraries to offer similar services.

## INFORMATION LANDSCAPE FOR RESOURCE SHARING

Academic ILL staff members are information-discovery experts and the exploration of information sources has been an essential part of the process that has migrated from a check of the National Union Catalog to the verification of citations on the Internet. The ILL process usually starts with a check of local holdings in a library catalog or a check of OCLC holdings. Resource-sharing employees check local holdings because, generally, about 10-15% of ILL requests are available in the library and have to be cancelled. A check of the OCLC database for a particular on-line title can mislead if it is a title from an aggregated database that may not be cataloged or the library's online holdings may not be reflected in OCLC because the libraries bibliographic record for the title is based on a print format. One of the challenges faced by users and resource-sharing staff alike is a lack in online public-access catalogs (OPAC) of a simple comprehensive search function that encompasses information resources, holdings, and services. While this frustrates the user, it is even more so to the ILL staff which, to be effective, must understand the strengths and weaknesses of several library systems and tools as well as explore beyond traditional bibliographic systems.

From a user's perspective the lack of a simple and comprehensive access point to information resources that are available in the library, regardless of format, complicates the process and delays content-delivery. Resources that often fall into this category include titles held in aggregators; specialized information sets such as ERIC documents; open access journals; and unpublished works. Many libraries limit the full expression of their electronic holdings to originating database sources or alternative resource database services such as CUFTS, Gold Rush, SerialsSolutions, SFX, or TDNet.

Although the rise of ubiquitous information and the associated growth in source options challenges, equally, mediated and unmediated ILL processes, the consistent value of the services offered to users by resource-sharing librarians is to locate and deliver information that is not otherwise conveniently discovered.

## WORKFLOW CHANGES

Perhaps the greatest change in resource-sharing workflow can be attributed to online resources. For libraries that, primarily, lend, those changes derive from the shift away from ownership of print-based collections to the license of ER. For those libraries that, primarily, borrow, it is the need to augment resources borrowed from other libraries with alternative resources from the free Web.

### Lending Workflow Migration: From Print to Licensed Resources

As libraries began to shift from the ownership of print-based serials to the license of access to online resources, the rules that govern the resource-sharing of a collection have undergone significant changes. While ILL staff have always been aware of copyright laws they must now learn licensing provisions, which may restrict access to ER. For example, licenses may specify how ER can be posted to the Web; or faxed or transmitted over Ariel™, a proprietary library to library file-transfer application. Many ILL terms in contracts mandate a print and scan of articles rather than the use of the source database's e-mail function or a digital transfer of the file that contains the article to Ariel™ for subsequent transmission to the borrower.

David Fowler provides background research into the basics of licenses and their impact on ILL. Fowler notes that early licenses were so unique that "every publisher re-invented the wheel," which caused great variations in their acceptability, quality, and usefulness.[6]

Because of this lack of information about the acceptable terms of use lending staff would rarely provide e-content to borrowers. According to Fowler, this began to change in 1995 when JSTOR and Project Muse became two of the earliest e-information vendors to employ a standard model of license terms that allowed ILL; the development of model licenses soon became common.[7]

For example, as part of a California Digital Library (CDL) license, "Vendors allow interlibrary loan between libraries for non-commercial purposes in compliance with Section 108 Interlibrary Loan provisions of copyright law."[8]

John Cox states that the "driving force behind the development of standard license language is a recognition of the need for a predictable environment in which model language can be found and used to express the outcome of most negotiations."[9]

Another driving force was the partnerships of resource-sharing professionals, serials staff, attorneys, and ER librarians who advocated to vendor/publishers favorable ILL terms for libraries. Besides work to negotiate better terms and provisions for ILL in licensed resources many librarians developed workflow to accommodate those terms and conditions. Janet Brennan Croft describes this approach, where library employees are "developing tools and procedures which aid . . . in complying with licensing terms that differ from the copyright regulations" as well as a few of the tools, i.e., the creation of title lists, the addition of local notes to MARC records, electronic rights/resources management software, etc.[10]

In the spring of 2002, OCLC introduced automatic-deflection and now a library can set the settings for resource-sharing in WorldCat to automatically cancel requests received to copy/lend electronic titles. Before the implementation of these automated deflections librarians must evaluate their long-term impact on access. Lynn Wiley makes a case for librarians to negotiate ILL friendly terms and concludes that, "Libraries must remain focused on maintaining access for their users . . . Remember that copyright in the USA was based on the principle that all need access to information for the good of all."[11]

While the use of standard license terms has made the use of a library's ER more congruent with workflows in lending units there are other types of licenses now emergent that have highly customized terminologies. Professionals with Creative Commons have imagined an innovative set of licenses that provide a range of protections for authors. These highly customized distinct instruments are usually favorable to educational use.[12]

While Creative Commons improves access, others that apply micro-rights management to content may prove too much of a challenge for scholarly works because they may never be visible enough to be effective or unobtrusive enough to be useful.

Some have questioned the future viability of resource-sharing in the face of increased availability as well as consortial purchases of ER. According to an ILL assessment project that looked at two other studies conducted in the State of Illinois (1995-1996 and 1999-2000), ILL use had increased 9% even though users had more ER available to them.[13]

It is clear from the latest study that the increased availability of ER increased the need for ILL, which may indicate that library users expect resource-sharing services to act like reference services; to find resources that are not obvious in library catalogs and databases.

### *The Borrowing Workflow Shift to Alternative Sources*

Another significant resource-sharing workflow change is the recognition of non-traditional sources from which to obtain digital information. Many members of ILL staffs now incorporate searches of the Internet into processes of requests, usually as a verification tool for incomplete or wrong citations, but also as a means to locate resources that are available on the free Web.

To illustrate the challenges of the traditional approach and the opportunities offered on the free Web that may be encountered by a resource-sharing professional who attempts to fill a user request for an online resource, consider this example:

An attempt to fill a request for the full-text of:

Atsushi Fujii and Tetsuya Ishikawa, "Organizing Encyclopedic Knowledge Based on the Web and Its Application to Question Answering," chapter in *Proceedings of the 39th Annual Meeting of the Association for Computational Linguistics (ACL-EACL 2001).*

A traditional ILL process of this request would start with a check of the availability of the item in library's catalog. Next, the search to locate and deliver the requested information might proceed as follows:

- A search in OCLC on title finds: six bibliographic records with 80 holdings; only one record with one holding has a link to the full-text (OCLC # 58973515). That link can be followed to: http://acl.ldc. upenn.edu/P/P01/P01-1026.pdf where a *browse by author* will locate the article in *ACL Anthology, A Digital Archive of Research Papers in Computational Linguistics* at the University of Pennsylvania.
- A search on Amazon for "ACL-EACL 2001" finds: the conference proceedings, which contains the article. The complete work can be purchased for $80.00.
- A search of the title on Google and Yahoo finds among the entries at the top of the hit list:

  - arXiv.org, an e-print service from Cornell University that covers the fields of physics, mathematics, non-linear science, computer science, and quantitative biology at: http://arxiv.org/abs/cs.CL/0106015
  - *ACL Anthology, A Digital Archive of Research Papers in Computational Linguistics* from the University of Melbourne at: http://www.cs.mu.oz.au/acl/P/P01/P01-1026.pdf
  - CiteSeer, IST Scientific Literature Digital Library from Pennsylvania State University at: http://citeseer.ist.psu.edu/fujii01 organizing.html

This example highlights how the electronic resource environment provides many access points, sources, and potential versions of requested items. While the location and delivery of requested information is still at the heart of the service the depth, breadth, and complexities of the information universe requires librarians to chart new paths beyond the traditional boundaries of the library. As more content is stored, indexed, and made available by digital repositories and libraries; open access journals and Web sites; and self-archiving by authors, free Web services, platforms, and search engines have become essential tools to locate content and verify citations. ILL staff often use free Web services to verify bibliographic citations, rather than use slower subscription-based databases in the library. The use of free Web services allows ILL staff to fill requests more quickly and more cost effectively.

Heather Morrison points out those articles found in pre-print or post-print digital repositories complicate the discussion of non-traditional ILL because multiple versions of an item may be discovered.[14]

However, in the case of Morrison's article as with many others the presence of a free pre-print online may be a benefit to a user as well as to library staff. Versions of Morrison's article exist as an online pre-print, which is available in a repository, and as a traditional publication in the *Journal of Interlibrary Loan, Document-Delivery & Electronic Reserve (JILLDDER)* 16(3) (2006). If there had been a request for this article in September 2005, an ILL specialist might have submitted the request to OCLC, which would have meant a long wait until the request was filled by a library (once it had received the JILLDDER issue that contained the article); a significant delay would be entailed as is the case with all ILL requests for upcoming issues of a journal or requests that are prompted as a result of pre-publication alert services. However, as in the case of Morrison's article, many articles can be located in pre-print repositories.

In her article, Morrison concludes that the paradox is that although open access may decrease the number of traditional ILL requests it also may mean an increase in "more complex requests requiring more expert knowledge and/or more advanced search skills."[15]

Indeed, the complexity of the information environment ensures that ILL personnel will handle more problem requests, and more communication with users and other library professionals will be required in order to solve problems in an effective fashion.

As resource-sharing workflow adapts to the existence of and requests for licensed resources and alternative sources library staff have developed strategies to better satisfy the information needs of patrons. Determinations as to whether or not a resource may be borrowed/lent through the ILL process and which version is it that the user really wants are two examples. In an environment of information ubiquity it is important to make sure that emergent library workflows and strategies meant to respond to the exigencies of the digital information age are networked in a process-oriented fashion designed to empower decision-making that spans the entire library organization; a collaborative structure of information nodes that looks at partnerships, Web services, communication, and the library community in new ways.

## EMERGENT STRATEGIES

The emergent strategies to deal with the challenges and opportunities to share online information through traditional and non-traditional ILL are indicative of the overall transformation of the library; as librarians adapt services to emergent user needs the demarcations among and between traditional library functions are blurred. Strategy-based convergence and partnerships with acquisitions personnel, collection development staff, managers of digital initiatives, reference librarians, and ILL workers help to increase the capability/efficiency of library services through the foster of better communication/service frameworks. Beyond internal partnerships, external collaborations with other libraries, vendor/publishers, and other content-providers extend the capability/capacity of librarians to meet the needs of users in the digital environment.

## PARTNERSHIP STRATEGIES

### Partnering with Digital Libraries

ILL professionals can be powerful partners to those involved with digital library initiatives as both are often involved in aspects of digitization. The opportunities (and convenience) offered by the capture of ILL scans and citation metadata, which encompass considerable information content, should not be overlooked. In an assessment of five years of ILL requests, which were scanned in order to be lent, at the University of Virginia, over 14,000 articles and chapters that were scanned or obtained from other libraries could have been contributed to a digital repository.[16]

Besides a reconfiguration of workflow to allow the deposit of a copy into a digital archive, the ILL system could automatically add the bibliographic data as well. If this workflow was centrally administered, i.e.,

OCLC's digital archive at http://www.oclc.org/digitalarchive/about/default.htm, the collection would grow based on, to some extent, patron demand and take advantage of the work that is already done at thousands of libraries.

## Partnering with Reference, Bibliographic Instruction, and Collection Management

A partnership among reference, bibliographic instruction, collection management, and ILL professionals is the process of requests for grey literature/unpublished material. Gray or grey literature has many definitions that include pre-prints, proceedings, technical reports, unpublished works, working papers, and other materials that are not commercial publications. This is often unique information/bibliographic citations that are discovered by users on the free Web. ILL services have often appeared ineffective at locating/obtaining grey literature. In an effort to provide a more effective service to researchers, the ILL workflow for grey literature at Portland State University was refocused on collaborative problem-solving through the combination of a number of functions:[7]

- Evaluate the nature of grey literature requests through the identification of the sources of the citations
- Collaborate with subject specialists, authors, and users to locate and collect the grey literature
- Provide bibliographic instruction on grey literature
- Use ILL data to assess collection needs for grey literature

The short-term implication for the library is clear: collaborative engagement by reference, bibliographic instruction, collection management, and ILL professionals is the best service scenario to aid researchers who use unpublished works.

## Partnering with Cataloging

Effective partnerships among cataloging, collection management, and ILL staff are important to make open access resources more accessible to library users. The Directory of Open Access Journals (DOAJ) lists 2,334 scholarly journals (as of 6 August 2006) that offer free, full-text access. However, library users often initiate an ILL request for open access content because:

- The knowledgebase that populates the library's link-resolution tool may not include the resource
- The library OPAC/OCLC holdings may not include the resource
- Users may overlook the relevant open access link because the print and online records are separate in the OPAC

## Partnering with Acquisitions and Web-Based Book Sellers

ILL professionals have a long history of collaboration with staff from the acquisitions and collection management units in the identification of frequently requested titles to consider for purchase. Librarians have begun to see ILL requests as an opportunity for an acquisition request through the parsing of selected requests based on established collection-building criteria. In a recent study of ILL requests, Holley and Ankem conclude that "for monographs, purchase may be a reasonable substitute for interlibrary loan."[18]

Out-of-print booksellers have made the process to discover and obtain printed books as well as online books and chapters on the Internet easy and straightforward.

Alibris demonstrates its recognition of the convergence of acquisitions and ILL requests as it offers book purchases via OCLC ILL requests. This service convergence will lead to the development of advanced technologies and tools as better ways to evaluate ILL requests are developed. Through the use of automated-parsing based on machine-readable profiles, the cost and availability of out-of-print resources may be taken from vendor/publisher databases.

Such emergent partnerships are important because they create a new library service framework with convergence based on user needs and strategic opportunities.

> Through new partnerships ILL professionals provide a *resolving function* in library services that attempts to provide strategic pathways to information within the library that are needed by users. Libraries "should move beyond the role of collector and organizer of content, print and digital, to one that establishes the authenticity and provenance of content and provides the imprimatur of quality in an information rich but context-poor world.[19]

At the intersection of users and information, an ILL staff handles more than a user information request; they deliver an authentic content experiment through the use of new collaborative service models that encourage work with alternative information suppliers that are competitors as well as partners.

## EXPERIMENTING WITH WEB SERVICES STRATEGIES

Emergent resource-sharing strategies include experimentation with Web services library customers often already use, e.g., the purchase or rent of videos in lieu of a borrow of them and the use of peer-to-peer sharing networks. Librarians frustrated with unsuccessful or slow attempts to borrow popular video titles from other libraries have discovered alternatives, i.e., the purchase of videos from online companies and the use of subscription-based rent services, e.g., Netflix. In addition to the purchase of videos online, e.g., through Amazon.com, other new e-sources have emerged, e.g., iTunes at http://www.apple.com/itunes/videos/ and Google Video at http://video.google.com/. Peer-to-peer networks designed as reader resource-sharing groups are Web services that provide opportunities to experiment with new sources for ILL work. For example, Paperbackswap.com allows readers to post, in an online database, the titles they will exchange; if a title is requested and delivered, the sender receives credit to use to order a book from the service. In tests of this service, the University of Virginia Libraries ILL staff made 24 requests; the average turn-around time was six days. These and other Web services offer all library users attractive options that librarians can also offer; this is especially true of titles that have proven difficult to borrow through traditional means, audio-visual materials, and popular literature. In addition to the use of Web services as sources of content, librarians must also evaluate emergent Web services for a host of other applications in communication and education.

## COMMUNICATION STRATEGIES

While libraries, especially ILL units, have excelled in the early stages of global-networking, communication and collaborative technologies have not expanded as well as other technologies have.[20]

However, the introduction of VoIP (Voice-over-Internet Protocol) and other technologies has begun to change that situation rapidly. "VoIP will serve as a platform for more strategic communications that combine voice with other data-so-called 'converged communications.'"[21]

At the University of Virginia Interlibrary Services, a test has begun in the use of Skype™, VoIP software that provides additional internal communication tools and is used for some external communication with other libraries. Benefits of VoIP applications include:

- Resource-sharing networks with virtually free long-distance calls between libraries and customized delivery systems for article and file transfers along with phone and voice notifications
- Social contact awareness that allows users to see an icon that indicates a contact is available to receive a call
- Chat, conference calls, broadcast calls, and file transfers

UVA librarians foresee VoIP software incorporated into a global library and policies directory and interoperable with request management software. Through the incorporation of VoIP as a platform, library systems personnel could strategically connect library services through a strengthening of the global network and the improvement of communication with users. The range of partnerships, Web services, and communication tools as emergent strategies underlies one of the most important aspects of the future of resource-sharing in libraries.

## EDUCATION AND TRAINING STRATEGIES

A renewed effort to provide better education and training in libraries has been the most critical strategy to emerge in the area of resource-sharing in the face of so much change brought on in the digital age. While much of the effort over the last two decades focused on the implementation of new request management and imaging software and other new technologies, a shift towards best practices, mentoring, and e-learning has taken hold in the resource-sharing community. Best practice topics range from fast/cost-effective workflow, i.e., purchase-on-demand (a form of just-in-time acquisitions), to a variety of issues associated with copyright and licensing, tips to find resources on the Web, and international ILL. These are all strong efforts towards community knowledge-building. At the same time, networks within national and regional associations have developed new strategies, tools, workshops, and tutorials in order to better anticipate and meet the needs of users as well as changes in the information environment.

ILL professionals have actively networked in order to satisfy their education and training needs so that they may in turn meet user information requirements and overcome challenges associated with the delivery of information. This trend is evident in the resource-sharing discussion list at http://lists.webjunction.org/mailman/listinfo/ill-l as well as in the development of guides like those found at ILL Web: http://www.law.northwestern.edu/lawlibrary/illweb/.

Further, there are ILL 101 tutorials and workshops in ALA RUSA STARS. However, there is still a need for cooperative training programs that stretch across library functions and anticipate principles of service convergence and hybridization. A starting place for the development of library-wide training programs is to identify core competencies or essential knowledge and skills for success. Examples of Library core competency are easily found:

- Reference & User Services Association (RUSA), a division of the American Library Association (ALA)

  o Professional Competencies for Reference & User Services Librarians: http://www.ala.org/ala/rusa/rusaprotools/referenceguide/professional.htm

- California Library Association (CLA)

  o Technology Core Competencies for California Library Workers: http://www.cla.net.org/included/docs/tech_core_competencies.pdf

- Special Library Association (SLA)

  o Competencies for Information Professionals of the 21st Century: http://www.sla.org/content/learn/comp2003/index.cfm

Core competencies help clarify employment expectations and they are variously implemented within an organization, i.e., hiring, interviewing, training programming, evaluating and supervising. Established core competencies are useful in the development of training programs that are informed by organizational requirements. UVA ILL staff has piloted a practical example with the creation of a Library and Information Architecture Certificate Program (see Figure 1), which provides core library knowledge for ILL services and other areas of the library. The basic requirements to earn the certificate are to attend a series of training sessions:

- ○ MARC Basics
- ○ Finding ER, Part I: University Library Resources and Finding ER, Part II: Alternative Resources
- ○ Bibliographic Verification

The certificate/program represents an effort to share knowledge about the changing information environment and to prepare staff for a future of resource-sharing activities that will encompass a greater variety of workflow options and responsibilities.

## THE FUTURE OF RESOURCE-SHARING

"One can state one of the major challenges facing libraries in these terms. Historically, users have built their workflow around the services the library provides. As we move forward, the reverse will increasingly be the case. On the network, the library needs to build its services around its users' work- and learn-flows."[22]

### Resource Sharing Tools:
### Request Management and Context Sensitive Workflow

The challenge to design new staff interfaces and workflows that are flexible enough to take advantage of a variety of service options parallels the library user's information environment. The plethora of discovery and fulfillment/get options must be ameliorable to the needs of the individual user as well as the institution. If a user needs an article that is not available in a library subscription database, they should be made aware of copies in other institutional repositories. If the article cannot be found there, the ILL request system and workflow must be able to interface with Web searches to verify the record or locate the item without the need for an ILL request from another library. For popular titles or videos that are a challenge to borrow, the ILL request system must display the cost to rent/buy the item and interface with supplier systems.

ILL workflows must be designed to take advantage of the same information environment as that encountered by library users. They must be simple, flexible realistic interfaces that accommodate variations in institutional policies and practices.

FIGURE 1. UVA ILL Information Architecture Certificate Program

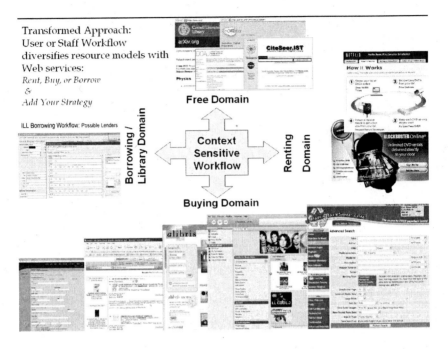

## THE FUTURE OF SERVICE

Self-service and pre-service are models for user experiences and service expectations. While it is, currently, quite easy to place ILL requests or download articles from a list of citations based on a keyword search, libraries must develop better tools to provide context and guides in both unmediated and mediated settings. The information-seeker has many options to find information online. Librarians must guide and provide services that are specific to the user's situation and purpose. How services, such as resource-sharing, are shaped in order to provide context at points of need will inform the design and workflow of ILL and lead to the redesign of relational services offered by reference and other library units. One of the goals of the library of the future must be to resolve many of the ambiguities that surface as a result of attempts to provide access to online resources and services.

## THE FUTURE OF LIBRARIES

Scholarly publishers; peer-to-peer and social networks; and blogs, wikis and other learning communities have created an information environment crisis for librarians. Resource-sharing employees must determine their role to help information-seekers. Librarians must provide innovative services that are collaborative learning networks/communities, e.g., SourceForge, an Open Source software development site that provides a variety of Web services; it hosts over 100,000 projects that serve over 1,000,000 users;[23] social networking and bookmarking tools; or architectures of collaborative participation, e.g., Connotea, del.icio.us, CiteULike, and Flickr.[24] Libraries have an enormous stake in the cultivation of learning communities, which thrive on the sharing of high quality information and the creation of new knowledge. Library ILL personnel are well-equipped to partner with these innovative services. As e-resources become entangled with social networks, and scholarly content from online communities increases, resource-sharing and reference staff will, necessarily, work closer to resolve the future challenges that they and library patrons will face.

In order to provide that resolution librarians must better understand and engage in the emergent online environment. An important way for that process to begin would be to utilize the strength of social networks and online communities and use them to communicate and share locally and regionally generated knowledge and training. Librarians must create a community framework that stores, shares, and repackages library projects, work, and information across the functional divides of libraries, i.e., acquisitions, cataloging, reference, etc. The approach requires several components:

- Develop or use an existing central repository of library information, i.e., documents like LIS e-prints at: http://eprints.rclis.org/
- Develop or use an online learning community, e.g., the Multimedia Educational Resource for Learning and Online Teaching (Merlot) at http://www.merlot.org/Home.po, which has over 130 LIS learning objects (see: http://www.merlot.org/artifact/BrowseArtifacts.po?catcode=235&browsecat=233). Other online learning communities include Online Programming for All Libraries at http://www.opal-online.org/about.html and the Blended Librarian at http://blended librarian.org/, which uses LearningTimes, LLC as its online learning environment (see: http://home.learningtimes.net/library

- Create a director or namespace registry in order to link the projects and resources of libraries and related organizations together

## *CONCLUSION*

Knowledge-sharing is very similar to resource-sharing in that they both rely on partnerships. In order to address the opportunities and challenges of electronic information resources as well as to endure the successful digital transformation of the library world, partnerships must be formed and exploited. ILL staff will play a powerful role in this transformation as they develop new strategies for the delivery of e-information; promote learning and research; and encourage learning communities. In addition, they must advocate for the creation of new partnerships in order to transform library services because the nature of user requests/expectations links libraries to outside organizations and beyond traditional services. Innovative services must be designed in order to affect satisfactory user and staff experiences that reflect a changed world. Librarians address, on a daily basis, the dichotomy between the familiar/traditional and the remade in their efforts to meet the needs/expectations of information consumers. As a result, ILL workers focus as never before on education and training as critical requirements to gain the knowledge and skills required for the work. The changes ahead for librarians will be a shared experience. The creation of new partnerships, enhanced workflows, the utilization of Web services, and effective communication are fundamental to the reshaping of library services to the user community. The development and sharing of knowledge and resources provides opportunities to build pathways to a successful transition for libraries in the digital age.

## NOTES

1. "Reports: Technology and Media Use," http://www.pewinternet.org/PPFr/184/report_display.asp (viewed February 19, 2006).

2. Edward O'Neill, Brian F. Lavoie, and Rick Bennett, "Trends in the Evolution of the Public Web," *D-Lib Magazine* 9(4) (April 2003); (viewed February 19, 2006).

3. "2004 Information Trends: Content Not Containers," http://www5.oclc.org/downloads/community/2004infotrends_content.pdf (viewed February 19, 2006).

4. "Community Membership Reports: Perceptions of Libraries and Information Resources (2005)," http://www.oclc.org/reports/2005perceptions.htm (viewed February 19, 2006).

5. "Reports: Education," http://www.pewinternet.org/PPF/r/71/report_display.asp (viewed February 19, 2006).

6. David C. Fowler, "Licensing: An Historical Perspective," *Journal of Library Administration* 42(3/4) (2005): 177-197.

7. Ibid., 181.

8. "Acquiring Digital Resources: The Licensing Process," http://www.cdlib.org/vendors/licensingprocess.html (viewed February 19, 2006).

9. John Cox, "Model Generic Licenses: Cooperation and Competition," *Serials Review* 26(1) (2000): 3.

10. Janet Brennan Croft, "Interlibrary Loan and Licensing: Tools for Proactive Contract Management," *Journal of Library Administration* 42(3/4) (2005): 44-45.

11. Lynn N. Wiley, "License to Deny? Publisher Restriction on Document-delivery from E-licensed Journals," *Interlending & Document Supply* 32(2) (2004): 101.

12. "Creative Commons: Enabling the legal sharing and reuse of cultural, educational, and scientific works," http://creativecommons.org/ (viewed February 19, 2006).

13. Lynn Wiley and Tina E. Chrzastowski, "The Illinois Interlibrary Loan Assessment Project II: Revisiting Statewide Article Sharing and Assessing the Impact of Electronic Full-text Journals," *Library Collections, Acquisitions, & Technical Services* 26 (2002): 30.

14. Heather G. Morrison, "The Dramatic Growth of Open Access: Implications and Opportunities for Resource Sharing," *Journal of Interlibrary Loan, Document-delivery & Electronic Reserve* 16(3) (2006): 21); http://eprints.rclis.org/archive/00004558/ (viewed September 23, 2005).

15. Ibid., p. 23.

16. Cyril Oberlander, "Collaborative Strategies for Collection Development and Resource Sharing," presentation at the 3rd Annual NW Interlibrary Loan and Resource Sharing Conference, September 15, 2005; http://www.oclcwestern.org/nwill/2005/oberlander.ppt (viewed February 19, 2006).

17. Sherry Buchanan, Rose Jackson, and Cyril Oberlander, "Can Cooperative Service Solve the Grey Literature Challenge?" *OLA* 10(2/3) (fall 2004): 8-9.

18. Robert Holley and Kalyani Ankem, "The Effect of the Internet on the Out-of-print Book Market: Implications for Libraries," *Library Collections, Acquisitions & Technical Services* 29 (2005): 118-139.

19. "2004 Information Trends," http://www5.oclc.org/downloads/community/2004infotrends_content.pdf (viewed February 19, 2006).

20. "The Social Landscape," http://www.oclc.org/reports/escan/downloads/social.pdf (viewed February 19, 2006).

21. Kevin Werbach, "Using VoIP to Compete," *Harvard Business Review* 83(9) (September 2005): 140.

22. "Lorcan Dempsey's Weblog: On Libraries, Services, and Networks," http://orweblog.oclc.org/archives/000933.html (viewed August 8, 2006).

23. "Document A01, SourceForge.net: What Is SourceForge.net?" http://sourceforge.net/docs/about (viewed February 19, 2006).

24. Tony Hammond et al., "Social Bookmarking Tools (I): A General Review," *D-Lib Magazine* 11(4) (April 2005): http://www.dlib.org/dlib/april05/hammond/04hammond.html (viewed February 19, 2006).

doi:10.1300/J105v32n01_14

# Improving Access to Electronic Resources (ER) Through Usability Testing

## Laura S. Wrubel

**SUMMARY.** Electronic resources (ER) constitute an increasingly significant portion of library collections, both in usage and cost. It is vital to design easy, efficient access to these collections as users have other online options to meet their information needs. Thus, an important goal for ER librarians is to provide a usable ER site. Formal usability testing is a powerful tool to help librarians create the most useful site for their customers. This chapter will cover the basic components of usability testing and suggest ways in which ER librarians can lead efforts in their institution to improve the customer experience with library Web sites. ER librarians can create buy-in from library staff for usability testing as a worthwhile method to improve access to ER through involvement in the process and sharing results of the testing. The responsibilities of ER librarians vary from one institution to another, but all share in the mission of the profession to serve its customers' information needs. This chapter addresses the possibilities of usability testing as a force to maximize the user experience with the collections ER librarians manage. doi:10.1300/J105v32n01_15 *[Article copies available for a fee from The Haworth Document Delivery Service: 1-800-HAWORTH. E-mail address: <docdelivery@haworthpress.com> Website: <http://www.HaworthPress.com> © 2007 by The Haworth Press. All rights reserved.]*

---

Laura S. Wrubel, MLS, is ER and Systems Librarian, McKeldin Library, University of Maryland, College Park, MD 20742-7011 (E-mail: lwrubel@umd.edu).

[Haworth co-indexing entry note]: "Improving Access to Electronic Resources (ER) Through Usability Testing." Wrubel, Laura S. Co-published simultaneously in *Collection Management* (The Haworth Information Press, an imprint of The Haworth Press) Vol. 32, No. 1/2, 2007, pp. 225-234; and: *Electronic Resources Librarianship and Management of Digital Information: Emerging Professional Roles* (ed: Mark Jacobs) The Haworth Information Press, an imprint of The Haworth Press, 2007, pp. 225-234. Single or multiple copies of this article are available for a fee from The Haworth Document Delivery Service [1-800-HAWORTH, 9:00 a.m. - 5:00 p.m. (EST). E-mail address: docdelivery@haworthpress.com].

Available online at http://col.haworthpress.com
© 2007 by The Haworth Press. All rights reserved.
doi:10.1300/J105v32n01_15

**KEYWORDS.** Usability testing, user research, Web site design, electronic resources

## *INTRODUCTION*

Imagine a library with a wide-ranging, expensive book collection, but no catalog, no call numbers, and no librarians available to help patrons locate the books they need. This is the situation users may face when they try to use a library's Web site for online research. While librarians have designed Web sites to steer users to the best databases and e-journals, each library may arrange e-resources differently. Some librarians approach the organization of electronic resources (ER) by creating lists and subject directories. Others offer search tools or use the catalog to provide access. As a result, users have to learn a new interface for each site they visit.

Because of the complex and varied nature of online resources, these collections can be difficult to present in a clear, easily navigable way. The public has become accustomed to performing daily tasks online, e.g., banking, making travel reservations, and keeping up with news.[1] They expect to be able to use the library's ER as quickly and without assistance, much as they use Google and other Internet search engines to find information.

A well-designed library Web site takes into consideration the goals and needs of its audience, whether that audience includes students, faculty, professionals, or the general public. Library Web sites are, usually, well- designed and implemented, but how can librarians be sure that their customers are able to use the site effectively? What assumptions do users make about how online research should be conducted and how do those assumptions affect their ability to find the ER they need? In the face of such questions, to provide a *usable* ER site is an important goal for an ER librarian. Usability testing can be a powerful tool to help answer such questions and to help librarians create the most useful sites for their customers.

For ER librarians, usability testing is a new endeavor and, if an institution has a usability testing program, it might be managed in any number of departments. What are the advantages of ER librarians leading usability testing at their institution and how might the process be managed across departments? What skills and education are needed for usability testing efforts? How might the process change the library's workflow, and what might be the end result for users?

## WHAT IS USABILITY?

Usability encompasses characteristics such as effectiveness, learnability, usefulness, helpfulness, and satisfaction.[2] The International Organization for Standardization (ISO) has defined usability as "the extent to which a product can be used by specified users to achieve specified goals with effectiveness, efficiency, and satisfaction in a specified context of use."[3] Usability goes beyond whether a site is functional and comprises the ability of users to learn, understand, and navigate the site easily. Ultimately, user ability to accomplish work when they use the site determines its success.[4]

There are a number of factors which can affect a library site's usability. The navigational structure must make sense to a user who has little experience with research or who approaches the research process in a different way than might a librarian. The user should be able to predict link destinations and how each section of the site is different from others.[5] The language used on the site is closely related to the link structure. Do users understand the meaning of terms they read on database, e-journal, and e-resource Web sites? Do terms on the site used to describe concepts match user language, or are they library jargon? The ability of a site to be easily scanned and quickly understood also affects usability. Large blocks of text with well-intended instructions can undermine a site's usability as the elements users look for are obscured and navigation obstructed. The factors described above contribute to or detract from usability more than colors, images, fonts, or other graphic elements. While graphic design has a role in the creation of a visually pleasing Web page, engineers have found that it plays little role in a site's usability.[6]

To provide a usable site is good customer service.[7] An easy-to-use site earns user loyalty while an unusable site frustrates and drives users away. A site's usability will determine whether or not customers return to the site, which is an important consideration in a world where libraries must compete with other online information providers. Librarians know the value of their ER collections, but unless they provide easy-to-learn systems for access in an unmediated, online environment, users will go elsewhere.

### Why Formal Usability Testing?

User research, e.g., focus groups, surveys, and interviews, can provide valuable information about user assumptions, needs, and goals. Heuristic analysis, or a "usability audit," in which evaluators review a site for particular usability problems, can also be an effective evaluation technique.[8] However, there is no better way to understand how users interact with a site than by direct observation of users in the course of their work. This chapter will focus on formal usability testing as an important tool in the assessment of the success of a site. Early on, basic usability testing can reveal major problems and allow librarians to offer users the best site possible. Dumas and Redish characterize formal usability testing as follows:

1. The primary goal is to improve the usability of a product. For each test, there are also more specific goals and concerns that are articulated when a test is planned.
2. The participants are representative of real users.
3. The participants perform real tasks.
4. The evaluators observe and record what participants do and say.
5. The evaluators analyze the data, diagnose the problem, and recommend changes to fix the problems.[9]

Through direct observation of users, librarians can gather rich data about real user behavior on their site and thus gather data which will have the greatest impact on an evaluation of the usability of their site. Later in this chapter, the components of a formal usability test and how to share results of those tests will be discussed.

## THE ROLE OF THE ER LIBRARIAN

ER librarians are in a unique position to initiate and lead usability testing in their organizations. As keepers of usage and cost-benefit data on licensed resources, they understand the stakes involved in ensuring that patrons can find and use the library's ER. Their involvement in all aspects of delivery of ER allows them a broad perspective as they guide development of e-content delivery systems. For example, the terms and conditions of licenses as well as technical requirements impact the design of databases and e-journal Web sites. Licenses often require that librarians make a reasonable effort to notify users about conditions on use of licensed content. Librarians might be required to immediately post information about copyright or the number of permitted simultaneous users. Other resources may require instructions to obtain usernames and passwords or directions on the use of the library's proxy server for remote access.

Usability testing gives ER librarians an opportunity to develop an informed understanding of the problems users face in their online research as well as common usability problems they encounter when they use electronic collections. Many ER librarians have duties in more than one department and have regular contact with the library's customers. They may learn about user difficulties with ER while they provide technical support for patrons who encounter error messages and other access problems with databases and e-journals or while they provide virtual or in-person reference assistance, during bibliographic instruction, or through other public services activities.

In addition to being able to influence design of the library's access to electronic collections, ER librarians also play a role in the development of the interfaces which vendors provide for access to their databases and online journals. Librarian relationships with e-resource vendors/publishers provide them with an opportunity to provide feedback on common problems which are encountered by users with product interfaces. They can also help vendors/publishers understand the issues librarians are concerned with and the challenges they face to provide access to digital products. Vendors/publishers may offer ER librarians opportunities to serve on advisory boards or participate in product usability studies of their own. The results of library-sponsored usability testing may also be of interest to vendors/publishers whose products were included in the test.

In the development and implementation of a usability testing program, there are a number of individuals an ER librarian might involve in the process. Those most involved with the design and maintenance of the library's Web site, such as the Webmaster or Web designer, should be included as should members of the library's Web advisory or Web administration committee. Those responsible for collection management are stakeholders who may not need to be involved in the testing itself, but have an interest in the usability of a costly segment of the library's collection. Reference and user education staff can contribute through their knowledge of user experiences and questions as well as through their understanding of user assumptions and expectations. Other staff may have to be recruited to help with the testing process itself.

## AREAS OF THE WEB SITE TO TEST

While the ER librarian may already be aware of problem areas in the Web site, basic user research can reveal other trouble spots and focus the testing. Pre-assessment techniques might include print or online surveys and focus groups.[10] These tools can help the usability testing team gather information about typical tasks users want to perform on the site and their expectations concerning access to ER.

The areas of the library's Web site that provide access to databases and e-journals are often among its most heavily used sections and should be the primary focus of the ER librarian. The design of upper-level pages, e.g., the home page, which serve as gateways to ER should also be a focus of the testing. At many libraries, link resolvers, portals, and meta-search systems are available to users and may be so integrated into the user experience with ER that they should be included in any testing of e-resources delivery as well. Finally, the program might be expanded to address other areas of the Web site, e.g., the catalog, subject guides, and other pages designed to aid library customers. Involvement and partnerships with stakeholders in other areas of the Web site may help build a broader and stronger usability testing program.

Usability testing can play a role in collection development decisions. A database's search interface affects the user's ability to successfully find what he or she needs. An interface that frustrates users may cause them to turn to other online resources or leave the library's site altogether. Some databases and e-journals are available from more than one vendor, and ER librarians and collection managers should consider the usability of each vendor's interface in the selection of resources. Formal usability testing can be a helpful technique in the evaluation of these interfaces. Of course, an improvement of a vendor interface is beyond the librarian's immediate control. The greatest improvement is possible with those sites to which librarians can directly apply the findings of usability testing.

### Conducting Formal Usability Testing

After a determination is made as to which areas of the Web site are to be tested, the next step is to consider the goals of the site and develop a set of task scenarios which users should be able to accomplish. The results of preliminary user research may guide the development of sample tasks, but page authors and other librarians familiar with the content may also be able to point out potential trouble spots.[11] These should be tasks which are commonly performed by users on the site as well as popular sections uncovered by user research. In academic institutions, there may be information literacy goals for students, and those might be considered in the creation of sample tasks. Tests of pages which provide access to ER might include the selection of a database, a search for a particular article, and locating a specific issue of an e-journal. Scenarios which users might encounter in everyday life, e.g., background research for a report, might also be included.

During the usability test, a facilitator, usually a neutral party not directly involved in the design and management of the Web site, will present a list of tasks to a participant. This participant will then try to use the Web site to accomplish each task; as the test progresses the participant will be asked to speak his or her thoughts and reactions aloud. Approaches to usability testing may vary, but the "think aloud" protocol, where participants use the site while they describe their experience out loud, offers a balance of efficiency in terms of time commitment and quantity versus quality of data gathered.[12] The facilitator prompts the participant to explain choices and expectations as they use the site; the facilitator must avoid any tendency to lead the user.

A simple way to record the test is to set up a video camera to monitor both the computer screen and the participant. Software can also be used to capture the screen display and, when connected to a digital camera, the participants' comments and facial expressions. If possible, allow others in another room to view the tests by running a cable from the video camera or use software to remotely view the session.

An effective usability test does not require a large number of users. In fact, as few as five participants can discover 85% of the problems with a particular site.[13] What is more important is to test continuously as the site is improved and ensure that each attempt to address user problems accomplishes its goal.[14]

> When participants are recruited, consider categories of users. At an academic library, categories might include faculty, undergraduate and graduate students, administrators, and library staff. A special library may find it appropriate to include researchers, members, or the general public. An offer of incentives may help in recruitment, but some participants may find the experience itself enough reward. An academic library with student workers might require participation in usability testing as a part of its training process. The library benefits by having a local pool of test participants who gain an understanding of the problems library patrons may face.

No matter who participates in a usability test, obtain informed consent before recording a session and protect participants from feeling as though they are being tested or evaluated.[15] The site is being tested, not the participants. In an academic setting, follow any policies and procedures for working with human subjects.

## INTERPRETING AND USING TEST RESULTS

Usability testing produces rich data, but testers can be overwhelmed by the length of the recordings which must be transcribed and the amount of notes which must be taken and summarized. An alternative is to write and share brief reports. Through the course of the tests common problems with the Web site will emerge, e.g., difficulty understanding labels, problems with the general concept of the page, or an inability to find particular items on a busy page.[16] One way to summarize testing data is to create a list of frequently encountered problems. This may be done task by task or in consideration of the tests as a whole. Other methods of analysis might include an evaluation of how long it took each participant to complete each task, or a count of the number of clicks or steps needed to complete each task.[17]

The results from the first round of tests should allow the ER librarian to improve the Web page by an implementation of recommended changes, and then test again. Usability testing is an iterative process and ongoing rounds to test, evaluate, and revise will lead to the best end result.[18]

In order to integrate usability testing into the library's overall approach to providing access to ER, the ER librarian should share results on the progress of usability testing with interested parties in the organization, e.g., reference and instruction committees; Web design teams; and public relations staff and administration. Sharing results is part of the process to create buy-in for usability testing and to demonstrate its worth as a method to improve the Web site. Those who see the test results may be surprised by what they reveal about what library users found difficult with the site. To view recorded video-clips of the tests or read transcribed comments may be an eye-opening experience for librarians. As Dumas explained,

> One of the important assets of testing is that it sells itself. Watching a few minutes of live testing can be very persuasive. . . . When people see their first live test they are almost always fascinated by what they see. They gain an understanding of the value of the method. . . . Some of them will even become advocates for testing.[19]

A quick demonstration of a usability test, at a staff meeting or for smaller groups, can be powerful persuasion for others of the value of usability testing and may dispel misconceptions about the cost and complexity of testing. Marty and Twidale developed a thirty-minute, high-speed demonstration of live usability testing which was aimed at the education of others about usability and to create a "culture of usability."[20] To watch remotely a testing session in progress may help others understand the worth of usability testing.

In addition to sharing results, the ER librarian can build an understanding of usability testing by becoming the local expert.[21] A number of practical manuals on usability testing are available and can provide guidance to run tests, analyze data, and integrate usability testing into the Web development process. E-mail lists, such as Web4Lib and Usability4Lib, may also provide support.[22] As others in the organization become interested in usability testing, an information workshop or discussion group may help further broaden buy-in.[23]

Beyond the improvement of user experience with a library's ER, usability testing may challenge librarian assumptions about library customers.[24] As librarians better understand what customers want and expect from the library, their attitudes may change. Users may have their own ideas about the Internet and the role of the library in their research and education which may encourage librarians to reconsider their approach to meet library patron information needs.

## NOTES

1. Deborah Fallows, *The Internet and Daily Life* (Washington, DC: Pew Internet & American Life Project, 2004); http://www.pewinternet.org/pdfs/PIP_Internet_and_Daily_Life.pdf (viewed September 5, 2005).

2. Judy Jeng, "What Is Usability in the Context of the Digital Library and How Can It Be Measured?" *Information Technology and Libraries* 24(2) (June 2005): 49.

3. Ibid., 48.

4. Joseph S. Dumas and Janice C. Redish, *A Practical Guide to Usability Testing*, rev. ed. (Portland, OR: Intellect Books, 1999), 4.

5. Jared M. Spool et al., *Web Site Usability: A Designer's Guide* (San Francisco: Morgan Kaufmann, 1999), 33.

6. Ibid., 9.

7. Deborah G. Mayhew and Randolph G. Bias, "Cost-Justifying Web Usability," in *Human Factors and Web Development*, 2nd ed. (Mahwah, New Jersey: Lawrence Erlbaum, 2003), 65.

8. Mary Pagliero Popp, "Testing Library Web Sites: ARL Libraries Weigh In" presentation at the ACRL Tenth National Conference, Denver, Colorado, March 15-18, 2001), 278.

9. Dumas and Redish, 22.

10. Elaina Norlin and CM! Winters, *Usability Testing for Library Web Sites* (Chicago: American Library Association, 2002), 24-26.

11. Dumas and Redish, 160-163.

12. M. J. Van den Haak, M. D. T. de Jong, and P. J. Schellens, "Employing Think-Aloud Protocols and Constructive Interaction to Test the Usability of Online Library Catalogues: A Methodological Comparison,"*Interacting with Computers* 16(6) (December 2004): 1168-1169.

13. Jakob Nielsen, "Why You Only Need to Test with Five Users," http://www. useit.com/alertbox/20000319.html (viewed September 3, 2005).

14. Ibid.

15. Steve Krug, *Don't Make Me Think: A Common Sense Approach to Web Usability* (Indianapolis, IN: New Riders, 2000), 155.

16. Ibid., 178.

17. Dumas and Redish, 185.

18. Nielsen, "Why You Only Need . . ."

19. Paul F. Marty and Michael B. Twidale, "Usability@90mph: Presenting and Evaluating a New High-Speed Method for Demonstrating User Testing in Front of an Audience," *First Monday* 10(7) (July 2005); http://www.firstmonday.org/issues/issue10_7/marty/index.html (viewed September 3, 2005).

20. Ibid.

21. Norlin and Winters, 20.

22. "Web4Lib (Web Systems in Libraries)," http://lists.webjunction.org/web4lib/ (viewed September 3, 2005); "Usability4Lib," http://www.lib.rochester.edu/index.cfm? PAGE=652 (viewed September 3, 2005).

23. Norlin and Winters, 23.

24. Dumas and Redish, 32.

doi:10.1300/J105v32n01_15

# FUTURE PARADOX: PARADIGM SHIFTS AND BUSINESS AS USUAL

## Can This Orthodoxy Be Saved? Enhancing the Usefulness of Collection Plans in the Digital Environment

Carolynne Myall

Sue Anderson

**SUMMARY.** This chapter discusses collection plans in the context of the current information environment with its mix of formats and its accelerated migration towards digital resources; and identifies problems with regard to the development of useful plans. The authors present the re-

Carolynne Myall is Head of Collection Services (E-mail: cmyall@mail.ewu.edu); and Sue Anderson is Acquisitions/ER Librarian (E-mail: sanderson@mail.ewu.edu, both at Eastern Washington University).

The authors thank the respondents to their survey. They also thank Marty Kurth (Cornell University) for reviewing their survey questions, and Jonathan Potter (EWU) and Sydney Chambers (Gonzaga University) for reviewing their draft.

[Haworth co-indexing entry note]: "Can This Orthodoxy Be Saved? Enhancing the Usefulness of Collection Plans in the Digital Environment." Myall, Carolynne, and Sue Anderson. Co-published simultaneously in *Collection Management* (The Haworth Information Press, an imprint of The Haworth Press) Vol. 32, No. 3/4, 2007, pp. 235-258; and: *Electronic Resources Librarianship and Management of Digital Information: Emerging Professional Roles* (ed: Mark Jacobs) The Haworth Information Press, an imprint of The Haworth Press, 2007, pp. 235-258. Single or multiple copies of this article are available for a fee from The Haworth Document Delivery Service [1-800-HAWORTH, 9:00 a.m. - 5:00 p.m. (EST). E-mail address: docdelivery@haworthpress.com].

Available online at http://col.haworthpress.com
© 2007 by The Haworth Press. All rights reserved.
doi:10.1300/J105v32n03_01

sults of an informal mailing list survey of collection development and electronic resources (ER) librarians; questions pertain to collection plans and, also, to professional preparation and continuing education, patterns of collaboration, and additional topics related to the work of the plan and management of collections that include digital resources. The authors provide suggestions for the improvement of the long-term value and immediate usefulness of collection plans in the digital environment and speculate about the qualities of the individuals who might bring about these changes. doi:10.1300/J105v32n03_01 *[Article copies available for a fee from The Haworth Document Delivery Service: 1-800-HAWORTH. E-mail address: <docdelivery@haworthpress.com> Website: <http://www.HaworthPress.com> © 2007 by The Haworth Press. All rights reserved.]*

**KEYWORDS.** Collection plans, collection development, electronic resources, collection development librarians

## INTRODUCTION

*Collection management* is an umbrella term that covers activities in the development and maintenance of a library's array of information resources: not only selection of resources for purchase or license, but, also, determination of budgets and allocations; inclusion or exclusion of free or donated resources; assessment of collections and their use; preservation; and de-selection, among other related activities.[1] Policy documents that define the goals and objectives of these activities and provide guidance for their systematic implementation and management are known, variously, as collection management policies, collection development plans or policies, or, more broadly, as collection plans.

Librarians, generally, accept the value of the creation and regular review of collection development policies and plans. Though not all libraries have collection plans, there is a professional expectation that libraries *should* have them. A committee of the Reference and User Services Association (RUSA) even identifies as its purpose: "to encourage libraries to establish and regularly review collection priorities, develop systematic approaches to collection development and management, and document those priorities in written policies . . . ."[2]

Indeed, states one of the leading writers in this area, "libraries without collection development policies are like businesses without business plans."[3]

Still, some question the value of collection management plans–at least beyond service as general policy statements, and in comparison to the amount of effort required to create and maintain them. In a era of financial constraints on libraries, new purchase patterns, and a transition to electronic formats, do collection plans serve as sturdy, but flexible frameworks for decision-making, or are they *smoke and mirrors* that are, primarily, useful to distract funding authorities and provide cover for the *real work*? What are the perceptions of librarians who have responsibility for management of electronic resources (ER) as they concern the need for, value of, or daily usefulness of collection plans? Do collection policy documents aid librarians, hinder them, or have little bearing on their work? Do collection plans help ER librarians organize their work and set priorities, or is it just a burden to create and maintain them?

This chapter begins with a brief discussion of collection plans in the context of the current, information environment with its mix of formats and its accelerating migration towards digital resources. Some difficulties with regard to the usefulness of collection plans in the current environment are identified.

Next, in the spirit of this volume's theme–the people who work with ER–the results of an informal, mailing list survey of collection development and ER librarians are presented. Many of the survey questions pertained, directly, to collection plans, systems of fund allocations, and other collection-related policies while others addressed professional preparation and continuing education; patterns of collaboration; and additional topics related to the work to plan and manage collections that include digital resources. Although the responses to this second set of questions are not related to collection plans *per se*, they help create a picture of the professional context in which collection plans are created, revised, used, ignored, and/or abandoned.

Finally, having picked the brains of their colleagues through a literature review and mailing list survey the authors venture to forward some suggestions to improve the long-term value and immediate usefulness of collection plans in the digital age and speculate about the qualities of the individuals who will be responsible to lead the implementation of these changes.

## *COLLECTION POLICIES: PLANS, MAPS, PROBLEMS*

Collection development plans and policies are written to guide the selection, acquisition, de-selection, and preservation processes of a library–in theory with regard to all formats. Collection plans synchronize the library's collection activity with the mission of the library and its parent institution and relate this activity to the needs of identified clientele such as undergraduate students and faculty researchers.

Frequently cited discussions of the purposes and value of collection plans appear in the American Library Association's *Guide for Written Collection Policy Statements*,[4] Peggy Johnson's *Fundamentals of Collection Development and Management*,[5] and Mary J. Bostic's, "A Written Collection Development Policy: To Have and Have Not."[6]

Collection plans guide the identification of priorities for selection, explain reasons for exclusion, establish directions to plan and direct development and change, and assist in the establishment of priorities of staff and budget for collection support activities. Collection plans are both internal documents and public relations tools; they are a means to communicate with partners in collection development outside the library and may be used to negotiate for funds within the parent institution. When accreditation agencies visit, collection plans help provide answers about support for programs. Detailed plans can assist libraries to make the best use of funds through cooperation in selection with other institutions.

In addition to general directions, a collection plan provides a framework to provide answers to questions about selection decisions: why did librarians select one resource and not another, or why did they add certain gifts-in-kind to the collection and send others to a sale? In fact, a collection plan can serve as a line of defense against challenges of all sorts; from the inclusion or exclusion of controversial, sectarian, or mission-inappropriate materials to decisions about the allocations of funds. As one author summarizes, "We use collection development policies to defend our frontiers."[7]

Yet, there are skeptics who doubt that formal collection plans and policies are worth the investment of time necessary for their creation and suggest that, although collection plans may have been defined by some as professional requirements, they have not been, convincingly, demonstrated to be useful. Two authors of cogent, thoughtful papers on this subject employ the word "orthodoxy"[8] to describe the library profession's belief in the value of collection plans.

Orthodoxy? A doctrine declared to be true by authority and tradition? A conviction justified by faith, rather than evidence? Or, a position rigidly held? In an era–and, perhaps, a profession–that valorizes change, innovation, flexibility, agility, shifting the paradigm, breaking out of the mold, thinking outside the box, etc., etc., does the collection plan have value?

Concerns about collection plans in general fall into a few categories:

- *Collection plans are, typically, static descriptions or containers of a dynamic enterprise.*

  Curricula change quickly; available funds change quickly; these days, publication and distribution systems change quickly as well. Yet, collection plans are rarely revised on a regular or frequent basis. As statements of principles, collection plans may retain value over several years; as guides for the annual work of selectors, collection plans may be seldom consulted. Dan C. Hazen calls collection plans "enshrinements of obsolescence."[9]

- *The principles that govern collection plans are, typically, not linked to the economic realities of the institution.*

  During the last decade, library purchases have been limited by a combination of inflation in journal prices and static/reduced budgets. Libraries that once collected comprehensively in certain areas now have to be selective; libraries that once collected selectively in an area may now acquire little at all in that area. Yet, collection policies often do not highlight, or even mention, the link between collection activity and available funds. This is akin to an architectural blueprint for a structure that does not take into account future, on-going costs, e.g., heat, maintenance, etc.

- *Collection plans purport to define objective standards and promote interchangeability of data. Actually, though the terminology of collection-levels may be standardized, in their application these terms and standards are, largely, subjective.*

  The Conspectus of the Research Libraries Group established a vocabulary of collection-levels, but, as one author comments, "What one bibliographer considers a '5' in the Conspectus system, another considers only a '3.'"[10]
  Terminology cannot, necessarily, be assumed to be consistent from one situation to the next, or across time. And, while levels may be related to proportion of available materials collected and, thus, to quantity of materials, they "do not imply value. Reporting a level of 4 or 5 does not mean a library is better . . ."[11]—only that its staff has attempted to collect more comprehensively. In addition, the staff in question may have interpreted the levels differently.
  There are further difficulties associated with the identification of a core collection of monographic or serial titles for undergraduate

education; yet, the support of basic undergraduate education is a primary mission of academic libraries.

- *Assessment remains a difficult though critical enterprise; particularly for libraries that must be selective, rather than comprehensive in selection. Collection plans, often, provide minimal, realistic guidance.*

It is tough to determine if a collection meets its objectives, i.e., to support undergraduate students in a particular discipline; particularly when there is no recent core, bibliography available for the discipline, or the discipline is in a state of change.

- *To remain current, the maintenance of collection plans requires regular attention from high-level personnel.*

While collection plans are intended to serve as foundations for library-planning and development, their own foundations may be weak. Thus, it may not be cost-effective to invest the time of professionals with multiple responsibilities in their maintenance.

## ADD E-RESOURCES AND STIR?

"It is evident that library operations were built on a paradigm of scholarly communication based on printed sources."[12]

So, also, collection plans. What happens when digital resources, in particular remote ones outside the physical control of librarians, are added to the collection plan mix?

In the past, collection policies described how tangible items would be incorporated into the library's holdings. With the advent of ER, the idea of access versus ownership changed this focus.

ER has, irrevocably, changed the process of collection development and acquisitions . . . Library professionals have had to revisit not only how they select and add resources to their collections, but, also, their relationships with the communities they serve and, even, their awareness of other library collection efforts.[13]

To incorporate licensed and other remote, ER, librarians, typically, have to rewrite collection plans or add new sections. Johnson notes that the separate document(s) or element(s) of a policy should "address both the acquisition of digital information and the purchase of rights to access remote digital resources."[14]

*Core Elements of Electronic Resource Collection Policies*, a Web resource from RUSA's Collection Development Policies Committee, contains a list of elements or criteria that are recommended for inclusion in ER collection policies. These include the policy's relationship to the overall library policy, the relationship between print and electronic sources, and hardware and software considerations. The document, also, includes a list of evaluation criteria that range from ease of search methodologies to the availability of backfiles to cost.[15]

In the past, collection plans have not, typically, addressed the questions that follow. In fairness, it, probably, has not seemed necessary since, in the print-based environment, some basic assumptions were so widely shared that they could be assumed and left unspoken. In the digital environment, however, assumptions may not be fully shared or their implications fully understood. Collection plans that are intended to guide library activities in the digital information age should provide answers, even provisional ones, to the following questions:

- *In the digital environment, what does it mean to "collect?" What does it mean to "select?"*

Selection, in the case of tangible information resources, has, usually, meant the purchase of an item or the acceptance of a gift, which is then added to the collection and the library's catalog. As libraries began to acquire access to remote databases, they often extended the definition of *selection* to include purchased-access to digital resources. But, with the appearance of peer-reviewed, open-access journals; free, high-quality, ready-reference sites; and collections of public-domain monographs on the web, a new definition of *collection* and *selection* must be developed; presumably, on a basis that is less purchase-driven. Otherwise, librarians may not be able to offer the most appropriate resources available and maintain the relevance of the library to users.

- *What is the information "object" that the library collects; particularly, with regard to journal literature?*

In the print-based environment, librarians, typically, collect journals at the title-level (although they may, of course, acquire copies of specific articles). In the digital environment, has the object that is collected shifted downward to the article, rather than the title-level? Or, at institutions that support basic undergraduate education, has the object collected shifted upward to, say, a body of peer-reviewed articles in specified disciplines, rather than in specified publications? In some cases, the objects that librarians collect may be included in all three categories: specific, discipline-critical journals; mixed databases of articles to support curricula; and individual articles as requested by clients.

- *Given the purchasing complexities of the electronic environment, how are subject coverage, subject balance, and equity of funding for different subject areas achieved?*

Allocation formulas in academic libraries, particularly libraries that do not collect comprehensively, help guarantee coverage in all areas of the curriculum. They are, generally, based on the assumption that journals may be selected and paid for on a title-by-title basis. When libraries shift to the purchase of multidisciplinary bundles of resources, how do they determine that resources are distributed equitably across the curriculum?

- *What does it mean to de-select? To track and manage losses?*

One objection to the addition of digital resources to the online catalog that represents the library's collection is that they are ephemeral and appear and vanish, often without warning. If the definition of the *selection* of digital resources is their inclusion in the online catalog or in databases, then a collection maintenance plan should include a description of a formal method or process for the removal of dead/inactive links similar to the *weeding* unusable books from a library's shelves.

- *To what extent, in what ways, and for what reasons, does format matter?*

When writing collection plans, librarians have assumed that content is the primary basis for collection decisions. There has always been some consideration of format, i.e., printed and recorded music, film, and other non-textual materials. With client expectations of remote access and distance education programs; and the preference among some groups, e.g., young people, for digital resources format can no longer always be a secondary consideration. Additionally, the maintenance of the last print-based copy of a title by a consortium or regional group may, also, be an element of collection maintenance that needs to be identified formally when more and more libraries have migrated to an electronic version.

The effort to provide access to digital resources introduces a number of fundamental questions about the definitions and nature of the selection, maintenance, and assessment of collections–or, perhaps more accurately, places some old questions in a different light. The consideration of these issues in a mixed, information environment requires an *across the board* thought process that is not limited to one set of library resources. Digital resources are just one part of the array of library resources. They bear a relationship to all the others and all of them are intended to enable the library to fulfill its mission. It is doubtful that a collection plan that is intended to guide decision-making and promote the library's relevance to its users in the mixed digital and print-based environment can simply add e-resources and stir.

## RESPONSES TO A MAILING LIST SURVEY OF ER AND COLLECTION LIBRARIANS

How should librarians proceed toward a new manifestation of the collection management plan? What do librarians who have responsibilities with collection development and/or ER think about collection plans and the digital environment, and how do individual librarians met the objectives identified in their libraries' collection policies? To find out, a survey (see Appendix A) was posted on two electronic discussion lists.

The Orbis Cascade Alliance ER discussion list has 32 subscribers from member institutions of the alliance, a consortium of academic libraries in Oregon and Washington. The alliance has a shared catalog that is used to share resources; negotiate licenses for ER for participating members; and provide other services. Six subscribers responded.

Their responses were compared with those from the ER in Libraries (ERIL-L) discussion list, which has 1,667 subscribers. Ten ERIL-L subscribers responded. This was not, of course, a random sample. Rather, the sample is a focus group of librarians who have thought about this topic and offered their observations.

Although some respondents had collection development, collection management, or ER job titles, many did not. Some were members of reference, systems, or technical services departments and their specific responsibilities with ER varied greatly, including selection, budget management, contract negotiation, licensing, setting up access to or providing training for new databases, usage data analysis, and vendor/publisher/consortia liaise. Librarians have adopted many different models in the assignment and organization of ER.

## Question: Has the Transition to ER Driven Changes in Collection Development Work and Its Organization?

General comments indicate that more work is required to maintain ER. Migration to digital resources appears to have promoted the development of collaborative groups in libraries. In one case, the collection development model changed into a team approach while in two others a more collective and collaborative approach to the purchase of ER is taken among units. Librarians indicated a need for increased support from other areas in the library as well as enhanced communication between personnel and departments. Only one respondent reported no changes in organization although there were some new duties and complications.

## Question: What Is Your Background for Working in Collection Development and/or ER?

Experience ranged:

- none in either area
- many years in collection management or acquisitions
- ten years work with ER

Julie Blake, Serials and ER Acquisitions Coordinator at Johns Hopkins University, said: "I'm a former director, although that probably doesn't prepare me for much of anything."

## Question: How Have the Responsibilities of Collection Development/Management Librarians Changed with the Transition to ER?

A few librarians said they take the view that their responsibilities haven't changed; they are just responsible for the management of a wider variety of formats. Others report drastic changes and greater complexity, and describe a shift from the management of subscriptions with one journal vendor to the license of databases and the negotiation of prices with multiple vendor/publishers or through consortia; liaise with sales, technical support, and billing clerks; and learning to understand technology and access issues. Many assume additional tasks, assignments, and decision-making responsibilities.

According to JHU's Blake: "I have to multitask, and I need to have various systems for organization. Maybe an ERM would take care of a lot of things for me, but we don't have one."

## Question: What Do You Think Are the Most Critical Skills and Abilities for Collection Librarians in an Electronic Environment?

Some of these skills are new to the librarian repertoire, but many are not. Skills used and valued in other areas of library work apply to the electronic environment; they are just applied differently.

Respondents identified personal and intellectual qualities such as:

- ability to think critically and independently
- ability to multitask and set priorities
- good organizational skills
- ability to deal with detail
- good outreach and communications skills
- flexibility and willingness to adapt quickly to change
- confidence, curiosity, and persistence
- ability to be proactive with a willingness to take risks
- commitment to continuous learning
- ability to develop a *comfort level with the unknown* [emphasis by the authors]

Other qualities identified involved professional competencies such as:

- knowledge of budget management
- ability to gather and analyze expenditure data
- ability to evaluate best deals
- knowledge of licensing issues, contract negotiation, and legal terms
- knowledge of publishing and the vendor landscape
- understanding technology
- leadership and teamwork skills
- ability to work with other librarians, teaching faculty, and consortia
- ability to analyze and select databases with curricular and user needs at the center of the process

## Question: How Has Formal and Continuing Library Education Served Participants in Terms of Your Current Responsibilities?

Several respondents reported that attendance at local and national conferences, workshops, and seminars provided valuable information. Classes on specific ER topics, also, provided additional benefit. An important element is to communicate with colleagues and find out what others do and how they adapt and keep up with specific topics. Reading professional literature was mentioned.

Susan Hinken, Head, Technical Services and Collection Development, University of Portland, said, "My formal education was a good foundation, but it would not have sustained me without access to additional education through conferences, workshops, committee work, and networking. Learning from my colleagues in peer institutions has also been an important element in developing the skills and knowledge I need."

Several respondents said their library science education gave them a solid theoretical background as regards the history and value of print, research methods, modes of access and ownership, and understanding the nature of publications and the needs of users. Others cited the value of backgrounds in cataloging, strategic planning, and public services as well as knowledge of data standards. Others stated they had gained most of their knowledge from reading and activity in the library professional community and on the job, rather than from formal or continuing education.

Melissa Holmberg, ER/Science Librarian, Minnesota State University at Mankato, said: "[Formal library education] hasn't [served well]. There are no best practices. There are electronic resource managers all over who keep trying different ways of doing things, often feeling overwhelmed, but still enjoying the constantly changing landscape."

Blake added: "I could have used a lot more training in business concepts, figuring out cost-effectiveness, assessment, data collection, etc. E-resources were only taught in library school as online searching when I went through, too, but I get a lot from conferences."

### *Question: What Sort of Professional Education, Formal and Continuing, Is Now Necessary to Prepare Individuals to Function Effectively as Collection Librarians?*

Core degrees include a BA or BS and a master's, particularly the ALA-accredited MLS, and coursework in the basics of collection development. Also identified were:

- presentations and coursework on licensing, negotiation, and analyzing use data
- opportunities to learn management and technological concepts and generalities that can be applied in a variety of situations
- information about how organizations, especially libraries, evolve and change, particularly as a result of technological advances

- networking and learning from peers, and sharing information on best practices

According to Blake: "I honestly don't know. You can't really train in common sense, and yet I think that's really what's needed–how to evaluate different deals, how to compare one format to another, budget management, as well as the theory behind selection."

Mori Lou Higa, Manager, Collection Development, University of Texas Southwestern Medical Center, said: "I really question whether grad school can prepare someone to walk into the job without still having a huge learning curve. I think one's individual qualities are more critical than learning specific functions. If grad schools can provide some of the basics (collection development strategies, licensing, budgeting, assessment) and communicate the unpredictability of this particular arena, I think that's all schools can do to prepare students. First-hand work experience in a library setting of some kind should also be mandatory. Even if the student doesn't work with collection functions specifically, they will be exposed to issues that arise in support of the collection by working in a library."

### *Question: Does Your Library Have a Collection Management Plan?*

Seven respondents said yes, three said no, and one replied "sort of." Others had partial or informal plans, or were in the process of rewriting their plans.

### *Question: Is the Collection Management Plan a Policy of the Library or of the University/College?*

All respondents indicate that their plans are policies of their libraries and about half of the collection policy documents are available on the Web.

### *Question: Do Current Collection Management Plans Have a Separate Section or Policy Regarding ER, or Are ER Considered in Various Sections of the Plan?*

Some policies have no provisions for ER while others include provisions in each subject area subdivided under format. Some have separate sections, documents, policies, or sub-policies for ER. Several respondents stated that ER is a format, policies govern all formats, and, thus, ER is covered.

However, between print-based/tangible journals that are subscribed to and retained in collections and intangible ER that are licensed and accessed through a vendor/publisher and not retained in on-site collections, there is an obvious difference in format and the *manner of purchase.* Licensing is a large part of ER management and collection plans do not, always, reflect this new reality.

### Question: Is a Collection Management/Development Plan Still Regarded as Useful by the Library or Is the Collection Plan Merely a Pro-Forma Statement with Little Impact on Decision Making?

Some respondents said that their collection development plans are useful to make decisions, either on a day-to-day basis or as a general guideline. One comment was that the plan provides overall guidance, but has little impact on day-to-day decision-making. Other respondents said the plan is useful, but could be better or should be updated, or expect the rewritten plan to be useful. One respondent likes the idea of good policies to support decisions and supports the ideas of collection plans in principle.

Peggy Firman, Associate Director for Technical Services, University of Puget Sound said: "It's both important, and has little impact. If you keep your plan and policy up to date, it can be a powerful tool; if you allow the plan to become out of date, then it does little use."

### Question: Are Collection Development Plans Regularly Updated? What Are the Procedures for Updating Them, and Who Is Responsible?

All respondents report that it is not a high priority to keep the plan updated; none of the libraries had a current guide to use to formulate policy or procedures, except in very general terms. In many cases, the update process was indicated not to be as regular as it should be; no specific schedule or procedure for updates is in place. Some policies are, currently, in the update stage. The responsibility for the initiation/completion of the update process ranged from one librarian to a team; once updated, plans are presented to an individual or a library committee.

### Question: Has the Transition to ER Created Changes in the Collection Fund Allocations or Other Collection Funding Models?

Some respondents reported that they provide funding for ER by moving money from serials or monographs while others create an ER fund to purchase full-text databases. In one state, libraries receive legislative support via bond money to purchase databases. In another library, extensive microform and duplicate subscriptions were cancelled in order to fund early, ER needs; money for ER was allocated to subject areas. Libraries report they have moved money from books to journals; from humanities and social sciences to science, technology and medicine; and that they, constantly, adjust priorities among books, other media, and ER.

Comments:

- Liza Rognas, Reference Convener, The Evergreen State College, said: "We've had some problems with core materials suddenly disappearing when publishers drop their contracts with aggregators who then do not notify us. We've lost access to key titles in the sciences in this way, and then had to scramble to find money for renewed access."
- Hinken, at the University of Portland, said: "Because so many e-resources are interdisciplinary, this year we are removing all funds from departmental allocations to a single fund overseen by the Head of Technical Services and Collection Development. We are implementing a more focused, team approach with the collection development librarians working together to evaluate and select titles."
- Higa, at the University of Texas Southwestern Medical Center: "We don't use allocations. Since many of our electronic resources are consortial packages, I find that a subtle collection development shift and strategy is to react to consortial opportunities. This is often difficult to budget for and plan."

## *Question: Have Collection Development/Management Plans or Policies Been Revised in Terms of Coverage or Content, Driven by the Transition to ER?*

Answers range from yes to we're getting there. Some policies address ER as one format of many. Some libraries have no written policy, but decisions on ER are made in meetings and documented in minutes. If policies are outdated, librarians follow undocumented strategies when they make decisions. If policies do not include references to ER, librarians add or drop periodical subscriptions and cancel multiple-formatted items in an effort to make realistic decisions within budget constraints.

## Question: Do Collection Development Plans Include Policies About Canceling Print Subscriptions Based on Electronic Availability?

One respondent reported that the library's policy is to switch print subscriptions to electronic only, if this is possible for specific titles, while another policy has a broad statement on duplicates that includes reference to ER. Three libraries regularly cancel print subscriptions in favor of electronic only access, although this policy is not stated in their collection plans.

## Question: Has Responsibility for Writing the Collection Management Plan Changed, Driven by the Transition to ER?

Almost all respondents affirmed that there has been no change. One did report that the library's plan had changed because "there are two separate [information] worlds now, with no connection." Another stated that ER had, recently, been incorporated into the library's overall collection development policy.

## Question: What Role Do You Play in Regard to Creating and Updating the Collection Management Plan?

While some respondents propose ideas, write plans, draft revisions, provide overall direction during the process, or have ultimate responsibility for the plan, others contribute to initial discussions or current revisions. One participated in writing an ER policy in 2001, and said it hasn't been updated since; another who oversaw the creation of the initial collection development policy anticipates overseeing the revision. Blake wrote: "I write it, I live by it."

## SUGGESTIONS TO ENHANCE COLLECTION PLANS IN THE DIGITAL ENVIRONMENT

Literature review, survey responses, and our own experience suggest that collection plans have some problems and lacunae in the mixed digital and print-based environment. Collection plans are widely considered to be useful in principle as general guidelines–there's a high-level of belief in this library orthodoxy–but they may have limited impact on most decision-making.

A particular problem is that collection plans are perceived as outdated and, therefore, a bit off the mark in the address of the real collection development/management problems of the library world today. Perhaps this library orthodoxy need not be abandoned or, at least, reformed, simplified, and opened to the possibility of continuing revelation. The following suggestions are based on the responses to the survey, the observations of the respondents, and the reflections of the authors:

- *Address the issue of obsolescence in advance, through a written commitment to an identified review process with a regular rolling review schedule.*

  A review process might concentrate on different sections of the plan from year-to-year and include consultation with different groups on different schedules. Every element does not have to be rewritten every year for a regular review to be effective. A rolling review, like a rolling inventory, guarantees that nothing is overlooked forever while it limits expectations over a specific time period. In an effort to improve constituent communication, librarians may find it useful to identify and include in the planning process individuals in the library, teaching faculty, and other stakeholders to participate in the review process.

- *Address the issue of obsolescence in advance; adopt a structure for the collection plan that facilitates an update process, emphasizes principles, and leaves room for specifics, in attached documents, that can be changed frequently.*

  It is recommended that when a will is written that a list of personal property with legatees be prepared. However, the list will not be included in the will proper. If this structure is used, the personal property list can be updated regularly without a change to the will itself. In the development of a collection development/management plan, librarians might adopt a comparable structure with a brief foundation policy that contains references to other, more time-limited documents, which could help address more effectively and with less time spent in the rewrite of the entire document the issue of obsolescence.

- *Emphasize processes of assessment and update, rather than holdings counts and discipline-related specifics.*

  Librarians construct plans that specify level of collection, etc., for a myriad of individual classification areas and then assess collections on the basis of numbers of titles held as well as the extent of those holdings. As curricula and knowledge develop in unexpected directions or shift with changes in faculty specialties, these plans are almost immediately out of date. A specification of, in a collection development/management plan, a structured process of annual contact with department faculty in order to identify curriculum change and discipline direction may result in better service to the institution's mission. Analysis of circulation and other use statistics, bibliographies of student projects in key courses, and ILL requests, along with the use of focus groups of specific client populations may reveal collection successes and needs in a timely manner. An acknowledgment of the subjectivity inherent in collection development and assessment might, also, be a positive step forward in LIS philosophy in order to create a collection plan that has vision, but is still based in reality.

- *Define collection and selection within the current information environment of print, other media, and digital resources, with various types of access, both open and licensed/purchased.*

Although these definitions may be provisional, the acknowledgment of the need for remote digital resources as well as onsite digital collections; and the specification of the reasons to dedicate librarian time to the selection of open-access resources as well as licensed/purchased resources, is useful to plan for the deployment of staff time and for communication with teaching faculty and other constituents.

Some librarians have already begun to redefine collection and selection in ways that reflect the digital information environment. As an example, the collection development policy of the library at Brown University reads, under the heading *Developing and Managing the Brown University Library Collections*:

> In support of [its] mission, the Library *acquires information resources* in a variety of formats . . . We also *acquire access to information*, through direct licensing from authorized providers, establishing connections to free resources, or making consortial or exchange agreements with publishers, libraries, or other organizations. This document will refer to all of these resources as the Library's *collections*, whether they are owned, leased, or borrowed, and whether or not they reside physically in the Library.[16] [*emphasis by authors*]

- *Identify the objects the library collects in terms of journal literature: titles, articles, and databases.*

  When librarians refer to a *core collection*, they may mean high-quality resources to support student research across the undergraduate curriculum. When librarians consider those core resources, their thoughts may run to subject coverage, service to students, and aggregations of resources, rather than of specific titles. Teaching faculty, however, may interpret the phrase core collection in a discipline to mean the most important or heavily cited titles in the discipline. For the sake of good/effective communication among collection development/management policy stakeholders, librarians should document/ explain the levels of acquisition that are pursued. Of course, librarians will continue to collect at the journal title level, but the digital information environment presents alternatives and requires adjustments to this title-orientation in order to make the best use of limited resources. This transition is not always clear to the library's constituents.

- *Reflect economic reality, both in terms of available funds and available models to sell, license, and purchase. Specify the role of consortial licensing in the definition of an institution's collection.*

  A credible collection plan, one that is useful for planning over a period of years, "must take into account the eventuality, and perhaps the inevitability, of . . . changes in the fiscal and commercial environment."[17] Publishers of digital resources have tried out various models to bundle and price e-resources. These initiatives impact the library's ability to purchase specific titles. This dynamic nature of the economic side of digital resources management should be acknowledged along with some basic guidelines (if possible!). To the extent librarians of a particular library work in collaboration with librarians of other libraries, its digital collection may be defined by the consortium, not the individual library; a fact that, also, needs incorporation into the overall collection plan.

- *Integrate ER into the overall collection development/management plan.*

  ER present some specific issues that may need separate acknowledgement in the collection plan or, at least, may require references to separate, more dynamic documents. But, e-resources are no longer a separate or add-on part of most academic library collections;

they are central. Decisions about digital resources, like decisions about print-based titles, must be made in the context of the total collection.

- ***Abandon the pursuit of perfection and comprehensiveness that has dogged many library collection projects.***

  Perfection and comprehensiveness will not happen in the digital world with its constant expansion and churning oceans of resources. No collection will be permanent, no map of knowledge will be finished, no catalog will be complete. They never were, of course, and it was, also, not possible in the print-based world, but librarians hoped and found the pursuit of the impossible dream to be motivational and meaningful. In the digital information environment, however, this hope and its pursuit are not useful.

### WHO WILL REFORM COLLECTION-PLAN ORTHODOXY?

Many traditional skills and attributes of collection development librarians are, obviously, transferable to the electronic environment. Deegan and Tanner note, for example, that subject skills are implicit in librarianship and they do not change when the information changes from print to electronic; the focus "is on the content, rather than the container"[18] and subject skills are as valuable as ever. The interview skills used in reference can, also, be used in collection development teams charged with the selection of ER, whether in a single library or in consortia.[19] And as one respondent to the survey observed, common sense remains important.

Effective management of a mixed information environment, also, requires new or enhanced business and negotiation skills. Cortez maintains that, although technical knowledge is important, "business functional knowledge and interpersonal/management skills are considered to be the most important."[20]

Some survey respondents, also, stated that they need more business knowledge and background. Certainly, the ability to perceive the implications, both financial and service-oriented, of the many newly developed license models is critical.

Many areas of professional knowledge will need to be used in order to rewrite collection plans to accommodate the integration of all resources: knowledge of trends in publication and distribution, access modes, licensing, archiving, use patterns, and client preferences are just a few examples.

Nevertheless, to lead the efforts of librarians to write a new kind of collection plan, the attributes that are likely to produce success are intellectual and personal, rather than strictly professional competencies:

- the ability to think in conceptual and theoretical terms, while not losing sight of the details that, ultimately, will support or debunk the theory
- the ability to communicate the *big picture* to colleagues and constituencies–and do so in terms of the details that are meaningful to them
- the ability to engage these individuals and groups in collaborative efforts
- the ability to move back and forth between narrative mission and budgets, as two languages that express, ideally, the same idea
- the ability to negotiate within the library, within library consortia, with vendor/publishers, and with varied constituencies with varied interests
- the willingness to accept less than perfection and tolerate ambiguity
- the ability to listen, regroup, and consider multiple perspectives
- a commitment to principles of equitable coverage of curricula, service to constituencies, and best use of limited resources

## NOTES

1. G. E. Gorman, "Collection Management," in *International Encyclopedia of Information and Library Science*, 2nd ed. (London: Routledge, 2003), 81.

2. "Core Elements of Electronic Resource Collection Policies," http://www.ala.org/ala/rusa/rusaourassoc/rusasections/codes/codessection/codescomm/ (viewed October 4, 2005).

3. Peggy Johnson, *Fundamentals of Collection Development and Management* (Chicago: American Library Association, 2004), 72.

4. *Guide for Written Collection Policy Statements*, 2nd ed. Chicago: American Library Association, 1996.

5. Peggy Johnson, *Fundamentals of Collection Development and Management* (Chicago: American Library Association, 2004).

6. Mary J. Bostic, "A Written Collection Development Policy: To Have and Have Not," *Collection Management* 10, no. 3/4 (1988): 89-103.

7. Dan C. Hazen, "Collection Development Policies in the Information Age," *College & Research Libraries* 56 (Jan. 1995): 29.

8. Ibid., 31; Richard Snow, "Wasted Words: The Written Collection Development Policy and the Academic Library," *Journal of Academic Librarianship* 22 (May 1996): 191.

9. Hazen, 29.

10. Snow, 193.

11. Johnson, 78.

12. Kris D. Schmidt, Pongracz Sennyey, and Timothy V. Carstens, "New Roles for a Changing Environment: Implications of Open Access for Libraries," *College & Research Libraries* 66 (Sept. 2005): 415.

13. Joan Conger, *Collaborative Electronic Resource Management* (Westport, CT: Libraries Unlimited, 2004), 98.

14. Johnson, 80.

15. "Core Elements of Electronic Resource Collection Policies," http://www.ala.org/ala/rusa/rusaourassoc/rusasections/codes/codessection/codescomm (viewed October 4, 2005).

16. "Developing and Managing the Brown University Library Collections," http://www.brown.edu/Facilities/University_Library/collections/colldev/general.html (viewed October 4, 2005).

17. James H. Spohrer, "The End of an American (Library) Dream: The Rise and Decline of the Collection Development Policy Statement at Berkeley," *The Acquisition Librarian* 30 (2003): 42.

18. Marilyn Deegan and Simon Tanner, *Digital Futures: Strategies for the Information Age* (New York: Neal-Shuman Publishers, Inc., 2002), 221.

19. Edwin M. Cortez, Sanjay K. Dutta, and Edward John Kazlauskas, "What the Library and Information Professional Can Learn From the Information Technology and Project Management Knowledge Areas," *portal: Libraries and the Academy* 4 (1) (2004): 137.

20. Ibid., 134.

doi:10.1300/J105v32n03_01

## APPENDIX I. Listserv Survey Questions

We are working on a project intended to identify the competencies and abilities collection librarians need to function effectively in the electronic publications environment, and especially the abilities they need to develop meaningful collection management plans in this environment.

We would appreciate your sharing your thoughts on this subject with us, by responding to the following questions. Of course, we will attribute your comments to you, unless you request otherwise.

We would be grateful for any response–INCLUDING BRIEF RESPONSES, OR RESPONSES TO SOME QUESTIONS AND NOT OTHERS. We know you are all very busy, and we appreciate even a few minutes of your time.

The environment:

During the last decade, academic libraries have shifted toward acquisition of resources, particularly serials, in electronic format. This ongoing transition hasn't been a simple switch from purchasing specific titles in print form to purchasing them in an electronic form, however. Instead of primarily acquiring resources on a title-by-title basis, libraries are acquiring packages, including aggregations of articles (such as ProQuest), (electronic archives such as JSTOR), and publishers' databases of varying types, among other possibilities.
Many of these electronic "packages" are interdisciplinary in content. Their purchase/licensing may complicate libraries' use of formulas to allocate funds to specific disciplines. Many e-packages are dynamic in content, which may complicate decisions concerning retention of print subscriptions. To obtain the best price, selection and licensing may take place at a consortial level, rather than at the level of a single library matching its resources to one institution's curriculum. The process of licensing, whether consortial or at the single-institution level, is itself complicated and dynamic: many publishers appear to be experimenting with a variety of pricing models, and rights for various forms of traditional library usage (e.g., interlibrary loan) are not always assumed.

- Our questions:
- What is your job title? What is the job title of the individual to whom you report?
- What are your responsibilities with regard to electronic resources?
- With whom do you collaborate, in your work as e-resources collection librarian? Has this changed during the past decade?
- What is your background for work in collection development/electronic resources?
- In your experience, how have the responsibilities of collection development/management librarians changed with the transition to electronic resources?
- In your experience and observation, what are the most critical skills and abilities for successful collection librarians, in the emerging electronic environment? Have these changed over the past decade? Are collection librarians now primarily managers, public relations officers, negotiators, technicians?
- Does your library have a collection management plan? Is it on the Web, where we could see it?
- If your library has a collection management plan, does it have a separate section or separate policies regarding electronic resources, or are e-resources considered in most sections? If not, are electronic resources treated in a separate document?
- If your library has a collection management plan, is it a policy of the library, or is it a recognized policy of the university/college, subject to shared governance procedures, etc.?

## APPENDIX I (continued)

- Is having a collection management/development plan still regarded as useful by your library? By your larger institution? Or is it just a pro forma statement with little impact on decision-making?

- If you have a collection management plan, is it regularly updated? What is the procedure for updating it, and who is responsible?

- Has the transition to electronic resources driven changes in your collection fund allocations or other collection funding models? If so, in what ways?

- Apart from changes to allocations formulas, has your collection development/management plan or policies been revised in terms of coverage, content, etc., driven by the transition to electronic resources? If so, in what ways?

For example:
Does the collection management plan include policies about canceling print subscriptions based on availability electronically?

Does the collection management planning include policies adding back titles deleted from e-resources packages?

Does the collection management plan provide greater or lesser detail than in the past, with regard to level of collecting in specific subject areas?

- Has responsibility for writing the collection management/development plan changed, driven by the transition to electronic resources?

- What is your role, with regard to the collection management plan?

- Has the transition to electronic resources driven changes in the organization of collection development work at your institution? If so, in what ways?

- In what ways has your library education, both formal and continuing, served you well, or not, in terms of your current responsibilities?

- What sort of professional education, both formal and continuing, do you believe is now necessary to prepare individuals to function effectively as collection librarians?

# Description of and Access
# to Electronic Resources (ER):
# Transitioning into the Digital Age

Elaine McCracken

**SUMMARY.** Traditional description and access of library materials has
undergone a transition for over a decade now as catalogers and librarians
as well as information and computer scientists have worked with the
challenges to identify and provide access to various types of digital resources such as electronic journals; electronic books and reference resources; electronic government publications, Web sites and databases;
and geospatial maps and digitized special collections. Along with the provision of measures to internationalize and accommodate the nature of electronic resources (ER) to Anglo-American cataloging description and
standards, catalogers have assessed workflow and technology issues and
now look ahead to new ways to describe and catalog resources, i.e., the
Functional Requirements for Bibliographic Records (FRBR) concept
model, various metadata schemes, and management tools called electronic resource management systems (ERMS). The goal is to continue to
identify, manage, and preserve digital materials today and into the future

---

Elaine McCracken, MLS, is Serials and ER Cataloger/Librarian, Davidson Library–Serials Department, University of California, Santa Barbara, Santa Barbara, CA
93106-9010 (E-mail: emccrack@library.ucsb.edu).

[Haworth co-indexing entry note]: "Description of and Access to Electronic Resources (ER): Transitioning
into the Digital Age." McCracken, Elaine. Co-published simultaneously in *Collection Management* (The
Haworth Information Press, an imprint of The Haworth Press) Vol. 32, No. 3/4, 2007, pp. 259-275; and: *Electronic Resources Librarianship and Management of Digital Information: Emerging Professional Roles* (ed:
Mark Jacobs) The Haworth Information Press, an imprint of The Haworth Press, 2007, pp. 259-275. Single or
multiple copies of this article are available for a fee from The Haworth Document Delivery Service
[1-800-HAWORTH, 9:00 a.m. - 5:00 p.m. (EST). E-mail address: docdelivery@haworthpress.com].

doi:10.1300/J105v32n03_02

in order to provide the best access to information for library users. doi:10.1300/J105v32n03_02 *[Article copies available for a fee from The Haworth Document Delivery Service: 1-800-HAWORTH. E-mail address: <docdelivery@ haworthpress.com> Website: <http://www.HaworthPress.com> © 2007 by The Haworth Press. All rights reserved.]*

**KEYWORDS.** Electronic information resources, digital resources, cataloging, library catalogs, descriptive cataloging rules, metadata, workflow

## *INTRODUCTION*

Experienced catalogers are well aware of the historical significance and benefits of the traditional library catalog. However, in an era where the number of available digital resources has rapidly expanded, online public access catalogs (OPACs) and the rules of description have been unable to keep pace with user demands for instant access to full-text resources brought on by their exposure to and expectations for simple-to-use search engines. The challenges presented by new technologies have prompted dialogue and collaboration among information scientists from across specialties, disciplines, and countries for a number of years and the results have come to fruition in ways that, at last, play out, not in laboratories, but in the backrooms of library technical services units and on the workstations of patrons who use OPACs in the library lobby or via remote access from home or office.

For those catalogers who work, specifically, with electronic resources (ER) the past decade has been an experience of intense transition. The Anglo-American Cataloging Rules (AACR), which were adopted in 1967 and have served much of the library community well for almost a half century, do not, necessarily, translate in the same manner for digital materials as they do for print-based materials. This is particularly important since electronic access has increased our patron base from a mostly local stance to one that is international in scope. Even though the AACR's chapter 9 for ER was revised in 2002; new rules for continuing and integrating resources were adopted; and the rules were aligned with international standards, there has been a continued realization among library professionals of a need to drastically rethink how digital materials are packaged and presented. Hence, librarians have discussed new models for cataloging, particularly the International Federation of Library Association (IFLA) Functional Requirements for Bibliographic

Resources (FRBR); enhanced database search and retrieval features; and electronic resource management systems (ERMS) to use to keep track of a library's digital titles, subscription and vendor/publisher information, and link resolution with more accuracy and less duplication. In addition, a Joint Steering Committee for the Revision of the Anglo-American Cataloging Rules has worked on a major restructure of AACR that will apply in the digital age. This new version of the AACR, expected to be complete in 2008, will be called Resource Description and Access (RDA).[1]

In this transitory phase between a catalog based, primarily, on print-based materials in local collections and a new era of digitization, aggregator databases, collaborative collections, and marked increases in material costs coupled with significant budget cuts and no increases in staffing over the past twenty years, how can the balance between cataloging the material at hand in accordance with the current rules while, at the same time, looking ahead to improved services with new technologies, resources, and patron expectations be maintained? It is only necessary to look at student research patterns to see how Google has influenced directions for catalogs and search engines. The current hybrid approach to provide traditional cataloged records and A-Z lists of aggregator databases and electronic journals on the library Web site seems an interim approach effective only in the short-term. Librarians must realize that they can only continue to serve customers and provide access to the best information resources if they actively collaborate with one another, with vendor/publishers, and with computer science engineers. They must be involved in the design of better search engines and continue the process of the evaluation and update of metadata standards. It has taken time to get classification schemes, subject headings, AACR, and MARC to work well internationally. With digital resources that elude cataloging librarians must continue to find ways to resolve the complications these materials present as well as work to maximize the benefits of digital access.

## A BIT OF DESCRIPTION AND ACCESS HISTORY

Catalogers continue to reorganize and enhance major guides for description and coding, i.e., *AACR* and *MARC21*, in addition to work on other metadata schemes. This is a given in a profession that seeks to provide the most intelligent, convenient access to information with the technology of the day. Though librarians have exerted great effort to move forward with description codes in the past decade and have witnessed progress to align AACR with international standards (achieved with *AACR2 Revised 2002*) the rules remain based on the print-card catalog and do not work well with digital resources. *RDA* is intended to resolve problems encountered with AACR as the authors work to build in rules that will aid in the identification and collocation of various formats in a digital environment.

The library catalog's objectives, i.e., identification and collocation, have always been known to library staff. However, for the principles envisioned to bring about these objectives we owe a debt of gratitude to professionals like Antonio Panizzi, Charles Cutter, and Seymour Lubetzky.

Antonio Panizzi offered a new concept for the catalog at the British Museum in 1841 where he worked as Keeper of the Department of Printed Books. "Panizzi's rules conceived of books as editions of particular works, with those representing the same work to be integrated and arranged in the catalog in a prescribed order, so that the reader who came to the library for a particular book would find it in context with other books representing editions of the same work and might select the edition or editions that would best serve his or her interests."[2]

According to Panizzi, a work should be described in full-length only once and any subsequent editions should be cross-referenced. These concepts of main entry and collocation were embraced by the library world in 1961 at the International Conference on Cataloging Principles and have come to be known as the Paris Principles.[3]

This is an important point to recall in this chapter's discussion on bibliographic description of titles available in multiple formats.

In addition, in 1876 Charles A. Cutter, in his *Rules for a Printed Dictionary Catalogue*, outlined similar principles for cataloging books. He proposed that a library's catalog should enable the patron to find all books by an author, or title, or all editions of the book, or all books on a specific subject.[4]

This is an excellent synopsis of the catalog and librarians might view this more comprehensively today to include materials in multiple formats.

Any discussion on ER must consider the Library of Congress's introduction of technology to the process of cataloging. Around the turn of the century the Library of Congress (LC) made its printed catalog cards available to all libraries for a small fee that included distribution costs. This service led to cooperative cataloging and, ultimately, to OPACs, OCLC, RLIN, and interlibrary loan 9ILL).[5]

The LC, long respected as a leader in the library community, continues to address issues of technology and access. The report *LC21: A Digital*

*Strategy for the Library of Congress*, published in 2000, outlines findings and recommendations for a transition to a collection and access plan for management that focuses on digital resources.[6]

With the recognition that no paradigm has emerged for the collection, organization, and provision of access to digital materials the authors of the report recommend a definition of clear long-term goals. No one library can collect every digital resource available on the Internet, so the LC (and other library institutions that follow their example) should define the materials they will be responsible for collecting and preserving. In respect to description and organization the report recommends the development of more complex metadata and active participation and collaboration with others in the information community.[7]

The LC has recently developed and tested Access-Level MARC/AACR records for electronic monographs and integrating resources that are important enough to add to the LC catalog, but don't merit the time and expense of full-level cataloging.[8]

Access-Level records use core data elements, conform to AACR2 and Library of Congress Subject Headings (LCSH), and were developed with the principles of FRBR in mind. The success of Access-Level records will likely influence future national cataloging practice.

## How Has the Nature of Digital Resources Driven the Creation and Development of Cataloger's Positions and Their Responsibilities?

While much of the major think-tank work of the past decades has related to the reconsideration and redesign of cataloging rules and the improvement of search engines, thanks to the tireless efforts and hard work of many librarians who serve on various steering committees, the day-to-day work of catalogers often appears to have been turned on its head. OPACS and other cataloging utilities, e.g., OCLC and RLIN, follow AACR rule revisions and the CONSER Editing Guide and Cataloging Manual (particularly Module 31 for Cataloging Remote Access Serials), but electronic resource cataloging still presents new complexities and concerns. Catalogers must know the specific rules for the description of digital materials and must factor in to their decision-making related issues, i.e., license agreements, remote access, link resolution, and the addition of resources to an A-Z list.

The sheer number of ER, often purchased in large vendor/publisher packages, and user demand for online, full-text resources has required the consideration and adoption of new ways to manage technical services workflow. Vendors have developed new tools to help organize these resources. Companies such as SerialsSolutions and EBSCO have developed A-Z lists and other tools for the management of e-resources and new software, e.g., Ex Libris' Verde, aim to resolve many electronic resource management issues that encompass the consolidation of cataloging, acquisitions, and license data into one interactive management module. The A-Z lists can be indispensable for smaller libraries without the necessary staff to catalog and maintain ER and, also, for larger libraries with thousands of titles. Still, many of these tools, electronic resource management systems (ERMS) in particular, are new and in an evolutionary stage. ERMS are a great aid in the overall management of electronic materials. They help librarians and staff track packages, invoices, and order payments and place all pertinent information into one database.

Currently, library managers continue to evaluate staff needs as workflow shifts and ask the question: *Do we need less staff to check in journals or receive books, now that we have cut back on print purchases and many items are delivered electronically?* or *Can we shift a staff person out of the bindery unit into cataloging/reference/digital processing?* or *Do we need to create a separate unit to process and maintain digital resources?* There is no one answer to workflow and staff organization. A decision must be made that is appropriate to the library as the need arises. A manager must, also, keep in mind the skills, abilities, and personalities of individual staff members when any major assignment changes are planned.

There is a need today for catalogers who specialize in ER cataloging, who understand the ways in which AACR2 2002 rev. should be applied, just as special rules have been applied to audiovisual and cartographic materials, manuscript collections, and serials. ER has unique description requirements as outlined in Chapter 9 of AACR2. In addition, with digital materials a cataloger must be trained to identify monographs from serials and integrating resources as outlined in LCRI 1.0.

For now, catalogers will continue to follow AACR, CONSER, MARC21 bibliographic format, LCSH, the LC Authority file, and other tools to provide consistency in the creation of cataloging records and databases. However, the public's demand for easier to use search engines, the library's fiscal considerations in a period of shrinking budgets, RDA and FRBR, and the proliferation of digital resources may change the way catalogers operate in the not too distant future. In addition, with continuously improved automation and the potential to purchase vendor/publisher-created catalog records catalogers will, it is likely, perform less basic descriptive and subject-analysis work. There may be opportunities to contribute expertise in the design and development of new technology such as new search engines that will work with the strengths of library catalogs and the creation of institutional repositories. However, this type of shift will require a willingness to learn new technological skills as well as necessary training, funding and administrative support.

Academic libraries use various organizational models to manage workflow and access to digital materials. In some cases, not much has changed as the charting follows the established flow of print-based materials. This is just one more format: selection remains the responsibility of bibliographers/collection managers and cataloging is still performed by catalogers (though some librarians have combined assignments). Where cataloging is separated by format such as monographic, serials, and government publications, the process of description and access to ER may continue to be the responsibility of staff in a standard cataloging unit. However, librarians in other libraries have created entirely new divisions to manage their digital materials and these new divisions control the entire process of selection, acquisitions, license, cataloging, and maintenance. In a small library where there are only one or two librarians or library assistants the staff will need to be responsible for multiple aspects of electronic resource management. Many librarians have come to rely on consortial arrangements to increase their purchase-power to obtain ER. Some also rely on vendor/publishers to supply catalog records and A-Z lists. As publishers make more materials available in the e-only format the need for collaboration among vendors, libraries, and publishers will increase.

The nature of electronic materials is often volatile and shape-shifting. While serials catalogers may understand resource title changes and alterations in the numbering schemes of serials they have not dealt with the scale of change inherent in online resources. In addition, titles are often purchased as part of package deals and vendor/publishers change the titles they offer from year to year. An electronic resource is not acquired, cataloged, and shelved like print-based and other physical resources. The essence of a library's holdings, its archived collection, is philosophically and realistically different in a digital environment.

As regards workflow, library organizations vary in the assignment of digital resources cataloging. Many librarians manage electronic materials in much the same way as other formats, while other librarians pull the process of digital materials, i.e., the order, acquisition, cataloging, and maintenance of, into one digital resources management unit.

Work with ER often involves cross-departmental or cross-sectional collaboration and there must be a willingness and ability among library employees to communicate well with each other as well as the proper training in order to identify problems. For example, what is the best treatment of an item in terms of the electronic record created for its management if the newest version of the resources is treated as a monograph, but a record already exists that treats the item as a serial? Other common communication challenges/opportunities might be when public service employees hear from patrons who have had trouble with access to an online resource or a collection manager who has identified a new digital resource for consideration. Catalogers often consult with acquisitions staff to establish subscription information or to determine a hyperlink address.

Even though library paraprofessional are weary of the need to constantly learn new procedures, rules, and computer systems, library procedures must be updated frequently to accommodate AACR revisions, CONSER updates, MARC updates, changes or upgrades in OCLC and RLIN, local practice, and ILS migrations. Policy and procedure-writing as well as training may fall upon the cataloging librarian, but is also often a responsibility of upper-level cataloging assistants. Training and communication are crucial in today's library because of the rapid changes, increase in cooperative partnerships, and availability of new technologies.

## *DESCRIPTION AND ACCESS*

ER cataloging librarians work with straightforward as well as complex digital resources such as integrating resources (updating Web sites, updating databases, updating loose-leafs), electronic journals, books, and government documents. Each resource requires unique coding considerations based on national rules and local practices.

Here are a few crucial AACR2 definitions that define specific formats:

*Continuing Resource:* "A bibliographic resource that is issued over time with no predetermined conclusion. Continuing resources include serials and ongoing integrating resources."[9]

*Integrating Resource:* "A bibliographic resource that is added to or changed by means of updates that do not remain discrete and are integrated into the whole. Integrating resources can be finite or continuing."[10]

*Monograph:* "A bibliographic resource that is complete in one part or intended to be completed within a finite number of parts."[11]

*Serial:* "A continuing resource issued in a succession of discrete parts, usually bearing numbering, that has no predetermined conclusion. Examples of serials include journals, magazines, electronic journals, continuing directories, annual reports, newspapers, and monographic series."[12]

[LCRI 1.0] : Decisions Before Cataloging–This Library of Congress Rule Interpretation provides guidelines to aid a cataloger to make the decision on what aspect of the bibliographic resource is being described and what type of issuance does the resource represent: monograph, serial, or integrating resource.[13]

The need for LCRI 1.0 clearly indicates the overlap that ER present: format decisions frequently are not clear-cut. Publishers have more options to update and present their product electronically and this provides challenges for bibliographic description, including the fundamental question: What type of resource is being described? This question is not as simple to answer with digital materials; the decision as to whether it is a print item that represents a monographic series or a serial is not always self-evident.

## What Makes Digital Resources Unique in Terms of Description and Access?

AACR2 Rev. 2002 incorporates a broader scope in order to provide bibliographic description for the international community. Chapter 9 details rules for the description of all forms of ER with direct or remote access.

The new rules allow more flexibility to catalog ER in recognition that this format may require catalogers to glean information about the item from a variety of sources. The identification of the chief source of information for digital materials has presented difficulties under past cataloging rules because the *title page* of a digital resource does not always encompass the most complete description of the resource.

The chief source of information for ER is outlined in Rule 9.0B1:

> The chief source of information for ER is the resource itself. Take the information from formally presented evidence (e.g., title screen(s), main menus, program statements, initial display(s) of information, home page(s), the file header(s) including "Subject": lines, en-

coded metadata (e.g., TEI headers, HTML/XML meta tags), and the physical carrier or its labels), including information that has been uncompressed, printed out, or otherwise processed for use.[14]

This revision differs immensely from the previous AACR, Chapter 9, which was called Computer Files, and reflects more familiarity with the difficulties and concerns of catalogers who work to accurately describe the many types of digital resources. The previous AACR rule 9.0B1 directed the cataloger to take the chief source of information from the title screen.[15]

Though this latest revision was a step-up from previous editions of AACR to try to get a handle on the fluid nature of ER, problems remain. Steve Shadle in, "A Square Peg in a Round Hole: Applying AACR2 to Electronic Journals," presents an excellent discussion of many of the problems encountered by catalogers in their efforts to catalog ER. Shadle notes that resources on the Internet differ from their print-based counterparts in several important ways: they may be organized differently, they are mutable, sometimes they have added functionality, and they don't follow the same display standards.[16]

Specifically, these differences lead to difficulties to determine title proper, first issue, and correct format. Journals may be organized in a database by article, rather than by issue and what was clearly a serial in print format may be part of an integrating database when repackaged electronically; format may have implications for the organization of the library's A-Z list as well as the bibliographic work form a cataloger chooses to describe the resource. Many A-Z lists are organized under separate headings for e-books, e-journals, indexes, and databases. If a patron uses an A-Z list to locate a journal by title and the journal has been repackaged into an aggregator database s/he might think that the library no longer has access to the resource, if only the journal title section is checked; many A-Z lists do not have the cross-reference capabilities of the OPAC so they are limited in their search usability. Journals with multiple title changes are particularly problematic for patrons who limit their search to an A-Z list. In time, search and retrieval options for tools other than the OPAC will become more powerful and effective.

## *SINGLE RECORD vs. SEPARATE RECORD vs. NO RECORD*

The debates on the merits to catalog serials with a single bibliographic record for all versions of a title as opposed to a separate record for each format has proliferated because e-journals have become a standard access point for the delivery of digital information to users. While each approach has benefits and drawbacks both are used to varying levels of success by librarians.

What is described when an electronic resource is cataloged? The rules are a synthesis of expression, rather than manifestation. Single e-journal records are, for the most part, based on a print-based item with access provided to digital versions in other MARC fields, e.g., 856. Separate records also have elements of a print-based description such as the fixed field dates and the publication/imprint information.

In the future, however, discussions among catalogers will go beyond the single versus separate record issue. Experiments with FRBR, new metadata coding and standards, and core data records, i.e., LC's access-level record, will continue to evolve national/local policies in bibliographic description.

Separate records are recommended by AACR Rule 0.24 that reads in part, "It is important to bring out all aspects of the item being cataloged, including its content, its carrier, its type of publication, its bibliographic relationships, and whether it is published or unpublished."[17]

In strict adherence to AACR a cataloger would create a separate record for each class of material; thus, a print and an electronic record would be created following the appropriate chapter instructions. For an electronic journal the cataloger would look to chapter 9 to find descriptive rules and chapter 12 for the continuing resource aspects.

As more library materials are delivered electronically, how much sense will it make to continue to create bibliographic records based on print resources? There has been an assumption among some librarians that electronic journals are, essentially, the same as their print-based counterpart with a minor difference being the carrier. However, not all journals are organized and displayed in the same fashion; publishers combine title changes under the most recent title or license individual articles to aggregator databases. While many librarians and patrons feel that separate records cause clutter in OPACs others think that a single record, which contains elements of several different formats, is just as clumsy.

Separate records do require more staff time and expense for creation and maintenance, but separate records purchased from vendor/publishers or shared through a consortium can be downloaded directly into an OPAC. Also, when a library drops a subscription to an electronic package, which can involve hundreds of titles, separate records can be deleted or suppressed by an automated systems program. Single records can be more difficult to untangle as individual MARC fields will need to be edited or removed.

The Government Printing Office (GPO), which has had a policy of single records for government publications since the 1970s, announced a major shift in a draft memo dated January 11, 2005 that notes that over 85% of FDLP titles are available electronically and states, "GPO cataloging policy must reflect the prominence of electronic publications by always providing full bibliographic access."[18]

This policy change has the potential to have a major impact on depository libraries that follow GPO practice, but to date, more than one year since the announcement; the policy change has not been implemented. Has it been reconsidered? Was there such a large outcry from the GODORT community that the GPO decided to continue with the single record approach?

There are many reasons why libraries look to CONSER for guidance to catalog e-journals. In Module 31 of the CONSER Cataloging Manual catalogers are offered a *non-cataloging* single record option as well as a *cataloging* aggregator-neutral option. If the online version has full-text access and can be considered a substitute for the original print resource or if only partial access is available and a separate record is not warranted then a single record is adequate. If an online version of a print resource has significant additional content not available in the original then a separate record is advised. Implemented in July 2003, the aggregator-neutral practice allows description based on any or all of the versions of an electronic publication.[19]

Differences among various aggregators that provide the same title do not require a new bibliographic record as they once did. It is much easier for catalog assistants to locate and export electronic journal records from OCLC since the aggregator-based records were collapsed into a single record for the online version.

CONSER advocates that catalogers regard the single record as easier for patrons to navigate with immediate expediency. Initial cost savings are another benefit of the approach to add fields to a single record, rather than to create separate records. In a serial record, a cataloger is instructed to add descriptive elements of the digital resource to the print record when the two formats have similar content, i.e., a print journal that retains the concept of volume/issue with the online format. If the content differs substantially, if the print format ceases and the journal is continued as online-only, or if there is no print counterpart (born online), the cataloger should create a separate record. CONSER outlines guidelines for both the single and separate record approach in Module 31.2.3.[20]

Should libraries eliminate all bibliographic records for ER and, simply, list the titles on the library's Web site in alphabetical order? Why bother to catalog these resources at all? They are slippery–linked one day to one vendor and then the next day to another vendor or back to the publisher. Why bother with subject analysis or title changes or any kind of description?

Controlled vocabulary, authorized subject headings, and authority control are all essential stalwarts of description and access. These practices, well-established throughout the international library and information science community, make bibliographic records interoperable. Briscoe, Selden, and Nyberg studied best practices to provide access to online journals in a law library in the "post-Google world."[21]

Researchers have different approaches to their searches for online materials so these authors advocate the use of multiple ways to create access to digital resources, i.e., create a bibliographic record and add a link; add icons to a library's Web site that link to e-resources; and create an organized list of titles and/or subjects to add to the library's Web site. Online resources should be cataloged along with the other materials the library holds so that users have one place where they can search the entire collection. A list of resources on the library's Web site is necessary to help patrons who won't use the catalog and are satisfied to find one or two articles of interest in an aggregator database.

## RESOURCE DESCRIPTION AND ACCESS (RDA): THE NEW AACR

Tom Delsey has been appointed editor of this latest edition of AACR that is called *RDA: Resource Description and Access.* The Joint Steering Committee for Revision of Anglo-American Cataloging Rules includes representation from the American Library Association's Committee on Cataloging: Description and Access (CC:DA). The joint committee is overseen by the Committee of Principals whose members represent the Canadian Library Association, the American Library Association, the Chartered Institute of Library and Information Professionals (CILIP), the British Library, the National Library of Canada, and the Library of Congress.[22]

There is agreement in the cataloging community that AACR has become too complex. One of the major goals of RDA is to simplify the code and make it more consistent/less redundant. RDA will include guidelines that describe analog and digital materials and should be applicable internationally as a resource description metadata standard that uses the FRBR model.[23]

*RDA* will be published primarily as a Web-based tool though a print edition will also be available. This update of AACR is necessary to address the problems of code that was designed for a card catalog environment that no longer exists. RDA will be structured in three parts: one for resource description, another for FRBR *relationship* guidelines, and a third for access point control. In addition, RDA will provide a glossary, index, and appendices.[24]

The guidelines for the description of the attributes and relationships of the FRBR entities, i.e., *work, expression, manifestation,* and *item,* are key to RDA. FRBR was developed by the International Federation of Library Associations (IFLA) in the 1990s. Its principles allow for better collocation of works with multiple manifestations such as Mark Twain's *Huckleberry Finn,* the Bible, or any of Shakespeare's plays. Since FRBR is a relatively new concept there is a certain amount of trepidation to use it on the part of catalogers. How should it be implemented in catalogs? Does the ILS need to be redesigned? Jennifer Bowen addresses the FRBR data model in light of its applicability to cataloging and the FRBRphobia of those who dread its implementation.[25] The Joint Steering Committee on Format Variation Working Group has studied the use of the FRBR entity expression as opposed to the current practice of cataloging at the manifestation-level. Significant difficulties such as the fact that libraries don't acquire multiple manifestations of the same expression at the same time (and, therefore, won't have all the necessary bibliographic data) led the joint committee to conclude that librarians should continue to catalog works at the manifestation-level.[26] The group continues to study how the best means of expression-level collocation can be provided. FRBR is less likely to be feared once RDA is published and hands-on FRBR catalog prototypes can be viewed and tried.

## CONSORTIUMS AND COLLABORATIONS

The University of California (UC) is a ten-campus system each of which with its own research specializations; in addition, its libraries collect general materials for undergraduate study. In 1997, UC developed the California Digital Library (CDL) to address issues related to electronic information delivery. An ER Task Force (TFER2) was appointed in 1998 to develop CDL cataloging standards and a plan to share records among the UC campuses. The Shared Cataloging Project (SCP) was established in 1999 to provide a means to centrally catalog ER that were purchased and licensed by the CDL and deliver the records to the campuses.[27]

This organizational structure has tremendous cost and time-saving benefits for all UC campuses.

Librarians have used cooperative bibliographic utilities such as OCLC and RLIN to download and create catalog records for many years. In the past, records were searched and exported title by title. With the acquisition of large packages of online materials that contain hundreds/thousands of titles, library managers look to options for the purchase of vendor/publisher record sets, which can be batched and downloaded quickly.

Outsourcing has often been viewed with suspicion by catalogers who have worked with vendors on retrospective conversion projects in the past. Among the problems identified with outsourced catalog records are poor-quality descriptions and missing or duplicate records.[28]

Partnerships and improved communication between vendor/publishers and catalogers may change this view. Regina Reynolds, Head of the National Serials Data Program at the Library of Congress, was one of the speakers at the Conference on Bibliographic Control in the New Millennium in 2000. She identified a number of potential partnerships for metadata creation/sharing and discussed initiatives such as the use of CORC to translate Dublin Core elements into MARC tags and the creation of standardized Web templates for resource creators to aid automatic metadata creation.[29]

## *IS THERE A FUTURE FOR CATALOGERS?*

Will ER continue to be described? Do search engines such as Google, necessarily, portend the demise of cataloging? At a seminar, a librarian asked, "In the age of digital information, of Internet access, of electronic keyword searching, just how much do we need to continue to spend on carefully constructed catalogs?"[30] Many catalogers believe that controlled vocabulary and authority control are as indispensable now as they have been in the past, perhaps more crucial than ever. Reliance on keyword searches does not impose order or structure to the ever growing World Wide Web of information. According to Barbara Tillett, the library world must identify where consistency is important, keep the basics of description and access, and forego special case laws.[31]

## CONCLUSION

In this exciting, sometimes chaotic, Google-ized environment where patrons demand instant access and prefer simple keyword searches, often at the expense of precision and accuracy, what can librarians offer researchers? What can they do differently? How can they contribute, as in the past 200 years, to the organization of information? Librarians must stay abreast of current trends in information technology, management, organization, and description and educate themselves and their staff as new technologies and new initiatives in cataloging metadata develop. The international library and information community must continue to move in positive directions, build new systems that enhance library catalogs, and integrate multiple database functions. These are roles that can be played by catalogers of digital resources who represent an important segment of the ER librarianship community. In an arena dominated by the digital and the cyber, these library professionals contribute on a regular basis to the improvement of the library catalog; to the understanding and implementation of new tools and technologies; to cooperation with all stakeholders of the information world; and to innovation and change. They are essential to the concept of a human element in the digital information age.

## NOTES

1. For more information, see the Joint Steering Committee for Revision of Anglo-American Cataloging Rules Web site: http://www.collectionscanada.ca/jsc/rda.html

2. Seymour Lubetzky and Elaine Svenonius, "The Vicissitudes of Ideology and Technology in Anglo-American Cataloging Since Panizzi and a Prospective Reformation of the Catalog for the Next Century," chapter in Tschera Harkness Connell and Robert L. Maxwell, eds., *The Future of Cataloging : Insights From the Lubetzky Symposium, April 18, 1998, University of California, Los Angeles* (Chicago: American Library Association, 2000), 4.

3. Ibid., 4-5.

4. Charles A. Cutter, *Rules for a Printed Dictionary Catalogue* (Washington, DC: USGPO, 1876), 10.

5. Lubetzky and Svenonius, 8.

6. *LC21: A Digital Strategy for the Library of Congress*, (Washington, DC: National Academy Press, 2000), 22; http://www.nap.edu/openbook/0309071445/html (viewed March 3, 2006).

7. Ibid, 122-143.

8. "Defining an *Access Level* MARC/AACR Catalog Record Project Report," http://www.loc.gov/catdir/access/report_final.pdf (viewed December 8, 2005).

9. *Anglo-American Cataloging Rules*, 2nd ed., 2002 rev. (Chicago: American Library Association, 2002), Appendix D-2.

10. Ibid., Appendix D-4.

11. Ibid.

12. Ibid., Appendix D-7.

13. *Cataloging Service Bulletin* 108 (Spring 2005): 14-21.

14. *AACR2 2002 rev.*, 9-3.

15. *Anglo-American Cataloging Rules*, 2nd ed., 1988 rev. (Chicago: American Library Association, 1988), 222.

16. Steven C. Shadle, "A Square Peg in a Round Hole: Applying AACR2 to Electronic Journals," chapter in Wayne Jones, ed., *E-Serials: Publishers, Libraries, Users, and Standards*, 2nd ed. (New York: Haworth Information Press, 2003), 124.

17. *AACR2 2002 rev.*, I-2.

18. "National Bibliography Policy: Separate Records for Titles in Multiple Formats," http://www.access.gpo.gov/su_docs/fdlp/cip/SeparateRecord.pdf (viewed March 24, 2006).

19. "Aggregator-Neutral Record," http://www.loc.gov/acq/conser/agg-neutral-recs.html (viewed September 20, 2005).

20. "Module 31: Remote Access Electronic Serials," in *CONSER Cataloging Manual*, 2002 edition, Update 1, Spring 2004, ed. Jean Hirons (Washington, DC: Library of Congress, 2004), Module 31.2.3, pp.14-19.

21. Georgia Briscoe, Karen Selden, and Cheryl Rae Nyberg, "The Catalog vs. the Home Page? Best Practices in Connecting to Online Resources," *Law Library Journal* 95(2) (spring 2003): 151-174.

22. See the *Joint Steering Committee for Revision of Anglo-American Cataloging Rules FAQ* at: http://www.collectionscanada.ca/jsc/rda.html

23. Ibid.

24. Ibid.

25. Jennifer Bowen, "FRBR: Coming Soon to Your Library?" *Library Resources & Technical Services* 49(3) (July 2005): 175-188.

26. Ibid.

27. Patricia Sheldahl French, Rebecca Culbertson, and Lai-Ying Hsiung, "One for Nine: The Shared Cataloging Program at the California Digital Library," *Serials Review* 28(1) (2002): 4-12.

28. Kyle Banerjee, "Taking Advantage of Outsourcing Options: Using Purchased Record Sets to Maximize Cataloging Effectiveness," *Cataloging & Classification Quarterly* 32(1) (2001): 55-64.

29. Regina Romano Reynolds, "Partnerships to Mine Unexploited Sources of Metadata," http://www.loc.gov/catdir/bibcontrol/Reynolds_paper.html (viewed March 3, 2006).

30. Deanna B. Marcum, "The Future of Cataloging : Address to the Ebsco Leadership Seminar, Boston, Massachusetts, January 16, 2005," http://www.loc.gov/library/reports/CatalogingSpeech.pdf (viewed March 24, 2006).

31. Barbara B. Tillett, "Change Cataloging, But Don't Throw the Baby Out with the Bath Water," http://www.loc.gov/catdir/cpso/Mittler.pdf (viewed December 8, 2005).

doi:10.1300/J105v32n03_02

# Electronic Resources (ER) Librarians, Usage Data, and a Changing World

Alea Henle

**SUMMARY.** What factors affect the handling of usage data? What skills does an electronic resources (ER) librarian need to work with usage data? How do they solve problems innovatively and contribute to the library's efforts to deliver digital information? First and foremost, ER librarians need a firm understanding of the libraries in which they work and what innovations or adaptations are appropriate. There are no *true answers* to the question of how to handle usage data, which leaves the field open for innovation and customization. doi:10.1300/J105v32n03_03 *[Article copies available for a fee from The Haworth Document Delivery Service: 1-800-HAWORTH. E-mail address: <docdelivery@haworthpress.com> Website: <http://www. HaworthPress.com> © 2007 by The Haworth Press. All rights reserved.]*

**KEYWORDS.** Usage data, technology, standards

Alea Henle, MS, formerly Assistant Professor and Electronic Resource Librarian, Colorado State University, is currentlyworking on a doctorate in history at the University of Connecticut, researching information issues in Early America (E-mail: alea.henle@huskymail.uconn.edu).

[Haworth co-indexing entry note]: "Electronic Resources (ER) Librarians, Usage Data, and a Changing World." Henle, Alea. Co-published simultaneously in *Collection Management* (The Haworth Information Press, an imprint of The Haworth Press) Vol. 32, No. 3/4, 2007, pp. 277-288; and: *Electronic Resources Librarianship and Management of Digital Information: Emerging Professional Roles* (ed: Mark Jacobs) The Haworth Information Press, an imprint of The Haworth Press, 2007, pp. 277-288. Single or multiple copies of this article are available for a fee from The Haworth Document Delivery Service [1-800- HAWORTH, 9:00 a.m. - 5:00 p.m. (EST). E-mail address: docdelivery@haworthpress.com].

## INTRODUCTION

In the time between the writing of these words and the publication of this book, the world usage data will have changed, significantly, again. In 2005, several publishers revised their usage data Web sites and reporting styles; MPS Technologies released ScholarlyStats, a usage data collection service;[1] and Thomson Scientific, a subsidiary of the Thomson Corporation, announced plans to develop a product that integrates usage data with Journal Citation Reports (JCR).[2] During the same time period, Counting Online Usage of NeTworked Electronic Resources (COUNTER) published *Release 2 of the COUNTER Code of Practice for Journals and Databases* http://www.projectcounter. org/r2/COUNTER_COP_ Release_2.pdf and *Draft Release 1 of the COUNTER Code of Practice for Books and Reference Works*[3] http://www. projectcounter.org/cop_ books_ref.html.

More innovations and shifts will follow throughout 2006, especially from the offices of the Standardized Usage Data Handling Initiative (SUSHI) working group whose members have developed a protocol that automates the delivery of usage data to Electronic Resource Management Systems (ERMS)[4] http://www.library.cornell.edu/cts/elicensestudy/ ermi2/sushi/.

These actions exemplify the two primary forces that drive and change the world of usage data: technology and standards. Electronic resources (ER) librarians operate within a framework that is, partially, dictated by external forces. However, success in addressing usage data is based, also, on internal factors. To date, the extant literature that concerns usage data has focused on standardization, with some reference to specific application, but with little discussion of the role and responsibilities of the individual(s) who are charged to handle the data. This chapter will discuss the environment within which ER librarians operate, the skills and characteristics of ER librarians that are desirable in order to ensure continued success in the acquisition and use of usage data, and how ER librarians apply usage data to contribute to the delivery of digital information.

## THE ENVIRONMENT

The environment within which usage data are processed comprises three main parts: two external and one internal. The external aspects are the evolution of standards and technology while the internal aspect is the institution within which the ER librarian operates. While knowledge of each factor is important, the internal factor plays the most vital role to determine the line between success and failure.

### Standards

The march to standardize the collection and dissemination of usage data is far from complete. Multiple entities have issued standards of one kind or another, but to ensure compliance with these standards is another matter. The earliest efforts included the Association of Research Libraries (ARL) E-Metrics Project[5] and the International Coalition of Library Consortia (ICOLC) guidelines.[6] These began the process of the definition of data categories and the establishment of minimum requirements with regard to their collection and dissemination by vendor/publishers. However, many vendor/publishers have focused their attention on the Codes of Practice issued by COUNTER.[7]

The benefit of the rush to offer COUNTER-compliant reports is that the COUNTER initiative incorporates an audit mechanism whereby compliance can be verified. The application of COUNTER reports provides data that can be considered comparable, but verification will raise the bar. COUNTER has issued two Codes of Practice applicable to journals and databases and a draft code with regard to books and reference works.

The adoption of standards is, clearly, of benefit to libraries: comparable data allows for improved analysis while fewer reporting formats mean less time and effort on the part of those who gather and disseminate them. However, there are several aspects that remain troublesome. First, the majority of ER librarians may and do comment on and contribute toward the further development of standards, but they have little to no direct influence. Second, despite the recent rush on the part of vendor/publishers to offer COUNTER-compliant reports, ER librarians still find that they have to work with multiple reporting formats delivered in a variety of ways. Also, the question of how to handle data from those vendor/publishers that do not yet offer COUNTER-compliant reports remains. In addition, standards for books and reference works are only in the draft stages and the adoption of and compliance with them will, obviously, only follow their final issuance. Last, technology will continue to change during the development stages. Federated searching and *pre-fetch* services such as Google Scholar have complicated the picture and may make necessary further adjustments in the approach to the collection and use of data. Standardization will always lag behind the technological innovations that make it a requirement.

### Technology

The winds of technological change buffet usage data from two very different directions. Many vendor/publishers offer tools to assist ER librarians in the diverse tasks that surround the collection of usage data. They are, also, at work on complementary products to assist in the tasks which support the analysis of such data. On the other hand, technological innovations continue to change the conditions under which data are collected. Both factors complicate the issue, to one extent or another.

On the beneficial side, vendor/publishers, with their products, approach usage data from multiple angles. The ScholarlyStats product from MPS Technologies is focused the collection of usage data from vendor/publishers and the delivery of unified reports. The SUSHI protocol will automate delivery of COUNTER reports between participating developers and data providers. The ERMS modules offered by information vendors include functions to store and analyze usage data, i.e., cost per use features.[8] These products are based upon COUNTER reporting practices and are in various stages of development. As development proceeds, it is likely that value-added features offered in one ERMS will make their way into other ERMS modules. Thomson Corporation, as mentioned earlier, has announced its intention to develop a product that will integrate usage data its JCR product, which will provide the opportunity for further analysis of the data. As such products flourish or fail, other vendor/publishers will enter the arena, while vendors that are already in the ERMS business will expand what they offer. Librarians should be proactive in their evaluation of these products and encourage the further development of collection and application tools.

The flip-side of the benefits of technological developments is the complications that arise from the application of new tools. For instance, federated searching can inflate the results from database searches and session counts; federated searching can also shut down access to databases when their use across a number of databases that have limits on the number of simultaneous users who can access the database at the same time resulting in a false indication to the system that the maximum number of allowed users has been reached. Google Scholar as well as other services pre-fetch documents that underlie the first three or more search results (the number varies by service) and load the documents into the browser cache–if the results were links to full-text, then the vendor/publisher records a request. When the searcher activates the link, another request is sent that might be separately counted.[9] In a presentation at the 2005 North American Serials Interest Group (NASIG) annual meeting, Oliver Pesch noted that "without some kind of control, this activity could result in significant over-counting, [but] vendors can change systems to recognize pre-fetch" and, thus, avoid the second count.[10] While remedies for these issues exist, they are not, for the most part, under the control of librarians.

## *Local Environment*

Evolving standards and technology, as noted above, play a large part to define the environment within which usage data is handled. However, the local environment is paramount. ER librarians perform their duties within the cultures and climates of their libraries and utilize the resources of these institutions. If this exigency is not understood or is disregarded, the job will be much more difficult. Less reference was made to ER librarians in the preceding sections because the extent to which standards and technology affect ER librarian work is determined, to a great extent, by the local culture and resources.

The local environment defines the world in which an ER librarian or ER unit operates. How many people are available to address the problems that surround the collection, organization, and dissemination of usage data? How much of their time is already occupied with other commitments? How much money is available to purchase vendor-offered, data analysis products? How many resources–databases, e-journals, and e-book collections–are involved? What resources are made available through arrangements with consortia? The answers to these and other questions will depend upon the size of the library as larger places with larger staffs inevitably, are in a better position to allocate the needed resources to the collection, analysis, and dissemination of usage data. Librarians who work in libraries with fewer resources may have to balance the way they handle usage data against competitive claims; work with usage data will not always win. Therefore, the myriad of issues that serve to define the local environment in regard to the way librarians handle usage data can be boiled down to two questions:

1. What data is valued and should be collected, and
2. What resources can be dedicated to the process?

Knowledge and understanding of the local environment are essential for the effective process and application of usage data.

## THE ER LIBRARIAN

The extant literature that analyzed the position of the ER librarian is in its early stages. Much of the discussion, thus far, has been on the less formal side, e.g., a discussion featured at NASIG's 20th annual meeting: a strategy session (repeated the following day with different attendees) that focused on the qualities that are desirable in an ER librarian.[11] On the more formal side, two articles exist which analyze job descriptions for ER librarians. Plus, there was an earlier article that described the creation of an ER librarian position description.[12]

While specific qualities may be better-suited to some libraries more than others and while the organizational structure of each library will be a factor as well, the discussion in this section will concentrate on characteristics with the broadest application. Also, as the topic of this chapter is usage data, the qualities that are discussed will be referenced in that context.

### Qualities Desired in the ER Librarian

Overall, flexibility surfaced as a key attribute in the discussion at the second NASIG session referred to above. This is a particularly desirable quality with regard to handling usage data. Since change is a given in the digital arena, librarians must be able to work with a constantly moving target. In addition, ER librarians are faced with the task to explain usage data–its applicability, changing structure, and limitations–to colleagues, administrators, and others. In short, in addition to being flexible, ER librarians must find a way to encourage flexibility–or, at a minimum, acceptance of the changing circumstances–in those they serve.

Another important quality in an ER librarian is technological savvy. At a minimum, it is necessary to understand electronic tools such as spreadsheets and their utilization. In addition, it is preferred that ER librarians will have–or be willing to work to achieve–the ability to design and/or adapt databases, whether simple or complex, to organize, analyze, and report usage data. Usage data are, inherently, fractious due to the way databases and journals are shifted from platform to platform and from publisher to publisher and because libraries often have separate subscriptions to backfiles and archives. An ER librarian who works in a library where there is an interest in a cost per use analysis may need to design a method to combine usage and cost data.

Usage information comprises thousands of individual bits of data and this fact makes attention to detail another desirable quality of the ER librarian. In the midst of work with myriad and massive amounts of information, an ER librarian must be attentive to errors that arise as well as to places where and circumstances under which errors may occur, and take action to correct the situation. Vendor/publisher usage reports have not proved infallible. Within the past year, at least two have reviewed and reissued usage data that was inaccurate when originally compiled and issued. The devil is in the details because inaccurate usage reports may impact, incorrectly, how a particular resource is viewed.

Communication skills are of high importance. In a study of position descriptions found in *American Libraries*, communication skills were mentioned in 220 of 298 job advertisements.[13]

In a look at the issue from the viewpoint of the creation of a position description, Bożena Bednarek-Michalska rated communication skills as eight on a scale of one to eight.[14]

Communication is closely related and necessary to understand the local, library environment, an issue important enough to warrant additional discussion. ER librarians must analyze local needs, interests, and resources on a regular basis because the best concatenation and presentation of data means nothing if it is not used. Communication skills are critical tools to use to gain an understanding of the local environment, which is vital to the effective accomplishment of several of the tasks that are outlined in the next section, e.g., setting priorities and the performance of public relations.

Patience, also, is a valuable trait for ER librarians as they attempt to explain to their colleagues the reasons that some information is important; that some information is difficult or impossible to acquire; or that some information costs too much to provide. Patience is also necessary for librarians who work with constant, technological shifts. It is a great plus to be able to wait out difficulties with technology and technological advances (and to encourage patience among others) as difficulties often sort themselves out.

## Organization

Who handles usage data? With whom do they work? To whom do they report? These decisions are dependent to a large extent on a given library's size and staffing level. ER librarian position announcements do not indicate a clear assignment of the position to technical or public services and there is no definitive description of the position.

However, in relation to the management of usage data, communication skills are the most important of the desirable qualities for ER librarians referenced earlier. ER librarians who work with usage data need to communicate well with individuals in units across the library–from acquisitions and serials to reference and circulation. In an article on cooperation between technical and reference services was a quote from a cataloger who noted, "frequent cordial interaction is the key" to a symbiotic relationship."[15]

## MANAGING USAGE DATA

How do ER librarians solve problems innovatively? How do they integrate and manage usage data so that it contributes to the library's delivery of digital information? As noted previously, the extent to which usage data are of import varies, dependent upon the library's size and staffing. However, regardless of size, certain commonalities apply across the board. The effective management and application of usage data relies on the performance of four over-arching tasks. From assessment through public relations, the tasks discussed here constitute the major issues that facilitate problem-solving and ensure the delivery of meaningful data.

### Assessment

Assessment offers to librarians an opportunity to understand the nature and use of digital resources within the local environment. A director of the American Association of Higher Education (AAHE) noted that:

> Assessment becomes a collective means whereby colleagues discover the fit between institutional or programmatic expectations for . . . achievement and patterns of actual . . . achievement.[16]

Although written in the context of student learning, the words are also applicable to the evaluation of digital resources. The conduct of assessment involves the review of available data and technology, i.e., vendor/ publishers, formats, standards, tools, unaddressed issues, etc., and interviews with users. Given the changes imposed by the external evolution of technology and standards, to perform an assessment of the management of usage data enables an ER librarian to identify problems and opportunities with regard to its acquisition, organization, delivery, and application. It is a truism that the first step to address a problem is to identify it. Once an issue is identified, assessment offers detailed information and empowers the ER librarian to draw on contributions from a wider community to track developments in usage data management, to jettison ineffective approaches, to identify effective responses to problems, and to design and implement solutions. Performing as assessments, on a small or a large scales, enables the ER librarian to tailor the effective delivery of usage data, which facilitates the evaluation of digital, information delivery.

## Priorities

"Just because you *can* do something does not mean you *should* [emphasis in original]."[17]

It is crucial to the provision of usage data in a helpful and timely manner that the ER librarian who is charged with the process prioritize the tasks involved, which may mean that some things will have to be moved to the back-burner. Judith A. Siess breaks down the process of prioritization into several steps, i.e., what to do, when to do it, how to do it, what not to do, and reevaluation.[18] Innovations in the areas of technology and standards offer an additional incentive for the ER librarian to evaluate priorities in the management of usage data.

## Tool Evaluation and Development

As noted earlier, this is a time of intense and continuous development within the realm of information technology; specifically, that designed to address the management of usage data. ER librarians must evaluate these tools and make recommendations for their purchase when needed. However, even in libraries that have the funds and the willingness to purchase new software and/or services to use to manage usage data, these resources may not address all the needs of the library in the management of usage data. Therefore, in addition to an evaluation of tools for local utility the ER librarian may face the need to develop tools to integrate information from a variety of sources, e.g., vendor/publisher-generated reports, local catalogs, or other tools, and reformat them into an end-product that contains the data and expresses the desired relationships for librarians to use in their evaluation of digital resources. This means familiarity with spreadsheets and databases, but also may mean the design and development of in-house databases. When local resources do not suffice for the development of a local solution, beta-testing new developments is an option as is a lobby of vendor/publishers for enhancements.

## Public Relations

There are many discussions in the professional literature on the topic of public relations between libraries and external groups/individuals–patrons, governing boards, etc. Although lower in profile, internal public relations between library departments and individuals also play an important role in library operations. Effective public relations contribute to a greater understanding of and consequent use of library resources. The subject of the management of usage data is complex and an ongoing, internal public relations initiative might counter the potential for confusion among librarians, which might lead to a lack of use of the supplied usage data. Good communication is vital. The ER librarian may be responsible for the collection, process, and dissemination of the usage data, but subject specialists, selectors, bibliographers, and administrators will be responsible to apply the data in their evaluation, selection, and liaise endeavors. Lack of communication, or public relations, opens the door to misapplication or non-use of usage data. Internal public relations involve the conveyance of technical information on where to go to find usage data. Of equal, if not greater import, is to ensure awareness of issues that might affect the accuracy interpretation of data, e.g., instances where vendor/publishers restrict access to usage data (or don't provide it at all), the adoption of standards by vendor/publishers, the impact of federated searching and pre-fetch on data, etc. One reason to establish and maintain good, internal public relations is quite practical: those who provide the resources needed to support the management of usage data will be more supportive if they find value in the data and understand its benefits to themselves.

In addition, librarians who interact with library users, in a reference or instruction, may be able to offer information that places digital resources and usage data in context to user needs and expectations.

## CONCLUSION

Given the evolving nature of the position and the resources with which the ER librarian is involved, the opportunity exists for each individual to put a stamp on the position within an organization. One way to do this is to make a contribution to the development and utilization of usage data. ER librarians, as they manage usage data, must exhibit effective communication skills, flexibility, and an understanding of technology. However, to understand the local environment is the critical step to solve problems, to be innovative, and to ensure the dissemination of meaningful usage data. In a changing world, ER librarians have the potential to effect global developments in the management usage data, but they still work for localized institutions and their most, effective decisions in the management of usage data will take that into account. As there is no one answer to the questions that surround the collection and dissemination of usage data, the ER librarian faces an ongoing quest to assess developments, set priorities, and adapt tools for local use. The arena is ripe for innovation.

## NOTES

1. Martha Sedgewick, e-mail message to LibLicense-L discussion list, May 9, 2005; Martha Sedgewick, e-mail message to author, November 16, 2005.

2. "Thomson Scientific Partners with University Libraries to Develop New Solution for Assessing Journal Use," http://scientific.thomson.com/press/2005/8281610/ (viewed August 25, 2005).

3. "Counting Online Usage of NeTworked Electronic Resources," http://www.projectcounter.org/; "Release 2 of the COUNTER Code of Practice for Journals and Databases," http://www.projectcounter.org/r2/COUNTER_COP_Release_2.pdf (viewed April 2005); "Draft Release 1 of the COUNTER Code of Practice for Books and Reference Works," http://www.projectcounter.org/cop_books_ref.html (viewed January 2005).

4. "Standardized Usage Statistics Harvesting Initiative (SUSHI)," http://www.library.cornell.edu/cts/elicensestudy/ermi2/sushi/ (viewed December 23, 2005).

5. "E-Metrics Activities," http://www.arl.org/stats/newmeas/emetrics/proj.html (viewed August 25, 2005).

6. "Guidelines for Statistical Measures of Usage of Web-Based Information Resources (Update: December 2001)," http://www.library.yale.edu/consortia/2001webstats.htm; "Guidelines for Statistical Measures of Usage of Web-based Indexed, Abstracted, and Full-text Resources (November 1998)," http://www.library.yale.edu/consortia/webstats.html.

7. "Counting Online Usage of NeTworked Electronic Resources Codes of Practice," http://www.projectcounter.org/code_practice.html (viewed January 12, 2006).

8. Vendors that offer Electronic Resources Management products include: Dynix, http://www.dynix.com/products/erm/; Ex Libris, "Verde," http://www.exlibris-usa.com/verde.htm; and Innovative Interfaces, http://www.iii.com/mill/digital.shtml#erm. In other cases, electronic resources management functions are integrated into extant products.

9. Oliver Pesch, "Project COUNTER: Ensuring Consistent Usage Statistics"; Alfred Kraemer, "Insuring Consistent Usage Statistics"; and Jenny Walker, "Cross-Provider Search," presentation sessions, annual meeting of the North American Serials Interest Group, Minneapolis, MN, May 19-22, 2005.

10. Oliver Pesch, "Project COUNTER: Ensuring Consistent Usage Statistics," handout, annual meeting of the North American Serials Interest Group, Minneapolis, MN, May 19-22, 2005.

11. Katy Giananni, "TALK ABOUT: E-Resources Librarian to the Rescue? Creating the Über Librarian, Turning Model Job Descriptions into Practical Positions," discussion

session, annual meeting of the North American Serials Interest Group, Minneapolis, MN, May 19-22, 2005.

12. William Fisher, "The Electronic Resources Librarian Position: A Public Services Phenomenon?" *Library Collections, Acquisitions, & Technical Services* 27(1) (spring 2003): 3-17; Rebecca S. Albitz, "Electronic Resources Librarians in Academic Libraries: A Position Announcement Analysis, 1996-2001," *Portal* 2(4) (October 2002): 589-600; Bozena Bednarek-Michalska. "Creating a Job Description for an Electronic Resources Librarian," *Library Management* 23(8/9): 378-383.

13. Fisher, 11.

14. Bednarek-Michalska, 382.

15. Naomi R. Sutherland and Valerie P. Adams, "Territorial Invasion or Symbiotic Relationship? Technical Services and Reference Cooperation," *College & Research Libraries News* 65(1) (January 2004): 12-15.

16. Peggy L. Maki, "Developing an Assessment Plan to Learn About Student Learning," *Journal of Academic Librarianship* 28(1/2) (January-February 2002): 8-13.

17. Judith A. Siess, *Time Management, Planning, and Prioritization for Librarians* (Lanham, Maryland: Scarecrow Press, 2002).

18. Siess, 162-174.

doi:10.1300/J105v32n03_03

# The Human Element in Digital Preservation

Jacob Nadal

**SUMMARY.** This chapter is a presentation of the major areas of digital preservation activity with reference to representative and well-known projects. It is also a presentation of the roles that Electronic Resources (ER) librarians may take to assist and advocate for digital preservation. The need for human mediation and decision-making during this early period of digital preservation development is emphasized. The roles and responsibilities of the ER librarian is described in the context of emergent business models for digital preservation as well as questions about the impact of licensing and ownership arrangements on ER preservation. doi:10.1300/J105v32n03_04 *[Article copies available for a fee from The Haworth Document Delivery Service: 1-800-HAWORTH. E-mail address: <docdelivery@haworthpress.com> Website: <http://www.HaworthPress.com> © 2007 by The Haworth Press. All rights reserved.]*

**KEYWORDS.** Digital preservation, digital archives, digital repositories, electronic resources, preservation management

---

Jacob Nadal is Field Service Librarian, Barbara Goldsmith Preservation Division, New York Public Libraries, and Visiting Assistant Professor, Pratt Institute and the Indiana University School of Library and Information Science.

Address correspondence to: Jacob Nadal, 5th Avenue and 42nd Street, New York, NY 10018 (E-mail: jacobnadal@nypl.org).

[Haworth co-indexing entry note]: "The Human Element in Digital Preservation." Nadal, Jacob. Co-published simultaneously in *Collection Management* (The Haworth Information Press, an imprint of The Haworth Press) Vol. 32, No. 3/4, 2007, pp. 289-303; and: *Electronic Resources Librarianship and Management of Digital Information: Emerging Professional Roles* (ed: Mark Jacobs) The Haworth Information Press, an imprint of The Haworth Press, 2007, pp. 289-303. Single or multiple copies of this article are available for a fee from The Haworth Document Delivery Service [1-800-HAWORTH, 9:00 a.m. - 5:00 p.m. (EST). E-mail address: docdelivery@haworthpress.com].

## INTRODUCTION

This chapter will cover the major areas of digital preservation activity with reference to representative and well-known projects. However, it should not be viewed as a comprehensive survey of digital preservation activities. The central issue here is not the endeavor to develop reliable digital preservation processes, but the role of electronic resources (ER) librarians who are in the forefront of that development. The endeavor to preserve digital resources is a necessary consequence of the digital library movement, which uses machine processes to enable sophisticated searches and novel uses of online materials. Likewise, many digital preservation activities will involve a great deal of automation, but this does not eliminate the need for human intervention and verification, especially in this adolescent period in digital preservation development. In his advocacy for mass digitization efforts, Michael Keller has proposed that "only a few considerations hinder us from providing our readers, our students, and our faculty with vastly improved opportunities to search, to read, to cite, and to exploit the digitized contents of our libraries."[1] Digital preservation is one of these considerations.

## STORAGE

Successful preservation of digital objects begins with secure and reliable storage. Digital storage media tend to be fragile and unstable, which means that they do not suffer physical stress well and will degrade from inherent chemical and physical exigencies. Even for media that have some potential for long term stability there has not been enough research to substantiate or disprove claims of longevity.

Although certain media fare better than others and may be sufficient for short-term storage, it is clear that digital preservation initiatives cannot rely upon digital media as the primary, preservation format. This approach to preservation is characterized as *media-independence* in discussions on digital preservation and is achieved through the process of copying data.

Copying data is one of the basic activities of computing and numerous strategies exist to perform this operation in a reliable fashion. This process is often referred to as *refreshing* or *bit preservation*, terms which indicate that the 1s and 0s that constitute the structure and content of a document will be maintained in proper order. A distinction must also be made between bit preservation and data backup, which creates a copy of the digital resource at a given point in time. A backup system, in its simplest sense, may only allow for a recovery from media or system failures, while a bit preservation system audits and maintains the integrity of a set of data independent of the media that are used to store them. Among the models that exist for the useful management of this process for digital preservation there are two that have significant differences in their design and methodology, but can fulfill the essential need to keep files viable over the long-term without dependence upon a physical, storage medium.

## *LOCKSS*

LOCKSS, an acronym for Lots of Copies Keep Stuff Safe, is an open-source project that originated at Stanford University. The project's creators, like those at the Federal Depository Library program, cite Thomas Jefferson's 1791 letter to Ebenezer Howard as inspiration for their model, but these 18th century ideas are managed through 21st century technologies.[2]

LOCKSS is a peer-to-peer system that offers reliable storage of digital information, repair of damaged data, and, a recent development, feasible data migration within the LOCKSS framework. The system uses multiple, remote computers (*LOCKSS Appliances*, to use the LOCKSS terminology) to cache data from selected Web sites. In practice, these sites are e-journal Web sites, but LOCKSS has the potential to harvest anything that can be transferred through the Hypertext Transport Protocol (http). Since LOCKSS is an open-source system, other methods to gather resources can be incorporated. A number of LOCKSS projects have sprung up to take advantage of this potential to harvest government documents (LOCKSS-DOCS) and other digital library content, e.g., the MetaArchive of Southern Culture. LOCKSS caches constantly update the network of LOCKSS appliances with information about their contents and the members of this network vote on the validity of one another's stored data. The design of the voting algorithm enables reliable repair of corrupted data across the system and ensures a high degree of resistance to malicious attacks as well. The viability of the process has been demonstrated in the laboratory as well as in real world scenarios, e.g., the fire at Los Alamos National Laboratory.[3]

In the event that the original copy of the resource becomes unavailable, the LOCKSS cache is activated to provide the requested content. LOCKSS cannot replicate server-side functionality, e.g., search tools, but it does store, repair, and reproduce individual instances of digital content. Each LOCKSS machine or peer constantly polls the other peers to determine if the content in its cache is accurate. If it is intact the system records the time when its validity was confirmed and if it is false it signals an alarm and begins to poll the other LOCKSS peers to determine how to correct its cache.

In a test of their system, LOCKSS researchers predicted "with undetected damage at each peer every five years, in the worst case the average rate of false alarms in the system is 44 days, that is, every 44 days some peer in the system sees an alarm. The average peer sees an alarm once in about 120 years." Even more promising is their conclusion that "in over 200 machine-years of the test deployment, we have observed only one peer in which such errors affected polls."[4]

LOCKSS is forthright about its approach to preservation. Central factors in the approach are to use the least complicated means which result in the lowest cost and the longest horizon of technological usefulness. The best summary of this approach may have been given by Maniatis and his fellow LOCKSS researchers in their paper for the 19th ACM Symposium on Operating Systems Principles:

> Digital preservation systems have some unusual features. First, such systems must be very cheap to build and maintain. Second, they need not operate quickly. Their purpose is to prevent rather than expedite change to data. Third, they must function properly for decades, without central control and despite possible interference from attackers or catastrophic failures of storage media such as fire or theft.[5]

## *BIG-BIT ARCHIVES*

The OCLC Digital Archive takes a centralized approach to the storage of data, colloquially called *a big-bit archive*. All data in the archive are stored in a Redundant Array of Independent/Inexpensive Disks (RAID) and are backed-up daily and weekly with backups stored at an off-site facility.[6]

Similar facilities, such as those developed by the High Performance Storage System (HPSS) alliance, are in use in many universities, scientific organizations, and other data centers. The HPSS defines several storage classes and methods to manage large amounts of data. These are referred to as hierarchical, storage systems in which hierarchies of storage media are used to manage various groups of data dependent upon their size and frequency of use.

Indiana University's HPSS service, for example, pairs two terabytes of hard disk space with 1.6 pedabytes of tape storage. Files are first deposited onto disk and then migrated into the tape library over time. Although system backup is not feasible for almost 2 pedabytes of data, the Massive Data Storage System (MDSS) is mirrored to a remote site to ensure that catastrophe does not result in loss of the data.[7]

This big-bit model, obviously, provides benefits in size and scalability. Hierarchical storage systems can grow in size to several pedabytes and can be expanded as far as resources allow. These systems, also, allow for centralized control as well as for activities to be audited in a familiar manner with clearly identified lines of responsibility assigned to various preservation tasks. However, massive capacity and expert staff come at a tremendous cost. For libraries associated with universities or other organizations that have large data centers, some of the cost may be absorbed by their parent organizations. Outsourcing data management may be the most (or only) feasible route for others that need large-capacity data storage.

It is also important to note that, beyond storage and data integrity checking, these data centers do not offer any preservation services, such as migration of content to new formats or emulation of obsolete software. Moreover, these services do not necessarily provide a facility for the addition of preservation services to their process. Although OCLC has stated its intention to incorporate these services in the future, it is not clear whether users will need to rely on OCLC to provide these services or if there will be interfaces to allow in-house or third party preservation services to operate on data in the Digital Archive.

At the present stage of digital preservation development, it is wise to invest in various solutions. Of course, basic backup and replacement of aging media are essential strategies. ER librarians must consider the appropriate use of other tools, as well. LOCKSS is a well-proven and low-cost method of ensuring ongoing e-journal access and has begun to develop services in other areas which concern digital content. Librarians may find it worthwhile to invest in the services enabled by the creation and maintenance of digital archives, especially if they have created digital collections for their institutions.

Tim DiLauro's observation that "the challenge here will be evaluating the strengths and weaknesses of the various systems and selecting one that satisfies or most closely matches your goals [and that] in some cases . . . it might be useful to implement more than one repository or to integrate complementary systems to achieve needed functionality" is well-taken.[8] Librarians must recognize that we are in a period of development and evolution. Digital preservation is not yet at a point where we can select a single tool and consider our obligations fulfilled.

## PRESERVATION STRATEGIES

If we assume that digital resources are maintained bit-perfect, the next digital preservation task is to render those bits in such a way that they are readable. The current approaches to this task are often viewed as competitive (presumably as they contend for scarce resources in time and money), but they are, in fact, complementary in many ways.

### *Migration*

One way to ensure that digital resources remain readable in the future is to migrate data from one format to another. On a small scale, this process is familiar to all computer users who have lived and worked with more than one generation of a software application. As new features and functions are added to programs, or when applications become obsolete the data in files must be converted in order to be usable in the future. Migration for the purpose of preservation is this familiar process writ large.

Advocates of migration see the batch conversion of files as the simplest, lowest-cost measure to ensure that the intellectual content of digital resources remains accessible. The basic function of migration is already widely available. It is migration when common, application programs can open files that were created with previous versions of the application. On a more complex level, numerous utilities exist for the batch conversion of files from one format to another. Familiar, to most, are utilities used in Web development for the creation of Web-viewable, derivative images from master images which are stored in richer, graphical formats. ImageMagick, Photoshop, or Graphic Converter all provide what amount to format migration tools.

The challenge of migration as a digital preservation strategy exists n t in the technicalities of the conversion process, but in its successful  p ication on a massive scale and in requirements which pertain to qu ity assurance. This is an area where expertise already exists in the librar/ community since the issues which surround the management of quality assurance for a large number of digital files are similar to those which are confronted in large-scale microfilming processes as well as in technical services processes which are, increasingly, automated. Although much can be done by machine, there is an important role for librarians in the final validation of the migration process and in the selective examination of migrated files.

There is concern that an error or alteration introduced in the process of a migration will be propagated in successive migrations which might lead to a steady increase in the level of error and inaccuracy in successive, digital files. This is the so-called *telephone game* effect where a phrase spoken by one person to another becomes altered after numerous repetitions. The likelihood of such an occurrence has not been established and the developers of the CAMiLEON project, in particular, have suggested that the possibility can be avoided, altogether, if all migrations begin from the original data.[9] In this model, called *migration on request*, the original data is kept and all migrations to contemporary formats are made from that source.[10] This idea assumes no true obsolescence, i.e., the original information must have been stored in a format which will always be understandable enough that a tool to read and translate it into a new format may be created.

### Emulation

Another approach to deal with information obsolescence is called emulation. Emulation relies upon new software to reproduce the functionality of older software, hardware, or both. Emulation, therefore, uses the coding of the original digital object, which is unaltered, and avoids the potential problems of the migration approach.

Although considered complex and, thus, cost-prohibitive, emulation is already in wide use. Technology developers use the approach as a way to test software and network designs without the cost and difficulties which arise from the use of numerous computers. Two other common uses of emulation are:

- A large, enthusiast community uses emulation to play video games of past eras on current computers.
- Emulators allow major operating systems to be run under other operating systems as well as on a variety of chipsets, i.e., VirtualPC to run Windows and Intel Linux or Unix builds on Macintosh or Windows machines, or WINE to run Windows in Linux computers.

Although these efforts are not recognized as digital preservation systems or intended as such, as Ross and Gow observe, "there has been a tendency to dismiss emulators as a possible solution to the problems posed by technological change. Given the increasing interest in emulation technology and the array of people working in the area from computer scientists to computer junkies, it is probably much too early to discount the likely success of this approach."[11]

Concerns with emulation as a strategy for long-term preservation rest on its technical complexity; the process necessary to replicate an entire, hardware architecture; and that the functionality of an older application may have greater, potential benefit than that which can be realized from a difficult and expensive mapping of one file format to another. There is still debate as to whether users are more comfortable with the use of digital resources in an emulated environment or in a migrated format accessed through contemporary software.

## *Archaeology*

Although little-discussed in the library literature, it is important to understand that digital archaeology is, also, a part of the digital preservation toolkit. It is costly and best avoided, to be sure, but these costs and risks should also be considered as important factors in the drive to develop a sound, digital preservation strategy. In their article for the United Kingdom's Joint Information Systems Committee (JISC), "Digital Archaeology: Rescuing Neglected and Damaged Data Resources," Ross and Gow provide an informative overview of the process and its varied success.[12]

It is helpful to draw a parallel between the emerging field of digital preservation and the established field of conservation science. Conservation science has led to the development and use, in libraries, of a variety of physical treatments–paper splitting, suction leaf casting, mass deacidification, and anoxic sterilization to give a few examples–each one with its virtues and controversial aspects. Professional opinion of these remedial strategies may be in flux, but there is agreement on the best practices for the creation and storage of artifacts to prevent damage that would require corrective treatment.

While these three approaches–migration, emulation, and digital archaeology–provide many options for the repair of digital objects, it is more important, in the first place, to create and properly maintain good digital objects. The ER (ER) librarian has a crucial role to play as an advocate for standards and good practice. By the promotion of standards-based creation of materials in-house and insistence upon standards-based ER for purchase, ER librarians can have an impact on the long-term viability of digital resources in libraries.

It is essential to frame this aspect of digital preservation in a context that invites action. Brian LaVoie concludes that, "If one considers information not just as abstract intellectual content, but as a combination of the intellectual content and the physical package or medium, in which it is delivered and accessed, it is much more meaningful to talk about the durability of information."[13] As resources are weighed against one another, selected, and licensed, this process will often fall into the hands of the ER librarian.

To ensure that resources can be preserved in the first place, a metric to use in the evaluation of a resource or a digital preservation system must be adopted. Such standards have begun to be formed and the promotion of these standards is just as crucial to the long-term preservation of digital content as the promotion of printing on permanent-durable paper has been to the preservation of print-based resources.

## METHODS OF ASSESSMENT

The assessment of resources to determine if they can be preserved is a key activity in a successful, digital preservation strategy. The profession is still in a speculative place in this area of preservation, as librarians have observed catastrophes as well as the potential for systemic problems, but it is still early enough in the development of digital libraries for theory to have had little practical application. Just as selection of acid-free paper by a publisher ensures the preserve-ability of a book, the selection of the correct file format, storage system, and metadata will facilitate long-term digital preservation.

Methodologies to help librarians make good decisions about various elements of the digital preservation process have developed alongside standards and guidelines for the creation of digital resources and assessment methodologies. Some of these methodologies focus on the digital objects themselves and examine the likelihood of the loss of information and its potential impact on individual digital resources. Others are directed toward the evaluation of preservation environments and are intended to guide decisions about secure and reliable storage and the long-term viability of preservation service providers.

The Consultative Committee on Space Data System's (CCSDS) *Reference Model for an Open Archival Information System*, or OAIS, has risen to prominence as a model for digital archives.[14] Although Section 4: The Detailed Models of the OAIS Entities might be omitted at a first reading, the remaining sections should top the reading list for any librarian who prepares to undertake serious involvement with the issues at stake in digital preservation.

Key concepts of the OAIS are the archival roles defined as Producers, Managers, and Consumers. Each of these is tied to a Submission Information Package (SIP), an Archival Information Package (AIP), or a Dissemination Information Package (DIP). It is likely that librarians will take on all three roles at various points: they will produce information as they digitize library collections, manage digital libraries, and disseminate ER among library patrons. It will be just as common, however, for librarians to work with others on these services as databases and other, digital content are licensed through vendor/publishers, data is stored by a third-party digital archive or as part of a LOCKSS-like collaborative project, and access to information is distributed across producer or aggregator-controlled systems, collaborative projects, or other systems, i.e., OAI harvesters or search engine crawlers.

In many of these scenarios, complexity of individual types of ER is not the most important preservation issue. The development of a preservation strategy for a complex ER might require a great deal of initial effort, but then that solution can be applied to future ERs with relative ease. Developing numerous solutions to a wide and changing assortment of ERs requires a high level of ongoing effort that must be renewed with each change in the resources. An analogy might be made to the preservation of recorded sound, where recorded sound archivists must deal with dozens of formats that may have only had a few years of use after their introduction as a recording medium, but now are part of collections to be maintained in perpetuity, and each requiring its own particular playback equipment. One strategy to manage this is to focus on simplifying what is added to the assortment of ERs in libraries, rather than to control the whole of the digital arena.

As mentioned earlier, ER librarians are in a position to be key advocates for standards and practices within the library community and among its partners. One worthwhile venture would be to encourage vendor/publishers to adopt standards and practices that align with those of the digital library community. This would help us gain the maximum impact from any preservation tool developed in the future since it would have some applicability to ERs from multiple creators. While there are many technical issues to resolve along the path towards interoperability, charting the course towards common standards is an entirely human activity and ER librarians occupy a crucial place in this process.

There are several tools available to help with this process. The Research Libraries Group (RLG) has drafted *An Audit Checklist for the Certification of Trusted Digital Repositories* with the conclusion of the development project scheduled for October 2006.[15] This document focuses on the certification of trusted providers of services. Rather than specify technologies and methodologies for preservation, the Trusted Digital Repositories Guidelines (TDRG) discuss, in general, their trustworthiness based on necessary requirements of accountability and transparency of operations.

The nature of digital objects, e.g., their file formats and the standards under which they are captured from analog sources, plays an important role in their preservation. The Digital Library Federation (DLF) promotes general standards and best practices for the creation of digital objects. In addition, efforts such as Harvard University's Global Digital Format Registry (GDFR) should provide a good place to start to investigate the current state of practice in the creation of digital content.

As with any library preservation activity, the best objects in the best environment are of little value without intellectual control. Important elements of intellectual control for digital preservation are technical and administrative metadata, which fall under the combined heading of preservation metadata. The RLG is, once again, at the center of this effort with their *Data Dictionary for Preservation Metadata*. This document grew out of the efforts of the Preservation Metadata: Implementation Strategies (PREMIS) working group and defines the elements necessary to implement the PREMIS data model.

In all these areas (digital repository services, creation of digital objects, and management of digital information) ER librarians are in a position to make a major contribution to preservation activities. One way to describe preservation management is the reduction of unknown or ill-defined problems in a collection. If the practices of vendor/publishers of digital information can be aligned with those of librarians, the number of unknowns that we pass on to future librarians will be smaller.

## HUMAN ELEMENTS

The scope of current, digital preservation activities would fill this book and it is important to emphasize that the initiatives described in this chapter are presented only as representative examples of a rich, new area of library science. More certain than the specific, future tools and standards in digital preservation is the change in role and responsibilities of individuals in the profession which are certain to change in scope and focus as the profession moves towards consensus on the best approaches to the preservation of digital resources.

It is obvious that computer professionals will be needed in any digital preservation initiative, but where they are to be located in the library organization is less clear. Thorin and Greenstein observe that digital library programs may be in any number of organizational locations and are often collaborative endeavors drawing on IT staff beyond the library itself.[16] This is especially true in Universities where faculty in computer and information science schools may be involved in digital library development.

In libraries where there is a concern with digital preservation, this organizational complexity presents a more, fundamental problem than the difficulty of scheduling a meeting. The RLG suggests that organizational commitment is a clear necessity for the development and implementation of a reliable, digital preservation project and such a commitment is difficult to guarantee across divisions. In the library organization, roles for an ER office might include being the location and focus of accountability for the development and implementation of a digital preservation initiative, to lobby for the required commitment in resources, and to prepare library personnel for and encourage their acceptance of frequent change.

Collection management professionals have a significant stake in digital preservation. Through the selection of licensed digital resources they impact on the long-term shape of library collections. With the legal status of creative work so much in flux collection managers must consider the risks inherent in licensed content, e.g., consideration of long-term availability, etc. ER librarians play a crucial role:

- to understand the effect of a license
- to envision and promote manageable, licensing standards
- to guide collection managers toward more, favorable licenses or purchase options
- to broker a balance between the needs of the collection and the user as expressed by collection development personnel and the restrictions imposed under the licenses that govern access to resources

Technical services staff as the creators and managers of metadata also have a key role to play in digital preservation and will be integral in the purchase and licensing of digital content. An important objective in the successful management of a digital collection is to help the technical services staff understand the various metadata that is needed for digital preservation and help them get this information from vendor/publishers.

In libraries that have a staff dedicated to preservation, there is, of course, a natural ally for the ER librarian. Many preservationists already take an active interest in digital preservation as an extension of their basic, professional obligations. Many preservation units are centers of digital content creation as a result of the transition from production microfilming to production digital imaging; and through the creation of images from special collection materials in conservation laboratories that are equipped to for security, safe-handling of materials, and photography.

As Stanescu writes on the INFORM methodology, "there are two necessary components in any measuring system–the units of measurement themselves and the process of applying those units of measurement."[17]

To make an organizational parallel, we might say that in digital preservation there is the adoption of standards and practices as well as the process to apply them.

It is in this effort, the adoption of and advocacy for digital preservation policies and practices, that the ER professional plays a necessary role to help the ER community develop a uniform consciousness about digital preservation.

Kelly Russell and Ellis Weinberger addressed this issue of separate responsibilities in a CEDARS paper: they identified two groups with separate, but dependant responsibilities for digital preservation who must consult with one another on issues that relate to the long-term retention of digital materials:

1. Collection managers (e.g., archivists, subject specialists) and
2. Systems managers

The collection manager can provide advice about usage or about the relative value of an object to the collection. The systems manager can discuss the cost of specific technical issues, i.e., required conversion, migration, or emulation, as well as the metadata or representation information required.[18]

Russell and Weinberger's main aim was to outline cost elements in the digital preservation process. The eight areas they identified are:

1. Selecting a particular digital object for preservation
2. Negotiating the right to preserve the object
3. Negotiating the right to provide access to the preserved object
4. Determining the appropriate technical strategy for preservation and continuing access

5. Validating the completeness of the object on delivery to the archive
6. Producing metadata
7. Storing files
8. Administering the archive

In library parlance, the first three might fall under the umbrella of collection development policies and licensing principles and the remainder under the province of systems managers with the assumption that, in some cases, step five: validation, would be an automated process. However, steps five and eight would require some level of human involvement to ensure that the automated processes yield the desired results. Step six points to one of the newest roles to emerge in the field of digital or ER librarianship. The creation and management of metadata has become a full-time job at some institutions and, while the choice of metadata formats and the creation of technical metadata may lie within the purview of Russell and Weinberger's systems managers, ER librarians will be asked to contribute much of what librarians think of as bibliographic information for digital resources in order to ensure that they are discoverable and useful to library users.

ER librarians occupy a crucial position in the world of digital libraries and ER. Because of their connections to the publishers and distributors of ER of every variety, they are the natural spokespersons in the library community for the implementation of good standards and practices. Through advocacy for standardized, license terms that will require vendor/publishers to adopt standards-based best practices from publishers and preferential treatment in terms of spending to digital information suppliers who engage in practices that are favorable to libraries, ER librarians can effect important change and, thus, limit the scope of preservation challenges to be faced in the future. If they help to coordinate local efforts to create digital information by following these same standards, librarians can limit potential difficulties in preservation and provide the framework for the creation of digital collections that are more easily adapted to changes in user needs and expectations.

## NOTES

1. Michael A. Keller, "Casting Forward; Collection Development After Mass Digitization or Doing One's Part: Thinking Globally, Acting Locally," presented at the Fiesole Collection Development Retreat, March 18, 2004: 2; http://digital.casalini.it/retreat/2004_docs/KellerMichael.pdf (viewed April 9, 2006).

2. "... let us save what remains: not by vaults and locks which fence them from the public eye and use in consigning them to the waste of time, but by such a multiplication of copies, as shall place them beyond the reach of accident." (Jefferson, Thomas. [1791] 1984. Thomas Jefferson to Ebenezer Hazard, Philadelphia, February 18, 1791. In Thomas Jefferson: Writings: Autobiography, Notes on the State of Virginia, Public and Private Papers, Addresses, Letters, edited by Merrill D. Peterson. New York: Library of America)

3. Vicky Reich and David S. H. Rosenthal, "LOCKSS: A Permanent Web Publishing and Access System," *D-Lib Magazine* 7(6) (June 2001); http://www.dlib.org/dlib/june01/reich/06reich.html (viewed April 9, 2006).

4. Petros Maniatis et al., "Preserving Peer Replicas by Rate-Limited Sampled Voting," presented at the 19th ACM Symposium on Operating Systems Principles (SOSP), Bolton Landing, NY, October 2003: 14; http://www.eecs.harvard.edu/~mema/publications/SOSP2003-long.pdf (viewed April 9, 2006).

5. Maniatis et al.

6. *OCLC Digital Archive Preservation Policy and Supporting Documentation. Last Revised: 20 January 2005* (Dublin, OH: OCLC, 2005); http://www.oclc.org/support/documentation/digitalarchive/preservationpolicy.pdf (viewed April 9, 2006).

7. "The Indiana University Massive Data Storage System Service," http://storage.iu.edu/mdss.html (viewed April 9, 2006).

8. Tim DiLauro, "Choosing the Components of a Digital Infrastructure," *First Monday* 9(5) (May 2004); http://firstmonday.org/issues/issue9_5/dilauro/index.html (viewed April 9, 2006).

9. "Creative Archiving at Michigan and Leeds: Emulating the Old on the New," http://www.si.umich.edu/CAMILEON/ (viewed April 9, 2006).

10. Phil Mellor, Paul Wheatley, and Derek Sargent, "Migration on Request, a Practical Technique for Preservation," http://www.si.umich.edu/CAMILEON/reports/migreq.pdf (viewed April 9, 2006).

11. Seamus Ross and Ann Gow, "Digital Archaeology: Rescuing Neglected and Damaged Data Resources," http://eprints.erpanet.org/archive/00000047/01/rosgowrt.pdf (viewed December 7, 2005).

12. Ibid.

13. Brian F. Lavoie, "The Incentives to Preserve Digital Materials: Roles, Scenarios, and Economic Decision-Making," http://www.oclc.org/research/projects/digipres/incentives-dp.pdf (viewed December 7, 2005).

14. "ISO Archiving Standards–Reference Model Papers," version cited: http://ssdoo.gsfc.nasa.gov/nost/wwwclassic/documents/pdf/CCSDS-650.0-B-1.pdf (viewed April 9, 2006: username and password required for access).

15. Further information and the draft *Audit Checklist* is available at http://www.rlg.org/ en/page.php?Page_ID=20769.

16. Daniel Greenstein and Suzanne Thorin, *The Digital Library: A Biography* (Washington, DC: Council on Library and Information Resources, 2001); http://www.clir.org/pubs/abstract/pub109abst.html (viewed April 9, 2006).

17. Andreas Stanescu, "Assessing the Durability of Formats in a Digital Preservation Environment: The INFORM Methodology," *D-Lib Magazine* 10(11) (November 2004); http://www.dlib.org/dlib/november04/stanescu/11stanescu.html (viewed April 9, 2006).

18. Kelly Russell and Ellis Weinberger, "Cost Elements of Digital Preservation (Draft of May 2000)," http://www.leeds.ac.uk/cedars/colman/CIW01r.html (viewed April 9, 2006).

doi:10.1300/J105v32n03_04

# Electronic Government Information Dissemination: Changes for Programs, Users, Libraries, and Government Documents Librarians

Robert A. Staley

**SUMMARY.** The federal government, "the largest single producer, consumer, collector, and disseminator of information in the United States,"[1] has begun to disseminate most of that information electronically. Legislation and more economic production and dissemination of government information have produced changes in the Federal Depository Library Program (FDLP) and federal agency dissemination. This chapter examines the dissemination of electronic government information from the Government Printing Office (GPO) through the FDLP and executive branch agencies and discusses the impact that this has on users, libraries, and government information specialists. doi:10.1300/J105v32n03_05 *[Article copies available for a fee from The Haworth Document Delivery Service: 1-800-HAWORTH. E-mail address: <docdelivery@haworthpress.com> Website: <http://www.HaworthPress.com> © 2007 by The Haworth Press. All rights reserved.]*

Robert A. Staley, MLS, MA, is Documents Coordinator, University of Wyoming Libraries, Department 3334, 1000 East University Avenue, Laramie, WY 82071 (E-mail: rastaley@uwyo.edu).

[Haworth co-indexing entry note]: "Electronic Government Information Dissemination: Changes for Programs, Users, Libraries, and Government Documents Librarians." Staley, Robert A. Co-published simultaneously in *Collection Management* (The Haworth Information Press, an imprint of The Haworth Press) Vol. 32, No. 3/4, 2007, pp. 305-326; and: *Electronic Resources Librarianship and Management of Digital Information: Emerging Professional Roles* (ed: Mark Jacobs) The Haworth Information Press, an imprint of The Haworth Press, 2007, pp. 305-326. Single or multiple copies of this article are available for a fee from The Haworth Document Delivery Service [1-800-HAWORTH, 9:00 a.m. - 5:00 p.m. (EST). E-mail address: docdelivery@haworthpress.com].

**KEYWORDS.** Government documents, government information dissemination, electronic government information, Government Printing Office (GPO), Federal Depository Library Program (FDLP), government documents librarians

## INTRODUCTION

The federal government, "the largest single producer, consumer, collector, and disseminator of information in the United States,"[1] has begun to disseminate most of that information electronically. Legislation and economically efficient production and distribution of government information have produced changes in the Federal Depository Library Program (FDLP) and federal agency dissemination. This chapter examines the dissemination of electronic government information from the Government Printing Office (GPO) through the FDLP and executive branch agencies and discusses the impact that this has on users, libraries, and government information specialists.

## THE FEDERAL DEPOSITORY LIBRARY PROGRAM

The idea of free public access to government information has been a feature of our republic from its inception, acknowledged both in the Constitution[2] and in the thoughts of the founding fathers. James Madison, in his letter to William T. Barry, then lieutenant governor of Kentucky, noted:

> A popular Government, without popular information, or the means of acquiring it, is but a Prologue to a Farce or a Tragedy; or, perhaps both. Knowledge will forever govern ignorance: And a people who mean to be their own Governors, must arm themselves with the power that knowledge gives.[3]

The depository library program was created in 1813 when Congress authorized the distribution of House and Senate Journals and other Congressional documents to universities, historical societies, libraries, and certain other institutions. Subsequent Printing Acts in 1852 and 1860 authorized a Superintendent of Public Printing to procure buildings, equipment, and supplies for public printing and gave oversight to the

Joint Committee on Printing to set standards, resolve disputes, and approve major purchases.[4]

The passage of the Printing Act of 1895 consolidated printing activities and established a Superintendent of Documents to catalog, index, and supervise the distribution of government documents to 4,200 depository libraries.[5]

That year also saw the publication of the Monthly Catalog and the beginning of the development of the Superintendent of Documents Classification System by Adelaide Hasse.[6]

These developments set in place a framework that librarians still work within today. Both the Monthly Catalog and the SuDocs classification system are still used in depository libraries.

Title 44 USC is the direct descendant of the 1895 Printing Act. Title 44, Chapter 19 USC, the *Government Printing Office Electronic Information Access Enhancement Act of 1993* (Public Law 103-40), and OMB Circular A-130 define the current legal and regulatory environment for the distribution of government information.[7]

Together they control the operation of the depository program, ensure public access to electronic government information, and require that all federal agencies make publications available for distribution in the FDLP.

Despite the fact that approximately 130 federal departments and agencies use the GPO for printing or distribution of information, agency non-compliance is a major problem. Non-compliance has been ascribed to ignorance of the requirements of Title 44, to a lack of enforcement provisions within Title 44, different statutory authority, or the unresolved constitutional separation of powers conflict between the Congressional Joint Committee on Printing (JCP) and the executive Office of Management and Budget (OMB). The result is the creation of a class of *fugitive documents*. Fugitive documents, or U.S. government documents that fall within the scope of the FDLP, but have not been included in the program, account for about half of all U.S. government printing.[8]

The GPO's push for legislative solutions to the issues that underlie the fugitive documents problem has, for the most part, not been successful. The GPO, the JCP, and the Senate Committee on Rules attempted to address some of the problems with Title 44 through printing reform proposals in the Wendell H. Ford Government Publications Act of 1998, but the bill (S. 2288) was not carried over to the 106th Congress.[9] In addition, the GPO's authority over executive branch printing is in question. The Department of Justice Office of Legal Counsel has argued that the GPO's involvement in executive branch printing is an unconstitutional violation of the separation of powers doctrine.[10]

Legislative issues aside, the GPO's FDLP has been successful enough that 1,248 selective (partial) and regional (full) depository libraries participate. According to the GPO, these depositories serve 9.5 million people annually and each library averages 7,000 patron visits per year.[11] Between FY1995 and FY2002, the GPO distributed 230,019 paper, microform, and CD-ROM titles to depository libraries.[12] By 2004, however, GPO Access, the official GPO gateway to electronic publications, provided access to 275,970 titles. The Public Printer, Bruce James, regards GPO Access as a mainstay of the FDLP and notes that downloads of documents from the site exceed 35 million per month.[13] The primary format for distribution of government information is now electronic. By FY2004, 65% of all government titles were accessible on the Internet and by July 2005 the Superintendent of Documents reported that distribution of new titles was 90% electronic.[14]

At the same time that electronic publication and dissemination increased the demand for printed products decreased. Between FY1993 and FY2003, sales of printed products declined from 24.3 million to 4.4 million copies. About ten years ago the Federal Register had 35, 000 subscriptions; in 2003 it had 2,700. During the same year, there were 4 million downloads of the Federal Register from GPO Access per month.[15] The result of these changes is a decline in revenue for the GPO. Its revolving fund, which funds procured printing and document sales, went from a $100 million surplus in FY1998 to a $19 million deficit in FY2003. Losses to the sales program, $77 million over five years, were the largest part of the decline.[16]

These losses, the decline in the demand for printed products, and the rise in the demand for electronic products stem from changes in the technology of printing and distribution. As Printing Industry of America spokesman Ben Cooper pointed out, digital technology has blurred the distinction between printing, desktop publishing, broadcasting, and other kinds of information management.[17]

Sophisticated and user-friendly publishing software enables printing with little or no involvement from traditional printing professionals or GPO printing services. With the Internet available for instant dissemination, federal agencies and other organizations can use tools like Extensible Markup Language (XML) to prepare documents for a variety of media, including Web sites.[18]

## GPO AND THE TRANSFORMATION OF THE FDLP

The GPO recognized that technological changes that underlie the printing industry and the electronic distribution of government documents would require a transformation in the agency's printing and FDLP operations. Changes to legislation like Public Law 103-40 were followed by Congressional mandates attached to legislative branch appropriations that directed the Public Printer to study "the functions and services of the [FDLP]" and identify measures "that are necessary to ensure a successful transition to a more electronically-based program."[19]

The GPO began to work with federal agencies, Congress, the depository library community, the information industry, users, and other stakeholders.

As part of the mandate, the GPO was directed to report on the transformation of the FDLP into an electronic program and include a strategic plan for implementation. The GPO noted widespread interest to expand the content of the FDLP, a decline in agency compliance with legal requirements to distribute or print information, the necessity for standards and location tools to maintain permanent public access, the costs of electronic information to depository libraries, and the legislative changes that would be required to support the program.[20]

As follow-up on the report to the Congress, the GPO submitted a transition plan with their FY1997 appropriations request. Comments from this document were included in *The Federal Depository Library Program: Information Dissemination and Access Strategic Plan, FY 1996–FY 2001*. The plan proposed a gradual transition period with FDLP to provide information in all formats and electronic information to supplement tangible formats with links to government and agency Web sites. To help make use of this information, the GPO would continue catalog operations and develop information locator services to maintain permanent public access to electronic information. The plan also called for an assessment of the standards used to create and disseminate electronic information.[21]

Representatives of the GPO met with the U.S. National Commission on Libraries and Information Science (NCLIS) in order to try to understand the issues that surround standards. The NCLIS's *Report on the Assessment of Government Information Products* outlined the need for policy to guide electronic publication and dissemination, permanent public access, metadata, authenticity, information life-cycle management, coordination at government, branch, and agency-levels, new product development, and Web design compliance with the ADA.[22]

At the same time that the GPO prepared the transition plan and worked with the NCLIS, Congress met to consider a number of related issues. Hearings were held to ensure permanent public access to government information; encourage advances in technology for greater public access without "creating a society of information 'haves' and 'have-nots'"; review Title 44 printing, procurement, and compliance issues; and revise the statute to "bring Title 44 into the 21st Century with a minimum cost to the taxpayers."[23]

By the end of the development of the strategic information plan, the GPO had garnered public support for the transition to an at least partly electronic FDLP, increased the number of online titles to 225,000, and decreased its workforce by 35% over 1993 levels. Despite these accomplishments, the agency had $45 million in losses, a workforce composed of 47% blue-collar occupations, e.g., plate-makers and electricians, and a building of 1.5 million square feet first occupied in 1903.[24]

The 24th Public Printer of the United States, Bruce James, was appointed in 2002 and charged to bring an essentially 19th Century organization into the 21st Century. The challenge for the GPO, like other manufacturing businesses in America, is to "re-engineer itself if it is to remain relevant and viable for the future." James, at his confirmation hearing, noted that, with agreement from customers, information users, and employees a plan "will present a new vision for GPO, set our specific and measurable short and long-term objectives and goals, and will have budget and timetable details."[25]

James took the first step towards the GPO's transformation from a traditional printing facility to a modern information enterprise when he imported an organizational model from private industry in order to reorganize management focus and direct it on the future. In this model, the Public Printer's role became organizational policy and long-range planning with the Deputy Public Printer in charge of daily operations. In collaboration with GPO senior management, the top-level organizational structure was reoriented to focus on customer needs. The reorganization established key management positions in the areas of customer relations, plant operations, and information dissemination as well as a chief information officer, a chief financial officer, a chief human capital officer, and a chief of staff.[26]

In addition to management changes, the GPO instituted voluntary retirement incentives; improvements to the printing procurement process (in cooperation with the OMB; closed money-losing regional bookstores and reduced inventories in order to reduce the operational costs of the sales program; and began negotiations for a new integrated library system (ILS) in order to enhance cataloging and access to the electronic FDLP. By FY2004, the GPO's financial position had improved for the first time in five years and the agency had a small surplus.[27]

Coincident with the Public Printer's reforms, the General Accounting Office (GAO), now known as the Government Accountability Office, was charged by the Senate Subcommittee on Legislative Branch Appropriations with a general management review of GPO operations. Assisted by the National Academy of Sciences (NAS), the GAO convened a panel of printing and publishing technology experts to assist the GPO's efforts to transform operations. The recommendations in the GAO reports[28] were incorporated into the GPO's modernization plans.

These recommendations as well as the GPO's analysis and consultation with employees, Congress, federal agencies, the printing and information industries, and the library community "have begun to develop a new vision for the GPO: an agency whose primary mission will be to capture digitally, organize, maintain, authenticate, distribute, and provide permanent public access to the information products and services of the federal government."[29]

*A Strategic Vision for the 21st Century* was released late in 2004 to outline the GPO's plan to address this mission.[30]

The plan noted that while the GPO's mission will not change in the future the agency will need to develop goals for the delivery of products and services to meet the needs of the federal government and other users. The plan's general goals for the reorganization are to develop a modern integrated enterprise approach for agency operations and finances and to use GPO assets to finance the agency's transformation.[31] Specific goals for the FDLP include a flexible digital information content system for federal documents, a new model for the FDLP which increases partner flexibility, and an increase in both the percentage of federal documents procured and processed for the FDLP as well as access and utility for users of federal information.[32]

To achieve these goals the GPO proposes a digital content system, the Future Digital Information System or FDsys,[33] to manage and preserve content. All FDLP documents, print-based or digital, will be authenticated and cataloged. GPO metadata and document-creation standards will be followed when documents are entered into the system; content may include text, graphics, video, audio, as well as new formats. This content will be available to search, download, and print; and as document masters for other requirements.[34]

The FDLP's role in the FDsys will be to determine content; set standards for and authenticate documents; and catalog, manage, and preserve content. In addition, the FDLP will set standards for and manage the digitization of all retrospective documents that can be authenticated all the way back to the *Federalist Papers*.[35] The GPO will use a new unit, Digital Media Services (DMS), to train 300 GPO employees for this project. The GPO estimates that 70% of this project can be completed by December 2007.[36]

The GPO has planned other changes to the FDLP that are designed to increase flexibility for participants. FDLP members will have free access via the FDsys to all past, present, and future federal documents in digital format. The GPO will provide Web search tools[37] and training for depository librarians. FDLP members will also have the option of print or digital copies of key federal documents.[38]

The 53 regional depositories extant will be allowed to combine tangible collections to reduce operational costs, but still offer public access.[39]

Two "collections of last resort" or "deep archives" will house all known tangible and digital document masters.[40]

The changes outlined in *A Strategic Vision for the 21st Century* and other planning documents as well as in presentations to Congress,[41] federal agencies, professional associations, depository librarians, and others[42] are far-reaching and controversial.[43] If the GPO and the FDLP are to continue in their role as the primary agencies to collect, catalog, produce, disseminate, and preserve federal information they must recognize that "the way the Government keeps America informed has been forever altered. . . . We can no longer afford to simply react to change in information . . . we need to lead it."[44]

## FEDERAL AGENCY INFORMATION DISSEMINATION AND E-GOVERNMENT

While much agency information has also been captured by the electronic FDLP, there is a significant amount of information that has originated in distribution programs operated under legislative or regulatory authorities other than Title 44 or as *gray literature* defined as "foreign or domestic open source material that usually is available through specialized channels and may not enter normal channels or systems of publication [or] distribution. . . ."[45] Much of this information is scientific and technical, and originates in the Department of Defense (DOD) or in the Commerce Department's alternative distribution system, the National Technical Information Service (NTIS).[46]

The Defense Technical Information Center (DTIC) is the major provider of DOD technical information and, historically, the largest contributor of technical reports to NTIS.[47] The DTIC operates the Scientific and Technical Information Network (STINET) that offers free public access to unclassified and unlimited (in distribution) technical information through Public STINET. The STINET technical reports collection database provides access to citations from 1974 to the present; many of the citations have links to the full-text of the reports.[48]

NTIS provides access to 3 million publications in 350 different subject areas and, as of FY2004; the agency provided more than 500,000 publications annually.[49]

While NTIS charges for the products that they distribute many of the product records contain links to the full-text of documents. NTIS has also established a portal site for government information. FedWorld. gov links to federal agency as well as science and technology Web sites; IRS forms and publications; Supreme Court decisions; and the FirstGov. gov portal.[50]

Other federal agencies that produce large amounts of scientific and technical information disseminate this information on their own Web sites. The Department of Energy (DOE) makes energy, science, and technology research and development available through online collections like *DOE Information Bridge, Energy Citations*, and the *E-print Network*.[51] The Environmental Protection Agency (EPA) databases, *National Service Center for Environmental Publications (NSCEP)* and the *National Environmental Publications Internet Site (NEPIS)* offer free public access to thousands of documents in paper or electronic formats.[52] The National Aeronautics and Space Administration (NASA) makes mission-related information available on the *NASA Technical Reports Server*.[53] By 2004, publications were accessible on 98% of the federal agencies and court sites identified in the Brown University report on e-government.[54]

Federal multi-agency sites dedicated to specific subjects serve as alternative access points to government information. The Science.gov portal provides public access to scientific and technical information, i.e., thirty scientific databases and 1,700 authoritative science Web sites with over 47 million pages that can be searched or browsed by topic.[55]

Multi-agency sites cover numerous topics:

- FedStats for statistical information from over 100 Federal agencies
- Healthfinder for medical information

- Consumer.gov for consumer information
- AgNIC for agricultural information
- Recreation.gov for recreational opportunities on public lands; and many more.[56]

The increased Internet presence of federal agencies as an alternative to the FDLP for access to government information has been driven by technology, economic considerations, and legislation. The *Information Technology Management Reform (Clinger-Cohen) Act* requires agencies to establish a process to ensure that agency information is available to the public in a timely manner. The *Freedom of Information Act* and the *Electronic Freedom of Information Act* have replaced a *need to know* information dissemination policy with one based on the consumer's *right to know*. Other legislation has addressed security and privacy concerns (*Federal Information Security Management Act*; *Computer Security Act*) and access by the disabled (*Rehabilitation Act, § 508*).[57]

The September 11th terrorist attacks have prompted a legislative response, but policies that deal with government information dissemination have presented relatively few changes. There were some reported incidences of agencies that removed information from Web sites, recalled information from depository libraries, and made it more difficult to access some types of information.[58] There were some changes made to FOIA policies; some restrictions on access to information on nuclear, chemical, and biological weapons were established; and there were changes made in the classification and declassification policies for information.[59] Overall, however, "the U.S. tradition of democracy and open government remains strong and will survive the attempts to limit information access. . . ."[60]

The most important recent legal influence on executive branch federal agency Web sites is the *E-Government Act of 2002*. One of the purposes of the act was to establish "a broad framework of measures that require using Internet-based information technology to enhance access to Government information and services . . ."[61] The finding and purposes section of the act noted that the federal government has had an uneven record of application of information technology to increase access to government information and that federal Internet services had been developed and presented separately with more attention given to agency boundaries than functionality for users.[62]

The OMB, with oversight responsibilities for the implementation of the act in executive branch federal agencies, issued guidelines and policies to change the design and content of federal agency Web sites to make them more user-friendly. The requirements, based on usability studies and best practices, specify search functions for all federal Web sites; standard formats for data and metadata; timely dissemination of information; compliance with the *Information Quality Act*; the establishment and enforcement of linking policies; the restriction of user domains to .gov, .mil, or fed.us; security and privacy controls; accessibility; and management of records throughout the time that they are in federal custody.[63]

Assisted by the Interagency Committee on Government Information (ICGI) the OMB has begun to address practices related to access, dissemination, and preservation of government information. The ICGL's Web Managers Advisory Group (WMAG) established webcontent.gov to address OMB and other federal Web site requirements.[64]

The focus of the act's implementation is on users–the federal government's customers. The ICGI noted that the goal of federal Web site policies was "to make the U.S. government websites the most citizen-focused and visitor-friendly in the world."[65]

The FirstGov.gov site was redesigned in response to the requirements of the act and has been cited as a successful example of customer-focused design.[66] It serves as the official executive branch Internet portal and as the public domain directory for federal agency websites. With access to 180 million pages of federal, state, and local information as well as direct feedback to 130 agency programs[67] FirstGov.gov is organized to allow users to navigate the federal bureaucracy without knowledge of organizational structure, program names, or acronyms. Public use of FirstGov.gov in FY2004 totaled 78 million visitors to 203 million pages of information.[68]

## USERS, LIBRARIES, AND GOVERNMENT INFORMATION

Changes in the way government information is presented have had measurable effects on users. Internet access is available in the homes of nearly 75% of the U.S. population and from almost all schools and public libraries. Government Web sites have as many unique visitors as *eBay* and *Amazon.com*.[69]

In 2003, 77% of all Internet users, or 97 million Americans, went online to search for information or to communicate with government agencies. Of users who search for information on government Web sites, 41% do research that involves official statistics or documents, 34% access recreational or tourist information, 28% access information on health or safety, and 23% access information on or apply for government benefits.[70] A significant number of these users (37%) found these sites with an Internet search engine.[71]

Library users have preferences in the way government information is presented. The virtual depository pilot study at the University of Arizona concludes that both users and library staff are comfortable with and in many cases preferred government information in electronic format.[72]

Electronic formats and the Internet have changed user expectations as well. The study, "What Students Want: Generation Y and the Changing Function of the Academic Library," notes that users want *one-stop shopping* when it comes to research, expect research to be fast and easy, feel Internet-based resources as fulfill all their research needs, no longer associate library resources with the library building in all cases, tend to work in groups more frequently, and view the Internet and technology as part of their lives.[73]

The availability of government information from federal agency Web sites has had an impact on depository libraries. According to Superintendent of Documents Judy Russell, more than 100 libraries have left the FDLP since 1998.[74]

Responses to surveys of library directors and libraries mention Internet access to government publications among the reasons they left the program. The loss of these depositories has prompted the FDLP to develop the "Stay With the Program" Web page[75] and the Depository Library Council (DLC) to the Public Printer to form a Subcommittee on Attrition and Retention.[76]

While these efforts may help the FDLP temporarily, without the GPO's transformation federal agency Web sites may supplant the FDLP as the first choice of users for the dissemination of government information.

When they offer Internet access to government information independently of the FDLP librarians may start "the age of the new depository."[77] With government information available from any library, school, or community information center "we are moving into an era where every library in the country has the potential to become a depository in the sense that each one could potentially provide users with access to government information at a level previously unavailable except by libraries in the current depository system."[78] In order for users to make effective use of government information these new depositories will need to provide expertise in the organization of government, the *architecture* of information produced by agencies, and the current depository system.[79]

Electronic information dissemination and changes in user needs and preferences has affected other types of libraries as well. In university libraries, particularly those with reference departments organized under the information commons model, librarians apply new skills in order to convey knowledge about library resources. Skills that involve Internet applications and Web site design, electronic resources (ER) of all kinds, search strategies, ILS applications, office applications, e.g., word-processing and spreadsheets, and equipment maintenance are used to deliver on user expectations.[80]

In public libraries, the most popular professional development activities involve many of these same skills. Over 80% of the respondents to a survey of public librarians reported that they had used professional development time to improve skills related to Internet applications and ER.[81]

The organization of these skills in order to serve user needs stretches the capabilities of traditional, hierarchical library organizations. Librarians have followed trends in corporations and federal agencies and have started to give a higher priority to user needs than to organizational structure.[82]

Most government information specialists now work in combined reference departments[83] as well as with technical services and systems units on issues or questions that involve ER, the Internet, or computer software applications and technology. Cooperative effort in these areas requires "flatter–indeed more Web-like–organizations and self-directed work groups [that] allow for more flexibility and more opportunities for communications" as well as the ability to make decisions on issues that directly affect the delivery of services.[84]

Institutional flexibility and new Internet applications and software have prompted libraries, organizations, and the LIS profession to explore new methods for the dissemination of government information. The University of Illinois at Chicago, the State Library of Illinois, OCLC, and thirty universities, public, and state libraries and archives in Illinois have started a pilot virtual reference service for government information at Government Information Online. The LOCKSS (Lots of Copies Keep Stuff Safe) project comprises over 80 institutions that cooperate in a project to ensure the archive of digital content locally. Librarians from the University of California at Santa Cruz and the University of Alaska sponsor a Web site and blog to provide news and discuss developments in government information.[41] As a current awareness service for depository librarians, the GPO has initiated RSS feeds to deliver new content and the DLC has a blog as a place for librarians to comment on government information policies.[85]

Libraries are in transition from the development and maintenance of repositories of printed materials to what the DLC calls a "non-exclusive government information environment," which has implications for the future role of librarians and government information specialists. For libraries, the DLC foresees greater access to current and historical government information via the proposed national digital collection as well as the flexibility to offer government information without the attainment of depository status. For future government information specialists, it is expertise in the structure and functions of government operations that will allow them to package information to meet user needs.[86]

## ELECTRONIC INFORMATION
## AND GOVERNMENT INFORMATION SPECIALISTS

To build professional skills to meet user needs requires training, but government information specialists are not, primarily, trained in library schools. When asked about the primary means to gain knowledge about government documents, surveyed documents librarians listed self-instruction and in-service training as more important than library school.[87] Most of the training for government information specialists is offered through the FDLP desktop; the annual Depository Library Conference and DLC meetings; and the annual Interagency Depository Seminar. Professional associations like the ALA Government Documents Roundtable (GODORT), the American Association of Law Libraries Government Documents Special Interest Section, and state and local organizations also provide training materials.[88]

The DLC provides recommendations on training needs to government information specialists who work with ER. The Electronic Transition Committee of the DLC notes that "for effective use of GPO Access databases as currently structured, patrons need a fairly sophisticated understanding of the federal government, FDLP organization, and bibliographic tools."[89]

The report calls for increased training for new depository librarians, non-depository librarians, and the public modeled on that offered at the annual Federal Depository Library Conference and DLC meetings. To reach the members of the public who are non-library users, Web-based tutorials and online training modules should be directed at users with various levels of expertise.[90]

Implicit in the report is the recognition of the future role of government information specialists as providers of expertise and interpreters of content.

Government information specialists recognize the importance of subject knowledge in their role to provide expertise. The most common undergraduate backgrounds of documents librarians include history and English, but "only 4.1% held an undergraduate degree with a major in political science, a major considered useful to librarians pursuing government documents librarianship."[91]

Moreover, while more than 25% of the documents librarians surveyed held an advanced degree none were in political science or any area of public policy. When asked about the education of future government documents librarians, many of those surveyed stressed "course work in U.S. history, American government, civics, political science, economics, and statistical analysis or interpretation."[92]

For government information specialists, the GPO's plan to provide online access to past and present government information in FDsys, better bibliographic control through their new ILS, and the proposed *National Bibliography of U.S. Government Publications* will change access to and retrieval of government information. Traditional tools like the *Monthly Catalog of U.S. Government Publications* and the Superintendent of Documents classification system are no longer sufficient to provide information to the public effectively. Provenance, the historical basis of access and retrieval for government information, has given way to the subject-oriented access and retrieval provided by Internet search engines and databases. Government information specialists, like their colleagues in other subject specialties, will increasingly rely on Internet applications and computer technology to deliver information.

The production of electronic government information, whether through the FDLP or other sources, has shifted the emphasis in depository libraries from the physical control of a tangible product to the provision of services to identify, organize, and preserve information on the Internet. Some see this as a moment of liberation for librarians who specialize in government information. "They become 'curators' of knowledge who package and explain related information resources to their communities."[93] Without possession of all the information that concerns their users, but with the expertise to locate and select the information that does, government information specialists will continue to build skills in order to collect and explain relevant information to their users.[94]

## CONCLUSION

For nearly 200 years, the Government Printing Office has been the leader in the dissemination of government information through the Federal Depository Library Program. From the beginning, the focus of the

FDLP has been to provide print-based collections to a limited number of the nation's libraries. Legislation and changes in technology have lead to a non-exclusive information environment and federal agencies now play a major role in the dissemination of government information. These legislative and technological developments have changed the nature of the FDLP, user access to information, librarian roles in the provision of access to information, and the way that government information specialists manage and present information.

The effort to change the focus of the FDLP to a digital content system that incorporates all current and past information will provide access to more government information than even the largest paper collections. Approximately 9.5 million people annually visit federal depository libraries for information, but the number who visit federal Web sites is ten times greater. The depository library of the 21st Century will be universal in that any computer with an Internet connection will be able to provide access to government information. The documents librarian of the 21st Century will be a government information specialist educated in how government works and how to manage and interpret the greater amount of information that will be available.

## NOTES

1. "Management of Federal Information Resources," Circular A-130, Revised. February 8, 1996, http://www.whitehouse.gov/omb/circulars/a130/a130.html (viewed July 7, 2005).

2. U.S. Constitution, art I, § 5, cl. 3.

3. James Madison, *Writings* (New York: Penguin Putnam, 1999), 790.

4. Sheila M. McGarr, "Snapshots of the Federal Depository Library Program," [Updated from an article in *Administrative Notes* 15/11 (1994): 6-14], http://www.access.gpo.gov/su_docs/fdlp/history/snapshot.html (viewed July 7, 2005).

5. *100 GPO Years 1861-1961: A History of United States Public Printing* (Washington, DC: USGPO, 1961), 75.

6. McGarr, "Snapshots."

7. Depository Library Program, U.S. Code 44 (2000), Chapter 19, http://www.access.gpo.gov/su_docs/fdlp/pubs/title44/chap19.html (viewed July 7, 2005); Access to Federal Electronic Information, U.S. Code 44 (2000), Chapter 41. http://www.access.gpo.gov/su_docs/fdlp/pubs/title44/chap41.html (accessed July 7, 2005); "Management of Federal Information Resources," http://www.whitehouse.gov/omb/ circulars/a130/a130.html (viewed July 7, 2005).

8. Gil Baldwin, "Fugitive Documents–On the Loose or On the Run," *Administrative Notes* 24/10 (2003): 5. Baldwin does not mention distribution under different statutory authority. National Technical Information Service distribution is authorized by the *National Technical Information Act of 1988*, U.S. Code 15 (2000), Chapter 63.

9. Harold C. Relyea, "Public Printing Reform: Issues and Actions," CRS Report to Congress 98-687, April 5, 2001, 1-2, http://www.ncseonline.org/NLE/CRSreports/government/gov-36.cfm?&CFID=9742212&CFTOKEN=26620095 (viewed July 10, 2005).

10. "Government Printing Involvement in Executive Branch Printing (May 31, 1996)," http://www.usdoj.gov/olc/printer.fin.htm (viewed July 10, 2005).

11. "FDLP Fact Sheet," http://www.access.gpo.gov/su_docs/fdlp/fdlp_fs.pdf (viewed July 10, 2005).

12. "Government Printing Office. LPS Annual Report" [Reprinted from *Administrative Notes* 23/13 (2002)], http://www.access.gpo.gov/su_docs/fdlp/pubs/annrprt/02lpsar.html (viewed July 10, 2005).

13. *Oversight Hearing on the Government Printing Office: Hearing Before the Committee on House Administration, House of Representatives, 108th Congress, 2nd Session* (April 28, 2004), 12.

14. *U.S. Government Printing Office 2004 Annual Report* (Washington, DC: USGPO, 2004), 9; http://www.gpo.gov/congressional/annualreports/04annrep/GPO_2004_ANNUAL_REPORT_web.pdf (viewed July 10, 2005); "Update for AALL," (July 2005,) http://www.access.gpo.gov/su_docs/fdlp/pubs/aall_update.pdf (viewed July 18, 2005).

15. Judith C. Russell, "The Federal Depository Library Program: Current and Future Challenges of the Electronic Transition," Paper presented to the Canadian Library Association and American Library Association Joint Program, How is Federal Government Information Reaching the Public in the 21st Century? Toronto, June 21, 2003, 2; http://www.gpoaccess.gov/about/speeches/062003_alatoronto.pdf (viewed July 10, 2005).

16. *Government Printing Office: Actions to Strengthen and Sustain GPO's Transformation: Report to Congressional Addressees* (Washington, DC: GAO, 2004), 8-12; http://www.gao.gov/new.items/d04830.pdf (viewed July 11, 2005).

17. *Public Access to Government Information in the 21st Century: Hearings Before the Committee on Rules and Administration, 104th Congress, 2nd Session . . . June 18 and 19, July 16 and 24, 1996* (Washington, DC: USGPO, 1996), 150.

18. *Government Printing Office: Actions to Strengthen and Sustain GPO's Transformation*, 10.

19. *Legislative Branch Appropriations, 1996. Senate Report 114, 104th Congress, 1st Session* (1995); http://www-lib.uwyo.edu/redirect.cfm?url=http%3A%2F%2Fweb%2Elexis%2Dnexis%2Ecom%2Fcongcomp%2F (viewed July 12, 2005).

20. "The Electronic Federal Depository Library Program: Transition Plan, FY1996-1998," *Administrative Notes* 16/18 (1995); http://www.access.gpo.gov/su_docs/fdlp/retired/transit.html (viewed July 12, 2005).

21. *Report to the Congress: Study to Identify Measures Necessary for a Successful Transition to a More Electronic Federal Depository Library Program as Required by Legislative Branch Appropriations Act, 1996 Public Law 104-53* (Washington, DC: USGPO, 1996); http://www.access.gpo.gov/su_docs/fdlp/pubs/study/studyhtm.html (viewed July 10, 2005).

22. *Report on the Assessment of Electronic Government Information Products* (Rockville, MD: Westat, 1999); http://www.access.gpo.gov/su_docs/nclisassessment/report.html (viewed July 12, 2005).

23. *Public Access to Government Information in the 21st Century*, 1.

24. *Public Printers Annual Report, FY2003, Management's Discussion*, 6; http://www.gpo.gov/congressional/annualreports/03annrep/Content/Financials/FiDocpdf.pdf (viewed July 13, 2005); *Advancing GPO's Transformation Effort Through Strategic Human Capital Management* (Washington, DC: GAO, 2003; http://www.gao.gov/new.items/d0485.pdf (viewed July 13, 2005).; *Actions to Strengthen and Sustain GPO's Transformation: Report to Congressional Addresses*, 8; http://www.gao.gov/highlights/d04830high.pdf (viewed July 13, 2005); Robert E. Kling, *The Government Printing Office* (New York: Praeger, 1970), 35.

25. *Hearing on the Nomination of Bruce R. James, of Nevada, to be Public Printer, October 3, 2002*; http://www.gpo.gov/congressional/pdfs/ppnom.pdf (viewed July 13, 2005).

26. *U.S. Government Printing Office 2004 Annual Report, Management's Discussion and Analysis*, 3; http://www.gpo.gov/congressional/annualreports/04annrep/GPO_2004_ANNUAL_REPORT_web.pdf (viewed July 13, 2005).

27. Ibid.

28. *Advancing GPO's Transformation Effort Through Strategic Human Capital Management; Actions to Strengthen and Sustain GPO's Transformation.*

29. *Oversight Hearing on the Government Printing Office*, 14.

30. *A Strategic Vision for the 21st Century* (Washington, DC: USGPO, 2004); http://www.gpo.gov/congressional/pdfs/04strategicplan.pdf (viewed July 15, 2005).

31. In the appropriations request for FY2006, the Public Printer noted savings from workforce reductions due to the retirement incentives plan and the closing of inefficient regional printing plants. The Public Printer is also seeking legislative authority to use money from the redevelopment of the main GPO building once the agency moves to a more modern facility; Bruce R. James, "Prepared Statement Before the Subcommittee on Legislative Branch Appropriation, U.S. Senate on the Appropriations Request of the U.S. Government Printing Office for Fiscal Year 2006," 2; http://www.gpo.gov/congressional/testimony/sapp06_stmt.pdf (viewed July 15, 2005)

32. *A Strategic Vision for the 21st Century*, 2-3.

33. "Future Digital System (FDsys)," http://www.gpo.gov/projects/fdsys.htm (viewed July 15, 2005).

34. *A Strategic Vision for the 21st Century*, 4.

35. "Information Dissemination Internal Policies," 71-73, http://www.access.gpo.gov/su_docs/fdlp/pubs/policies/index.html (viewed July 19, 2005); "Authentication (Draft) June 21, 2005," http://www.access.gpo.gov/su_docs/fdlp/pubs/proceedings/05spring/cdqa/authentication_white_paper.pdf (viewed July 19, 2005); "Version Control (Draft) June 21, 2005," http://www.access.gpo.gov/su_docs/fdlp/pubs/proceedings/05spring/cdqa/version_control_white_paper.pdf (viewed July 19, 2005); "GPO's Digitization and Preservation Initiatives," http://www.gpoaccess.gov/legacy/index.html (viewed July 19, 2005).

36. *A Strategic Vision for the 21st Century*, 4.

37. The GPO has developed a Web interface for the online public access catalog (OPAC) component of the new integrated library system (ILS). The OPAC replaced the Catalog of U.S. Government Publications in the fall of 2005 and offers better searching, more precise results, and new services for depository libraries. The replacement for the Catalog is called the National Bibliography of U.S. Government Publications. For more information, see the "National Bibliography Program," http://www.access.gpo.gov/su_docs/fdlp/cip/index.html (viewed July 19, 2005).

38. Although primary access to publications in the FDLP will be online, there are some titles that will remain available for selection in paper as long as the originating agency still produces them. These titles are generally important for reference or contain critical information on U.S. Government activities. See "Essential Titles for Public Use in Paper Format," http://www.access.gpo.gov/su_docs/fdlp/pubs/estitles.html (viewed July 20, 2005).

39. *A Strategic Vision for the 21st Century*, 2.

40. "Council Discussion, Questions and Answers from the Fall Meeting, 2004: National Collection of U.S. Government Publications–Formerly Known as the Collection of Last Resort," http://www.access.gpo.gov/su_docs/fdlp/pubs/proceedings/04cbt/nationalcollection.pdf (viewed July 19, 2005).

41. "GPO Testimony Before Congress," http://www.gpo.gov/congressional/testimony.htm (viewed July 18, 2005).

42. "Update for AALL (American Association of Law Librarians), July 2005," http://www.access.gpo.gov/su_docs/fdlp/pubs/aall_update.pdf (viewed July 19, 2005); *Proceedings of the Annual Spring Depository Library Council Spring Meeting, April 17-20, 2005* http://www.access.gpo.gov/su_docs/fdlp/pubs/proceedings/05spring/index.html (viewed July 18, 2005); Bruce R. James, "Transforming the Government Printing Office: Revitalizing Public Access to Government Information in the Electronic Age, University Forum, Brigham Young University–Idaho, Rexburg, ID, Thursday, February 17, 2005," http://www.gpo.gov/news/speeches/PP_IdahoSpeech.pdf (viewed July 19, 2005).

43. James A. Jacobs, James R. Jacobs, and Shinjuong Yeo, "Government Information in the Digital Age: The Once and Future Federal Depository Library Program," *Journal of Academic Librarian Librarianship* 31/3 (2005): 198-208. The authors argue that "the steps and plans [the GPO] is outlining are, at best, incomplete and, at worst, badly flawed."

44. Bruce R. James, "Prepared Statement Before the Committee on Appropriations, House of Representatives on the Appropriations Request of the U.S. Government Printing Office for Fiscal Year 2006," 3, http://www.gpo.gov/congressional/testimony/happ06_stmt.pdf (viewed July 19, 2005).

45. "What Is Gray Literature," http://www.osti.gov/graylit/whatsnew.html (viewed July 22, 2005).

46. *The Government Printing Office and Executive Branch Information Dissemination: Hearing Before the Subcommittee on Government Reform and Oversight, House of Representatives, 105th Congress, 1st Session, May 8, 1997* (Washington, DC: USGPO, 1997), 20.

47. Ibid.

48. "U.S. Defense Technical Information Center. Public STINET (Scientific and Technical Information Network," http://stinet.dtic.mil/ (viewed July 22, 2005).

49. *National Technical Information Service Financial Statements, Fiscal Year 2004*, 17, http://www.ntis.gov/pdf/annrpt2004.pdf (viewed July 22, 2005).

50. "FedWorld.gov," http://www.fedworld.gov/ (viewed July 22, 2005).

51. "Information Bridge," http://www.osti.gov/bridge/ (viewed July 22, 2005); "Energy Citations Database," http://www.osti.gov/energycitations/ (viewed July 22, 2005); "E-print Network," http://www.osti.gov/eprints/ (viewed July 22, 2005).

52. "National Center for Environmental Publications," http://www.epa.gov/ncepihom/ (viewed July 25, 2005); "National Environmental Publications Information System," http://nepis.epa.gov/ (viewed July 25, 2005).

53. "NTRS: NASA Technical Reports Server," http://ntrs.nasa.gov/ (viewed July 25, 2005).

54. Darrell M. West, *State and Federal E-Government in the United States* (New York: Brown University, Center for Public Policy, 2004), 4; http://www.insidepolitics. org/egovt04us.pdf (viewed July 25, 2005).

55. "About Science.gov," http://www.science.gov/about.html (viewed July 25, 2005).

56. "FedStats," http://www.fedstats.gov/ (viewed July 25, 2005); "healthfinder," http://www.healthfinder.gov/ (viewed July 25, 2005); "Consumer.gov," http://www. consumer.gov/ (viewed July 25, 2005); "AgNIC," http://www.agnic.org/agnic/index_ html (viewed July 25, 2005); "Recreation.gov," http://www.recreation.gov/ (viewed July 25, 2005).

57. *Information Technology Management Reform (Clinger-Cohen) Act, P.L. 104-106; Freedom of Information Act, P.L. 89-554; Electronic Freedom of Information Act, P.L. 104-231; Federal Information Security Management Act, P.L. 107-347; Computer Security Act, P.L. 100-235; Rehabilitation Act, § 508, P.L. 105-220.*

58. Laura Gordon-Murnane, "Access to Government Information in a Post 9/11 World," *Searcher* 10/6 (2002): 3-8.

59. "Memorandum for Heads of All Federal Departments and Agencies, October 12, 2001," http://www.usdoj.gov/04foia/011012.htm (viewed July 28, 2005); "Memorandum for the Heads of Executive Departments and Agencies, March 19, 2002," http://www.usdoj.gov/oip/foiapost/2002foiapost10.htm (viewed July 25, 2005); "Executive Order 13292 of March 25, 2005. Further Amendment to Executive Order 12958, as Amended, Classified National Security Information," *Federal Register* 68: 15315-15334.

60. E. Herman, "A Post-September 11th Balancing Act: Public Access to U.S. Government Information Versus Protection of Sensitive Data," *Journal of Government Information* 30 (2004): 19.

61. *E-Government Act of 2002, P.L. 107-347*, http://frwebgate.access.gpo.gov/ cgibin/getdoc.cgi?dbname=107_cong_public_laws&docid=f:publ347.107 (viewed July 28, 2005).

62. Ibid., § 2.

63. "Memorandum for the Heads of Executive Departments and Agencies. Policies for Federal Agency Public Websites, December 17, 2004," http://www.whitehouse. gov/omb/memoranda/fy2005/m05-04.pdf (viewed July 28, 2005).

64. "Chief Information Officers Council. Interagency Committee on Government. Information," http://www.cio.gov/documents/icgi.html (viewed July 28, 2005); "Webcontent.gov," http://www.firstgov.gov/webcontent/index.shtml (viewed July 28, 2005).

65. *Recommended Policies and Guidelines for Federal Public Websites: Final Report of the Interagency Committee on Government Information Submitted to the Office of Management and Budget* http://www.cio.gov/documents/ICGI/ICGI-June9report. pdf (viewed September 9, 2005).

66. *Becoming a Citizen Centered Government Through Best Practices. Open File Report 2004-1359*, http://erg.usgs.gov/isb/pubs/ofrs/2004-1359/ofr2004-1359.pdf (viewed September 9, 2005).

67. "FirstGov.Gov Fact Sheet," http://www.pueblo.gsa.gov/firstgov-fs.htm (viewed July 29, 2005).

68. *FY 2004 Report to Congress on the Implementation of the E-Government Act of 2002. March 1, 2005*, 7; http://www.whitehouse.gov/omb/inforeg/2004_egov_report. pdf (viewed July 29, 2005).

69. "Three Out of Four Americans Have Access to the Internet, According to Nielsen/ Netratings, March 18, 2004," http://www.nielsennetratings.com/pr/pr_040318.pdf (viewed August 24, 2005).

70. John B. Horrigan, *How Americans Get in Touch With Government–Internet Users Benefit From the Efficiency of E-government, But Multiple Channels Are Still Needed For Citizens to Reach Agencies and Solve Problems* (Pew Internet and American Life Project, 2004), 21; http://www.pewinternet.org/pdfs/PIP_E-Gov_Report_0504.pdf (viewed August 24, 2005).

71. Ibid., 17.

72. Atifa Rawan, Cheryl Knott Malone, and Luara J. Bender, "Assessing the Virtual Depository Program: The Arizona Experience," *Journal of Government Information* 30 (2004): 723.

73. Susan Gardner and Susanna Eng, "What Students Want: Generation Y and the Changing Function of the Academic Library," *Libraries and the Academy* 5/3 (2005): 407-413.

74. Judith C. Russell, "Federal Depository Library Adds and Drops, FY 1998-2005," Message posted to GovDoc-L mailing list (July 15, 2005).

75. Luke Griffin and Aric Ahrens, "Deposits and Withdrawals: A Survey of Depository Libraries That Have Recently Changed Status," Presentation at the Depository Library Council Meeting, Reno, NV (April 8, 2003), http://www.jsu.edu/depart/library/ government/depositories/ (viewed July 25, 2005); "Stay With the Program: Benefits of Being a Member of the FDLP," http://www.access.gpo.gov/su_docs/ fdlp/staywiththe program.html (viewed July 25, 2005).

76. "Committees of the Depository Library Council," http://www.access.gpo.gov/ su_docs/fdlp/council/dlccoms.html (viewed July 25, 2005).

77. Charles A. Seavey, "Documents to the People," *American Libraries* 36/7 (2005): 44.

78. Ibid.

79. Ibid.

80. Allison Cowgill, Joan Beam, and Linsey Wess, "Implementing an Information Commons in a University Library," *Journal of Academic Librarianship* 27/6 (2001): 436.

81. Ethel Auster and Donna C. Chan, "Reference Librarians and Keeping Up-to-Date: A Question of Priorities," *Reference & User Services Quarterly* 44/1, (2004): 61.

82. Michael Hammer and James Champy, *Reengineering the Corporation: A Manifesto for Business Revolution* (New York: HarperCollins, 2001); "E-Gov," http:// www.whitehouse.gov/omb/egov/index.html (viewed July 29, 2005); Cowgill et al., 438.

83. The majority (61%) of government documents units are not independently administered. They are most frequently combined with reference, cataloging, or acquisitions. *Biennial Survey of Depository Libraries: 2001 Results* (Washington, DC: USGPO, 2003), 6-7; http://www.access.gpo.gov/su_docs/fdlp/bisurvey/01survey.pdf (viewed July 6, 2005).

84. Paula Warnken, "New Technologies and Constant Change: Managing the Process," *Journal of Academic Librarianship* 30/4 (2004): 324.

85. "Government Information Online," http://govtinfo.org/ (viewed July 20, 2005); "LOCKSS Program," http://www.lockss.org/ (viewed July 25, 2005); "Free Government Information," http://freegovinfo.info/ (viewed July 25, 2005); "RSS Main Page," http://www.gpoaccess.gov/rss/index.html (viewed July 25, 2005); "DLC Vision Outline," http://dlcvisionoutline.blogspot.com/ (viewed July 25, 2005).

86. "The Federal Government Information Environment of the 21st Century: Towards a Vision Statement and Plan of Action for Federal Depository Libraries," Discussion Paper. Prepared by the Depository Library Council, (September 2005), http://www.access.gpo.gov/su_docs/fdlp/pubs/dlc_vision_09_02_2005.pdf (viewed September 9, 2005).

87. Zheng Ye (Lan) Yang, "An Assessment of Education and Training Needs for Government Documents Librarians in the United States," *Journal of Government Information* 28(2000): 429.

88. "Depository Management," http://www.access.gpo.gov/su_docs/fdlp/mgt/index.html (viewed July 29, 2005); "Proceedings of Federal Depository Library Conferences," http://www.access.gpo.gov/su_docs/fdlp/pubs/proceedings/index.html (viewed July 29, 2005); "FDLP Desktop: Events–2005 Interagency Depository Seminar," http://www.access.gpo.gov/su_docs/fdlp/events/interagency.html (viewed July 29, 2005); "GODORT Created Resources," http://sunsite.berkeley.edu/GODORT/created.html (viewed July 29, 2005); "Government Documents Special Interest Section," http:// www.aallnet.org/sis/gd/ (viewed July 29, 2005); "LLSDC's Source Book," http://www. llsdc.org/sourcebook/ (viewed July 29, 2005).

89. Maggie Farrell, "U.S. Depository Library Council Electronic Transition Report," *Government Information Quarterly* 17/3(2000): 332.

90. Ibid.

91. John Shuler, "Informing the Nation: The Future of Librarianship and Government Information Service," *Government Information Quarterly* 22(2005): 148.

92. Ibid., 149.

93. Yang, 428.

94. Yang, 434.

doi:10.1300/J105v32n03_05

# Challenges and Opportunities for Electronic Resources (ER) Librarians in Facing Down the Digital Divide

Tawnya K. Plumb

**SUMMARY.** The electronic resources (ER) librarian has a social responsibility to be knowledgeable about the digital divide. Discourse on the digital divide began in the mid-1990s and continues today. Data analysis reveals that divides still exist, particularly when considering income, education, region, disability, age, and race. Librarians face many challenges to take on the digital divide. These challenges include issues of access, content, technical literacy, privacy, civic participation, education, employment, non-use, and political debate. Yet for each challenge, there is an opportunity for the ER librarians to thrive while they face down the digital divide. doi:10.1300/J105v32n03_06 *[Article copies available for a fee from The Haworth Document Delivery Service: 1-800-HAWORTH. E-mail address: <docdelivery@haworthpress.com> Website: <http://www.HaworthPress. com> © 2007 by The Haworth Press. All rights reserved.]*

---

Tawnya K. Plumb, MLIS, is Electronic Services Librarian, George W. Hopper Law Library, University of Wyoming College of Law, Department 3035, 1000 East University Avenue, Laramie, WY 82071 (E-mail: tplumb@uwyo.edu).

[Haworth co-indexing entry note]: "Challenges and Opportunities for Electronic Resources (ER) Librarians in Facing Down the Digital Divide." Plumb, Tawnya K. Co-published simultaneously in *Collection Management* (The Haworth Information Press, an imprint of The Haworth Press) Vol. 32, No. 3/4, 2007, pp. 327-349; and: *Electronic Resources Librarianship and Management of Digital Information: Emerging Professional Roles* (ed: Mark Jacobs) The Haworth Information Press, an imprint of The Haworth Press, 2007, pp. 327-349. Single or multiple copies of this article are available for a fee from The Haworth Document Delivery Service [1-800-HAWORTH, 9:00 a.m. - 5:00 p.m. (EST). E-mail address: docdelivery@ haworthpress.com].

**KEYWORDS.** Digital divide, electronic resources librarian, ER librarian, electronic services librarian, electronic resources

## INTRODUCTION

As the position of electronic resources (ER) librarian becomes more prevalent in libraries, we must recognize the social responsibilities that come along with the position. The ER librarian is charged with the selection, acquisition, description, implementation, maintenance, and evaluation of ER. These are all tasks you will find in an ER librarian job description. What you will not find in one of these descriptions, however, is mention of social responsibility. As we push for the electronic, we must acknowledge those who will not benefit from our work. We are responsible to make sure that all persons have access to e-resources, regardless of income, education, region, disability, age, race, or sex. Though progress has been made over the years, a divide between the haves and have-nots still exists. The ER librarian has an integral role to fill to face down the digital divide.

## A HISTORICAL OVERVIEW OF THE DIGITAL DIVIDE

When did the term digital divide come into use? Andy Carvin from the Digital Divide Network provides us with some leads. The digital divide, in the context of how the term is used today, was introduced by author Dinty Moore and by columnist Amy Harmon of the *LA Times*.[1]

I also located an early reference in an article by Howard Wolinsky of the *Chicago Sun-Times* in 1996.[2]

The term gained more credence from its official use by Vice President Al Gore and later by President Bill Clinton in speeches delivered to promote their policy goal to connect every classroom in the United States to the Internet. The National Telecommunications and Information Administration (NTIA), a part of the United States Department of Commerce, published a series of reports called *Falling Through the Net*. These reports became foundation documents for the study of the digital divide.

*Falling Through the Net* was first published in 1995; later editions appeared in 1998, 1999, and 2000. I will refer to the research of Lisa Servon in order to summarize these reports.[3] The 1995 report proposed to connect households to the National Information Infrastructure (NII)

and to create public access for others. The 1998 report added a stronger urgency to meet the goal and was politically supported by Gore. The 1999 report followed the premise that universal connectivity is a given and should be seen as a national necessity with emphasis placed on a skilled workforce. The 2000 report, the last within the Clinton Administration, showed there had been progress in closing the digital divide. Some divides, such as usage between men and women, seemed to disappear altogether. Servon concludes from the *Falling Through the Net* series that "there is not one digital divide but many" and that "the digital divide is a dynamic problem, not a static one."[4] This is an opinion that reflects the shape of the digital divide today.

Under the current Bush Administration, NTIA has published the *A Nation Online* series. The first report of this series was titled, *How Americans Are Expanding Their Use of the Internet,* and demographic factors were considered. One theme that emerges from this report was that "Internet use is increasing for people regardless of income, education, age, races, ethnicity, or gender."[5]

The report is optimistic, and surprisingly, the term digital divide does not appear in the text a single time. The most recent *A Nation Online* report published by NTIA is *Entering the Broadband Age.*[6] Unfortunately, demographics were not considered at all in this study of broadband access. I agree that progress is being made, yet I argue that divides still exist. The divides should be acknowledged, and the divided must be served.

## Who Are the Divided?

Some of the most current data available on Internet use come from the Pew Internet and American Life Project (PIALP). I will refer to this data in addition to the NTIA reports to construct the face of the divided. Income, education, region, disability, age, race, and sex will be considered.

### Income

Today, 49% of those that earn $30,000 or less use the Internet. Compare this with 93% of those who make over $75,000.[7]

A clear relationship exists between income and Internet use. The more money one makes, the more likely he/she is to use the Internet. Although the number of lower-income Internet users is on the rise, not much has changed in the percentages since 2001. Most of our divided patrons will be those with less money and it does not appear that this will change soon.

## Education

PIALP has compiled data that reveals a strong correlation between education and use of the Internet.[8] The difference between the percentage of Internet users with less than a high school education (29%) and users with a college degree or more (89%) is enormous. Even the difference between users who have finished high school (61%) and users who have some college (79%) is significant. Education is one of the most important factors to determine who has access to the Web and who does not. Consider the technology that is available at universities; those who attend or work at college have better and readier access to computers than those who do not. In addition, those with college degrees are, often, rewarded with high-paid occupations where can be found top-of-the-line technology.

## Region

After a consideration of income, there will be few surprises as to what regions have populations that have the easiest access to the Web and which have the worst. Regions with high incomes, such as the Pacific Northwest, New England, and California, have the best connectivity. The poorest region of the U.S., the South, has connectivity rates 20% lower.[9] A divide also exists between urban and rural communities. In 2003, 67% of urban residents used the Internet, whereas only 52% of rural residents reported use.[10]

Though the divide has narrowed, in 2005 there was still a 13% disadvantage for rural users.[11]

But, factors are at play beyond those of income and education, which compounds the problem.

## Disability

One study confirmed that "just 38% of Americans with disabilities use the Internet" and about a fifth of the disabled indicate that their disability hampers their use,[12] which makes this a very large, very notable population without access. Individuals with disabilities not only need adaptive technologies to use computers, but, also, physical access, i.e., to be able to get to computers and assistance to be set up at a computer workstation.

*Age*

The persons who are least likely to use computer technology are aged 65 or older. In 2005, the percentage of seniors online was only 26%. Compare this with 84% of 18-29-year-olds who use the Internet and a divide clearly emerges.[13]

Comfort-level and available content that is relevant to the age group are factors in this divide. Older persons have not had the benefit to be raised with computers and must work and struggle in order to be comfortable with technology. Once they feel confident in their computer skills they often find a dearth of content on the Web that interests them. There is content available on the Internet that could be of service to the elderly, but it is not likely that it can be found through an AOL keyword search.

The outlook is positive for children aged 7-17. In 2003, 100% of public schools had some type of Internet access.[14]

With computer access at school, children have rapidly become comfortable with technology. There is, also, a wealth of Web content available on the Web that appeals to this age range.

*Race/Ethnicity*

In 2001, NTIA reported the percentages of various races that reported computer use. According to the report:

- Asian American/Pacific Islanders (71%)
- Whites (71%)
- Blacks (56%)
- Hispanics (49%)[15]

More recent data on the demographics of computer users are not available. A 2005 snapshot of Internet users shows that divides still exist, e.g., a 13% difference between Blacks and Whites, English-speaking Hispanics use the Internet as much as Whites, but Spanish speaking Hispanics as well as Native Americans are not included in the data.[16]

We know that unemployment and poverty rates on reservations are high and the income and education issues mentioned above can be added to the equation in terms of Native American access to the Internet. It is also known that only 39% of Native Americans who live in rural communities have telephone service, much less Internet access.[17]

The basic, technological infrastructure is lacked, which prevents the development of the foundation for the use of computer technology to search the Web, or to do anything else for that matter. Native Americans are, perhaps, the most digitally divided group in our nation, particularly they who live and work on reservations, and Kade Twist rightfully asks of NTIA, "A Nation Online, But Where Are the Indians?"[18]

## Gender

Today, a woman is statistically no less likely to be without computer access than a man. This represents progress because a divide between the sexes once existed. A 2005 survey noted a 2% usage advantage for men, but this was no greater than the margin of error.[19]

## Summary

Fortunately, the factors that contribute to the digital divide today are not as extensive as they were in the 1990s. Karen Mossberger confirms the data patterns covered, thus far, in this chapter. Those least likely to have a computer at home are poor, less-educated, aged, Spanish-speaking, or African-American.[20]

These are the individuals that ER librarians must identify in our communities and to whom they should provide special services, e.g., access to the Internet. This is the first step to work to eradicate the divide in Web access between those who have access and those who do not.

# CHALLENGES AND OPPORTUNITIES FOR ER LIBRARIANS

## Access

Users need access to computer hardware and they need a connection to the Internet and we know that some users visit libraries to get this access. Since 1994, NTIA's Technology Opportunities Program (TOP) has awarded grants to libraries, non-profit organizations, universities, community technology centers, hospitals, and local governments. Libraries have used these funds to provide much-needed, computer access as have other public institutions in our communities. The Bush Administration cut funding to TOP in 2005 and these grants are no longer available.

The initiatives that are of interest to the current administration are broadband and wireless access. In an executive memorandum, President Bush established the United States Spectrum Policy for the 21st Century that seeks to provide wireless services worldwide to governments, industries, and individuals.[21]

The administration is very interested in broadband technology as well with a goal of "universal, affordable access for broadband technology by the year 2007" in order that "consumers have got plenty of choices when it comes to [their] broadband carrier."[22]

These are solid initiatives for the computer user, yet I argue that everyone's needs for basic access have not been met.

Private benefactors, such as the Bill and Melinda Gates Foundation, still offer grants for libraries, but as TOP grants have been eliminated less funding will be available to institutions in need and the competition between institutions that seek grants will increase. Many libraries also rely on the government's E-Rate program to get connected. For how long will this service be available? Which libraries are in danger of a funding loss? I suspect that the most vulnerable libraries will turn out to be those whose users are the most needy: members of the digitally divided. Consider that libraries, generally, have a development board of some kind, a public relations department, a friends of the library group, and a fund-raising team. Then, consider the donation pool to which the library that is located in a suburban, middle-class neighborhood can petition. Libraries located in less-fortunate neighborhoods do not have the same avenues of support. The local users do not have the money to donate to their local library in poorer communities. Ultimately, the most vulnerable libraries are dependant on national, state, and local governments for funding. This will continue to be the case and is a challenge for librarians who seek to close the divide.

Another challenge is to modify library software and equipment to give access to all users, specifically those users with disabilities. Many libraries are not equipped with the software needed, by blind or deaf patrons, to access and use computer technology. Also, many library Web sites do not follow the rules provided by the Web Access Initiative (WAI) of the World Wide Web Consortium[23] to make Web pages accessible to the blind. The WAI asks librarians to learn new skills and seek training to serve disabled patrons.

These challenges give ER librarians opportunities to step up, create new programs, and promote and fight for extant programs. Within our communities, we have the opportunity to identify our own divided and then tailor new programs to fit their needs. If there are users with disabilities, identify their software needs and meet them. If they are trained, ER librarians would be able to introduce, manage, and evaluate accessibility tools to use to serve users. If you work near a reservation, support wireless networking as it is a cost-effective means to connect the divided.[24]

Native-run tribal colleges and universities have begun to play a large role to narrow the digital divide as their representatives help reservations gain access to technology.[25]

> Volunteer to help. To facilitate these programs, identify a local business sponsor or write grants to receive funding for equipment, software, and connections. Pay attention to E-Rate legislation and lobby for its continued support. Likewise, become an activist to get funds restored to federal programs, e.g., TOP grants. We need to continue to be vigilant to ensure our libraries receive the funds they need to provide computer access for everyone.

We need not do this work alone. Seek out network opportunities such as WebJunction, "an online community where library staff meet to share ideas, solve problems, take online courses–and have fun."[26]

Thanks to the Gates Foundation, WebJunction has received funds for their Spanish Language Outreach Program (SLOP) and for the Rural Libraries Sustainability Program (RLSP); both seek to serve the divided.[27]

The Digital Divide Network (DDN) is another place to network with others to find solutions to the digital divide.[28]

The "Tool Kit for Bridging the Digital Divide in Your Community" is a source of help as well. Archived by the United States Department of Education, the tool kit helps those who work to end the digital divide gather information, establish goals, plan, and write grants.[29]

This community-based approach, which caters to the needs of its local client-base, may be the most successful means to take on the digital divide.

### Relevant Content

Librarians become familiar with much of the information our users access on a regular basis. Shoppers visit eBay, adventurers toggle between Travelocity and Orbitz to get the best possible travel deal, current event enthusiasts visit a plethora of news sites, and writers create blogs and respond to the blogs of others; to offer just a few examples. But, what about the information needs of the divided. Many of the divided have little or no extra money and, therefore, the shopping and travel sites are of little interest. News sites may be of interest, but to what extent does CNN.com cater to the aged or low-income user? But, a lot of the problem, in terms of whether the Internet is used by the divided, may have to do with perception. Katz and Rice summarize the limitations of Web content:

> Although the Internet is extraordinarily useful to some, it is of little or no use to others. And even if it might be useful to them, many people still perceive that it is not. Such a view may be more important than any physical constraints that might limit access.[30]

Unless Web information is perceived as relevant to the divided, the divided will remain disconnected.

So, the question is: What is relevant content? For many, relevant content means practical and/or local, helpful information. Online interests for the low-income user might include information on low-cost child care, free legal services, or job training programs. For others, relevant might refer to material written at the basic literacy-level, such as easy-to-understand, online encyclopedias on health or medicine, or electronic tutorials that cover basic, computer skills. Relevance can also be reserved for vital, government information written in languages other than English, e.g., tax forms or social security documents. Finally, relevant can be assigned to cultural content. Although the cultural presence of many groups and communities has appeared on the Web, more diverse cultural content is desired.[31]

The availability for all of relevant, cultural content in a public medium is not a new idea related only to online information. Members of minority groups in the United States have complained for decades about the lack of television programming that is relevant to their lifestyles and cultures. Because of the difference between the mediums, however, an opportunity for change becomes apparent. Television programming is created and produced by a limited, select number of people whereas the potential number of contributors to the Internet is unlimited. Anyone, with a little training, can create a home page or start a blog. This is where ER librarians might step in, create and implement programs to empower the divided to make use of the net, teach basic Web-design skills with the use of WYSIWYG editors, and connect the divided with free Web hosts. Sampa.org[32] in Sao Paulo and HarlemLIVE[33] are models to be emulated of what can be accomplished when the divided come together to create their own high-quality, online content.[34]

The interest is out there; the ER librarian just needs to locate and train the interested.

In terms of practical, local information, librarians might create local pathfinders for users; Web pages that contain links that connect to information that is pertinent to the divided in the community, i.e., education, family, finances, government, health, housing, personal enrichment, and vocations.[35] The development of community databases that contain information resources needed by the divided, e.g., maps, local listings, and community resources, etc., would be beneficial as well.[36] The Children's Partnership publication titled, *The Search for High-Quality Online Content for Low-Income and Underserved Communities: Evaluation and Producing What's Needed* contains action plans, guidelines, and blueprints to help ER librarians take the steps necessary to get relevant content generated on Web sites in their communities. [37]

A simpler, more straightforward, library-oriented task for ER librarians to address the problem of the digital divide would be to consciously consider the divided community when collection development decisions are made. There is an opportunity to meet the needs of the divided each time a new digital resource is added to a library's collection.

### Literacies in the Digital Age

Technical literacy, information literacy, and basic literacy all contribute to the "skills divide."[38] Many users need help with technical literacy skills, but, for the divided, it is vital to get this help. If a patron does not know how to use a mouse or navigate the Web with the use of a browser, they won't have much luck with an online library catalog. Many others lack the information literacy skills they need to identify their research needs, locate a useful source of information, or evaluate the information they retrieve. Library patrons who most need technical assistance and help with information literacy are the elderly, the less-educated, the poor, and members of minority groups, such as African-Americans and Hispanics.[39] If librarians fail to identify these individuals and their needs, they will continue to be left behind; to be divided. At the most, basic level of literacy are patrons who are unable to read or write; this skills-divide represents the most formidable challenge for librarians who seek to face down all aspects of the digital divide.

In the arena of instructional technology, many opportunities exist to improve the technical literacy of library users. The specific type of training sought by the divided must be provided. Programs should be realistic and designed to meet the actual needs of the participants, not a librarian's perception of those needs. Also, an emphasis on communication is more meaningful to participants than an emphasis on information. Finally, barriers to Internet access are not only technological, but also cultural. Programs that recognize this are the ones that are best received.[40]

Not only do ER librarians have the opportunity to train users, but we also have the opportunity to train the trainers. Many school teachers and public servants train users in technical literacy in formal and informal settings. Some are comfortable with this task; others are not. We can improve the process when we support these trainers and offer our expertise when appropriate.

The ER librarian's skills are, also, integral in the improvement of the information literacy skills of patrons. Through the research interview the research needs of the user can be identified and, then, steps can be taken to help in the development of a research plan. It is important to understand that a search of the library's online catalog or subscriber databases is second nature to some, and downright foreign and impossible for others. ER librarians have advocated and, in some instances, led the implementation of simplified search interfaces and federated search engines in libraries. The simpler the access method, the easier and more effective it will be to train the divided. In line with this idea is the contention that "one-stop searching bridges the digital divide."[41]

Ease of use is always an issue for all users, and search interfaces that are difficult to understand and navigate may keep some non-users away. A significant role for ER librarians is to continue to encourage vendors and to advocate for improvements to interfaces to use to search databases and catalogs; this and support for effective federated search engines will benefit all users, especially the divided.

### Privacy Concerns

Some in our divided populations may choose not to use the Internet for fear that their privacy may be compromised. I have my own concerns about the information that is collected from and attached to me online; yet, I am aware of the risks and know how to minimize them. Others do not know how and are hesitant, understandably, to participate in online transactions or to provide any personal information as these activities may result in identity theft. The recent ChoicePoint breach of personal information is the type of incident that exacerbates this anxiety. Others fear their visits to so-called subversive or non-mainstream Web sites might be monitored/tracked by government bodies, law enforcement agencies, or employers. The Office of National Drug Control Policy used software to track users who viewed a drug advertisement through the attachment of a *cookie* to their computers in order to follow their subsequent Internet searches.[42]

Another example is the Federal Bureau of Investigation's e-mail interception software, Carnivore, used by law enforcement.[43]

Carnivore raises *big brother* flags for some users and could discourage them from taking advantage of the benefits of e-mail. Fear of a violation of privacy is a reasonable and justified concern and many divided users consider the risk of using technology greater than its benefits. These individuals, then, form another group of the digitally divided: the non-users.

Section 215 of the Patriot Act allows the FBI to request "any tangible things (including books, records, papers, documents, or other items) for an investigation to protect against international terrorism or clandestine intelligence activities."[44]

This section of the act has been tested in libraries, and users have learned that they do have reason to be concerned about their privacy in libraries. This has resulted, unfortunately, in a fear to use the Internet in our nation's libraries. With the American Library Association (ALA) and other library associations at the forefront, librarians continue to fight activities and policies that abuse patron privacy. To benefit, encourage, and reassure divided users, librarians must let them know that we will fight for their right to come to the library to access the Internet freely and anonymously.

On the other hand, each problem presents an opportunity for the ER librarian. An increase in public awareness on issues of privacy provides an opportunity to educate users on risky Internet behavior, i.e., the difference between entering personal information into an unknown .com Web site as opposed to a .gov or .edu site. As they are informed of and trained in ways to respond to Internet cookies, spamming, and security software, users will develop confidence in their ability to *surf the Web* safely. Another way to increase the confidence of users is to design and implement better and safer technologies in the library. ER libraries must encourage vendor/publishers to incorporate measures and safeguards to protect user privacy into licensed products. ER librarians must, also, continue to stand up and question the necessity of Section 215 of the Patriot Act in light of the abuses of personal privacy it has enabled. Of course, in those instances where users still have privacy concerns in their use of the Internet in libraries, ER librarians have the option to do what they can to provide viable alternatives as research options. However,

the creation, implementation, and adherence to privacy policies/proce-
dures will alleviate many privacy concerns in the library. If the library's
position on privacy issues is outlined and delineated in writing, library
users will feel less anxiety to use the library's resources to access the
Web; they must feel confident that librarians will do everything in their
power to protect user anonymity.

The San Francisco Public Library has such a privacy policy.[45]

> Maria Protti, the City Attorney for San Francisco, made a
> presentation on the creation of a privacy policy at a session of the
> 2005 AALL (American Association of Law Libraries) annual con-
> ference in San Antonio (Tex.). Topics of discussion included li-
> brary cards, circulation records, public computer use, web forms,
> reference questions, network security, law enforcement requests,
> radio frequency identification (RFID), and the Patriot Act.[46]

## *The Civic Disconnect*

Increasingly, the local, state, and national political processes are carried out online; a significant and, potentially, formidable shift in the political landscape. Grassroots e-mail campaigns, e-mail distribution lists,
and fundraising Web sites have taken hold of the public imagination and
will continue to be influential. Internet non-users are left out of this important aspect of the political process. The Internet has become "a deliberate public forum" and a "democratic divide" has been observed and
questioned.[47] In the future, e-voting may become an important way
(some would say the primary or only way) to cast a vote and those comfortable with technology will feel more confident in the process. Others,
who have a lower comfort-level, many of whom are members of the
various demographic groups that make up the divided, may not feel
comfortable with an online political process. This creates a civic discon-
nect for the divided.

The E-Government Act of 2002,[48] the goal of which is to provide
more government resources online, is a noble cause and many of us who
work in reference services appreciate Web access to government forms
and information, but this movement may pose a problem for voters, taxpayers, and citizens who do not have Web access. After an evaluation of
the E-Government Act, Jaime Klima concluded:

> By passing the E-Government Act, however, Congress over-
> looked the extent of the digital divide, and worse, assumed that

existing means of public access will allay any concerns about disadvantages that arise from e-government.[49]

In public libraries, it is common to have all public computers in use while other patrons wait for their thirty minutes of access. That scenario will not be sufficient to take care of all the public's government needs all of the time. Furthermore:

> Congress may have put the cart before the metaphoric horse. Rather than embedding an impact study within the Act, Congress should have assured that discrepancies in Internet access would not cause disadvantage under the E-Government Act *before* passing the bill.[50]

Libraries as well as other, public Internet sites are in a position of responsibility to connect the divided to the government via the Web. The more government information to which access becomes limited to the Internet, the more the need increases for ER librarians to make access to the Web as widely available as possible.

"Government websites . . . are the most important public face of the Internet."[51] An increase in public awareness through advertisements is the best means to connect the divided to e-government Web sites. If librarians offer programs that address health care, tax benefits, and other governmental topics, non-users may be brought into the library where electronic pathfinders can be used to guide them to the best, government resources to meet their needs. Government Web sites are not the easiest to navigate, so librarians must demonstrate exemplary patience to train new and experienced users.

Voting stations have, traditionally, been located in libraries and public schools and community members view libraries as a place of civic action. All political affiliations have a presence online, though one must know how to seek them out. What takes place on the Web, the newest political forum exemplified by Web sites, e-mail distribution lists, action alerts, political news, etc., could be useful enough to the non-user to encourage them to find a means to get connected.

### Loss of Education and Employment Opportunities

If the divided do not learn how to use computers and access information, they will not have the same education and employment opportunities available to computer users. In terms of education, distance learning via the Internet is widespread and a great benefit to those unable, for any number of reasons, to physically attend classes, which includes the divided/disconnected. But, Whites are the likeliest to take advantage of online courses as are the young, the educated, the affluent, and the employed; these are the connected.[52] An examination of the job market reveals, "there is a high demand for entry-level IT workers, present[ing] a unique opportunity for moving disadvantaged people into good jobs."[53] Obviously, opportunities exist, but the challenge is to unite the divided with these jobs; to help them gain the qualifications for these positions. The divided do not have access to Monster.com and the myriad of resources available online to hunt for jobs. Often, job advertisements and application forms are only available online and it has become common for employers to request resumés by e-mail. This type of perpetual cycle has been, historically, one of the biggest challenges for the disadvantages to overcome in order to improve their situation.

ER librarians can help to break this cycle when they identify the distance learning opportunities available in their communities. If they locate, organize, and publish this information, they might be able to reach the divided with it. If they work with distance education professionals, they should be able to bridge the gap between disconnected students who want to learn online and the educators who want to teach them. Likewise, programs to develop skills to hunt for jobs online would be of benefit with discussions and training on how to find and use employment Web sites and instruction on how to create and e-mail resumes.

It was pointed out, earlier, that the divided lose access to high-tech jobs due to their lack of computer experience and training. There should be programs offered within librarianship to train disadvantaged workers. At the University of Arizona School of Information Resources and Library Science and the University of Arizona Libraries, a program has been initiated called Knowledge River. The initiative's mission is "devoted to attacking the full spectrum of Digital Divide problems Hispanic Americans and American Indians face."[54] Knowledge River is an important model for such programming. One of its goals is to create an interdisciplinary, library education for Hispanics and American Indians. The LIS community can take on the digital divide through the active recruitment of members of the divided into their own ranks. Internships can be set up for members of disconnected groups in order to provide opportunities for the disadvantaged to enter the library profession and workforce. There are funds available for this kind of recruitment. The Institute of Museum and Library Services (IMLS) awarded over $21 million to universities, libraries, and organizations to recruit new librarians.[55]

The University of Arizona received $990,174 for their Knowledge River project, and there were 36 other grants awarded to similar programs.

## The Non-Users

Roughly, one-third of Americans are non-users of the Internet[56] and their reasons are many.

Cost and technical literacy as causes and challenges have already been discussed. However, Figure 1 reveals that the major reasons stated for non-use are "I don't want it" and "I don't need it." As librarians, we have learned to respect the wishes of patrons, but, in order to do the best job possible to help them find the information they need, we often probe to uncover the larger picture; the circumstance that underlies the decision or the belief. Of those who reported that they didn't want or need the Internet, there were some notable responses. One study participant re-

FIGURE 1. Pew Internet and American Life Project March-May 2002 Survey

| **The reasons non-users aren't online** *Major and minor reasons why non-users do not use the Internet* | | | |
|---|---|---|---|
| | **Major Reason** | **Minor Reason** | **Not a Reason** |
| I don't want it | 52% | 16% | 26% |
| I don't need it | 52 | 19 | 24 |
| I'm worried about online pornography, credit card theft and fraud | 43 | 14 | 37 |
| It is too expensive | 30 | 18 | 42 |
| I don't have time to use the Internet | 29 | 17 | 49 |
| The Internet is too complicated and hard to understand | 27 | 19 | 43 |
| Don't have a computer | 11 | n/a | n/a |

sponded that "the Internet isn't for people like me"; others felt that the Internet was "just for business."[57] These are troubling beliefs.

An argument can be made that *people like me* refers to persons who do not feel comfortable in the use of technology. Experienced computer users, it is true, develop a certain comfort-level and confidence over time. After a while they realize that they will not damage the computer with a few, incorrect clicks. Non-users do not have this knowledge and are understandably uneasy. There is a challenge here for librarians, especially librarians who work with digital resources, to identify the *people like me* and to determine the reasons that lie behind the comment and the uneasiness.

Then there is the belief that the Internet is *just for business*. A common thought among non-users, to rectify its incorrectness in the minds and for the benefit of the divided lies in demonstration; the solution of a problem through the use of the Web or the resolution of a patron need through reference to Web sites on employment, health, or other, practical matters. The personality and lifestyle of the non-user must, also, be taken into consideration by the librarian. "A person's media use is related to Internet use."[58] It's a paradox: the Internet may have more and better information to offer than the non-user's favorite media, e.g., television/ radio, newspapers/journals, etc., but, also, must be similar enough to those media to instill a sense of familiarity and, hence, confidence in use in the inexperienced user.

### Defending the Digital Divide

ER librarians face a challenge to defend the concept, itself, of the digital divide. In Compaine's book titled, *The Digital Divide: Facing a Crisis or Creating a Myth*, the argument is made that it is questionable whether there is a need for any, extraordinary work to erase the digital divide in technology as it seems as if it will take care of itself; after all, the gaps have narrowed.[59] Others contend that a *go slow* approach is necessary for economic and network concerns.[60] Then, there are individuals like Michael Powell who as Federal Communications Commission Chief dismissed the importance of the digital divide as he noted that there is a Mercedes divide as well.[61] Many are content to see the phrase fade from use, but this is not in the best interest of divided users.

This challenge places the ER librarian in the role of activist and researcher. The Bush Administration has not only ceased the use of the term, but has taken "steps to dismantle the digital divide initiatives of the Clinton-Gore era."[62] Cuts that result in a loss of funds for programs intended to right the wrongs of the digital divide must be actively opposed. Reports from NTIA have been more concerned with broadband access than with the demographics of users who have been denied basic, Internet access. Yet, there is data to show that a (or many) digital divide still exists. ER librarians must continue to follow as well as participate in the discussion and conduct and support independent research into the matter.

New conversations are emerging as to whether or not the digital divide is the most, useful construct in which to frame a discussion that may have wider significance. Warschauer asks, "Should the notion be broadened or conceptualized toward a different framework for analyzing technology access and social inclusion?"[63] However, regardless of the construct used to study and define the social implications of the digital divide, the ER librarian must continue to identify and serve the divided.

## *THE ER LIBRARIAN*

Within this discourse on the digital divide have been identified many, possible roles for the ER librarian (see Figure 2).

The technology specialist works to eliminate technical illiteracy. The content creator develops online Web sites that are practical and of interest to the divided. The educator teaches basic literacy along with information

FIGURE 2. The Many Roles of the ER Librarian in Facing Down the Digital Divide

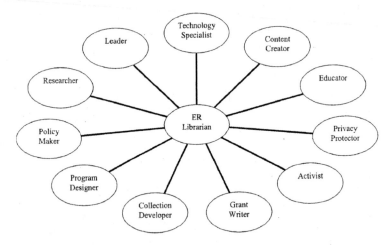

literacy. The privacy protector ensures the individual rights of patrons to search the Web without wondering who is watching. The activist fights for E-rate and federal programs and lobbies for funding. The grant writer seeks support for programs from both government and private sources. The collection developer selects databases and e-materials that are easy to use and relevant to the divided. The program designer identifies the divided within the community and tailors programs accordingly. The policy maker drafts and implements a solid, privacy policy for the library. The researcher studies the digital divide and its social implications and asks, where is work in still needed? Finally, the leader sets a goal to eradicate the digital divide. With such a diverse and integral skill set in mind, this chapter will be concluded with a discussion of who ER librarians are, what they know, and how they have been trained to take on the digital divide.

## *Who Is the ER Librarian?*

The ER librarian position is, apparently, so new that there is no research to be found that documents the demographics of its incumbents. The ALA has conducted a voluntary, demographics survey, but the results are not yet available. Further research is called for.

## *How Is the ER Librarian Trained?*

At library school, ER librarians may have had the opportunity to develop an assortment of skills to use to address the problem of the digital divide, i.e., drafting library policies and grant proposals. Of course, there are courses in collection development where students learn to construct and evaluate a library collection. There are classes in which to learn how to design educational library programs. In Web design and database coursework students may learn to become proficient with aspects of technology.

Upon graduation, of course, the ER librarian must pursue continuing education and professional development. There are skills that can be taught through library associations, e.g., ALA, AALL, etc. Among the skills to be learned and tested at conferences and that will be relevant to librarians who work on the issue of the digital divide are:

- Leadership roles within the association and within libraries
- Meetings and collaborations with others, which open up opportunities for research and scholarship

- Attention to challenges to face and encouragement for activism in library causes

These are all abilities needed to address the digital divide and to fill the role of the ER librarian.

Many ER librarians have had other library positions and have developed various, librarian skills, i.e., reference, cataloging, computer and database administration, and management, all of which are applicable to the requirements of the ER librarian position. Previous work experience of this nature helps ER librarians integrate ER into the traditional, library work environment while they maintain the broadest picture possible of the overall library functions. ER librarians have come from and worked in various, library settings as well, e.g., public and private libraries, academic institutions, and special libraries. As a law librarian, I know my experiences in a law firm, in a government law library, and in an academic law library have taught me the workings of legal databases and the needs of legal researchers.

Though most of this discourse has focused on those with the title of ER librarian, there are individuals in the library who do not hold the title, but have the same skill sets and responsibilities as ER librarians, e.g., librarians who work with digital resources or archivists who work with digital collections. Alongside the ER librarian, these professionals are leaders, collection developers, grant-writers, and program designers. Non-librarians who work with digital resources fit this mold as well; they work as researchers, policy-makers, and technology specialists.

## *What Does the ER Librarian Know?*

With collective knowledge realized through the selection, licensing, implementation, maintenance, and assessment of online products, ER librarians understand that ER are the future in libraries. They know how to teach users best practices to retrieve and evaluate Web-based information; and to use technology. They are cognizant of the best policies and procedures to serve our library community, that a digital divide still exists, and that the face of the divided will change. They know that there is a social responsibility associated with work to minimize or end the divided; to lower the numbers of the disconnected. And they are confident that, with their skills, training, and experience, they have what it takes to face down the digital divide.

# NOTES

1. "Andy Carvin's Waste of Bandwidth," http://andycarvin.com/archives/2004/08/diluting_digita.html (viewed August 17, 2005).

2. Howard Wolinsky, "The Digital Divide," *Chicago Sun-Times*, 17 March 1996, Sunday News, 6.

3. Lisa J. Servon, *Bridging the Digital Divide* (Malden, MA: Blackwell Publishing, 2002), 39-41.

4. Ibid., 41.

5. *A Nation Online: How Americans Are Expanding Their Use of the Internet* (Washington, DC: National Telecommunications and Information Administration, 2002), 1.

6. "A Nation Online: Entering the Broadband Age," http://www.ntia.doc.gov/reports/anol/ (viewed January 25, 2006).

7. "Demographics of Internet Users," http://www.pewinternet.org/trends/User_Demo_08.09.05.htm (viewed September 27, 2005).

8. Ibid.

9. Tom Spooner, *Internet Use by Region in the United States* (Washington, DC: Pew Internet & American Life Project, 2003), i.

10. Peter Bell, *Rural Areas and the Internet* (Washington, DC: Pew Internet & American Life Project, 2004), i.

11. "Demographics of Internet Users."

12. Amanda Lenhart, *The Ever-Shifting Internet Population* (Washington, DC: Pew Internet & American Life Project, 2003), 30.

13. "Demographics of Internet Users."

14. Wendy Lazarus, Andrew Wainer, and Laurie Lipper, *Measuring Digital Opportunity for America's Children: Where We Stand and Where We Go From Here* (Santa Monica, CA: The Children's Partnership, 2005), 2.

15. *A Nation Online*, 21.

16. "Demographics of Internet Users."

17. Therese Bissell, "The Digital Divide Dilemma: Preserving Native American Culture While Increasing Access to Information Technology on Reservations," *University of Illinois Journal of Law, Technology, & Policy* (spring 2004): 129.

18. "A Nation Online, But Where Are The Indians?," http://www.digitaldivide.net/articles/view.php?ArticleID=153 (viewed September 17, 2005).

19. "Demographics of Internet Users."

20. Karen Mossberger, Caroline J. Tolbert, and Mary Stansbury, *Virtual Inequality: Beyond the Digital Divide* (Washington, DC: Georgetown University Press, 2003), 30.

21. "Spectrum Management Policy Reform Issues," http://www.ntia.doc.gov/osmhome/spectrumreform/index.htm (viewed January 27, 2006).

22. "Promoting Innovation and Economic Security Through Broadband Technology," http://www.whitehouse.gov/infocus/technology/economic_policy200404/chap4.html (viewed January 27, 2006).

23. "Web Accessibility Initiative," http://www.w3.org/WAI/ (viewed September 30, 2005).

24. Bissell, 148.

25. Ibid., 144.

26. "WebJunction," http://www.webjunction.org (viewed September 30, 2005).

27. "Bill & Melinda Gates Foundation Awards Grants to WebJunction," http://www.oclc.org/news/releases/20057.htm (viewed September 30, 2005).

28. "Digital Divide Network," http://www.digitaldividenetwork.org/ (viewed July 6, 2005).

29. "Took Kit for Bridging the Digital Divide in Your Community," http://www.ed.gov/Technology/tool_kit.html (viewed August 2, 2005).

30. James E. Katz and Ronald E. Rice, *Social Consequences of Internet Use: Access, Involvement, and Interaction* (Cambridge, MA: MIT Press, 2002), 91.

31. Mark Warschauer, *Technology and Social Inclusion* (Cambridge, MA: MIT Press, 2003), 89.

32. "Sampa.org," http://sampa.org (viewed October 2, 2005).

33. "HarlemLIVE," http://www.harlemlive.org/ (viewed October 2, 2005).

34. Warschauer, 91-92.

35. Ibid., 88.

36. Ibid., 91.

37. Wendy Lazarus and Laurie Lipper, *The Search for High-Quality Online Content for Low-Income and Underserved Communities: Evaluating and Producing What's Needed* (Santa Monica, CA: The Children's Partnership, 2003).

38. Mossberger, 40-44.

39. Ibid., 47.

40. James E. Katz and Ronald E. Rice, *Social Consequences of Internet Use*, 94.

41. Roland Dietz and Kate Noerr, "One-Stop Searching Bridges the Digital Divide," *EContent* 27(7/8) (Jul/Aug 2004).

42. Raneta Lawson Mack, *The Digital Divide: Standing at the Intersection of Race and Technology* (Durham, NC: Carolina Academic Press, 2001), 29.

43. Ibid., 28.

44. *USA Patriot Act of 2001. U.S. Statutes at Large* 115 (2001): 272.

45. "San Francisco Public Library: Privacy Policy," http://sfpl.lib.ca.us/news/releases/privacy061704.htm (viewed October 2, 2005).

46. Maria Protti, "How to Create a Privacy Policy Statement" presented at the annual meeting of the American Association of Law Libraries, San Antonio, TX, July 2005).

47. Mossberger, 87.

48. *E-Government Act of 2002. U.S. Statutes at Large* 116 (2002): 2899.

49. Jaime Klima, "The E-Government Act: Promoting E-Quality or Exaggerating the Digital Divide?," *Duke Law & Technology Review* (2003): 13.

50. Ibid.

51. Pippa Norris, *Digital Divide: Civic Engagement, Information Poverty, and the Internet Worldwide* (New York: Cambridge University Press, 2001), 115.

52. Mossberger, 78.

53. Servon, 141.

54. "Knowledge River," http://knowledgeriver.arizona.edu/background.html (viewed July 6, 2005).

55. Norman Oder, "IMLS: $21M To Recruit Librarians," *Library Journal* 130(14) (September 2005): 17.

56. "Demographics of Internet Users."

57. Lenhart, 10.

58. Ibid., 28.

59. Benjamin M. Compaine, ed., *The Digital Divide: Facing a Crisis or Creating a Myth?* (Cambridge, MA: MIT Press, 2001), 268.

60. Ibid., 165-167.

61. Mossberger, 5.

62. Mark Warschauer, "Reconceptualizing the Digital Divide," *First Monday* 7(7) (July 2002); http://firstmonday.org/issues/issue7_7/warschauer/index.html (viewed September 22, 2005).

63. Ibid.

doi:10.1300/J105v32n03_06

# Open Access and Libraries

## Charles W. Bailey

**SUMMARY.** This chapter examines the major open access movement statements, analyzes the open access concept based on these statements, examines the two major open access strategies (self-archiving and open access journals), discusses the rationale behind the open access movement, discusses the impact of open access on libraries, looks at open access funding issues, and considers whether open access will transform electronic resources librarians jobs. doi:10.1300/J105v32n03_07 *[Article copies available for a fee from The Haworth Document Delivery Service: 1-800-HAWORTH. E-mail address: <docdelivery@haworthpress.com> Website: <http://www. HaworthPress.com> © 2007 by The Haworth Press. All rights reserved.]*

**KEYWORDS.** Open access, open access journals, self-archiving

Charles W. Bailey, Jr. is Assistant Dean, Digital Library Planning and Development, University of Houston Libraries, Building L, Room 220, 4800 Calhoun Road, Houston, TX 77004. From 1987 to 2003, Mr. Bailey served as Assistant Dean for Systems, University of Houston Libraries.

The author thanks Peter Suber for reviewing this paper and making very helpful suggestions.

[Haworth co-indexing entry note]: "Open Access and Libraries." Bailey, Charles W. Co-published simultaneously in *Collection Management* (The Haworth Information Press, an imprint of The Haworth Press) Vol. 32, No. 3/4, 2007, pp. 351-383; and: *Electronic Resources Librarianship and Management of Digital Information: Emerging Professional Roles* (ed: Mark Jacobs) The Haworth Information Press, an imprint of The Haworth Press, 2007, pp. 351-383. Single or multiple copies of this article are available for a fee from The Haworth Document Delivery Service [1-800-HAWORTH, 9:00 a.m. - 5:00 p.m. (EST). E-mail address: docdelivery@haworthpress.com].

## *WHAT IS OPEN ACCESS?*

Conventional fee-based publishing models fragment worldwide scholarly journal literature into numerous digital enclaves protected by various security systems which limit access to licensed users. What would global scholarship be like if its journal literature were freely available to all, regardless of whether the researcher worked at Harvard or a small liberal arts college, or he/she was in the United States or Zambia? What would it be like if, rather than being entangled in restrictive licenses that limited its use, journal literature was under a license that permitted any use as long as certain common-sense conditions were met? This is the promise of open access (OA). Needless to say, there are many challenges involved in trying to achieve this bold vision, and it is not embraced, or even viewed as being feasible, by all parties in the scholarly communication system. Without question, however, open access has significant implications for libraries, especially academic libraries.

For Electronic Resources (ER) Librarians, "open access" raises a variety of questions. What is OA? Is it different from free access, or is it the same? What is a Creative Commons License, which some OA providers use? What's an "e-print?" Are there different types of e-prints? What is "self-archiving?" What are the different ways that e-prints are made publicly available? What's an open access journal? Are there different types of OA journals? How can OA journals be made available at no cost? How do you search for OA materials? Why is OA desirable? Will OA flourish or fail? How will OA affect library collections and services? What can librarians do to support OA and to integrate OA materials into their collections? How will OA affect library budgets, especially collection budgets? How will OA affect ER librarian jobs?

### *Open Access Definitions*

#### *Budapest Open Access Initiative*

Although there are important historical precedents that noted open access advocate Peter Suber outlines in his "Timeline of the Open Access Movement,"[1] the open access movement's "constitutional convention" was in December 2001 at a meeting in Budapest convened by the Open Society Institute. The resulting statement of this meeting, the *"Budapest Open Access Initiative,"* was made public in February 2002. It still stands as the most important definition of open access. The key passage from the BOAI is:

The literature that should be freely accessible online is that which scholars give to the world without expectation of payment. Primarily, this category encompasses their peer-reviewed journal articles, but it also includes any un-reviewed preprints that they might wish to put online for comment or to alert colleagues to important research findings. There are many degrees and kinds of wider and easier access to this literature. By "open access" to this literature, we mean its free availability on the public internet, permitting any users to read, download, copy, distribute, print, search, or link to the full-texts of these articles, crawl them for indexing, pass them as data to software, or use them for any other lawful purpose, without financial, legal, or technical barriers other than those inseparable from gaining access to the Internet itself. The only constraint on reproduction and distribution, and the only role for copyright in this domain, should be to give authors control over the integrity of their work and the right to be properly acknowledged and cited....

To achieve open access to scholarly journal literature, we recommend two complementary strategies.

I.  Self-Archiving: First, scholars need the tools and assistance to deposit their refereed journal articles in open electronic archives, a practice commonly called self-archiving. When these archives conform to standards created by the Open Archives Initiative, then search engines and other tools can treat the separate archives as one. Users then need not know which archives exist or where they are located in order to find and make use of their contents.

II. Open-access Journals: Second, scholars need the means to launch a new generation of journals committed to open access, and to help existing journals that elect to make the transition to open access. Because journal articles should be disseminated as widely as possible, these new journals will no longer invoke copyright to restrict access to and use of the material they publish. Instead they will use copyright and other tools to ensure permanent open access to all the articles they publish. Because price is a barrier to access, these new journals will not charge subscription or access fees, and will turn to other methods for covering their expenses.[2]

## The Bethesda Statement on Open Access Publishing

In April 2003, a second influential meeting was held at the Howard Hughes Medical Institute in Chevy Chase, Maryland. This meeting resulted in the *"Bethesda Statement on Open Access Publishing,"* which further refined the definition of open access. Since the BOAI definition was in place, the Bethesda Statement did not recap all the characteristics of open access literature. Rather, it stated that an open access work meets two criteria:

1. The author(s) and copyright holder(s) grant(s) to all users a free, irrevocable, worldwide, perpetual right of access to, and a license to copy, use, distribute, transmit and display the work publicly and to make and distribute derivative works, in any digital medium for any responsible purpose, subject to proper attribution of authorship, as well as the right to make small numbers of printed copies for their personal use.
2. A complete version of the work and all supplemental materials, including a copy of the permission as stated above, in a suitable standard electronic format is deposited immediately upon initial publication in at least one online repository that is supported by an academic institution, scholarly society, government agency, or other well-established organization that seeks to enable open access, unrestricted distribution, interoperability, and long-term archiving (for the biomedical sciences, PubMed Central is such a repository).[3]

Note that, in contrast to the BOAI, the Bethesda Statement introduces the use of a license, specifies the creation of derivative works, and requires the deposit of open access works in digital repositories run by "well-established" organizations. The specification of "small numbers of printed copies" for personal use is also new.

## BERLIN DECLARATION ON OPEN ACCESS TO KNOWLEDGE IN THE SCIENCES AND HUMANITIES

The Berlin Declaration, which written as a result of the Conference on Open Access to Knowledge in the Sciences and Humanities in October 2003, is very similar to the Bethesda Statement, with only minor additions and word changes in its definition.

1. The author(s) and right holder(s) of such contributions grant(s) to all users a free, irrevocable, worldwide, right of access to,

and a license to copy, use, distribute, transmit and display the work publicly and to make and distribute derivative works, in any digital medium for any responsible purpose, subject to proper attribution of authorship (community standards, will continue to provide the mechanism for enforcement of proper attribution and responsible use of the published work, as they do now), as well as the right to make small numbers of printed copies for their personal use.

2.  A complete version of the work and all supplemental materials, including a copy of the permission as stated above, in an appropriate standard electronic format is deposited (and thus published) in at least one online repository using suitable technical standards (such as the Open Archive definitions) that is supported and maintained by an academic institution, scholarly society, government agency, or other well-established organization that seeks to enable open access, unrestricted distribution, interoperability, and long-term archiving.[4]

## ANALYSIS OF OPEN ACCESS DEFINITIONS

Suber refers to the BOAI, Bethesda Statement, and Berlin Declaration, which he considers to be the "major public definitions of 'open access'" as the "BBB definition of open access."[5]

Let's examine key aspects of the BBB definition in more detail.

### Open Access Literature Is Freely Available

While open access advocates may dispute some other aspects of the essential characteristics of an open access work, they are fully unified in believing that free availability is a mandatory characteristic. Suber states that "this is the element that catalyzed the open-access movement."[6] He indicates that providing free access removes "price barriers."[7]

### Open Access Literature Is Online

Open access literature is "online."[8]

The unique economics of digital publication, which entail minimal distribution costs after first copy production costs are met, are necessary for open access to be feasible. The Internet, the Web, and related digital publishing developments have made open access possible. However, as we shall see, for-fee print publications may be used to supplement online open access publications.

### Open Access Literature Is Scholarly and Royalty Free

Open access deals only with unpaid, scholarly works (Suber calls this "royalty-free literature.")[9] Typically, scholars are not paid to write journal articles. They do so for both selfless (contribute to the growing body of knowledge) and self-interested (career advancement) reasons. Open access literature includes journal articles that are published and unpublished (i.e., preprints).

While the BBB definition excludes textbooks, scholarly monographs, or other works that scholars are paid for, Suber has suggested that providing open access to "royalty-producing literature" may be possible as part of a potential future three-phase development of the open access concept:

Phase 1:  Provide OA to royalty-free literature and to all other content for which there is already permission. This includes public domain content and content for which the copyright holder already consents to OA or would consent after a little education. . . .

Phase 2:  Provide OA to royalty-producing literature and to content for which copyright holders are not yet consenting to OA. Since OA to copyrighted content must be consensual, this will require persuasion. . . .

Phase 3.  Enlarge and protect the public domain by rolling back copyright term extensions and assuring that federal copyright law preempts state contract or licensing law. Make permission-seeking less often necessary by establishing the first-sale doctrine for digital content and restoring fair-use rights denied by copy-protection technologies. If Phase 2 persuades copyright holders to reevaluate their interests, then Phase 3 persuades legislators to revise copyright law. Successes at Phases 1 and 2 would make Phase 3 largely unnecessary, and vice versa.[10]

### Open Access Literature Can Be Used with Minimal Restrictions

Open access goes well beyond simply making journal literature freely available: it must also be able to be used for any purpose as long as there is correct attribution and the integrity of the work is maintained.[11] Consequently, scholars, students, and other users do not need to seek permission to utilize open access works as they choose. Nor do they make payments to do so. This is a radical departure from conventional publishing, where use rights are constrained by hard-to-determine fair-use copyright provisions, restrictive publisher license agreements, and permissions fees.

Suber characterizes this aspect of open access as removing "permission barriers," and he states:

> Permission barriers are more difficult to discuss than price barriers. First, there are many kinds of them, some arising from statute (copyright law), some from contracts (licenses), and some from hardware and software (DRM). They are not like prices, which differ only in magnitude. Second, their details are harder to discover and understand. Third, different users in different times, places, institutions, and situations can face very different permission barriers for the same work. Fourth, authors who deposit their articles in open-access archives bypass permission barriers even if they also publish the same articles in conventional journals protected by copyright, licenses, and DRM. Finally, some rights may be retained by authors without interfering with open access, such as the right to block distribution of a mangled or misattributed copy of the work. So permission barriers do not arise from retaining rights as such but only from retaining some rights rather than others. For all these reasons, the literature on open access is rarely as clear and careful on permission barriers as it is on price barriers.[12]

The Creative Commons offers six main licenses that could be used to make operational the minimal use restrictions envisioned in the BBB definition.[13] Aside from legal jurisdiction and format considerations, there are two key factors that differentiate these licenses: (1) whether commercial use is allowed, and (2) whether derivative works are allowed, and, if so, whether these derivative works must be under the same license as the primary work. For example, the Attribution License allows users to "copy, distribute, display, and perform the work"; "to make derivative works"; and "to make commercial use of the work" as long as they "attribute the work in the manner specified by the author or licensor" and "for any reuse or distribution" the user "must make clear to others the license terms" of the work.[14] By contrast, the Attribution-NonCommercial License has all of the Attribution License's provisions, but forbids commercial use without permission, and the Attribution-NoDerivs License has all of the Attribution License's provisions, but forbids derivative works.

There are a variety of other licenses, such as the GNU Free Documentation License, that might also be used to provide open access.[15]

It should be noted that this removal of permission barriers through Creative Commons or similar licenses is not the same thing as putting the work in the public domain. In the former, the author or publisher retains copyright then, through a license, grants users specific rights. In the latter, the author or publisher relinquishes the copyright to the work completely, and there are no restrictions of any kind on its use.

Suber has underlined the importance of removing permission barriers in the BBB definition:

> All three tributaries of the mainstream BBB definition agree that OA removes both price and permission barriers. Free online access isn't enough. "Fair use" ("fair dealing" in the UK) isn't enough.[16]

Nonetheless, removing permission barriers is a controversial requirement within the open access movement. Prominent open access spokesman Stevan Harnad has debated this requirement at length in the American Scientist Open Access Forum mailing list and in other venues, asserting that open access simply requires: "free, immediate, permanent access to refereed-article full-texts online."[17]

In one message, he notes that his definition has been criticized because it omits reuse and redistribution criteria and does not make reference to the Creative Commons Attribution License, and then he states:

> And what is meant by "redistribute" when the text is already distributed all over the planet on the Web, and freely available to anyone who may wish to find, search, read, download, process computationally online or offline, and print off anywhere in the world, any time?
>
> Could this "reuse" and "redistribute" right perhaps be a spurious holdover from another medium–the Gutenberg medium, print-on-paper–where "re-use" of a printed text meant re-use in *another* printed text (i.e., republication), and "redistribution" meant the distribution of that other printed text? But why on earth would anyone want to bother doing that in the post-Gutenberg era, when

*everyone* already has access to the text, and each can print it off directly for himself?

Collected works? That's just a list of URLs in the post-Gutenberg era.

And that's where it stops. My text is not like data or software, to be modified, built upon, and then redistributed (perhaps as your own). You may use its content, but you may not alter it and then distribute the altered version, online or on-paper.[18]

## OPEN ACCESS STRATEGIES:
## SELF-ARCHIVING AND OPEN ACCESS JOURNALS

Open access can be accomplished through two complementary strategies: self-archiving and open access journals.

### Self-Archiving of E-Prints

"Self-archiving" refers to making "e-prints" available on the Web. An e-print is either a digital preprint or a post-print.

The typical preprint is an article that has been (or is intended to be) submitted to a scholarly journal for peer review and editorial acceptance and editing. However, the term is also commonly used to refer to articles submitted to serials that do not conduct peer review and to articles that will never be submitted to any serial.

A post-print is the final version of an article, which reflects changes made during the peer review and editorial process. It can either be the publishers' digital version or a preprint that the author has modified to mirror the publisher's changes. The author may, for legal reasons, choose to append a list of changes (errata) to the original preprint rather than incorporate those changes in the body of the document.

E-prints are typically made available in one of primary four ways: (1) the author's personal Web site; (2) a disciplinary archive that includes works by authors worldwide about one or more subjects; (3) an institutional e-print archive that includes e-prints by authors in a single academic unit, such as a department, or the entire institution; or (4) an institutional repository that includes diverse types of digital works (e.g., data sets, electronic theses and dissertations, presentations, and technical reports), including e-prints, by authors at a single institution.[19] Of course, given the flexibility of digital archiving tools and the inventive imagination of their users, there are other variations on the theme. For example, there are academic unit archives that include diverse types of works. A wide variety of free open source software is available to support digital archives and institutional repositories, and commercial vendors have begun to offer turnkey systems to support the latter.

Open access to e-prints rests on the foundation of copyright law. The copyright owner of the article, whether it is the author or the publisher, must permit open access to it. It should be noted that open access does not require that current copyright laws be changed.[20]

Historically, publishers have required that authors assign all rights to journal articles to them. However, authors still owned the rights to preprints that were created prior to the copyright transfer for the final, edited work, and this allowed them to make these preprints publicly available. Recognizing this, some journals have refused to publish articles if digital preprints of them were available; however, this practice appears to be dying out.

Primarily as a result of the open access movement, publishers are gradually becoming more open to letting authors retain copyright, with authors granting specific rights to publishers. Although many publishers still require a copyright transfer, most of them now have explicit policies that grant authors' specific rights to distribute their articles and to make other uses of them.

While these policies could hardly be characterized as uniform, they are often grouped by open access advocates in four broad classes in a taxonomy created by Stevan Harnad: "gold (provides OA to its research articles, without delay), green (permits post-print archiving by authors), pale green (permits, i.e., doesn't oppose, preprint archiving by authors), gray (none of the above)."[21] The SHERPA Project provides a very useful database of publishers' self-archiving policies.[22]

There is no uniformity in e-print copyright or license practices. E-Prints may have: (1) no copyright statement (under U.S. law they are under copyright by default); (2) a conventional copyright statement; (3) a copyright statement that is modified by specific use provisions (e.g., liberal use permitted for noncommercial purposes); (4) a Creative Commons or other license, which may or may not permit commercial use or derivative works; or (5) another variation.

Consequently, the removal of permission barriers in e-prints is extremely variable, and, from a conventional BBB open access definition point of view, not as common as might be desired. To some extent, this is because the copyright statement is that of a non-OA publisher; however, author indifference and resistance to the permissions barrier issue are other common causes. In practical terms, open access to e-prints currently means *free* access.

## Open Access Journals

Open access journals are e-journals that are freely available (some open access journals have supplementary fee-based print versions as well). They mirror the quality assurance practices of conventional journals, such as editorial oversight, peer review, and copy editing. The extent to which they have an organizational infrastructure similar to that of traditional publishers varies according to whether they are revenue generating (this includes both commercial and nonprofit publishers) or what I term "no profit," meaning they literally make no money from their publishing endeavors. The existence of fee-based add-on products, such as supplemental print versions, is another factor. As noted earlier, electronic-only publication offers some meaningful cost savings, since physical reproduction, storage, distribution, and claiming costs are eliminated.

Open access advocates recognize that it costs money to produce journals and that viable business models are required to accomplish this, even though they may be unconventional.[23]

There are a small number of young commercial (e.g., BioMed Central)[24] and nonprofit (e.g., Public Library of Science)[25] publishers, whose only function is to publish journals and who use only the open access business model (I will call these *"Born-OA journal publishers"*). These publishers use a variety of strategies to fund open access journals, but the key ones are author publication fees (grant agencies may pay such fees), library membership fees that subsidize author fees in whole or in part for authors affiliated with the library's institution, grants, and supplemental products (such as print versions). Author fees are usually waived in cases of financial hardship, leveling the playing field for less affluent authors, and author fees do not influence publication decisions.

Born-OA journal publishers typically let authors retain the copyright to their articles and use the Creative Commons Attribution License or a very similar license.

Biomedical journals from these publishers are usually archived in PubMed Central,[26] a digital archival run by U.S. National Institutes of Health, in addition to being archived at the publisher's site, ensuring perpetual access regardless of the financial health of the publisher. Given the Creative Commons Attribution License, any digital repository or archive that wanted to could also preserve these publications without asking permission.

Increasingly, conventional publishers are experimenting with publishing some open access journals or using a mix of traditional and open access models in their business. An example of this is the Oxford Open initiative of Oxford University Press, which uses full open access for some journals and "optional open access" for others (i.e., authors decide if they want to pay fees to make their articles open access, leading to journal issues that have a mix of restricted and OA content).[27] Author fees are reduced if the author's institution subscribes to the journal and/or if the author is from a developing country (for some developing countries, authors pay no fees). The license agreement is similar to a Creative Commons Attribution-NonCommercial License.

The precursors to today's open access journals were scholar-produced e-journals established in the late 1980s and early 1990s whose business model was to use volunteer labor and institutional resources to offer "*no-profit journals.*" Examples of such journals are *EJournal*,[28] *New Horizons in Adult Education*,[29] *Psycoloquy*,[30] *PostModern Culture*,[31] and *The Public-Access Computer Systems Review*.[32] These journals typically also had very liberal copyright policies (e.g., allowed authors to retain their copyright and allowed noncommercial use).

Given the relatively informal publishing arrangements that "no profit" journals can operate under, a significant issue can be their sustainability. They may have no formal business plans or funding base and their continued existence may be contingent on the ongoing enthusiasm and involvement of their founders.

While some of these journals have ceased publication or morphed into commercial journals, they demonstrated the viability of electronic journals at a time when it was in serious question and they offered a model for others to follow. And follow they did: scholars and nonprofit organizations have continued to establish and publish journals of this type to this day, and this task has been made progressively easier by the Web, declining hardware/software costs, increased hardware/software power, and the availability of open source e-journal publishing systems that provide editorial management and journal production functions. While all of these journals are freely available, their copyright and licensing practices vary widely, ranging from conventional (or no) copyright statements to using Creative Commons or similar licenses.

One size does not fit all when it comes to open access journal business models. There can be significant differences between STM journals and humanities/social science journals in terms of number of articles published per year, article submission and acceptance rates, the necessity for inclusion of high-end production features (such as high-resolution color graphics), and the impact of publication errors, and these factors influence production complexity and cost. Disciplinary differences can also affect scholars' receptiveness to open access options.

Sparked by Harnad, there is a lively debate in the open access movement about the relative merits of e-prints ("Green Road") versus open access journals ("Gold Road") as the best way to advance the cause: Harnad strongly favors the "Green Road."[33]

## *OPEN ACCESS LITERATURE METADATA CAN BE HARVESTED*

Since open access literature is not hidden behind technical access barriers (such as IP restriction) its full-text can be indexed and made accessible by conventional search engines; however, while very powerful, these search engines do not offer precise field-based searching of particular bibliographic elements, such as author. The e-prints in a digital archive or institutional repository are described by metadata records (typically in Dublin Core format) that provide such information and, using the Open Archives Initiative Protocol for Metadata Harvesting (OAI-PMH),[34] external search systems can retrieve this metadata using a standard protocol, combine it with metadata from other archives and repositories, and create composite databases that allow users to retrieve information about e-prints from diverse archives and repositories as well as retrieve the full-text of e-prints of interest from those systems. Unfortunately, conventional author home pages on the Web do not have this capability, and this is a limitation of self-archiving e-prints in this way.

## *WHY OPEN ACCESS?*

To a large degree, open access is a reaction to dysfunctions in the conventional scholarly communication system. Since many of its leaders have been scholars, it strongly reflects their concerns and perceptions. As such, it is not focused on dealing with the underlying causes of serials crisis and the scholarly publishing "*knowledge explosion*" (e.g., the proliferation of ever more specialized journals publishing an increasing number of articles), but rather on developing new scholarly communication strategies that will function effectively in that environment. Of course, there are also prominent open access advocates who are librarians, and they bring to the table strong concerns with fundamental scholarly publishing issues. While this has resulted in differences of perception, it has not caused any meaningful schisms in the movement.

For scholarship to advance, its global knowledgebase must be accessible so that it can be built upon. Although it is highly competitive, scholarship is, paradoxically, also highly cooperative. Scholars must compete with each other for jobs, publishing and presentation opportunities, grants, tenure, and other career opportunities. However, they must also be able to easily access and utilize other scholars work and to ensure that their own work is equally available for use by other scholars.

For scholars' careers to progress, other scholars must read, value, use, and cite their works. To be read, their articles must be visible to the scholarly community. If an article is published in a journal whose articles are highly cited, it is more likely to be visible. Consequently, a journal's *"impact factor,"* as measured by bibliometric formulas (the key one being the Thomson ISI formula created by Eugene Garfield) is important, and the importance of scholars' articles is often judged by promotion and grant committees by the impact factors of the journals they were published in.[35]

However, under the conventional system, not even scholars at the most affluent research institutions in the world can be assured of having the access that they need, much less be assured that their peers worldwide will have such access.

Suber has characterized the inadequacies of the conventional scholarly communication system and the resulting need for open access this way:

> It doesn't matter whether we blame unaffordable journals on excessive publisher prices or inadequate library budgets. If we focus on publishers, it doesn't matter whether we blame greed or innocent market forces (rising costs and new services). Blame is irrelevant and distracting. The volume of published knowledge is growing exponentially and will always grow faster than library budgets. In that sense, OA scales with the growth of knowledge and toll access does not. We've already (long since) reached the point at which even affluent research institutions cannot afford access to the full range of research literature. Priced access to journal articles would not scale with the continuing, explosive growth of knowledge even if prices were low today and guaranteed to remain low forever.[36]

While the focus of open access on journal articles is likely the result of the serials crisis making journals increasingly inaccessible, it also reflects the STM and social science background of some key open access advocates (the crisis is worse for STM faculty since they are heavily dependent on journal literature and their journals are very expensive) and the unique characteristics of journal literature itself that simplify transition issues: its royalty-free nature and its structural features (i.e., articles are short, discrete works and can be easily downloaded and printed). If humanists had mainly led the charge, there might be more emphasis on scholarly monographs, given their limited sales and the increasing difficulty in getting such works published, but the end-game problem of a pile of hundreds of unbound book pages would have remained–that problem is not easily solved without affordable, ubiquitous print-on-demand solutions that pop out books at low or no (due to being part of subsidized infrastructure) cost to the user.

With its current orientation, open access is designed to remedy the perceived failings of the traditional scholarly communication system. Open access always topples price barriers. Anyone anywhere in the world can freely access open access literature as long as they have Internet access (such network access is one of several barriers that open access can't remedy). Permission barriers also fall if the open access work is under an appropriate Creative Commons or similar license (or if the copyright holder's statement permits it).

The short version of the open access vision of a transformed scholarly communication system follows. It is certainly far more complex than this, and the reader is referred to the *Open Access Bibliography: Liberating Scholarly Literature with E-Prints and Open Access Journals* (especially sections 1.1 and 1.2) for more in-depth treatments.[37]

When both barriers fall, scholarly communication is transformed: the global knowledgebase is fully accessible on the Internet to users in both the developed and developing countries; scholarly works are fully visible to discovery tools such as search engines and OAI-PMH harvesters and are available for linking, increasing their likelihood of being found and being used by scholars; ease of discovery increases the probability that the OA works will have greater impact[38]; the creation of derivative works (as well as other new knowledge) is greatly facilitated; the use of scholarly works for instructional purposes is easy, convenient, and free of permission fees; the return on investment for scholarly research sponsored by governments, foundations, universities, and other funding agencies is maximized; and knowledge preservation is greatly enhanced because there are no legal obstacles that prevent it.[39]

Open access has a number of potential benefits for libraries, which will be discussed later.

Although open access is primarily aimed at solving key problems in the traditional scholarly communication system, its benefits are not confined to scholars and librarians because, despite it specialized nature, scholarly literature can be of potentially great utility to other users as well.

For example, Sharon Terry recounts her struggle to gain access to medical literature that might help her two children who suffer from pseudoxanthoma elasticum (PXE):

> We spent hours copying articles from bound journals. But fees gate the research libraries of private medical schools. These fees became too costly for us to manage, and we needed to gain access to the material without paying for entry into the library each time. We learned that by volunteering at a hospital associated with a research library, we could enter the library for free. After several months of this, policies changed and we resorted to masking our outdated volunteer badge and following a legitimate student (who would distract the guard) into the library.[40]

Although she and her husband had to teach themselves medical terminology to even read needed literature and faced major barriers to accessing it, they went on to establish a nonprofit organization devoted to PXE, and they discovered a key gene related to the disease and created a test to detect it. Admittedly, few people would be able to duplicate this feat; however, one does not need to look far to encounter average citizens who, when faced with a major medical crisis, try to conduct research that will help them overcome it.

## THE DIFFICULTY OF ASSESSING OPEN ACCESS IMPACTS

As we saw in the earlier analysis of open access definitions, there is disagreement about whether the removal of price barriers is sufficient to achieve open access or whether, as is more commonly believed, the removal of permission barriers is also required. In the self-archiving and open access journal discussions, we saw that, in reality, digital works commonly characterized as "open access" could be under a wide range of copyright and licensing arrangements. For example, many journals listed in the *Directory of Open Access Journals*[41] (a widely recognized and used finding tool) do not remove permission barriers and neither do many e-print authors.

Looking solely at journals for a moment, the information environment is even more complex because there is a further distinction between free access to the entire contents of a journal and some subset of those contents. With this in mind, I have suggested the following taxonomy for journals, reserving the term "open access" for those journals that meet the highest level criteria:

1. **Open Access journals** (OA journals, color code: green): These journals provide free access to all articles and utilize a form of licensing that puts minimal restrictions on the use of articles, such as the Creative Commons Attribution License. Example: *Biomedical Digital Libraries.*

2. **Free Access journals** (FA journals, color code: cyan): These journals provide free access to all articles and utilize a variety of copyright statements (e.g., the journal copyright statement may grant liberal educational copying provisions), but they do not use a Creative Commons Attribution License or similar license. Example: *The Public-Access Computer Systems Review.*

3. **Embargoed Access journals** (EA journals, color code: yellow): These journals provide free access to all articles after a specified embargo period and typically utilize conventional copyright statements. Example: *Learned Publishing.*

4. **Partial Access journals** (PA journals, color code: orange): These journals provide free access to selected articles and typically utilize conventional copyright statements. Example: *College & Research Libraries.*

5. **Restricted Access journals** (RA journals, color code: red): These journals provide no free access to articles and typically utilize conventional copyright statements. Example: *Library Administration and Management.* (Available in electronic form from *Library Literature & Information Science Full-text* and other databases.)[42]

So, once all types of free access are considered, the overall access picture becomes more complex. While no major open access advocate endorses embargoed or partial access as a substitute for complete free/open access, the "Washington DC Principles for Free Access to Science,"[43] a significant statement from important not-for-profit STM publishers, does.

These factors make it somewhat difficult to discuss the impact of open access in simple black-and-white terms. As noted earlier, a pragmatic assessment of the current state of open access suggests that OA materials are always free of price barriers and they may be free of permission barriers as well, depending on whether the copyright holder has authorized this through a license or copyright statement.

## THE IMPACT OF OPEN ACCESS ON LIBRARIES

Schmidt, Sennyey, and Carstens have outlined three scenarios that would affect how open access impacts libraries: (1) the open access movement collapses, (2) the open access movement triumphs, and (3) the open access movement partially succeeds, resulting in a mixed scholarly communication system that has elements of both traditional and open access publishing.[44]

The third scenario is the one that the authors feel is most likely, and their subsequent analysis is based on this scenario. Of course, the third scenario is also the one that libraries find themselves operating under today.

From my perspective, a complete failure of the open access movement seems unlikely. It appears to me that, at this point, the primary factors that will determine its degree of success are: (1) legislative, funding agency, employer and other mandates that require open access (and may provide author-fee subsidies or provide other types of financial support for open access efforts); (2) sustainable business models for open access journals, including nonprofit and "no profit" journals; (3) a commitment by universities and other organizations to establish, adequately fund, staff, and operate *permanent* digital repositories and archives; and (4) a successful campaign to win the hearts and minds of scholars so that they will support (e.g., serve as editors and editorial board members) and publish in those journals, deposit e-prints in digital archives and repositories, and recognize the validity of open access publications in promotion and tenure proceedings.

## Major Open Access Impacts on Libraries

Suber has identified a number of key ways that full open access trans-
forms library policies, procedures, and services when it removes both
price and permission barriers:

- You would own, not merely license, your own copies of electronic
  journals.
- You would have the right to archive them forever without special
  permission or periodic payments. Long-term preservation and
  access would not be limited to the actions taken by publishers,
  with future market potential in mind, but could be supplemented
  by independent library actions.
- If publishers did not migrate older content, such as the back runs of
  journals, to new media and formats to keep them readable as technology changed, then libraries would have the right to do it on their own.
- Access and usage would not be limited by password, IP address,
  usage hours, institutional affiliation, physical location, a cap on
  simultaneous users, or ability to pay. You would not have to authenticate users or administer proxy servers.
- You would have the right to lend and copy digital articles on any
  terms you liked to any users you liked. You could offer the same
  services to users affiliated with your institution, walk-in patrons,
  users at home, visiting faculty, and ILL users.
- Faculty and others could donate digital literature and software
  without violating their licenses, and you could accept them without limiting their usability.
- All use would be non-infringing use, and all use allowed by law
  would also be allowed by technology. There would be no need for
  fair-use judgment calls and their accompanying risk of liability.
  There would be no need to err on the side of non-use. Faculty could
  reproduce full-text for students without the delays, costs, or uncer-
  tainties of seeking permission.
- You would not have to negotiate, either as individual institutions
  or consortia, for prices or licensing terms. You would not have to
  remember, consult, or even retain, complex licensing agreements
  that differ from publisher to publisher and year to year.
- Users who object to cookies or registration would have the same
  access privileges as other users. Anonymous inquiry would be possible again for every user.

- You would never have to cancel a subscription due to a tight budget or unacceptable licensing terms. Researchers would not encounter gaps in the collection corresponding to journals with unacceptable prices or licensing terms.[45]

## THE ROLE OF LIBRARIES IN OPEN ACCESS

Open access does not *require* that libraries do anything for it to exist. It has not been designed with libraries as its foundation. From this perspective, open access is all benefit, and no cost. For example, if a traditional journal becomes fully open access or a new open access journal fully substitutes for a conventional one, that is one less journal the library has to buy, and it can deploy those collection development funds elsewhere. If it was a double-digit-cost STM journal, all the better.

However, the probability that libraries, especially academic libraries, will simply ignore open access materials is quite low, if not zero. The lesson of other freely available Internet resources is that, regardless of what libraries think, many users (especially undergraduates) love them and may well use them to the exclusion of conventional, vetted materials. Graduate students and faculty find riches in the Internet as well, and may be engaged in creating valuable new authoritative digital resources in that setting. Of course, they can distinguish between the real and the glass diamonds; less sophisticated users can't. So whether it was out of enthusiasm for new digital resources or out of a sense of obligation to steer users towards useful materials (or both), libraries have increasingly considered that vast sea of Internet materials to be a source of materials that are a potential part of a redefined collection, one that primarily includes purchased and licensed materials, but also, through inclusion in digital finding tools and instruction, free Internet materials.

### Libraries Can Provide Enhanced Access to OA Works

Providing access to open access materials has inherent challenges similar to those of other freely available digital works on the Internet. Schmidt et al. identify a number of these challenges: the effort required to effectively select and catalog (or otherwise create metadata for) high-quality OA materials from a pool of candidates that is not restricted by materials cost considerations; difficulties in tracking changes in dynamic OA materials and monitoring their availability when the library has no special relationship with the publisher or other supplier; lack of adequate coverage of OA materials in indexes, aggregator databases, and other conventional finding tools; the necessity of using search engines and specialized finding tools to identify relevant materials; and the broadened scope of information literacy programs to account for the peculiarities of these materials.[46]

They also point out a unique challenge involved with open access in the mixed scenario:

> The hybrid character of the MOA environment presents other serial maintenance challenges for the library. A library might contain parts of the same journal in print and microform, provide access to a part of the journal's back file through an open-access archive, and provide access to issues through an aggregator. Access for a particular resource may undergo constant change as license agreements are renegotiated, embargoes are put into effect, and publication strategies evolve. Keeping up with this constant change, while making all these variations in access transparent to the patron, is an additional maintenance challenge for the library.[47]

Consequently, the integration of open access materials into normal ongoing library operations requires, as other Internet resources do, additional staff time and effort, even though the materials themselves are free.

## Libraries Can Be Digital Publishers of OA Works

Libraries are no longer simply consumers of scholarly information. A growing number of libraries have become digital publishers, primarily offering free/open access journals and institutional repositories.

High quality free open source software is available to support digital publishing.[48]

Hardware requirements will vary according to the scope of the project; however, they may be more modest than you would imagine, and hardware cost/performance characteristics continue to regularly improve.

## Free/Open Access Journals and Books

Libraries have been publishing free electronic journals for at least 16 years: in 1989, the University of Houston Libraries established one of the first free scholarly e-journals published on the Internet, *The Public-Access Computer Systems Review*, and, in 1996, began publishing a freely available electronic book, the *Scholarly Electronic Publishing Biblio-*

*graphy*,[49] which has been regularly updated. Starting in the early 1990s, the Scholarly Communications Project of the Virginia Polytechnic Institute & State University Libraries[50] published a variety of e-journals, including the *Journal of the International Academy of Hospitality Research*.[51]

More recent examples of libraries as digital publishers of free/open access works include Cornell University Library's Internet-First University Press,[52] the University of Wisconsin Libraries' *The Journal of Insect Science*,[53] and the University of Idaho Library's *Electronic Green Journal*.[54] *The Journal of Insect Science* uses the Creative Commons Attribution License, and it is a full open access journal.

The staffing requirements for free/open access journals are proportional to the level of editorial and journal production support services that the library provides. Given the sophistication of contemporary open source e-journal production systems, it is possible to have faculty editors shoulder more responsibility for key functions and to limit the library's role; however, this is a decision that must account for specific local factors.

### Institutional Repositories

While the trend for libraries to assume the role of a formal scholarly publisher has evolved fairly slowly, that to establish institutional repositories has evolved more quickly and with more vigor (e.g., see the list of DSpace users.)[55]

Although supporting open access may not be the only motivation for such endeavors (especially for institutional repositories), they are highly congruent with it. As was noted earlier, the establishment and operation of permanent institutional repositories is likely to be a critical factor in the success of open access. Other institutional units, such as the information technology unit, could theoretically provide institutional repositories without library involvement; however, this is unlikely at many institutions (especially academic ones) and, if it occurs, may not be as successful as it would be with library involvement.

There is a remarkable harmony between the skill set needed to successfully support institutional repositories and those possessed by librarians. The experience of early adopters of institutional repositories suggests that the technical challenges involved with them are far less daunting than the author attitude change, information organization and metadata, intellectual property, policy and procedure, public relations, and training challenges.[56]

While institutional repositories and the relationship of libraries to them is a complicated topic, the following list provides insight into how one group of librarians (reference librarians) could effectively support institutional repositories.

1. Helping to create sensible IR policies and procedures and to provide feedback about how they work in practice.
2. Assisting in designing the IR user interface so that it is clear, easy to use, and effective.
3. Helping to identify current self-archiving activity on campus to aid the content recruitment effort.
4. Acting as change agents by promoting the IR to faculty and graduate students in their subject areas.
5. Informing faculty and graduate students about Creative Commons licensing options and publisher e-print policies.
6. Depositing digital materials for faculty in their subject areas if such assistance is desired.
7. Participating in the creation of IR metadata, such as local controlled vocabularies (e.g., subject categories for IR documents).
8. Preparing Web-based and paper documents that explain and promote the IR and advocate scholarly publishing reform.
9. Training users in IR deposit and searching procedures.
10. Assisting local and remote users with IR utilization, answering questions about IR policies and procedures, and using the IR to answer reference questions.[57]

As this list of potential reference librarian responsibilities suggests, staff involvement in institutional repositories is likely to extend beyond technical staff. If the library has collection development specialists other than reference librarians, they may also play some or all of the above roles. Depending on local decisions about how to handle metadata issues, IRs could require significant involvement by cataloging/metadata staff, and require increased staffing in this area. Electronic resources librarians and special collections librarians/archivists may also be involved, depending on local factors.

## Libraries Can Build Specialized OA Systems

Since the dawn of the computer age, libraries have built specialized computer systems to meet their unique needs. Single-function library automation systems (e.g., a punched-card circulation system at the University of Texas at Austin in the 1930s,)[58] were followed by integrated library automation systems (e.g., Northwestern University Libraries' NOTIS system in the 1970s),[59] and, in recent years, open-source institutional repository software (e.g., MIT Libraries/Hewlett Packard's DSpace[60] and the University of Virginia Libraries' Fedora[61]) and OAI-PMH search services (e.g., University of Michigan Library's OAIster).[62]

Obviously, there is an extremely strong connection between some recent system development activities and open access support, although libraries may have additional motives for creating such systems. Consequently, libraries have been an important source of innovative system tools for the open access movement, and there is every indication that libraries will continue to play this crucial role in the future. Needless to say, such system development projects can be expensive and labor-intensive, and they can have significant budgetary impacts on the libraries that engage in them; however, they are also excellent candidates for grant support and for computer industry partnerships.

## Libraries Can Digitize OA Versions of Out-of-Copyright Works

Library digitization efforts also harmonize with the open access movement, since the resulting digital materials are typically made freely available in whole or in part. While many digitization projects have focused on rare materials housed in special collections, there has been a recent spate of partnership projects aimed at digitizing standard scholarly library books, including Google Library,[63] the Million Books Project,[64] and the Open Content Alliance.[65]

While price barriers may be eliminated by such projects, permission barriers may not always be (e.g., some digitized works are not in the public domain).

For libraries engaged digitization projects, a key question is this: should the digitized works created from out-of-copyright works remain in the public domain (or be put under a Creative Commons license) versus being put under a standard copyright statement with the digitizing library as the owner? To do the former, is to remove both price and permission barriers to these works. Even if both are removed, technological barriers to usability can remain if long works, such as e-books, are only offered through one-page-at-a-time access.

## Libraries Can Preserve OA Materials

Another area of traditional library responsibility is preservation, and libraries have already begun to tackle the difficult task of digital preservation of e-journals, notably through the LOCKSS project.[66]

While the preservation of biomedical open access journals is ensured by PubMed Central, other types of open access journals do not have a similar digital archive. The most pressing need is the preservation of a significant number of "no profit" open access journals, which can be in real danger of ceasing to be available. Open access journals from conventional publishers have similar preservation needs as their traditional counterparts. While *"dark"* open access journal archives are unquestionably better than no archives, their contents need to come to light when the journals within them cease to be available on the Internet from their publishers.

As was noted earlier, libraries are likely to view institutional repositories as permanent entities, and, consequently, to have assumed the digital preservation burdens associated with their contents. Other digital archives may be in long-term danger (e.g., disciplinary archives that house digital materials about one or more disciplines created by authors worldwide). The preservation of e-prints has been a controversial topic in the open access movement, with the thought being that the publisher's copy is the archival copy.[67]

However, some e-prints may never be published. Moreover, there can be other types of digital objects in non-institutional digital archives, such as technical reports and digital presentations. Should these materials be preserved? If the answer is yes, then libraries may consider doing so.

## Libraries Can Subsidize Author Fees

Libraries can subsidize open access journal fees through institutional memberships with publishers, which either eliminate or reduce such fees for affiliated authors. There are several factors to keep in mind when thinking about these memberships. Open access institutional memberships are voluntary, not mandatory. They are not universal in the very diverse open access journal publishing world (only 47% charge such fees).[68] Since the publishers that offer institutional memberships are specialized, it only makes economic sense to consider them if the publisher's journals are highly likely targets for a significant number of institutional authors' submissions and if the majority of those authors will need assistance in paying fees (as has been noted, there are other potential sources for such payment). Moreover, institutional memberships are part of a broader number of funding strategies that some open access journal publishers are experimenting with: it is difficult to predict their future.

If every journal in the world would suddenly (and magically) become open access, it would not mean that libraries would have to substitute open access institutional membership fees for subscription fees for all journals that were crucial to them unless: (1) every open access journal publisher had such membership fees, and (2) no other significant sources of support for open access journal publishers existed, and, consequently, the journal publishing system would fail if they were not paid.

Open access institutional membership fees can also be looked at another way: by supporting open access journals, they make their benefits available to all, and this is a collective good.

## FUNDING FOR OPEN ACCESS EFFORTS

As we consider library roles in support of open access, the natural question is: where will the money come from to support such efforts? While there are no easy answers to this question, it is important to realize that open access can potentially reduce certain costs, leaving these funds to be redeployed elsewhere.

Since libraries may not view preprints as the full equivalent of published articles, incremental cost reductions as a result of open access are primarily proportional to the prevalence of open access journals and post-prints.

The primary potential impact is on collection development costs as a result of having free access to a growing number of open access journals. These savings will be realized if libraries cut journal subscriptions because competing open access journals are viewed as being an adequate substitutes for conventional ones; if journals that previously required subscriptions fully convert to the open access model, eliminating their subscription costs; or if publishers reduce the cost of mixed-model journals (those that include both open access articles subsidized by author fees and traditional articles) in proportion to the number of open access articles published annually (e.g., Springer Open Choice).[69]

Aside from collection development budget savings, other potential savings as a result of open access for libraries may be in acquisitions and serials functions (fewer journals to buy and control), licensing management (fewer licenses to negotiate and track), restricted access enforcement (fewer journals to restrict), interlibrary loan (no need to loan articles that are freely available), and reserves (no need to assess fair use or pay permission fees).

## WILL OA TRANSFORM ELECTRONIC RESOURCES LIBRARIANS' JOBS?

Will OA *change* electronic resources librarians' jobs? Yes, if their libraries want to provide access to open access materials.

To do so, electronic resources librarians must understand OA concepts and systems, including search systems such as the *Directory of Open Access Journals*, the Institutional Archives Registry, OAIster, and Google Scholar.[70] They will need to establish (or help establish) collection development policies for OA materials, devise strategies for incorporating selected materials into appropriate electronic resource finding tools, track OA resource URL changes and maintain links, and facilitate user access to selected external finding tools. The identification of desirable OA materials is more challenging than the identification of conventional electronic materials because there are a large number of potential suppliers, not a limited number of commercial vendors, and these suppliers typically have no special relationship to the library. Electronic resources librarians will not need to license OA materials or restrict access to them.

Electronic resources librarians will play a major role in helping their libraries to determine whether to go further than mere access and to support OA through institutional memberships that subsidize author fees or through other mechanisms. If such support is desired, they will help deal with the collection development implications of this decision and handle the arrangements for such support.

The extent to which OA flourishes will determine the extent to which electronic resources librarians shift their work focus from licensing commercial materials to facilitating and fostering access to OA materials. Given prior experience with other types of free Internet materials, this shift will not result in a radical change of duties, except that licensing and access restriction tasks will diminish.

Will OA *transform* electronic resources librarians' jobs? That depends on two things: (1) will their libraries engage in transformational OA activities, such as operating institutional repositories and acting as formal electronic publishers, and (2) will electronic resources librarians be directly involved in such activities. If the answer to both questions is "yes," then their jobs are likely to be transformed to some degree. However, both factors are library-specific, and, at this early stage, the crystal ball is cloudy regarding the general outcome.

## CONCLUSION

The open access movement has gained considerable traction in the last six years. It has become the most successful scholarly publishing reform movement in modern times, and it has begun to transform the scholarly communication system.

Understandably, it has been met by hostility and skepticism by traditional publishers; however, a growing number of them are overcoming their initial reactions, and they are testing whether open access offers them a viable business model.

Open access has stuck a sympathetic cord in the library community, which has long suffered the debilitating effects of the serials crisis; however, libraries have been somewhat cautious in their embrace of open access, uncertain about its destabilizing effects on the scholarly publishing system and its ultimate impact on their budget and operations.

A growing number of scholars, especially in STM disciplines that have been hard hit by high serials prices, have either become open access advocates or have been swayed by its arguments; however, disciplines that are less dependent on journal literature have shown less enthusiasm and many scholars still have concerns about credibility issues associated with new digital publishing efforts and have not yet seen that the benefits outweigh the risks and costs in terms of time and effort (e.g., to create and deposit e-prints).

Primarily as a result of the open access movement, there is now a rare opportunity to truly transform the scholarly communication system. There has not been such an opportunity in living memory, and, if it is not seized, it is unclear if there will be another one in our lifetimes. If you want change, now is the time to act. Action does not require total agreement with the open access movement's beliefs and proposals, but it requires an active engagement with them. The movement is not monolithic, but diverse. Not closed, but participatory. Not dogmatic, but argumentative as it vigorously debates its future. It can be influenced by new voices and perspectives.

The open access movement is not the only potential solution to the serious problems that libraries face in the conventional scholarly communication system, but it is a very important one, and it does not require that other strategies be abandoned. The voice of libraries needs to be heard more strongly in it.

## AUTHOR NOTE

Bailey has been a digital publisher for over seventeen years, producing works such as PACS-L, an early Internet mailing list; *The Public-Access Computer Systems Review*, one of the first freely available scholarly electronic journals published on the Internet; *Public-Access Computer Systems News*, an electronic newsletter; the *Scholarly Electronic Publishing Bibliography*, a free electronic book that has been updated over 60 times; the *Open Access Bibliography: Liberating Scholarly Literature with E-Prints and Open Access Journals*, a printed book that was made freely available in digital form on the Internet; and *DigitalKoans*, a Weblog. For more details, see "A Look Back at Seventeen Years as an Internet Digital Publisher" (http://www.digital-scholarship.com/cwb/seventeenyears.htm).

In recognition of his early electronic publishing efforts, Bailey was given a Network Citizen Award by the Apple Library in 1992 and the first LITA/Library Hi Tech Award for Outstanding Achievement in Communicating to Educate Practitioners Within the Library Field in Library and Information Technology in 1993. Bailey was profiled in *Movers & Shakers 2003: The People Who Are Shaping the Future of Libraries* supplement to the March 15, 2003 issue of *Library Journal*.

Bailey has written numerous papers about open access, scholarly electronic publishing, and other topics. See http://www.digital-scholarship.com/ for a description of his publications.

## NOTES

1. Peter Suber, "Timeline of the Open Access Movement," http://www.earlham.edu/~peters/fos/timeline.htm.

2. Budapest Open Access Initiative, "Budapest Open Access Initiative," 14 February 2002, http://www.soros.org/openaccess/read.shtml.

3. "Bethesda Statement on Open Access Publishing," 20 June 2003, http://www.earlham.edu/~peters/fos/bethesda.htm.

4. "Berlin Declaration on Open Access to Knowledge in the Sciences and Humanities," 22 October 2003, http://www.zim.mpg.de/openaccess-berlin/berlindeclaration.html.

5. Peter Suber, "Praising Progress, Preserving Precision," *SPARC Open Access Newsletter*, no. 77 (2004), http://www.earlham.edu/~peters/fos/newsletter/09-02-04.htm-progress.

6. Peter Suber, "How Should We Define 'Open Access'?" *SPARC Open Access Newsletter*, no. 64 (2003), http://www.earlham.edu/~peters/fos/newsletter/08-04-03.htm.

7. Peter Suber, "Open Access Overview: Focusing on Open Access to Peer-Reviewed Research Articles and Their Preprints," http://www.earlham.edu/~peters/fos/overview.htm.

8. Ibid.

9. Ibid.

10. Peter Suber, "Creating an Intellectual Commons Through Open Access," http://dlc.dlib.indiana.edu/archive/00001246/01/suberrev052804.pdf.

11. Suber, "Open Access Overview: Focusing on Open Access to Peer-Reviewed Research Articles and Their Preprints."

12. Suber, "How Should We Define 'Open Access'?"

13. Creative Commons, "Creative Commons Licenses," http://creativecommons.org/about/licenses/meet-the-licenses.

14. Creative Commons, "Attribution 2.5," http://creativecommons.org/licenses/by/2.5/.

15. Lawrence Liang, "A Guide To Open Content Licenses," http://pzwart.wdka.hro.nl/mdr/research/lliang/open_content_guide.

16. Suber, "Praising Progress, Preserving Precision."

17. Stevan Harnad, "Re: Free Access vs. Open Access," *SPARC-IR*, 15 December 2003, https://mx2.arl.org/Lists/SPARC-IR/Message/167.html.

18. Ibid.

19. Charles W. Bailey, Jr., *Open Access Bibliography: Liberating Scholarly Literature with E-Prints and Open Access Journals* (Washington, DC: Association of Research Libraries, 2005), xvii-xviii, http://www.scholarship.com/oab/oab.htm.

20. Suber, "Open Access Overview: Focusing on Open Access to Peer-Reviewed Research Articles and Their Preprints."

21. Ibid.

22. Sherpa Project, "Publisher Copyright Policies & Self-Archiving," http://www.sherpa.ac.uk/romeo.php.

23. Suber, "Open Access Overview: Focusing on Open Access to Peer-Reviewed Research Articles and Their Preprints."

24. http://www.biomedcentral.com/.

25. http://www.plos.org/.

26. http://www.pubmedcentral.nih.gov/.

27. http://www.oxfordjournals.org/oxfordopen/.

28. Edward M. Jennings, "EJournal: An Account of the First Two Years," *The Public-Access Computer Systems Review* 2, no. 1 (1991): 91-110, http://info.lib.uh.edu/pr/v2/n1/jennings.2n1.

29. Jane Hugo and Linda Newell, "New Horizons in Adult Education: The First Five Years (1987-1991)," *The Public-Access Computer Systems Review* 2, no. 1 (1991): 77-90, http://info.lib.uh.edu/pr/v2/n1/hugo.2n1.

30. Stevan Harnad, "Post-Gutenberg Galaxy: The Fourth Revolution in the Means of Production of Knowledge," The *Public-Access Computer Systems Review* 2, no. 1 (1991): 39-53, http://info.lib.uh.edu/pr/v2/n1/harnad.2n1.

31. Eyal Amiran and John Unsworth, "Postmodern Culture: Publishing in the Electronic Medium," *The Public-Access Computer Systems Review* 2, no. 1 (1991): 67-76, http://info.lib.uh.edu/pr/v2/n1/amiran.2n1.

32. Charles W. Bailey, Jr., "Electronic (Online) Publishing in Action . . . *The Public-Access Computer Systems Review* and Other Electronic Serials," *ONLINE* 15 (January 1991): 28-35; and Pat Ensor and Thomas Wilson, "*Public-Access Computer Systems*

*Review: Testing the Promise," The Journal of Electronic Publishing* 3, no. 1 (1997), http://www.press.umich.edu/jep/03-01/pacs.html.

33. Stevan Harnad, "Fast-Forward on the Green Road to Open Access: The Case Against Mixing Up Green and Gold," *Ariadne*, no. 42 (2005), http://www.ariadne.ac.uk/issue42/harnad/.

34. Marshall Breeding, "Understanding the Protocol for Metadata Harvesting of the Open Archives Initiative," *Computers in Libraries* 22, no. 8 (2002): 24-29.

35. Richard Monastersky, "The Number That's Devouring Science," *The Chronicle of Higher Education*, 14 October 2004, A12, http://chronicle.com/weekly/v52/i08/08a01201.htm.

36. Suber, "Open Access Overview: Focusing on Open Access to Peer-Reviewed Research Articles and Their Preprints."

37. Bailey, *Open Access Bibliography: Liberating Scholarly Literature with E-Prints and Open Access Journals*, 3-10.

38. Steve Hitchcock, "The Effect of Open Access and Downloads ('Hits') on Citation Impact: A Bibliography of Studies," http://opcit.eprints.org/oacitation-biblio.html.

39. Suber, "Open Access Overview: Focusing on Open Access to Peer-Reviewed Research Articles and Their Preprints."

40. Sharon Terry, " In the Public Interest: Open Access," *College & Research Libraries News* 66, no. 7 (2005): 522, http://www.ala.org/ala/acrl/acrlpubs/crlnews/ backissues2005/julyaugust05/publicinterest.htm.

41. http://www.doaj.org/.

42. Charles W. Bailey, Jr. " The Spectrum of E-Journal Access Policies: Open to Restricted Access," *DigitalKoans*, 13 May 2005, http://www.escholarlypub.com/ digitalkoans/2005/05/13/the-spectrum-of-e-journal-access-policies-open-to-restricted-access/. Note: Since the publication of this paper, *College & Research Libraries* has changed to an embargoed access journal.

43. "Washington D.C. Principles For Free Access to Science: A Statement from Not-for-Profit Publishers," 16 March 2004, http://www.dcprinciples.org/statement.pdf.

44. Krista D. Schmidt, Pongracz Sennyey, and Timothy V. Carstens, "New Roles for a Changing Environment: Implications of Open Access for Libraries," *College & Research Libraries* 66, no. 5 (2005): 408-409.

45. Peter Suber, "Removing Barriers to Research: An Introduction to Open Access for Librarians," http://www.earlham.edu/~peters/writing/acrl.htm.

46. Krista D. Schmidt, Pongracz Sennyey, and Timothy V. Carstens, "New Roles for a Changing Environment: Implications of Open Access for Libraries," 409-414.

47. Ibid, 413.

48. Raym Crow, *A Guide to Institutional Repository Software*, 3rd ed. (New York: Open Society Institute, 2004), http://www.soros.org/openaccess/software/; and SPARC, "Publishing Resources," http://www.arl.org/sparc/resources/pubres.html.

49. Charles W. Bailey, Jr., "Evolution of an Electronic Book: The Scholarly Electronic Publishing Bibliography," *The Journal of Electronic Publishing* 7 (December 2001), http://www.press.umich.edu/jep/07-02/bailey.html.

50. http://scholar.lib.vt.edu/about/.

51. Lon Savage, "The Journal of the International Academy of Hospitality Research," *The Public-Access Computer Systems Review* 2, no. 1 (1991): 54-66, http://info. lib.uh.edu/pr/v2/n1/savage.2n1.

52. http://dspace.library.cornell.edu/handle/1813/62.

53. http://www.insectscience.org/.

54. http://egj.lib.uidaho.edu/.

55. http://wiki.dspace.org/DspaceInstances.

56. Charles W. Bailey, Jr., " Early Adopters of IRs: A Brief Bibliography," *DigitalKoans*, 2 May 2005, http://www.escholarlypub.com/digitalkoans/2005/05/02/early-adopters-of-irs-a-brief-bibliography/.

57. Charles W. Bailey, Jr., "The Role of Reference Librarians in Institutional Repositories," *Reference Services Review* 33, no. 3 (2005): 266, http://www.digital-scholarship.com/cwb/reflibir.pdf.

58. Frederick G. Kilgour, "Historical Note: A Personalized Prehistory of OCLC." *Journal of the American Society for Information Science* 38, no. 5 (1987): 381.

59. W. Boyd Rayward, "A History of Computer Applications in Libraries: Prolegomena," *IEEE Annals of the History of Computing* 24, no. 2 (2002): 10.

60. MacKenzie Smith, Mary Barton, Mick Bass, Margret Branschofsky, Greg McClellan, Dave Stuve, Robert Tansley, and Julie Harford Walker, "DSpace: An Open Source Dynamic Digital Repository," *D-Lib Magazine* 9, no. 1 (2003), http://www.dlib.org/dlib/january03/smith/01smith.html.

61. Thornton Staples, Ross Wayland, and Sandra Payette, "The Fedora Project: An Open-Source Digital Object Repository Management System," *D-Lib Magazine* 9, no. 4 (2003), http://www.dlib.org/dlib/april03/staples/04staples.html.

62. Kat Hagedorn, "OAIster: A 'No Dead Ends' OAI Service Provider," *Library Hi Tech* 21, no. 2 (2003): 170–81.

63. Charles W. Bailey, Jr., "The Google Print Controversy: A Bibliography," *DigitalKoans*, 25 October 2005, http://www.escholarlypub.com/digitalkoans/2005/10/25/the-google-print-controversy-a-bibliography/.

64. Denise Troll, "Frequently Asked Questions About the Million Book Project," http://www.library.cmu.edu/Libraries/MBP_FAQ.html.

65. http://www.opencontentalliance.org/.

66. Vicky Reich and David S. H. Rosenthal, "LOCKSS: A Permanent Web Publishing and Access System," *D-Lib Magazine* 7, no. 6 (2001), http://www.dlib.org/dlib/june01/reich/06reich.html.

67. Stephen Pinfield and Hamish James, "The Digital Preservation of e-Prints," *D-Lib Magazine* 9, no. 9 (2003), http://www.dlib.org/dlib/september03/pinfield/09pinfield.html.

68. Suber, "Open Access Overview: Focusing on Open Access to Peer-Reviewed Research Articles and Their Preprints."

69. http://www.springer.com/sgw/cda/frontpage/0,11855,1-40359-12-115391-0,00.html.

70. For an extensive OA directory, see: Adrian K. Ho and Charles W. Bailey, Jr., "Open Access Webliography," *Reference Services Review* 33, no. 3 (2005): 346-364, http://www.digital-scholarship.com/cwb/oaw.htm.

doi:10.1300/J105v32n03_07

## APPENDIX
## Creative Commons Licenses

Creative Commons (CC) licenses allow copyright owners to grant specific rights to users without the need for the users to request such rights. The licenses are not negotiated with the copyright owner. With the exception of the Public Domain Dedication license, works under CC licenses are not in the public domain. Their use is not restricted to open access materials. Any copyright owner can choose to put his or her work under a CC license.

Authors typically indicate that their works are under a CC license through a standard written statement, which is adjacent to the copyright statement that includes the license name, link information to the chosen license, and, optionally, a postal service address for the Creative Commons. If the license is on a Web page, there is also machine-readable license information that is not visible to the user.

Works under a CC license can be found using advanced search features in Google and Yahoo. The major CC licenses are:

1. **Attribution Non-commercial No Derivatives:** The work must be attributed to the author. It cannot be used for commercial purposes without permission. Derivative works (e.g., a translation) cannot be created without permission.
2. **Attribution Non-commercial Share Alike:** The work must be attributed to the author. It cannot be used for commercial purposes without permission. Derivative works can be created without permission, but they must be under the same CC license as the original work.
3. **Attribution Non-commercial:** The work must be attributed to the author. It cannot be used for commercial purposes without permission. Derivative works can be created without permission.
4. **Attribution No Derivatives:** The work must be attributed to the author. It can be used for commercial or noncommercial purposes without permission. Derivative works cannot be created without permission.
5. **Attribution Share Alike:** The work must be attributed to the author. It can be used for commercial or noncommercial purposes without permission. Derivative works can be created without permission, but they must be under the same CC license as the original work.
6. **Attribution:** The work must be attributed to the author. It can be used for commercial or non-commercial purposes without permission. Derivative works can be created without permission.

# Index